THE JOURNAL

OF

MARY FRAMPTON.

LONDON:
PRINTED BY GILBERT AND RIVINGTON, LIMITED,
ST. JOHN'S SQUARE.

THE JOURNAL

OF

MARY FRAMPTON,

FROM THE YEAR 1779, UNTIL THE YEAR 1846.

*INCLUDING VARIOUS INTERESTING AND CURIOUS
LETTERS, ANECDOTES, &c., RELATING
TO EVENTS WHICH OCCURRED
DURING THAT PERIOD.*

EDITED, WITH NOTES, BY HER NIECE,

HARRIOT GEORGIANA MUNDY.

London :

SAMPSON LOW, MARSTON, SEARLE, & RIVINGTON,
CROWN BUILDINGS, 188, FLEET STREET.

1885.

THE JOURNAL

OF

MARY FRAMPTON

FROM THE YEAR 1779, UNTIL THE YEAR 1846

*INCLUDING VARIOUS INTERESTING AND CURIOUS
LETTERS, ANECDOTES, ETC., RELATING
TO EVENTS WHICH OCCURRED
DURING THAT PERIOD*

EDITED, WITH NOTES, BY HER NIECE

HARRIOT GEORGIANA MUNDY

Elibron Classics
www.elibron.com

INTRODUCTION.

MARY FRAMPTON, the writer of this Journal, was born in 1773. She and her brother James (born 1769) were the only children of James Frampton, Esq., of Moreton, Co. Dorset, who died 1784, by his second wife Phillis, daughter and heiress of Samuel Byam, Esq., of the island of Antigua, and widow of Charlton Wollaston, Esq., by whom she had two children, Charlton Byam and Phillis Byam. Dr. Wollaston was a very scientific man, and his death was occasioned by opening a mummy, he having previously by accident cut his finger. Mrs. Frampton survived her husband many years, dying in 1829 at the age of ninety-two. Mary Frampton died at Dorchester, November 12th, 1846.

CONTENTS.

1779—1788.

PAGE

Journal 1

1789.

Journal 20

Mary Frampton to her Sister, Mrs. Shirley 20

Prayer written by the Queen during the King's illness in the
winter of 1810 24

Prayer written by Queen Charlotte at the same time as the
preceding 26

1790.

Journal 28

C. B. Wollaston to his Mother 29

1791.

Journal 34

From James Frampton 35

The Same to his Mother 35

Charlton Byam Wollaston to the Same 36

	PAGE
From James Frampton	37
From C. B. Wollaston	38
From the Same to Mrs. Frampton	39
James Frampton to his Mother	41
From C. B. Wollaston	43
The Same to Dr. Arnold	44
C. B. Wollaston to his Mother	48
From the Same	49
From James Frampton	52
C. B. Wollaston to Dr. Arnold	52
From James Frampton	54
From the Same	55
C. B. Wollaston to his Mother	57
From the Same	58
The Same to the Same	61
C. B. Wollaston to Miss Fauquier	63
From James Frampton	66
From C. B. Wollaston	67
The Same to Mrs. Frampton	69
From the Same	71
From James Frampton	72
From C. B. Wollaston	73
From James Frampton	74
C. B. Wollaston to Mrs. Frampton	76

1792.

Journal	78

1794.

From Lady Susan O'Brien to her niece, Lady Mary Talbot, at Penrice	79

1795.

PAGE

Journal 80

1796.

Extract from the Journal of Miss Ann Agnes Porter, for many
years the much-valued Preceptress and Friend in Lord
Ilchester's Family 86

1797.

Lady Mary Talbot to her Sister, Lady Harriot Fox Strangways . 90
Lady Elizabeth Talbot to Lady Harriot Fox Strangways . . 93
From Miss Porter to Lady Harriot Strangways 94
John Newbolt, Esq., to Lady Harriot Strangways . . . 95
Julia, Lady Sheffield, to Mrs. Mundy 96

1798.

John Newbolt, Esq., to Lady H. Strangways 100
Miss Porter to Lady H. Strangways 100
Charles Digby to his Cousin, Lady Harriot Strangways . . 101

1799.

From Mrs. Gumbleton to her Niece, Lady Harriot Strangways . 103
Mrs. Frampton to her Sister-in-law, Mrs. Heberden, at Windsor . 105

1800.

Journal 108

1802.

C. Burrell Massingberd, Esq., of Ormsby, Co. Lincoln, to F. N. C.
Mundy, Esq., of Markeaton 109

1803.

PAGE

Anecdotes of Paris, from Mr. W. Churchill, arrested in May, 1803, and kept there until January, 1804.

1804.

Extract from a Letter from Mr. Fox to Mr. O'Brien, in reply to an application for his intercession on behalf of Mr. W. Churchill when a "Détenu" at Paris 116
The Queen to Maria, Countess of Ilchester 117
From Mary Shirley to her Great-aunt, Mrs. E. Fauquier, at Sudbury 118
From the Same to the Same 120
From the Same to the Same 122

1805.

Journal 124
From Mrs. Campbell to Lady H. Frampton 125
Extract from the Diary of Lady Susan O'Brien 127
The King to Lord Eldon 127
From H.R.H. Princess Sophia to Maria, Countess of Ilchester . 128
From Lady Louisa Strangways to her Sister, Lady Harriot Frampton 129
Mrs. Kerby to Mrs. E. Fauquier, from Antigua 131
Extracts from Letters from the Countess of Ilchester to Lady Harriot Frampton, written from Windsor in this year . . 136

1806.

Lady Elizabeth Feilding to Lady Mary Talbot 137

1807.

From H.R.H. Princess Elizabeth to Mary Frampton . . . 137
From H.R.H. Princess Elizabeth to Mary Frampton . . . 138

1809.

PAGE

From H.R.H. Princess Elizabeth to the Countess of Ilchester . 139

Extract from the Journal of Lady Susan O'Brien . . . 139

1810.

From Lady Elizabeth Feilding to Lady Harriot Frampton . . 140

From the Same 141

Maria, Countess of Ilchester, to Lady Harriot Frampton . . 142

Lady Susan O'Brien to her Niece, Lady Harriot Frampton . . 143

The Same to the Same 144

From Lady Harriot Acland to Lady Harriot Frampton . . 145

State of the Expedition from Canada as laid before the House of

    Commons by Lieut.-General Burgoyne, 1780 . . . 146

Hon. George Eden to Lady Harriot Frampton 151

1811.

From Maria, Countess of Ilchester, to Lady Harriot Frampton . 153

C. B. Wollaston to Mary Frampton 153

1812.

Extracts from various Letters written to Mary Frampton by her

    Brothers in this year :—

  From Charlton B. Wollaston 155

  From James Frampton 155

  From C. B. Wollaston 157

  From the Same 158

1813.

From Lady Elizabeth Feilding to her Sister 158

From James Frampton 160

From the Same 161

PAGE

The Marchioness of Lansdowne to Lady Harriot Frampton .   .   161

Maria Dowager Countess of Ilchester to her Son, the Honourable
     Giles Fox Strangways   163

Letter from the Crown Prince of Sweden to Mrs. Bogue, whose
     Husband commanded the Rocket Brigade, and was killed at
     the Battle of Leipzig, Oct. 16th and 18th, 1813. (Commu-
     nicated to Lady H. Frampton, by Lieutenant Thomas
     Strangways)   166

C. B. Wollaston to Mary Frampton   167

1814.

The Marchioness of Lansdowne to Lady Harriot Frampton   .   169

Fragment of a Letter from Lord Harcourt to Lady Vernon .   .   170

From Mr. Wollaston   172

From the Same to Mary Frampton   173

From the Same to the Same   175

From the Same to the Same   176

Fragment of a Letter to the Same   178

C. B. Wollaston to the Same   178

From Georgiana Lady Vernon to the Same   .   .   .   179

From the Same to the Same   182

C. B. Wollaston to Mary Frampton   183

The Same to the Same   185

From the Same to the Same   186

From Georgiana Lady Vernon to the Same   .   .   .   187

Extract from a Letter from Captain Usher, R.N., of H.M.S.
     "Undaunted"   190

The Marchioness of Lansdowne to Miss Vernon .   .   .   195

From Miss Vernon to Lady H. Frampton   197

Sir George Paul to Lady H. Frampton   199

Journal   202

From C. B. Wollaston to his Sister   203

PAGE

The Dowager Lady Vernon to Mary Frampton 205
From James Frampton to Mrs. Frampton 207
Mrs. Shirley to her Sister, Mary Frampton 210
From Mrs. Fisher to Mary Frampton 212
C. B. Wollaston to Mary Frampton 214
James Frampton to his Mother 216
Mrs. Shirley to her Mother, Mrs. Frampton 220
Lady Harriet Frampton to Mary Frampton 221
Mr. Frampton to his Mother 222
Lady Harriot Frampton to Mary Frampton 224
The Dowager Lady Vernon to Mrs. Frampton 225
James Frampton to his Mother 227
From the Same to the Same 228
The Dowager Lady Vernon to Mary Frampton 229
The Same to the Same 230
Mr. Wollaston to Mary Frampton 231
James Frampton to his Mother 231
The Dowager Lady Vernon to Mary Frampton 233
James Frampton to Mrs. Frampton 234
From Lady Harriot Frampton 236

1815.

Hon. Caroline Fox to Lady Elizabeth Feilding 237
From the Same to the Same 240
Charles Lemon, Esq., to his Sister-in-law, Lady Harriot Frampton. 244
From the Same to the Same 246
Extracts from Letters of Mrs. Campbell, in attendance on H.R.H.
    the Princess Charlotte, to Lady Harriot Frampton . . 248
From the Princess Charlotte to H.R.H the Duke of York . . 251
The Dowager Countess of Ilchester, in attendance on the Princess
    Charlotte, to the Same 251
C. B. Wollaston to Mary Frampton 253

PAGE

Charles Lemon, Esq., to Lady H. Frampton 254
Journal 256
Mr. Stapleton Cotton to William Mundy 258

1816.

Maria, Countess Dowager of Ilchester, to Lady Dowager Frampton 259
Mrs. Campbell to Lady Harriot Frampton 262
Dowager Countess of Ilchester to Lady H. Frampton . . . 263
Mrs. Campbell to the Same 265
The Countess Dowager of Ilchester to the Same 267
Mrs. Campbell to the Same 268
The Dowager Countess of Ilchester to the Same 269
Mrs. Campbell to Lady H. Frampton 270
From H.R.H. Princess Charlotte to Lady H. Frampton . . 271
Mrs. Campbell to Lady Harriot Frampton 273
The Dowager Countess of Ilchester to the Same 275
Mrs. Campbell to the Same 276
From Caroline, Countess of Mount-Edgcumbe, to Mrs. Mundy . 277
The Dowager Countess of Ilchester to J. Frampton, Esq. . . 277
The Countess Dowager of Ilchester to Lady H. Frampton . . 278
Mrs. Campbell to the Same 280
The Dowager Countess of Ilchester to the Same 282
The Marchioness of Lansdowne to Lady H. Frampton . . . 283
Charles Lemon, Esq., to Lady H. Frampton 284
From the Same to the Same 286
Journal 288

1817.

C. B. Wollaston to Mary Frampton 288
From the Same to the Same 289
The Same to the Same 291
Charles Lemon, Esq., to Lady Harriot Frampton 292

	PAGE
Mrs. Campbell to Lady H. Frampton .	294
The Dowager Countess of Ilchester to Lady H. Frampton .	295
Lady Charlotte Lemon to the Same .	296
The Dowager Countess of Ilchester to Lady Harriot Frampton .	296
The Dowager Countess of Ilchester to the Marchioness of Lansdowne	298
From Mrs. Campbell to Lady H. Frampton .	299
The Dowager Countess of Ilchester to the Same .	301
Mrs. Campbell to the Same	301
Mrs. Campbell to the Same	303
The Dowager Countess of Ilchester to the Same .	304
From Mrs. Campbell to the Same	304

1818.

From Mrs. Campbell to Lady H. Frampton .	306
From Lady Susan O'Brien to her Niece, Lady Harriot Frampton .	308
Lady Susan O'Brien to her Niece, Lady Mary Cole, at Penrice Castle	310

1819.

From H.R.H. Prince Leopold of Saxe Coburg to Mrs. Campbell .	311
Mrs. Campbell to Dowager Countess of Ilchester .	314

1820.

The Dowager Lady Vernon to Mary Frampton .	317
C. B. Wollaston to Mary Frampton .	318

1821.

C. B. Wollaston to Mary Frampton .	319
The Same to the Same .	320

PAGE

From the Same to the Same 321
The Same to the Same 323
The Same to the Same 323
From Mrs. Campbell to Lady H. Frampton 324

1823.

From Henry Ker Seymer, Esq., to Mary Frampton . . . 324

1824.

From the Same to the Same 325

1825.

From Lady Harriot Frampton to Mary Frampton . . . 325
From Colonel Addenbrook to J. Frampton, Esq. 327

1827.

From James Frampton to his Sister, Mary Frampton . . . 327
From the Same to the Same 328
From Mrs. Shirley to Mary Frampton 330
James Frampton to Mary Frampton 330
From C. B. Wollaston to Mary Frampton 331

1828.

Reminiscences 333
Lady Caroline Damer 333
Rev. J. L. Jackson 335
Extract from a Letter from Ennis 335
From C. B. Wollaston to Mary Frampton 336

PAGE

From Sir Charles Lemon, Bart., to his Niece, Louisa C. Frampton   338

From Mrs. Shirley, of Lough Fea and Ettington, to Mary
Frampton   339

From Major William Shirley, 7th Hussars, to his Mother   .   . 341

1830.

Journal 342

From James Frampton to Mary Frampton 346

From the Same to the Same   347

Journal 348

Extract from Mr. Frampton's Note to Mary Frampton .   . 351

Extract from a Note from Harriot Frampton to the Same   . 356

From the Marchioness of Lansdowne to Lady Harriot Frampton . 363

Journal 365

From Lady Elizabeth Feilding to Lady H. Frampton .   . 366

1831.

Journal 367

From Harriot G. Mundy to Lady H. Frampton .   .   . 373

From Lady Theresa Strangways to her Cousin, Mrs. Mundy . 374

From Lady Louisa Fitzmaurice to the Same   .   .   . 375

Journal 377

From the Rev. J. L. Jackson to C. B. Wollaston, Esq.   .   . 384

From Harriot G. Mundy to Lady H. Frampton .   .   . 386

The Same to the Same   387

The Earl of Ilchester to his Niece, Mrs. Mundy .   .   . 389

The Earl of Ilchester to the Same   390

From Mrs. Mundy to Lady H. Frampton 391

From William Mundy to Lady H. Frampton   .   .   . 393

1832.

Journal   395

1833.

PAGE

Anecdote of the Duke of Wellington, from Colonel Gurwood . 397
Anecdote of Maria Louise, Widow of Napoleon, Grand Duchess
 of Parma, &c., told of herself in confidential correspondence
 with Lady Burghersh 399

1838.

From Lady Theresa Digby to her Cousin, Miss Frampton . . 402
From Mrs. Mundy to her Aunt, Mary Frampton 403
From the Same to Lady H. Frampton 404
From the Same to the Same 406
The Same to the Same 409

1840.

From the Dowager Countess of Ilchester to Lady Harriot
 Frampton 409
From Miss Charlotte Neave to the Countess Dowager of Ilchester
 (enclosed in the preceding). 410
The Marchioness of Lansdowne to Lady Harriot Frampton . . 412
From the Same to the Same. (After the Queen was shot at the
 first time.) 413

1842.

The Marchioness of Lansdowne to Lady H. Frampton . . 414
From Lady Caroline Fox Strangways to Lady Harriot Frampton . 415

1843.

Extract from a Letter from the Hon. Colonel Dawson Damer, of
 Came 417
From Mrs. Mundy to her Aunt, Mary Frampton . . . 418

1845.

PAGE

From the Hon. Mrs. George Dawson Damer of Came . . . 423

1846.

Journal 424

THE JOURNAL OF MARY FRAMPTON.

1779.

I CAME into the world with the American War, and the first political impression I received was from being taken in my father's coach to some hills above Lulworth—about six or seven miles from Moreton, to see Sir Charles Hardy's fleet retreating up the Channel.[1] I think I can even remember the degree of disgrace which I thought attached to it, though probably this idea might have been given me, not, however, in the nursery, for the fear of invasion from the combined Spanish and French fleets, though not equal to the present alarms (1803), was sufficient to cause a great degree of terror amongst the lower orders. I well remember an old house-keeper of Lord Dorchester's, at Milton Abbey, saying

---

[1] June, 1779. The French fleet, having effected a junction with the armament of Spain, insulted the English channel, showed themselves before Plymouth, and captured the *Ardent* of 64 guns, whose commander mistook the united fleet for that of the British Admiral. Sir Charles Hardy, with about thirty-eight sail-of-the-line, was still inferior to the united squadrons of the enemy. Happily, however, jealousy between the commanders of the combined fleet and sickness amongst the crews obliged them to retire into Brest in the month of September with the loss of nearly 10,000 men.

B

after a violent storm of thunder and lightning, " Oh,
dear ! I was so terrified, and the noise was so violent, I
thought it had been ' the Combined.' "

My father and mother generally went to London for
two or three months once in two years. The last time
that we were there *en famille*, we had a house in Hill
Street, very fancifully fitted up, which makes me mention
it. The house belonged to the learned Mrs. Montagu,[2]
who published some criticisms on Shakespeare, and was
well known both in the literary and great world. Her
fortune was very large, and she made a very benevolent
use of it. She built and fitted up magnificently a very
large house at the corner of Portman Square. I have
been in it at a breakfast given by her to the fine world,
and I have more than once been present there at an
assembly of a different kind, as on every May Day she
used to give roast-beef, plum-puddings, and beer to all
the chimney-sweepers' boys in London; the scene was
always pretty and gratifying. Mrs. Montagu was a very
old woman when I knew her, and I quite a girl. To
return to the furniture of her house; one room was
entirely hung with peacock's feathers, which made by no
means a pretty ornament; another painted with loves
and cupids.

1780.

My sister, Phillis Wollaston, now between sixteen and
seventeen, was beginning to be produced a little in the
world. At that time everybody wore powder and
pomatum; a large triangular thing called a cushion, to

---

[2] Elizabeth, daughter of Matthew Robinson, Esq., of West Layton,
Co. York, &c., married, 1742, Edward Montagu, grandson of first Earl
of Sandwich, and nephew of Lord Crewe, Bishop of Durham. Mrs.
Montagu died at her house in Portman Square, in 1800, aged eighty.

which the hair was frizzed up with three or four enormous curls on each side ; the higher the pyramid of hair, gauze, feathers, and other ornaments was carried the more fashionable it was thought, and such was the labour employed to rear the fabric that night-caps were made in proportion to it and covered over the hair, immensely long black pins, double and single, powder, pomatum and all ready for the next day. I think I remember hearing that twenty-four large pins were by no means an unusual number to go to bed with on your head. The perfection of figure according to the *then* fashion was the smallness of the circumference into which your unfortunate waist could be compressed, and many a poor girl hurt her health very materially by trying to rival the reigning beauty of that day, the Duchess of Rutland,[3] who was said to squeeze herself to the size of an orange and a half. Small hoops were worn in a morning and larger for a dress, some going outwards as they went downwards, something in the form of a bell. Sacques were very common ; my mother constantly wore them. They were dresses with loose backs and a stomacher. Gauze handkerchiefs trimmed with blonde were worn on the neck. On account of my sister's initiation into the dissipations of London society, it was deemed absolutely necessary that she should give a great deal of money—I forget the precise sum—for a ticket which was to introduce her to one of the finest fêtes in the French style, given under the direction of M. le Texier, since deservedly famous for his excellent reading, but I believe infamous in character (for although at war with France, and having Frenchmen to thank for the loss of thirteen colonies

---

[3] Mary, daughter of fourth Duke of Beaufort, married, 1775, Charles, fourth Duke of Rutland, K.G., Lord-Lieutenant of Ireland, 1784.

to the British Empire, nothing but what was French was the fashion). At the hour appointed, between ten and eleven, away went my sister to enjoy this grand spectacle at the Opera House; there all the fine world were assembling. Eleven o'clock came, no M. le Texier; no sight. Twelve o'clock struck; all London was at the Opera House, but nothing to amuse them. M. le Texier was loudly called for, but no M. le Texier appeared. At length a man came forward with the pretty excuse that he was very sorry to be forced to say that M. le Texier had disappeared, and nothing more was to be expected. The world, grumbling, departed, and this very same man established a "Theatre à Lecture" in Lisle Street, Leicester Fields, and John Bull crowded to hear him read, four or five years after this imposition. His reading was certainly inimitable, by changing his voice, he gave the effect of acting to three or four different characters, and did it with a French vivacity and boldness which increased the effect. Operas were at that time coming into fashion, and it began to be the *ton* to have a box, though ladies who had boxes went into the pit to see the dancing, and then returned to their box.

The riots that took place this year roused even the attention of a child, and the day on which we left London I remember seeing the smoke from the fires occasioned by the mob, raised through the madness of Lord George Gordon,[4] who, after his sentence of imprisonment turned Jew, and died not many years since in Newgate.

We left many friends in London who were under con-

---

[4] On June 9, 1780, Lord George Gordon was committed to the Tower. Subsequently tried for high treason, but was acquitted. He died 1792.

siderable alarm. The language of both town and country at this time was very desponding; Lord North's administration universally unpopular, and the Funds said to be so low that I was told I should never have any fortune, for that they would certainly break. Thank God, the danger from that was soon weathered, and I have good hope, if my life is spared, to smile when looking back upon the present certainly much more alarming times.

To show the progress of luxury, I must here mention that at that time my father, with a fortune of £4000 a year, with an excellent house, &c., lived entirely in one of the worst rooms in it, where we breakfasted, dined and supped; and even with company in the house, excepting on the rare occasion of a large party. We used to go out of the room for a short time after dinner, and return to it again to tea. Silver forks,[5] rugs, and

---

[5] Italy claims the merit of the invention of forks. In Coryate's "Travels in Italy," published 1611, he says: "The Italians always at their meals use a little forke when they cut their meat. They are for the most part made of yron, steele, and some of silver, but these are used only by gentlemen." They were not employed even by the higher classes in England until the middle of the seventeenth century.

About the period of the Revolution few noblemen had more than a dozen forks of silver, together with a few of iron or steel. The general introduction of silver forks into Great Britain can only be dated from the opening of the Continent to English travellers at the termination of the French War [1814].—*Chambers' Cyclopædia.*

However, in a list of the plate at Markeaton Hall, of the date of 1772, mention is made of "Three dozen silver forks;" also " 2 carving knives with silver hafts," and " 2 forks with 2 prongs, with handles to match."— H. G. M.

Carpets in bedrooms were also unknown until long after this period— at least covering the whole floor. Narrow strips of carpetting, woven on purpose, were laid down at the sides of the bed, and this continued until certainly about 1820, even in well-furnished gentlemen's houses.

When the Royal Family were at Weymouth at the beginning of the

foot-stools, were luxuries unknown, or, if the former *were* just known, it was only amongst people of very high rank, or who had lived much on the Continent.

1781.

IN the following year my sister married Mr. Shirley. His father, a son of Earl Ferrers, lived at Ettington in Warwickshire, in a house that had been partly built and had been in their family before the Conquest, but the principal estate was in Ireland. She was not quite eighteen, Mr. Shirley twenty-five when they married. As I profess to write occasionally on the most frivolous topics, I must mention her wedding clothes, which cost between £300 and £400. Polonaises were at that time the fashion; they consisted of a gown and petticoat of the same, frequently of coloured linen with borders of linen in patterns, with long sleeves, the train of the gown drawn up in a festoon behind, and fastened at the bottom of the waist by a loop to a button. My sister was married in a white lutestring. My mother was in a very dark blue or purple silk, called at that time from old Vestris, the famous opera dancer, an old Vestris blue, trimmed with spotted muslin. I was an extremely happy being, wearing a pink silk slip (*alias* body and coat) and a figured gauze frock over it, and my sorrow

present century, the King's Lodge was so ill-furnished that the floors of the small apartments occupied by the Princesses were entirely bare ; and the difficulty of obtaining even such an article as a bedside carpet was so great, owing to the application having to pass through so many inter-mediate hands before reaching the proper official—I believe the Lord Steward—that one of the King's Equerries (General Garth I think it was), actually procured and presented them to their Royal Highnesses at his own expense. One of the Princesses herself told this to my mother, when complaining how very uncomfortable they were when staying at Weymouth.—H. G. M.

for the loss of my sister's company, though I really felt it much, was considerably softened by being so finely clad. It was the old-fashioned custom to keep the new-married pair to dinner, and not dismiss them till evening, and the house where Mr. Shirley then resided was only two and a half miles' distance.

The wedding was attended only by the people in the house: the dinner was very handsome, but the day seemed long to all parties, notwithstanding an expedition to Lulworth Castle in the morning, to which, for fear of spoiling my dress, I was not permitted to belong—*Point de rose sans épines*.

I was at this time very indifferent to the politics of the day. The successes of Lord Rodney in the West Indies, towards the conclusion of the American War, is all that I remember to have made an impression on me—that interested *me* from a great friend of my father's (Captain Houlton,[6] afterwards an admiral, and my guardian) being the Captain of the *Montague*, a 74-gun ship, belonging to Lord Rodney's squadron. In spite of the brilliant successes under their commander, he was very unpopular in the navy; from Admiral Houlton I have heard various instances of Lord Rodney's hauteur to inferior officers, which, perhaps, accounted for it. He would occasionally shut himself up in his cabin, forbid all access to him; and if on particular business any one requested to be admitted, "Tell him," Lord R. would answer, "I am writing to my sovereign, and cannot see him." I cannot refuse myself the pleasure of recording one proof amongst thousands of British valour. I have it from undoubted authority, that of Lord

[6] John, son of Joseph Houlton, Esq., of Farley Castle, Co. Wilts. Rear-Admiral. He died, unmarried, 1791.

Dorchester (then George Damer)[7] serving in some regiment on board one of the ships at the time of Lord Rodney's great naval victory.

The ship, in which was Lord Dorchester, was warmly engaged with the enemy; the captain was killed, Lord Dorchester was sent to fetch up the first lieutenant to take the command, who came on deck, and in a few minutes was no more, the same fate befell the second lieutenant. The command then devolved upon an absolute youth, to whom—when Lord Dorchester announced the fate of the second lieutenant, and that consequently he must go on deck, and immediately take upon him the command—the intelligence seemed like a clap of thunder, and he, almost trembling, said, " To me, sir, it is impossible that I *can* command." Lord Dorchester trembled for him, but in a few minutes perceived that it was diffidence and not fear that made him turn pale, and refuse the office.

The instant the young man was persuaded that it was his duty, he flew on deck, gave his orders with the greatest judgment, prudence, and intrepidity, and succeeded in capturing the enemy's ship. After the action was over there was a still greater difficulty to make the

---

[7] Second son of Joseph Damer, Esq., of Milton Abbey, Co. Dorset, who was created Baron Milton, 1753, and in 1792 Viscount Milton and Earl of Dorchester. Mr. Damer served in the army under Lord Cornwallis during the American War; was M.P. for Dorchester, and subsequently for New Maldon; Secretary to Earl Fitzwilliam when Lord Lieutenant of Ireland, &c. On the death of his father, 1798, Lord Milton (as he had then become) succeeded to the earldom, his eldest brother (whose wife, the daughter of the Right Honourable Seymour Conway, is so well known from her talents as a sculptor) having unhappily destroyed himself in 1776. Lord Dorchester was colonel of the Dorset Regiment of Yeomanry Cavalry. He died unmarried, 1808, when the title became extinct.

modest youth wait upon his admiral, and he could not be persuaded to do so till Lord Dorchester promised to accompany him, as, although he had been victorious, and, in singular circumstances, had commanded the ship in the most masterly manner, he thought it would be too much presumption to visit his admiral. Lord Rodney, after complimenting him, rather in a cool manner, on his noble conduct, *put him under arrest immediately* for some very trifling omission of etiquette. Could such a commander be popular? The arrest might be right, according to Spartan or Roman discipline, but surely English gratitude might have dispensed with it. I wish I could recollect the name of the young man.

Peace soon succeeded, and though it gave occasion to much abuse of Lord Lansdowne, the pacificator, I cannot but say, in the words of a tetrastich composed on the occasion,—

> " Tho' we are cuff'd and kick'd and spit on,
> Let's make the best of our mischance.
> We still at least are little Britain,
> Thank God we are not petty France." [8]

---

[8] This alludes to the localities thus called, of some celebrity in London during the 17th and 18th centuries. Little Britain comes out of Aldersgate Street by St. Botolph's Church. Milton lodged for some time at the house of Millington, the famous auctioneer, who sold old books in Little Britain, and who used to lead him by the hand when he went abroad. Little Britain is also mentioned in the *Spectator*. The name is supposed to be derived from the circumstance that the Earls of Brétagne lodged near Aldersgate when in England (*temp*. Edward II.) Petty France in Westminster, now York Street, from having been the London residence of the Archbishops of York during the early part of the last century. From 1652 to 1660, Milton resided in a "pretty garden house" in Petty France, opening into St. James's Park.

1784.

IN October, 1784, I had the misfortune to lose my father. He died at Bath, whither my mother and I had accompanied him. On my father's illness increasing my brother was sent for from Winchester School. Charlton Wollaston was at Cambridge at the time.

When one object makes a deep impression on the mind it imprints every trifling occurrence equally deep; the rooms we were in, the books we read, are all as familiar to me as if it were yesterday. I was reading at that time "Les Veillées du Château," just come out from the pen of the celebrated Mme. de Genlis. It was her second publication. "Le Théâtre d'Education," so simple, so natural, so deservedly admired by old and young, was the first, and to my taste, the best of her works, some parts of "Les Veillées du Château" are also excellent. "Olimpe et Théophile," as a little interesting novel, is remarkably good, but not calculated for a *child*, any more than the "Histoire de M. de la Palinière." The story of Pamela is what she wishes you to believe was the real history of her own encounter with the Pamela whom she herself educated, and who is universally supposed to be her daughter, by the wretched Duke of Orleans, afterwards "Egalité." Her Pamela married Lord Edward FitzGerald,[9] who lost his

[9] "Pamela's daughter, Pamela Fitzgerald, married Sir Guy Campbell. She told me that she did not believe her mother to have been Egalité's daughter, but to have been brought over as a child to teach the young princes English. Pamela remembered a conversation, or sort of quarrel, between her mother and Madame de Genlis, in which the latter declared that she was not her daughter; and also said that there were some letters extant mentioning that a commission given by the Duke of Orleans had been executed, and that the little girl should be sent over at the same time."—Letter from Lady Louisa Howard to Mrs. Mundy, 1876. This is corroborated by the following extract from the Mémoires de

life for treason in the Irish Rebellion of 1798. She married afterwards a person of property at Hamburg, and became a dissolute character.

1785-86.

THE winter of 1785-86 was a very severe one. My brother, on his return to school, was obliged, from the quantity of snow, to take a route several miles round. We, I mean my mother and myself, removed early to London. We passed one night at Winchester *en route*, and thus the journey was easily performed in two days. Our house was in Clarges Street, directly opposite one inhabited by Colonel, now General Lake, who has since covered himself with laurels by his consummate bravery and skilful conduct in the Indian war against Scindiah and the Rajah of Berar. He was then a young man, married to a pretty though painted lady, and had at that time several children. He was in the Prince of Wales' family, and a great favourite of the Prince's, as well as one of his oldest servants. The Prince in his youth had promised him the Auditorship of the Duchy of Cornwall whenever it should be vacant, but pretending or really having forgotten this (equally culpable when it related to so old a friendship), when it became so, during

Madame de Genlis:—" M. le Duc de Chartres écrivit à Londres pour charger une personne de sa connoissance de lui envoyer une jolie petite Anglaise de cinq ou six ans. M. Forth en trouva une : il la confia à un marchand de chevaux, chargé par M. le Duc de lui acheter un beau cheval Anglais. Il annonça à M. le Duc de Chartres cet envoi dans ces termes : 'J'ai l'honneur d'envoyer à votre Altesse Sérénissime la plus jolie jument, et la plus jolie petite fille de l'Angleterre.' Cette enfant était en effet ravissante. Elle s'appelait 'Nancy Syms,' je la nommai Paméla : elle ne savait pas un mot de Français."—Mém. de Madame de Genlis.

General Lake's absence in India, he bestowed it on Mr. Sheridan.

My aunt, Georgiana Fauquier, was in May married to Lord Vernon. I fear, however, that I cannot enliven this year by either politics or literature. We returned and spent the summer and autumn quietly at Moreton. The expense of living began to increase. Butcher's meat, which when my mother took the management of Moreton House, immediately after my father's death, was at 2½*d*. per pound, rose to 3*d*., 3½*d*., and 4*d*. very soon after. The price of butter and other articles also increased, bread always fluctuating.

At this time the connection of Mrs. Fitz Herbert [1]

---

[1] Mary Anne, daughter of Walter Smythe, Esq., second son of Sir John Smythe, Bart., of Eske, Co. Durham, born 1756. She married, 1774, Edward Weld, Esq., of Lulworth, Co. Dorset, who died in 1775. Her second husband, Thomas Fitz Herbert, Esq., of Swinnerton and Norbury, Co. Stafford (married 1778), also died (s.p.) at Nice in 1781. Mrs. Fitz Herbert was married to George, Prince of Wales, at her own house in London, by a Protestant clergyman, December 21, 1785. The certificate of the marriage is still extant, signed by the Prince and herself. Mrs. Fitz Herbert died at Brighton, March 29, 1837, and was buried in the Roman Catholic Church at that place.

1845, March 4.—The following curious anecdote was related to me by the Honourable Mrs. George Dawson Damer, née Seymour, who on the death of her parents (Lord and Lady Hugh Seymour) was adopted and educated by Mrs. Fitz Herbert. She was dining with me at Dorchester, and my brother, James Frampton, and Major Horatio Shirley were also present:—"On the death of George IV. in 1830, some jewels and trinkets were directed to be given to Miss Seymour (then Mrs. Damer); amongst others was the counterpart of a kind of brooch, containing a miniature of George IV., set with a diamond instead of a glass. The diamond had been cut in half, and the other part, set in the same way, contained a miniature of Mrs. Fitz Herbert herself. Great search was made at Windsor for this valuable jewel, but without success. Rundell and Bridge, who had the setting of the two articles, were employed with others to examine, but in vain, and all hope of regaining the lost treasure was at an end. Some time afterwards the Duke of

with the Prince of Wales had not long existed. She held out long against him, and went on the Continent, and did not consent until a marriage ceremony, at least according to the Roman Catholic religion, to which she belonged, had been performed. She ought, however, to have been sensible that the ceremony, in the eye of the English law, was perfectly nugatory. Mrs. Fitz Herbert had known my mother well when she lived in Dorsetshire, having been first of all married, when very young, to Mr. Weld, of Lulworth Castle, a neighbour of ours. She was then very beautiful. She dined at Moreton on the day she was eighteen, perfectly unaffected and unassuming in her manners, as I have heard from my

Wellington, when one evening sitting next to Mrs. Damer, said to her, with some hesitation, 'I dare say you may like to know something of the lost jewel;' but added, 'perhaps I had better not tell you.' She pressed him, however, to continue, when the Duke proceeded to state, with some confusion, that in his office as First Lord of the Treasury it had been his duty to remain till the very last with the body of the King, who had given him strict injunctions not to leave it, and had desired to be buried with whatever ornaments might be upon his person at the time of his death. The Duke was quite alone with the body, then lying in an open coffin, and his curiosity being excited by seeing a small jewel hanging round the neck of the King, he was tempted to look at it, when he found that it was the identical portrait of Mrs. Fitz Herbert, covered with the diamond for which the unsuccessful search had been made. The Duke added, "I leave it to you to communicate this or not to Mrs. Fitz Herbert, as you may think best for her." As Mrs. Fitz Herbert scarcely ever alluded to her former connection with George IV., Mrs. George Dawson Damer doubted as to the propriety of naming this to her; but one day, when the conversation between them led that way, she ventured to tell the discovery. Mrs. Fitz Herbert made no observation, but some large tears fell from her eyes."

Mrs. Damer showed us the corresponding portrait of the Prince of Wales, which she was wearing at the moment, and which appeared very like him when he was a young man. This is a strong proof of how sincerely George IV. continued attached to Mrs. Fitz Herbert to the end of his life.—MARY FRAMPTON.

mother at that time, and as I have myself since seen.
Her husband dying very soon after this, my father and
mother, knowing Mrs. Weld to be so young, and without
any friend with her, sent to offer her to remove to Moreton, or to give her any comfort or assistance in their
power. This friendly conduct was on her side always
repaid with great civility and attention; she found out
my mother's residence in London and called upon her, to
my great joy, who of course wished to see a person so
much talked about, and who would certainly have been
a much greater as well as happier woman could she have
resisted the allurements of a Prince who, however, beyond all doubt, possessed beauty, talents, and the most
enchanting manners. Can it, therefore, be wondered at,
however much one may lament, that human nature did
not withstand the temptation held out! If ever the
Prince loved any woman, it was she; and half London,
had he thrown the handkerchief, would have flown to
pick it up. Mrs. Fitz Herbert's very uncomfortable life
since her connection with the Prince affords as strong a
lesson as ever was given in favour of virtue, for she never
derived any benefit from it. When she came in to my
mother I thought her certainly very handsome, though
too fat. A very mild, benignant countenance, without
much animation, and rather heavy than brilliant in conversation. Her chariot was without any armorial bear-
ings, nor has she ever worn any, since her liveries by
accident resembled the Royal ones, the Fitz Herbert
livery being red turned up with green, and she had gold
ornaments.

A year or two after this, when Mrs. Fitz Herbert was
living in Pall Mall, within a few doors of Carlton House, we
were at one of the assemblies she gave, which was altogether the most splendid I was ever at. Attendants in

green and gold, besides the usual livery servants, were stationed in the rooms and up the staircase to announce the company, and carry about refreshments, &c. The house was new and beautifully furnished—one room was hung with puckered blue satin, from which hangings the now common imitations in paper were taken. A whole-length portrait of the Prince of Wales was conspicuous in one of the drawing-rooms, and his bust and that of the Duke of York ornamented the dining-room. Her own manners ever remained quiet, civil, and unpretending, and in the days of her greatest influence she was never accused of using it improperly. The Prince and, I think, his brother, the Duke of York, came in late to the assembly.

1788.

IN 1788 the impeachment and trial of Warren Hastings [2] were the subjects of frequent conversation, and the attendance at his trial for the first few *years* was the object of every one's desire. I was fortunate, and had a ticket for the Duke of Newcastle's [3] Gallery, where, besides the advantage of getting to your seat in West-minster Hall quite quietly through a fine house, in the passage which communicated with that gallery there was, for the first year or two, a handsome cold collation regu-

[2] The trial of Warren Hastings began February 15th, 1788, when Burke opened the charge, which lasted three days.

On April 23rd, 1795, the House of Lords brought the trial to a conclusion, when he was acquitted. Hastings died in 1818, at the age of 85.

[3] Henry Clinton, first Duke of Newcastle of that family, to which title he succeeded in 1768, when he took the name of Pelham. He married, 1744, Catharine, eldest daughter and co-heir of the Right Honourable Henry Pelham, brother of Thomas, Duke of Newcastle. He was Lord of the Bedchamber to Kings George II. and III. K.G. The duke died 1794.

larly set out for those admitted by the duke's ticket. My aunt, Elizabeth Fanquier, attended with me constantly one year, and I heard Mr. Burke make his opening speech, and several of the other managers declaim against Mr. Hastings, and, being very young, was, of course, carried away by their eloquence to believe all the charges. Mr. Grey[4] pleased me particularly by his person and manner. The *coup-d'œil* was magnificent: that fine building, Westminster Hall, full in every part, with gentlemen and ladies full dressed, and the peers in their robes. The Prince of Wales's bow to the throne on entering and before taking his seat was universally admired, and the beauty of the then young Duke of Bedford,[5] but he wanted the grace and *air noble* which the other possessed in the highest degree. The length of the trial put an end by degrees not only to the Duke of Newcastle's collations, which were omitted certainly after the second year, but to all interest respecting the parties concerned on either side, and empty benches and woolsacks, as well as empty galleries, succeeded to the crowding and pressure for places and tickets of admission.

The opera at this time was in high fashion. Paesiello's *Schiavi per Amore*, with Storace and Morelli as performers, were deservedly great attractions.

Mrs. Siddons in tragedy at the English Theatre was making ladies faint and gentlemen weep whenever she performed. Drury Lane Theatre was not then enlarged, and her voice was not strained and spoiled as in later days.

Miss Farren, afterwards Lady Derby, and Miss Pope

---

[4] Charles, subsequently second Earl Grey, 1807 ; Prime Minister, 1830 to 1834. K.G. (Died 1845.)

[5] Francis, fifth Duke of Bedford. He died unmarried, deeply lamented, 1802.

were, in their different ways, inimitable, and about this time appeared the enchanting romp, Mrs. Jordan, whose voice alone was music to the ear.

Mrs. Siddons was received and courted, I would almost say, by the best society; amongst others she lived much in the company of Lord and Lady Harcourt,[6] where she met Mr. Mason the poet, Mr. Whitehead, poet laureate, and many other *literati*. She was always a dull woman in conversation, spoke very slowly, as if she were declaiming a set speech, instead of talking, of which many ludicrous stories were circulated at the moment. I recollect two of these. At dinner one day she turned to a gentleman next her, saying, "I am very ignorant, but I thirst for information; pray, what fish is that?" Another time some one was relating a melancholy story of a clerk in office having died suddenly in his bureau. Upon which Mrs. Siddons said, "Poor gentleman, I marvel how he got there!" not knowing evidently the sense of the French word. She had a considerable talent for modelling as well as acting, and was extremely kind and good-natured in affording information on the subject, to which I can speak, as I visited her with my Aunt Fanquier for some instructions in an art which, however, I did not take to. Her talent for reading and personating the different characters in plays, by change of voice and countenance, had not the liveliness of the Frenchman Le Texier, but

---

[6] George Simon, second Earl Harcourt, succ. 1777. Master of the Horse to Queen Charlotte. Married, 1765, his cousin Elizabeth, daughter of George Venables, first Lord Vernon, and died (s.p.) 1809. The intimacy between the families of Fanquier and Harcourt was great, particularly with my aunt, Elizabeth Fanquier. Lady Harcourt accepted the post of Lady of the Bedchamber to the Queen. She was a clever woman, and agreeable, though stiff; dressed in the extreme of fashion, and wearing much rouge.

The first Lord Harcourt had been preceptor to George III.

was equally good in its way. For some years after she left the stage, Mrs. Siddons still continued occasionally to delight her friends by her reading. She was very handsome, but had a heavy figure. Her conception of the character of Rosalind failed from the entire want of the playfulness which belongs to it.

Mrs. Jordan's failure in the same character was from the contrary error of making Rosalind a vulgar romp, instead of either a lady or a princess; and the cuckoo song she introduced, in spite of her silver tones, was what Rosalind *could never have sung.* I saw both these celebrated actresses in this pretty but difficult character, which requires to be acted by a *lady born*, to give it ease and playfulness, without a particle of stiffness or vulgarity.

Mr. Kemble was also much received in society, and it was said that one lady of rank was so captivated by him that her father sent to Kemble and promised him a certain sum on condition of his immediate marriage to some other person, which, according to the wishes of the peer, took place very soon after.

Many years previous to this, and indeed before my existence, the same prudence on the part of a father and mother might perhaps have prevented the union of the celebrated actor, Mr. O'Brien, with Lady Susan Strangways.[7] They were thrown together by the private theatricals carried on at Holland House,[8] and all London

----

[7] Eldest daughter of Stephen, first Earl of Ilchester, born 1743. She married, 1764, when scarcely above twenty years of age, William O'Brien, Esq., who died 1815. Lady Susan was one of the ten young ladies, daughters of dukes and earls, who were bridesmaids to Queen Charlotte on her marriage. The beautiful and renowned Lady Sarah Lennox was another. Lady Susan O'Brien died at Stinsford, 1827.

[8] The residence of Henry Fox, first Lord Holland. He was second son of Sir Stephen Fox, and younger brother of Stephen, Earl of

was wild with admiration of his person and his inimitable
manner of acting a fine gentleman in comedy. He was
himself of a gentleman's family in Ireland, left by some
accident for education with a Roman Catholic priest; and,
considering his education, his turn for the stage, and the
society into which that taste must have thrown him, he
was certainly a very extraordinary and amiable character.
He lived in Dorsetshire, respected and beloved by every
one, for many years, at Stinsford, a house belonging to
Lady Susan's brother, Lord Ilchester.

She, when young, was reckoned the proudest of the
proud, and the highest of the high; her elopement,
therefore, was the more wondered at. They went to
America for some years after the marriage, where her
friends had procured him some trifling office—I believe,
as commissary. Mr. O'Brien followed the law, and went
the western circuit for a short time after his return from
America, until they finally settled at Stinsford. They
remained always most affectionately attached to each
other. Lady Susan was a woman of a very strong and
highly improved understanding, extremely agreeable in
society, a steady, warm-hearted friend, and a person in
whose conversation anything like gossip or abuse of your
neighbour never held a place, but to the very latest hour
of her existence her lofty character was most strongly
marked. Her principles and education, as well as her
husband's, had been neglected; but whatever their errors
might be, in both they were redeemed by very valuable
and amiable qualities, and no two people were more liked
or their society more courted in the middle and close of

Ilchester, consequently uncle to Lady Susan Strangways.   Lord Holland
married, 1744, Lady Georgiana Caroline Lennox, daughter of Charles,
second Duke of Richmond, and died 1774. Their second son was the
celebrated Charles James Fox.

their lives.   He had most amenity, she most strength of
character.   *Requiescant in pace.*

1789.

IN 1788-9 party ran high from the melancholy state of
the King's mind and the agitation of the Regency question.   The welcome recovery of the King in the spring
of 1789 produced as strong expressions of affection from
a people to their sovereign as could possibly be witnessed,
and his going to St. Paul's to return thanks for his
restoration to health was a magnificent sight.[9]   I
returned from Eatington in Warwickshire on purpose to
see it, and the crowd and difficulty of access was so
great that I slept at a friend's in Doctors' Commons
over-night.

MARY FRAMPTON TO HER SISTER, MRS. SHIRLEY.

" *London, April 24th*, 1789.

" MY DEAR SISTER,—I must begin by telling you that
the King was not the worse for his fatigue yesterday,
and that everything was conducted with the greatest
order and regularity.   My brothers, Martha, and I set
out to sleep at Dr. Arnold's,[1] in Doctors' Commons; we
did not arrive at his house till very late, all the small
streets near St. Paul's being barred up to prevent carriages from going into Fleet Street by those streets; from
Temple Bar it was gravelled to St. Paul's, and we were
obliged to walk part of the way.   The next morning we

[9] 1789, Thursday, April 23rd.
[1] James Henry Arnold, Esq., of Ilsington, Co. Dorset, LL.D., F.R.
and A.S., King's Advocate in his office of Admiralty (1811-31), Vicar-
General to the Archbishop of Canterbury, Chancellor of the Diocese of
Worcester, &c., died 1836.   He was a relative of the Frampton family.

were up very early, breakfasted at Dr. Arnold's, and then went to Mr. Silk's, the upholsterer, where we arrived by a back way about eight o'clock, and got most excellent seats for the sight.

"Soon after that hour the members of the House of Commons began the procession, and after them the Lords. What pleased us much was that the populace huzza'd Mr. Pitt, but hooted and hissed Mr. Fox—at least, the greatest number did so. Mr. Fox, in consequence, sat quite back in his coach, not to be seen. The Lords and Commons had all arrived by about half-past eleven. The Dukes of Gloucester and Cumberland in their state coaches followed, then the Duke of York in a *vis-à-vis*, with a coach and six for his attendants, then some guards, and after them the Prince of Wales's attendants in a very handsome coach drawn by six beautiful black horses. The Prince himself followed in his own coach, drawn by six of the handsomest grey horses possible; and they were most elegantly ornamented, so that nothing could be finer than his equipage.

"Next followed the King's attendants, and after them the King and Queen in a coach made with glass all round; they were drawn by eight beautiful cream-coloured horses. While they were coming up to the door of St. Paul's, the band played 'God save the King,' and every hat was in the air, and the acclamations very great, but still louder on his coming out of the church. The Princesses' carriage followed the King's. The King looked very well, but thinner. We returned to Dr. Arnold's during the time of the King's stay in the church. Every one who was fortunate enough to get a seat within St. Paul's speaks of it as a most affecting scene. On the King's entrance, the 6000 children in the dome struck up the Hundredth Psalm; the King and Queen were much affected.   The service lasted rather more than two hours; an excellent sermon was preached by the Bishop of London."[2]

When the King and Queen had returned to Buckingham House, the three regiments of Guards fired a *feu-de-joie*, and the Prince of Wales and the three royal dukes had changed their dresses and appeared on horseback at the head of their respective regiments.   In short, throughout *this* day they behaved well.   The crowd was greater than anything you can conceive.   We are to go into the city to-day to see the illuminations; they are to be finer, it is said, than even last time, and the Queen is again to go about to see them.   The ball given by Brooks' Club is abused even by their own members; it is said that the Queen spoke again to her people, by the King's desire, to prevent their absenting themselves from it from party motives.

Several great fêtes [3] were given late in the spring, on

[2] Dr. Beilby Porteus.   Died 1808.   "I have heard my mother say that Bishop Porteus was the first Prelate who restored the custom of additional services during Lent, and that he did much good by giving lectures on weekdays, and preached most forcibly for the better observance of that season."—H. G. M.

Extract of a letter from Lady Elizabeth Feilding to her sister, Lady Mary Talbot.   1805, May 15th:—"The Bishop of London has written to Lady Salisbury, Lady Hertford, and Lady Stafford, to tell them how much he disapproved of their Sunday concerts.   The two last have promised him to discontinue them *in future*, after the present subscription closes; but Lady Salisbury is very angry, and will go on in her old way."

[3] 1789.—The most sumptuous of the entertainments given to celebrate the king's recovery was that of H.R.H. the Princess Royal, at Windsor, on May 1st.   The cards of invitation were in the name of H.R.H. to the unmarried branches of those persons of distinction who were honoured on this occasion; the married were invited by the Lord Chamberlain, in the name of the Queen.   The company, including the foreign ambassadors, amounted to 228 persons.   The dresses were the Windsor uniform, the

the occasion of the King's recovery. I was not out in the world, but was permitted to go to one of them given by Boodle's Club, at Ranelagh, on May 7th. I was dressed as a grown-up person for the first time, and wore powder, then the mark of distinction of womanhood. My dress was a black body and pink slip, with a crape petticoat, ornamented with pink bows, puffings, &c., and feathers in my head. The Rotunda at Ranelagh was ornamented for the occasion, and the numerous and excellent bands were stationed in the middle. There were temporary supper-rooms annexed for the occasion. I did not get home till between six and seven o'clock in the morning, but was as happy as possible, and the impression of all I saw is still fresh in my mind.

Ranelagh[4] itself in those days was a very agreeable assembly; it was lighted up two or three times a week,

old ladies wearing a long purple train, the young ladies without any. The gown was of white tiffany, with a garter-blue body; the sleeves were white, and ornamented, like the coat, with three rows of fringe, corresponding with that at the bottom of the gown. All the ladies wore bandeaux round the front of their head-dresses, with the words, "God save the King;" and many of them had beautiful medallions of his Majesty, some plain, some in pearl, and some set in diamonds. The dancing began a little before ten o'clock. All the six Princesses were present, as well as the Prince of Wales and the royal Dukes. The supper exceeded anything of the kind ever before given. The King led the Queen to a table under the throne appropriated to the royal party, which was exclusively laid out with gold plate; and then wishing the company a good night, retired.

[4] "Ranelagh" was erected about 1740, on the site of the gardens of a villa of Viscount Ranelagh. The principal room, the Rotunda, was 185 feet in diameter, with an orchestra in the centre, and tiers of boxes all round. The *coup-d'œil* was declared by Dr. Johnson to be "the finest thing he had ever seen."

The last great event at Ranelagh was the ball at the installation of the Knights of the Bath, in 1802. The site, of which no traces remain, is now part of the gardens of Chelsea Hospital.

and frequented by all the world as a promenade.   There were boxes round for tea and other refreshments, and as long as the fashion lasted, every one delighted in it; the fashion ceased, and no one went near it, and the building has long been pulled down.

It was during a subsequent attack of the King's sad illness that the Queen composed the following prayers, which I insert here, although somewhat prematurely.

The copy from which I write them was given me by the Lady Caroline Damer,[5] and the one she had was written out for her by one of the Princesses.

WRITTEN BY THE QUEEN DURING THE KING'S ILLNESS IN THE WINTER OF 1810.

" 1 Pet. v. 7 : ' Cast all your care upon the Lord, for He careth for you.'

" Now to Thee, O faithful Preserver and Father of Thy creatures, to Thee I recommend my afflictions, and the divers cares which put me to disquiet.   Thou alone canst remove them from my heart, to Thy wisdom and goodness I commit them all.   In Thy hands are

---

[5] Daughter of the first Earl of Dorchester, and heiress to her brother, the last earl.   Lady Caroline was one of the bridesmaids to the Princess Royal on her marriage with the Hereditary Prince of Wurtemberg Stuttgard, May 17th, 1797.   The royal family were much attached to her, and she was on terms of intimacy with the princesses to the end of her life. Lady C. Damer resided at Dorchester House, Park Lane, when in London, where I frequently accompanied my mother on a visit to her. That was a very handsome house, but was pulled down after the purchase of the property, in 1848, by R. S. Holford, Esq.

I have heard my father mention that he was one day dining in company with Lord Dorchester at a house in Bruton Street, when on the party breaking up, Lord Dorchester prepared to walk home, to the great surprise of the others ; and he was strongly advised, but in vain, not to run so great a risk as to return *by himself* and on foot, at night, to so lonely a spot as Dorchester House !   This was at the beginning of the present century.—H. G. M.

the destinies of mankind. Thou hast to each man assigned his days of happiness and days of sorrow; with all my reflections and endeavours I should not have it in my power to avert what it is Thy pleasure to impose on me.

" O give me but the prudence to comply with these circumstances, guide me to the proper means for lessening the causes of my affliction. Grant me steadiness to trust in Thee with a firm belief and comforted spirit, even in the midst of adversities. Thou art the Almighty, no danger is too great for Thee to remove. Thy wisdom knows the way to restore me to rest, and to the enjoyment of undisturbed prosperity. In Thee I hope. Thou art my God, my Father, reconciled to me through Christ, my chief consolation. To Thee I herewith surrender all my affairs and concerns. Guide Thou the hearts of men to my best advantage. Let all that gives me pain have a happy conclusion: fulfil in me Thy promise that they who faithfully seek Thy help shall not be confounded.

" I believe, and am certain that I shall yet see the goodness of the Lord in the land of the living. The Lord is my strength and my shield, in Him my heart hopes, and I am helped. The Lord is with those that are of a troubled heart. He helps those whose spirit is cast down. O Lord, look on my grief and my wretchedness, and forgive me all my sins. Forsake me not, Lord, my God! hasten to stand by me, O Lord, my help! Why art thou so heavy, O my soul, and why art thou so disquieted within me? I put my trust in God, for I will yet give Him thanks, which is the help of my countenance and my defence. Amen."

WRITTEN BY QUEEN CHARLOTTE AT THE SAME TIME AS THE PRECEDING.

"Psalm xxxvii. 5 : ' Commit thy way unto the Lord, and put thy trust in Him, and He shall bring it to pass.'

"To Thee, O Father, Who art faithful, and in Whom I trust, I recommend all my undertakings and designs, my troubles and my cares. Thou orderest my destiny with goodness and wisdom. Thou hast the power to make all circumstances tend to my best advantage; but I, with all the circumspection I can employ in my affairs, may easily fall into something contrary to my true interest. I know not what will happen in future, I dare but little confide in the favour and assistance of men, a single accident might suddenly destroy the greatest part of my hopes. To Thee, Omniscient and Almighty Ruler of the whole world, I surrender myself with all my designs and occupations. Thou hast seen from all eternity what is necessary for my true and lasting welfare. Thou guidest the hearts of all men according to Thy wise counsel. Thou hast promised that to them who love Thee all things shall turn out for the best, I hope in Thee, let me not be confounded. Govern my thoughts that I may ever do what is pleasing to Thee. Bless my undertakings, guard me against the attempts of those who are not favourable to me. Lead me but in the ways that are well pleasing unto Thee. Strengthen in my soul a lively confidence in Thy mercy through Jesus Christ. Establish content in my too often inquiet heart.

"Preserve me in the hope of those joys that await me in a better world, so I shall care for nothing anxiously. Thou, Lord, wilt bring all things well to pass. Amen."

In the summer of this year, 1789, the first royal visit

to Weymouth took place, the King and all his family coming thither to recruit his health, and vary the scene after his illness. His brother, the Duke of Gloucester, left them the house he had long possessed there, and which, with all the lodging-houses adjoining, from Gloucester Lodge to the hotel, were afterwards purchased by the King. The Duke of Gloucester had once, in my father's lifetime, visited Moreton for shooting, the sport on my father's manors being reckoned particularly good. In my extreme youth I remember seeing frequently, in my walks, so many pheasants together in a field that we doubted at a distance from the colour whether it was a ploughed field or not, and have counted when near them, more than 100 brace feeding, yet *then* no arts were used to entice them by giving them corn, &c.

The Duke of Gloucester breakfasted at Moreton, and, when pheasants were so plenty, royalty was much less common, and the fuss and attention paid was very considerable. The Duke had a small table set by itself for his *déjeûner*. I was too young to appear. A collation was prepared for him after shooting, but in those days dinners were at three or four o'clock, and, much to the dismay of my poor mother, the Duke returned from his sport, and requested to *dine* at Moreton, instead of merely taking a luncheon. I perfectly remember the distress in the house when this was announced, but what sort of dinner his Royal Highness got I know not. I was permitted to see him after dinner, just before he set off for Weymouth, and this was my first introduction to anything royal. The Weymouth visits made me, to a certain degree, familiar with the good, the excellent George III., his Queen, and most of the Princesses, but not in their *first* visits there. The pleasure I derived through them this year was going on board the *Magnificent*, a 74-gun ship stationed off Weymouth during their stay.

1790.

WE spent part of the year in London, and afterwards my mother and myself passed the early part of the summer with my aunt Lady Vernon, at Lord Vernon's beautiful place at Britton Ferry in Glamorganshire, at the mouth of the Neath River.[6]

We had two or three public days during the two months' stay by way of receiving the Welsh neighbours, and they afforded me considerable amusement. Not so my aunt, who grudged every moment spent within doors in that charming place. The service in church was, I believe, entirely performed in Welsh when Lord Vernon's family were not at Britton Ferry, and the First Lesson was constantly read in Welsh, and the text given out in that language. The peasantry were dirty and full of animals, and as numbers of poor came to be fed at the house, it was really difficult to keep free from them. The housemaids hired for the time all went about the house without shoes or stockings, and were not famous for honesty, at least pins, ribbons, &c., disappeared quickly if left about carelessly.

My eldest brother, Charlton Wollaston, made a summer excursion with two friends to Switzerland and Paris. The following extracts are from the letters we received:—

---

[6] Lord Vernon possessed this estate through his first wife, the Hon. Louisa Barbarina, daughter and heiress of Bussy, Lord Mansel, who died (s.p.) 1786. On his own death, in 1813, it devolved upon the Earl of Jersey, who sold the property.

C. B. WOLLASTON TO HIS MOTHER.

"*Rheims, July 18th,* 1790.

"On Wednesday, 14th July, was held the ceremony of the 'Fedération.'[7] All the Bourgeois were dressed in the national uniform, with arms, &c., to the number of between 2000 and 3000, and were drawn up on the promenade, a fine spacious walk near the town. At half-past eleven all the bells in the city began to ring, and some guns were fired, when the mayor pronounced the oath,to which they assented by holding up their hand, after which the *Te Deum* was sung. It rained so exceedingly hard during the ceremony, and there was such a mob of people, that we could hardly see anything that was going on, and indeed there was little to be seen. This ceremony was performed at precisely the same hour in every town in the kingdom, and there is something very well conceived and magnificent in the idea of the bells all over the kingdom ringing at the same instant of time, and the whole nation assembling to take the oath."

From Rheims Mr. Wollaston proceeded to Châlons, thence to Vitry, St. Dizier, and Joinville, the situation of which he says "is very romantic and fine on the banks of the Marne, with high-wooded hills and vineyards. At Compiègne we went to see the palace, and having lately perhaps seen the largest and handsomest palace of our king, I could not but draw comparisons between that and what we are told is one of the least superb mansions of the King of France. At Compiègne there are complete apartments for every one of the royal family; those of the

[7] "Confederation of Paris," held on the anniversary of the taking and destruction of the Bastille, at which the King was obliged to be present. He, the National Assembly, the army, and the people, solemnly swore to maintain the new Constitution, and also fidelity to the "Patriot King." Great rejoicings followed, and Paris was illuminated.

King and Queen fitted up in the most elegant modern style with Gobelin tapestry, which is very curious and very handsome, and the most superb hangings. Besides these there are separate apartments for all their suite. The road from Compiègne to Soissons, partly through the Forest of Compiègne, is very pretty, and from St. Dizier to Joinville it is beautiful.

" At Joinville is a fine old castle on the point of a very steep hill, formerly the residence of the Dukes of Guise. It *now* belongs to M. Philippe d'Orleans, who, we are told, is to be sent here *en exil*, and that the château is getting ready for him, but I do not believe this. There is a small room in the castle called the ' Cabinet de la Ligue,' in which the leaders of that party met to consult together. The church contains many curious monuments of the house of Joinville and the Guises." . . .

" At Dijon we saw realized the old French pictures, as on the Sunday evening there the public walk was quite full of ladies in dress caps, and gentlemen in fine coats without hats sitting down on the grass, walking about, &c. We put on our cockades (the national tricolour) and walked amongst them without being taken notice of, excepting that Dr. Arnold's spectacles attract much attention in this country. We have seldom used our cockades, except at Rheims on the day of the Fédération, as they are very little worn excepting by the National Guard in the country we have passed through, but in this town (Dijon) they are very general. We were stopped at the gate for a passport, which we had procured at Calais.

" About half a mile from the town is a Convent of the Chartreuse, which we have been visiting; in the church are some fine monuments of the Dukes of Burgundy.[8]

---

[8] On the suppression of La Chartreuse, these monuments were removed to the Church of St. Benigne, but in 1793 the Council of the Commune

" The cloisters are very large and handsome, and enclose a garden which is now suffered to go to ruin, as the building is to be sold and turned into a manufacture, and only the chapel and apartments of the monks to be left for them. They are to be allowed pensions for life instead of the immense revenues they possessed before.''

*   *   *   *

" Lyons, August 8th, 1790.

" To-morrow we mean to set out for Paris, but the journey will occupy some days.

" The country is everywhere perfectly quiet, as much so as if no change whatever had taken place, and yet *everything is* totally changed. There is no Intendant to be found, all is in the hands of the Municipalité. We were told that in Champagne there never had been any disturbance during the whole of the Revolution.

" We hear that there have been some commotions here, and we see the red flag now actually hoisted and cannon placed at the end of the street we are living in, with the match ready lighted, but everything is as tranquil as in any town in England, and men, women, and children are amusing themselves all day long in the Saône, which is running under our windows."

" Paris, August 17th, 1790.

" We went to Versailles a few days ago, and were highly gratified by a complete view of the magnificent

decreed their destruction. Fortunately, however, although the figures had been separated from their bases and dispersed, they were not destroyed, and in 1818 it was resolved to restore them, which has been most successfully accomplished. They are now placed in the Museum, arranged in the ancient Salle des Gardes, in the palace of the Dukes of Burgundy, now called Le Palais des États, where we saw them in September, 1852.—H. G. M.

palace, gardens, &c. . . . The chapel is magnificent,
and the apartments, theatre, &c., in the highest style of
grandeur. Having been so lately the scene of such
interesting events, it was particularly interesting to us.

" The hall where the National Assembly met whilst
they were at Versailles, and which was built on purpose,
is a very fine room, but is now made no use of. The
stables belonging to the palace are much larger than
those of any of the royal palaces in England. I am
sure that I saw at least 300 horses in them, all kept in
the finest order, although now seldom used. We
heard at Versailles that the King and Queen were at
Paris that day, and were to return to St. Cloud the
next, and that by going to St. Cloud we might see them
pass by. Accordingly, on Sunday night we slept at St.
Cloud. We were told there that we might go into the
palace and see them get out of their carriage; we therefore waited two or three hours in the apartments, to
which everybody had free access; they were full of
strangers and the National Militia. About two o'clock
the King, Queen, Dauphin, Madame Royale, and Madame
Elizabeth, the King's sister, arrived in one carriage. We
saw them get out, pass close by us going upstairs, and
afterwards we stood in the antechamber, where they
passed by two or three times, and stood talking for ten
minutes before they went to dinner. I shall never
forget the Queen's stepping out of the carriage and then
waiting and taking the Dauphin by the hand, leading
him upstairs, and afterwards appearing at a balcony
between her two children. I assure you, Mrs. Siddons
was never finer in any of her parts. We visited this
morning the Champ de Mars, where the great ceremony
of the 14th was performed. They were destroying the
scaffolding, &c., very fast; the place is immense, and it

must have been a fine sight to have seen it full of people, but it is so large that it is impossible to know at one end what may be going on at the other."

"*Paris, August,* 1790.

"I have been twice to the National Assembly, on Thursday through the whole of the sitting, and this morning for two or three hours. You shall hear more when we meet, at present I can only say that the President's 'bell' does not keep such good order there as the Speaker's mace in the House of Commons in England.

"The Duke of Orleans[9] was there on Thursday. He does not make his appearance much in public. He has some friends, but the generality of people look very shy upon him. You may have seen in the papers that he has been accused of having been concerned in the affair at Versailles[1] in October last, and of a design to murder the King; this, however, is not true.

"One of the members of the National Assembly made use of some strong expressions relating to that affair, for which he was reprimanded, and has since been imprisoned for eight days for publishing a pamphlet to the same effect. It was supposed that he alluded to the Duke of Orleans and Mirabeau.[2]

---

[9] Louis Philippe, surnamed "Egalité," father of Louis Philippe, King of the French.

[1] October 5th, 1789, when the King and royal family were *forced* to move to Paris.

[2] Honoré Gabriel, Comte de Mirabeau, né 1749, élu premier Deputé de la Sénéchaussée d'Aix, 1787; Membre du Département de Paris; et le 31 Janvier, 1791, *Président de l'Assemblée Nationale*. Il mourut 2 Avril, 1791.

Mirabeau was more than suspected of aiding the manœuvres practised

"Paris is certainly a very pleasant residence. Every-body dresses in the English fashion, and even to the extreme, as boots are not uncommon in the first boxes at the opera. This is fortunate for us. It is much less expensive living at Paris than in London; we dine every day at one of the first coffee-houses in the Palais Royal, where there is always very good company, and get our dinner very good and cheaper than in the coffee-houses in the neighbourhood of Lincoln's Inn.

" Yesterday we visited the remains of the Bastille, and picked off a bit of stone as a present for Miss Fauquier."

1791.

PARTY spirit ran high this year, the revolutionary spirit in France giving ground for warm disputes as to what ought to be approved or disapproved here as to the pro-ceedings in that country. The marriage of the Duke of York[3] to the Princess Frédérica, daughter of the King of Prussia, took place in the autumn.

She was a very short woman, with a plain face, but neat little figure, with a remarkably small foot. Consequently it became the fashion for every one to squeeze their feet without mercy, in order to be like her Royal Highness, and as she wore heels to her shoes, so did the rest of the world. I was very short, and of course wore high heels, raising my heels from the ground about two inches. The position, I think, made the ankle thinner and neater than the flat sole which after some

---

in Paris to seduce the troops, and of favouring the project to subvert Louis XVI., in order to place the Duke of Orleans on the throne of France.

[3] He married, September 29th, Frédérica Ulrica, eldest daughter of Frederic William II., King of Prussia. She died 1820; the duke survived her till 1827.

years succeeded, but the high heel is perfectly unnatural, and gives a bad movement in walking.

The Duke of York and his duchess did not live happily together, although appearances of union were kept up to the last.

At the beginning of June both my brothers set off for a few months to the Continent. The following extracts are from the letters received during their tour.

FROM JAMES FRAMPTON.

" Harwich, June 4th, 1791.

" Our carriage is all pulled to pieces and on board the packet. Our luggage has been examined by the Custom House officers, and although the wind is high and immediately against us, we leave this place for Dutchland as soon as the foreign letters arrive. The vessel we are to sail in is 100 tons burthen, and is called the *Diana* (as I see by our passport). We have laid in provisions for three days.

" This is a strange little town upon a small nook of land almost surrounded by the sea; but though this is a very comfortable inn, we have had almost enough of it."

THE SAME TO HIS MOTHER.

Helvœtsluys, June 6th, 1791.

" After a voyage of fifty hours from Harwich we are safely arrived here. We performed it with much greater satisfaction to ourselves than we expected. This is the cleanest, neatest place I ever saw; the inn is kept by an Englishman. The town is fortified.

" Pray tell Mary that Mr. Stewart's tail would be rather laughed at here for a short one, as they wear them in general quite down to their seats; at least, all the soldiers do so." (I insert this trivial remark and message to myself to mark the fashion of the times when all gentlemen wore queues, or tails of considerable length and thickness near the head, dwindling by degrees towards the extremity, with a little bow of ribbon near the head, and a small brush of hair at the end, the whole well plaistered and powdered, and great curls frizzed, powdered and pomatumed at the ears, called sometimes canons from their shape. The ladies wore the hair flowing down their backs and high in front, with much pomatum and powder put on with different kinds of puffs. The finishing powder had a brown hue and a strong perfumed smell, and was called "Maréchale" powder. This powder was applied at a distance, that every hair might be frosted with it. One pound, and even two pounds, of powder were sometimes put into the hair or wasted in the room in one dressing.) I return to the letter.

" We were obliged to put orange cockades in our hats, or tie some orange ribbon through our button-holes. The women wearing hoops has a strange appearance."

CHARLTON BYAM WOLLASTON TO THE SAME.

" *The Hague, June 9th,* 1791.

" The morning after we reached Helvœtsluys we set out for Rotterdam, and travelled about twenty-five miles in seven hours, with four horses to the carriage ; the roads are very sandy, but good enough at this time of the year. We had three ferries to cross, the last which carried us over to Rotterdam very wide, but the carriage was drawn in and out without difficulty. The country is extremely singular, being perfectly flat excepting for the dykes. Rotterdam has a striking appearance ; the canals run up most of the streets between rows of large elm-trees, and are crossed by drawbridges. Very large vessels by this means come up into the middle of the town, in which there are some very handsome buildings. On Wednesday we passed through Delft to the Hague. This place seems quite built for the Court, and the houses of the nobility, ambassadors, &c., are very large and much ornamented. There appears to be little going on, as the Prince of Orange[4] and his Court are not here at present, he being gone a progress, reviewing regiments and visiting the frontier towns. As we approached the Hague the Orange cockades increased by degrees, and here they are immense. I have a letter for a 'Mr. Hope,'[5] a great man at Amsterdam, who we are told is disposed to be very civil to the English."

FROM JAMES FRAMPTON (same date).

" We went this evening in one of the open cabriolets of the country to Scheveningen, a fishing town on the sea coast, where there is nothing worth seeing. All the carriages, by the way, are curious to see, being more like my Lord Mayor's or the Chancellor's state coaches than anything else, most superbly gilt. On the way to it is a villa belonging to Madame Bentinck, the grounds about which are laid out something in the English style, and as pretty as a perfect flat can be, but as there is no such thing

---

[4] William V., Prince of Orange and Stadtholder, succeeded 1751. His mother was the Princess Anne, daughter of George II., King of England. The Prince married Frederica Sophia, sister of Frederic William, King of Prussia, and died 1806. Their son (William Frederic) was the first who had the title of *King of the Netherlands* in 1815.

[5] John Hope, Esq., who was then residing at Amsterdam, and one of the richest merchants in Europe.

When subsequently driven from Holland by the revolution there, and the advance of the French armies, Mr. Hope settled in London.

as gravel in the country, the walks are over one's shoes in sand. The whole of which journey (N.B., as H. would say) is only between two and three miles, when we could not help thinking of my Uncle Toby and Stevinus's Flying Chariot![6] We are now sitting over a very good fire."

FROM C. B. WOLLASTON.

"Amsterdam, June 13th, 1791.

" We left the Hague on Saturday morning, dined at Leyden, and slept at Haarlem. The country is prettier than I could have conceived, as the road passes all the way through a thick wood, interspersed with divers Dutch villas, but when next I travel through this country I will have nothing to do with a carriage, as they are very little used to them, and you can go almost as conveniently in the trackshuts.

" The large organ at Haarlem has a very fine tone ; they were playing a Presbyterian Psalm tune and an odd sort of Voluntary upon it yesterday after church. We stayed there yesterday to dine with Mr. Hope, who has a most princely seat close to Haarlem. I had a letter for him which we left in the morning, and very soon received a very civil invitation to dinner, and were received in the most easy and pleasant manner. There were about twenty people at dinner, which was a magnificent one, and the house is more like a palace than the seat of a private gentleman. There is a picture-gallery which is one of the finest rooms I ever saw. Mr. Hope purchased two collections of famous pictures to furnish it, and he selected the best, which are of the first masters. Nothing could be more civil than they were, and we are to see them again here and to change money. We have seen

<hr/>

[6] Sterne's "Tristram Shandy."

but little of this town, as we only arrived to dinner, but the Stadthouse is magnificent, and in our walk this evening we got into a Jews' synagogue—a very large and handsome building. I never saw such a set of ill-looking wretches; they say there are upwards of 40,000 Jews in this town. I may add that the canals stink abominably.

" This being Whit Monday, the Post Office was closed, but we went into a coffee-house, where we met with several English papers. I find the Parliament is up, and am sorry that the Libel Bill is put off by the Lords. I suppose it is true that Dundas [7] is Secretary of State, and Barrington Bishop of Durham, by the manner in which it is mentioned. Not a word, however, of Dr. Vernon.[8] I am anxious to know whether he will be *be-bishoped !*

The French papers talk much of preparations for making an attack upon France. If it happens in Alsace, which is the scene they fix upon, we shall be in the midst of it."

FROM THE SAME TO MRS. FRAMPTON.

Antwerp, June 20th, 1791.

" MY DEAR MOTHER,—We arrived here yesterday, after two days' very tiresome travelling, though from Amster-

---

[7] The Right Honourable Henry Dundas, Secretary of State for Home Department, 1791, created Viscount Melville, 1802.

[8] The Honourable Edward Venables Vernon, third son of George, first Lord Vernon, Bishop of Carlisle, 1791, but translated to the metropolitan see of York, 1807. He married Lady Anne Leveson, daughter of Granville, first Marquis of Stafford. The archbishop took the name of Harcourt on succeeding to the Harcourt Estates on the death of the last Earl Harcourt (s.p.) in 1830, and died 1847. The Archbishop of York was brother-in-law to Mr. Wollaston's aunt, Lady Vernon.

dam to Utrecht is only a journey of about twenty miles; and the road, good and really very pretty for *that* country, for the greatest part was through an enclosed country, with villas on each side—very odd and very pretty. The next day we were in the carriage by half-past six, and reached Gorcum, about twenty miles, by twelve o'clock. There we dined and changed horses, and were upwards of seven hours getting from thence to Breda, having to cross three ferries. Breda is very strongly fortified and regularly kept up, so that we had a soldier walk before us into the town till we met with an officer at the inner gate, who took our names. There is a very fine old palace belonging to the Prince of Orange. He and his suite had been there for some time, and had left it only a few days previously. Yesterday we were more than eight hours in accomplishing the thirty miles from Breda to Antwerp, including the time we stopped to bait. We have been all day looking at very fine pictures, either in the churches or in private collections, and have as many more to see to-morrow, so that in time we may perhaps become connoiseurs.

"There are no end of monasteries and convents, with Crucifixes, Virgins, and Saints at every possible corner of the streets. I fear it is not respect for them that has made all quiet here again after the piece of work there has been for some time, but rather suspect it is owing to the presence of upwards of 3000 Hungarian and Austrian troops, which are quartered in and about the town. An army is a marvellous peace-maker in some popular commotions. The fortifications, though large, do not seem to be much attended to; but we had the same ceremony as at Breda on coming into the town.

"A Paper I saw to-night says, very particularly, that

the Prince de Condé [9] and the Comte d'Artois,[1] as well as several other French refugees, are arrived at Mayence, which is one of the towns we are to pass through. I hope we shall soon be in a land where they talk French, for, excepting at the inns, they still continue to speak a sort of Dutch, which they call the Brabançon language.

"We have visited Brock and Saardam, which are two of the lions from Amsterdam. The painted houses, with little gardens cut out in a fantastic manner, together with the neatness of the canals and the painted boats upon them, reminded me of a Chinese screen."

Madame de Genlis, in the third volume of her "Adèle et Théodore," has immortalized, by her amusing description, these two places mentioned by Mr. Wollaston.

JAMES FRAMPTON TO HIS MOTHER.

"*Brussels, June 23rd,* 1791.

"MY DEAR MOTHER,—As probably this letter will reach you sooner than your English newspaper, and the account will certainly be more authentic, I write to say that I have just seen Colonel Gardiner, the resident here for Lord Torrington, who has told us that the King, Queen,

[9] Louis Joseph, born 1736. In 1800 he retired to Amesbury, in England, but returned to France, 1814. The prince married, first, Charlotte, daughter of Charles, Duc de Rohan-Soubise, who died 1760; and secondly, in 1798, Cathérine de Brignole, Princesse Douairière de Monaco, who died 1813. His son, Louis Henri, Duc de Bourbon, accompanied his father to England, and went back with him to France. The Prince de Condé died 1818, but the Duc de Bourbon never took any other title. He was the last of his family, and unhappily destroyed himself at the Château de St. Leu, August 25, 1830.

The only son of the duke, by his marriage with Louise, daughter of Philippe, Duc d'Orléans (who died 1822), was the unfortunate Louis, Duc d'Enghien, shot at Vincennes, by order of Buonaparte, March 21, 1804 (s.p.).

[1] Charles, younger brother of Louis XVI., succeeded to the throne of France as Charles X.

and royal family of France have escaped from Paris.[2]
They walked in disguise from the Tuileries to the
Barrière, about two miles and a half, where they met a
coach which was to take them to some frontier town;
but where he could not tell. They had got twenty-five
miles from Paris when this account left them. We
expect to hear more every hour.

" Monsieur has escaped also, and was heard of at
Mons, which is within fourteen leagues of this place,
asking his way to join the Comte d'Artois and Prince de
Condé, who are somewhere in the neighbourhood of
Mayence.

" We saw several French officers setting out late
yesterday evening to join Monsieur at Mons. This is a
most critical moment, certainly, and there will be bloody
work, I fear.

" The Emperor has a vast body of troops here and in
the neighbourhood. I should think the King would
never have taken this step without having friends at
hand.

" We have this morning been seeing a magnificent
procession on account of to-day being the " Fête Dieu."
The Host was carried under a canopy by the bishop or
archbishop, and behind walked the Archduchess and her
husband, who returned to their Government only a few
days ago, followed by their suite. They ended at the
cathedral, where, by the way, Charlton heard a very
pretty ' Agnus Dei' at mass one morning.

" This town is as full as it can cram with refugee
French. They say that there are about 8000. You may
guess the stir this news makes. The whole business was

---

[2] June 21, 1791. Louis XVI. and the royal family fled from the
Tuileries.

conducted with the utmost secrecy.   You may depend
upon hearing anything authentic we can pick up."

FROM C. B. WOLLASTON.

"*Brussels, June 24th*, 1791.

" I have only a moment to tell you that Colonel Gardiner has just told us that undoubted intelligence is received
of the King, Queen, Dauphin, and Princess having been
stopped and conducted back to Paris.   'Monsieur'[3] and
'Madame' and Madame Elizabeth[4] have escaped, and are
expected here to-night.   The French here, from being in
the greatest spirits, are become miserably depressed :
indeed the consequences may be lamentable.   The officers
bespoke 'Richard Cœur de Lion' at the theatre last
night, and at every sentence applicable to the King's
deliverance, and particularly at the song of ' O Richard,
O mon roi ! ' the applause was amazing, and the actors
were obliged to repeat several sentences over and over
again."

" *June 25th*.—This morning everything is dismal, and
the long faces of the French people are most pitiable.

" The inauguration of the Emperor[5] as Duke of Brabant is fixed for Thursday.   He is not, however, to be

---

[3] Louis, Comte de Provence, brother of Louis XVI. ; succeeded as
Louis XVIII., 1814. He married Marie Joséphine, daughter of
Amadeus III., King of Sardinia ; dite "Madame."

[4] Sister of Louis XVI. She did not escape, but was arrested with
the King and Queen at Varennes, and was beheaded, June, 1794.

[5] Leopold II. succeeded 1790. At the Peace of Rastadt and of Baden,
1714, the Emperor Charles VI. received the Pays-Bas Espagnols, the
Milanais, Sardinia, Mantua, and the Tuscan Ports. France gave up
all her conquests on the Rhine as far as Landau. Bavaria and Cologne
were withdrawn from the ban of the empire, and all their dependancies
and dignities restored to them.

here, but the Duke Albert [6] is to represent him, though whether it will take place now is uncertain, as the Archduchess is sister to the Queen of France.

" We have this morning most fortunately met with Lord Albemarle,[7] and we shall stay over Thursday if this ceremony takes place.

" We have been much struck by the frivolity of the French, who, on hearing the account of the royal family having been arrested at Varennes, immediately ordered the Comédie of 'L'Obstacle imprévu' to be performed that night at the theatre. We dine at Colonel Gardiner's on Monday."

THE SAME TO DR. ARNOLD.

" *Brussels, June* 30*th*, 1791.

" The ceremony of the Inauguration took place to-day, though the day was rainy, especially towards the evening, which obliged the illuminations which were to have taken place in the public gardens to be postponed, so we have resolved to stay another day for the chance of better weather, as we hear that they will be well worth seeing. It was a fine sight altogether. We had a window directly opposite, and had the fun of seeing people scramble for medals which were thrown from the windows amongst them.

" I wished much for you, if only to see ' Toison d'Or,'

[6] Albert Casimir, Duke of Saxe-Teschen, son of Augustus III., Elector of Saxony and King of Poland, Gouverneur des Pays-Bas, 1780-92. He married the Archduchess Mary Christina, daughter of the Empress Maria Theresa.

" Her monument, by Canova, in the Augustine Church at Vienna is extremely fine."—W. M.

[7] William Charles Keppel, fourth Earl of Albemarle. He was a constant friend both of Mr. Wollaston and Mr. Frampton till his death in 1849.

a very fine fellow I assure you, dressed in a most rich coat all bedaubed with coats of arms, with a fine plume of feathers on his head, and mounted on a courser, which pranced about most majestically. There were besides four other heralds representing Brabant and the other counties—very fine creatures.

"This part of the procession, which preceded the Duke's carriage, was very rich, but the rest of the train was but shabby.

"They first went to hear mass at a superb altar erected on purpose in the great church, and then came into the handsome large square, on one side of which a fine throne had been built up. Here the Prince of Saxe-Teschen took the oaths for the emperor, which were administered by the Cardinal Archbishop of Malines [8] in his full-

[8] At the period when these letters were written, the laws relating to Roman Catholics were still extremely stringent, although they had to a certain degree been modified ; and no priest could venture on wearing an ecclesiastical dress, even within the house where he might be residing as chaplain, much less out of doors, until long afterwards. There was no English cardinal, with the exception of the Cardinal of York, from the death of Cardinal Philip Howard at Rome, in 1694, until Cardinal Weld, 1829.

His life was a curious one. Possessor of Lulworth Castle, Thomas Weld, Esq., married, 1796, Lucy, daughter of the Honourable Thomas Clifford, by whom he had an only child, Mary Lucy, subsequently, 1818, married to Lord Clifford, of Chudleigh ; and, on the death of his wife, Mr. Weld took holy orders, soon became a bishop, and obtained a cardinal's hat in 1829. He died at Rome, highly esteemed and deeply regretted from his charities, &c., April 10, 1837.

The refugee French clergy were allowed to live in England, where their residence was connived at, and a small colony of the order of "Trappists," when driven from Normandy by the French Revolution, took refuge at Lulworth, in Dorsetshire, where, under the protection of Mr. Weld, they were permitted to cultivate the wild heath-land unmolested.

They even wore a kind of monastic dress, but never spoke, according to the rules of their order. The buildings and land formerly occupied

dressed robes, which was a thing we were very desirous to see.

" At the conclusion of the ceremony, Toison d'Or came forward and proclaimed the Emperor's magnificent titles, which was followed by a triple discharge of artillery, guns, trumpets, &c., which sounded very fine. The popular applause, however, was very small, but when upwards of 10,000 men are about that did not much signify. The Archduchess was most coldly received, and there seemed to be very few hearts and not many hands that bid her and her husband welcome. She is a very sour, ungainly-looking woman, and not at all like her sister, the Queen of France.

" The Comte d'Artois arrived here a few days ago. Monsieur and Madame, who had been here some days previously, went out to meet him, and he was attended into the town by most of the French officers. We saw him come in and get out of his carriage. He and Monsieur appeared on the parade yesterday, but they have not otherwise shown themselves, and neither of them were present at the ceremony to-day. The Comte d'Artois is a fine, handsome man, like the family, but very different in figure from his brothers. He goes to Coblentz to-morrow. Monsieur and Madame stay some time longer, though they say the Archduchess wants to get rid of them.

" I never saw, I must confess, so fine a set of young men as the French officers here are. There is a manly

by the Monastery of La Trappe lie between Lulworth Castle and the sea-coast. It is now called the " Monastery Farm."

In the autumn of 1815, H.R.H. the Princess Charlotte, who was then staying at Weymouth, went to see the Trappist Convent at Lulworth, as the royal family can go into any monastic establishment in England which they may be pleased to visit.

gracefulness in them which few English fine men can boast. They always appear in the uniform of their regiments, and with a white cockade, and those who belong to no regiment wear a contre-revolution uniform.

"I have seen a very accurate account of the King's arrival in Paris, and a most stormy scene it must have been. The National Assembly had taken precautions to prevent any violence from the mob, and they were conducted to the Tuileries in a dead silence through a vast concourse of people. M. Barnave,[9] as soon as he had set them safe, came to the Assembly, which had continued sitting from the Tuesday on which the King escaped till the Saturday night without adjourning, and related what he had done. It seems to be believed here that the King, Queen, and Dauphin are each under a separate guard, without any communication with each other, and that when their deposition has been taken, they will proceed to a regular trial."

"*Friday, July* 1*st.*

"Though we have stayed to-day for the illuminations, I believe we shall be disappointed, as there has been some very heavy rain, and it looks as if it would continue. I have gained something, however, by the delay, as I have been to hear High Mass performed at a magnificent altar erected before the choir in the Cathedral of St. Gudule, which is only placed there on great occasions. The instruments, organ, and singers (who were but moderate), were behind and out of sight, and some of the music was exceedingly fine.[1]

[9] In 1790, President of the Assemblée Constituante, but after the dissolution of the National Assembly in 1791, he retired to Grenoble. The following year Barnave was denounced, arrested, and thrown into prison. He was executed November 30, 1793.

[1] Mr. Wollaston was a great musician. He composed and published

" I can send you no French news, as the French post to this place is stopped.

" The Comte d'Artois has left Brussels to-day, but they say the French will stay about here yet for some time; they expect something or other to take place in six weeks, what it is I know not. I was told this morning that the National Assembly had appointed a Regent. The King of Sweden is at Aix-la-Chapelle. I should like to see him. We go from hence to Spa, but our further movements depend much on the state of French politics."

C. B. WOLLASTON TO HIS MOTHER.

" *Aix-la-Chapelle, July 5th,* 1791.

" I have not written to you since my short letter from Brussels. It was quite melancholy to see the poor French people after the news arrived of the King being taken. Their joy, however, at his escape was, I thought, carried too far, as they seemed to have imagined the thing done, when at least there must have been a good deal of hard fighting before they could have returned home. They might as well have waited another day before they were so sanguine.

" You have, I suppose, seen the 'Declaration,' as it is called, of the King and Queen, though it had better be called *Examination*. That of the King is miserable; a little spirit on such an occasion might have had some effect.

" There is a most admirably written address to the National Assembly from Bouillé,[2] who commanded the

some very beautiful sacred music—Chaunts, Sanctus, Kyrie Eleison, &c. He was also the author of a translation of the " Satires of Persius," &c., which was much admired; but this was printed only for private distribution amongst his friends.

[2] François Claude, Marquis de Bouillé, General, born 1739. He de-

troops which were to have joined the King. I dare say
you will see it. He says that if they dare to touch a
hair of the King's head, there will not be left one stone
upon another in Paris, for that all the Powers in Europe
will unite in his favour. I believe, however, that he says
a great deal more than will appear to be true, and I also
hear that it is doubted whether it is really written by
Bouillé or not. If, however, the King had escaped and
had done as Bouillé says he intended to do, he would
probably have been joined by the most rational people,
and he might have succeeded.

"Colonel Gardiner was extremely civil and attentive
to us, and meeting Lord Albemarle at Brussels, made
our week there vastly pleasant. The upper part of the
town and park are beautiful, and there is something
sociable and entertaining in the style of the place. We
dined one day with Sir William Jerningham, where we
met Lord and Lady Cholmondeley[3] and several French
people. It was one of the hottest days I ever felt."

FROM THE SAME.

"*Aix-la-Chapelle, July 5th*, 1791.

"We passed through Liege on our way to Spa. The

voted himself, though unsuccessfully, to ensure the flight of Louis XVI.,
by placing detachments of troops between Châlons and Montmedy to
protect his route. A delay of twenty-four hours in the departure of the
King, and a mistake, attributed by Bouillé to the Duc de Choiseul,
were the cause of the royal family being stopped at Varennes. Bouillé
arrived two hours too late to save the King. He left France the same
day, and eventually went to England, where he died in 1800.

[3] George James, fourth Earl Cholmondeley, Lord Steward of the
Household, 1813, K.G., created marquis 1815, died 1827. He married
Georgiana, daughter and coheir of Peregrine, third Duke of Ancaster,
who, with her sister, the Baroness Willoughby de Eresby, was Joint
Hereditary Great Chamberlain of England. She died 1838.

Emperor is so good as to put soldiers in every corner of
the streets there to keep the good people in order; and
indeed I suspect they may want some such keepers, for
a more miserable set of people I never saw, nor a more
dirty, ill-built town than Liege. There are coal-pits in
the neighbourhood, and the colour of the streets and
people is many degrees deeper than those of Birmingham
or Bristol. We have been very lucky in meeting our
friends; we found the Ryders[4] at Spa, and stayed there
another day on that account.

" The Rooms at that pretty little place are very handsome, and there are assemblies of one sort or other all
day long, first at the Wells, afterwards at the Vauxhall,
and in the evening at the Assembly Rooms. There is
Faro and divers other games at all times going on, but
people do not play so high as in England."

" *Cologne, July 6th.*—I did not finish my letter last
night, as we went out to see the King of Sweden,[5] who
is staying at Aix-la-Chapelle. It is a vile, dirty, ill-built
town, and what can bring him or anybody else there I
cannot conceive, but for some reason or other he and a
great number of princes *are* there at present, and the
place is as full as it can hold. The company assemble
in the Rooms every evening, as at Watering-places[6] in
England, and there we went. At first it was a kind of

[4] The two elder sons of Nathaniel, Lord Harrowby. Both the brothers
were intimate and lifelong friends of Mr. Wollaston.

[5] Gustavus III. Stabbed at a masked ball, 1791. He married Sophia,
daughter of Frederick V., King of Denmark.

[6] At the end of the last and beginning of the present century, at the
few places of resort in England—Bath, Cheltenham, Harrogate, &c.,
then in vogue—the company regularly met of an evening in the Pump-
room, which corresponded with the Kursaal of the German baths.

The celebrated "Beau Nash" was Master of the Ceremonies at Bath
during the early part of the last century. He died there 1761.

Circle[7] like a Drawing-room. The King of Sweden, the Elector of Cologne, Prince Ferdinand of Prussia,[8] and princes, princesses, stars, and ribands appeared there without number, whilst all sorts of ill-looking people in no sort of dress stood round staring.

" I had a great curiosity to see an active fighting king, but I must say that of the three Majesties I have seen our own King is the best to look at.

" The King of Sweden is a short man, and his countenance is very disagreeable. He has, however, some spirit in his eye. He was in conversation most of the time with a Russian General, whose name I forget, who, not above a year ago, was actually fighting in person against him, which is curious enough. I should never have guessed that his Majesty had ever drawn his own sword by his appearance.

" The Elector of Cologne, who is brother to the Emperor, looks like a vulgar English patriot; he wears black distinguished only by a cross and star, with his hair cut straight behind, and his head bald in front. (At this time in England it was only strong party men approaching to revolutionists, and calling themselves patriots, who wore no powder in their hair, and cut off their queues.)

" Monsieur, Madame, and the Comte d'Artois had dined yesterday at Aix-la-Chapelle with the King of Sweden, but did not appear at the assembly in the evening. They

---

[7] During the reign of George III. the Drawing-rooms held every Thursday, and when the royal family were in London, usually on Sunday also —were principally attended by the *habitués* of the Court, excepting on occasions of a royal birthday or after a royal marriage, &c., and the King and Queen used to walk round the apartment, speaking to every one whom they knew. I have heard from my father and mother that the same kind of ceremony took place when they held receptions of an evening during the royal visits to Weymouth.—H. G. M.

[8] Brother of Frederic William II., King of Prussia.

are, I believe, gone to Bonn. Have you read Necker's làst publication on his own administration? You would be much pleased with many parts of it."

FROM JAMES FRAMPTON.

"*Cologne, July 6th*, 1791.

"Conceive our being driven the last stage this evening by a man in a full dress, olive-green coat lined with light blue, with a cap something in the form of a hunting cap, the crown of which was of red cloth with a gold tassel on the top, and the under part of the brim in front, and a sort of turning up behind of green velvet, with a long carter's whip, with which he could not possibly strike either of the horses. They carry, too, a vile horn, which they blow on purpose (I believe) to stun you.

"Hitherto our travelling has been fully as expensive as in England, not to mention the going very slow, and generally over a bad *pavé;* but to-day we got into a more Christian-like road. It may truly be called so from the quantity of crucifixes, &c., which are everywhere stuck about. The Bishop of Winchester,[9] whom we saw at Brussels, and afterwards at Spa, on his way to Italy, travels in very great style, with three coaches painted green and numbered, the doing which, though it seems grand, certainly is of use, as otherwise they would not know into which to put the baggage which belonged to it."

C. B. WOLLASTON TO DR. ARNOLD.

"*Upon the Rhine, Sunday, July* 10.

"MY DEAR FRIEND,—We are just going to sleep a third

---

[9] The Honourable Brownlow North, son of Francis, first Earl of Guilford, died 1820.

night upon the Rhine, without being tired with lodging
so long in the boat which we hired at Bonn to take us
to Mayence, so that you may conclude we have been well
amused.   It is a sort of barge with three rooms below in
which you might stand up, stretching your neck to its
full extent, and seats with an awning above and room
besides for the carriage.   The beds are really very
comfortable.   I had an odd sort of accident which we
have laughed at since, though it was disagreeable at
the time.   James and I were sitting on the fore part of
the boat on two chairs.   The horses which draw it
stopped to water, and when they stopped the rope by
which it is drawn hung down over my chair.   This I did
not remark.   When the horses went on the rope was
stretched, and carried my chair and me over into the
river.   I perceived, when it was too late, what was
coming, and found I could not save myself, so in I went
over head and ears.   It was out of my depth, but I
swam and soon recovered myself.   I took a dram of Eau
de Cologne and water (for want of brandy), which we had
bought at Cologne, and which the paper says is good for
every disorder in the world.   I had a cold before, but it
certainly cured me.   Yesterday we passed Coblentz and
Ehrenbreitstein.   Below the latter is a very large though
desolated palace, formerly the residence of the Elector of
Trêves.   On the opposite side in the town is a new and
very fine palace built by the present Elector [1] in 1786,
which he now inhabits.   We stopped there for two or

---

[1] Clement Wenceslaus, son of Augustus III., King of Poland.   The
building was degraded by the French into barracks, and is now used
as a Court of Justice.   The beautiful palace chapel has been conceded
to the service of the Church of England.

The original *castle* of the Electors of Trêves, built 1558, is now a
manufactory (1840).

three hours, and visited the castle and town. The Elector's palace is very handsome within, the apartments elegantly furnished in the modern taste, and some very rich. He appeared to have the same complacency which some people in England possess, but which if I was an Elector or even a country squire with a fine place, I believe I should *not* have, as we were stopped at the entrance to his apartment for some minutes, and when we went in he had evidently only just left his writing table, where his papers, &c., were lying about. He had an odd-looking harpsichord in his room which I should have liked to have sounded. A great table was preparing for a dinner the Elector was to give to the French aristocrates ; it looked as if it would hold upwards of a hundred. Monsieur and the Comte d'Artois have plagued us more than I ever thought they were likely to do, as from Aix to Cologne we could get no post-horses, owing to them, but were obliged to hire from people who cheated us.

" The Prince de Condé is, or at least was, at Mayence. I think something must come of it. The last paper I saw says that a party is set up for a Republic. If you can get it, I advise you to order the *Moniteur*, a French newspaper which gives a very accurate account of all that passes in the National Assembly."

FROM JAMES FRAMPTON.

" *Mayencè, July* 11*th.*

" It is incredible the number of French we have seen at Bonn, Coblentz, and at this place. They are coming in tribes every day, and I hope they will soon be able to do something against the present uppermost party, for you must know that I am more of an aristocrate than ever. They wear the white cockade and contre-revolution uniform, which they have made on purpose.

"I heard at the *table-d'hôte* to-day a story which makes me pity the poor King of France more than ever. He and the Queen are still kept separate, and he was extremely anxious to see her, and insisted on going to her apartment, which was refused him; however he persisted, and was going out of the room, when the Guards presented their bayonets and made him go back again. The King was so extremely hurt by this refusal and harsh treatment that in his vexation and despair he broke everything that lay in his way. They have not yet appointed the Dauphin a governor.

"We are in doubt whether we shall pass through Alsace or not. There is not any real danger in going through that country, but they are now so very precise, and give persons so much trouble about passports, examining luggage, &c., as to be very disagreeable.

"By the help of cherries, champagne, and Rhenish wine, we contrived to keep life and soul together very comfortably during our fresh-water sailing.

From the Same.

"*Donaueschingen, July 17th,* 1791.

"At Mannheim we saw the Elector Palatine's [2] palace and pictures, from thence to Kehl, where we slept. A French aristocrate refugee advised us so strongly not to go through France, and we heard from other quarters so much of the difficulty to which travellers were put, that we determined to keep on the German side of the

---

[2] Charles Philip Theodore, Duke of Bavaria, died 1799 (s.p.). The palace was built by the Elector Prince Charles Philip in 1720, when he permanently removed from Heidelberg.

river. At Kehl, however, they told us we might go
into the town of Strasburg, and out again without difficulty, if we left our baggage behind us; so as we were
anxious to get our letters, and curious to see the place,
we yesterday morning took a carriage, and, leaving
everything but our pocket handkerchiefs and a little
money, crossed the bridge with a passport. Both going
into and coming out of Strasburg, we were made to get
out of the carriage, they felt our pockets, behind our
waistcoats, and even down my half-boots, and into the
crown of our hats for letters; made us show our purses
to see how much money we had, and examined every
part of the carriage; they were, however, perfectly civil.
When we got into the town it was ridiculous enough
that the first thing to be done was to get a passport to
secure our retreat, which detained us at the Hôtel de
Ville almost half the time we were in the place, although
there was no other difficulty than waiting till other
people were served. We then went after our letters,
which, however, we were forced to tear up before leaving
the town, and having dined at eleven o'clock (our dinner
was literally over before twelve, dessert, wine, and all),
and visited the cathedral, returned to Kehl. There was
no appearance of disturbance in Strasburg, and the
place seemed empty; the waiter told us they had had
no kind of riot there, and that everything went on as
usual.

"In the afternoon we came on a very beautiful drive,
three or four posts towards this place, to a little vile
inn called Hasslach, from whence we set off very early
this morning, hoping to reach Schaffhausen to-day; but
the roads proving bad and hilly, and the gates of that
town being shut at nine o'clock, we thought it prudent
to stop here. They tell you that the Danube rises in

the courtyard of the Prince of Furstenberg's [3] palace here; be this as it may, we have stepped over it in imitation of Mr. Coxe.[4] The prince is not here at present, but is hunting wild boars at one of his châteaux—of which he has five—in the Black Forest: if none of them are better than this (which, however, they say they are), they are bad enough, as this appears as if no gentleman could live in it."

C. B. Wollaston to his Mother.

" Schaffhausen, July 18th, 1791.

" We are now arrived in Switzerland. Our road from Kehl to this place was across Suabia; the country very fine, especially that part through the Black Forest. The Germans are absolutely square, some oblong the wrong way, especially the women: at least this is the opinion of James; they certainly are altogether the ugliest set of people I ever saw.

"At Mayence we ate some wild boar, to say we had done so, but think it was baddish food enough.

"I could pick up no news from Paris, excepting that the King, Queen, and Dauphin are still kept under a guard, and separate. The National Assembly seem not to know what to do, and to be a good deal divided amongst themselves.

"In this town there is not even a newspaper.

"At Schaffhausen is the bridge [5] mentioned by Coxe,

---

[3] Joseph Maria Benedict. He married Maria Antonia, daughter of Joseph, Prince of Hohenzollern-Hechingen, 1778.

[4] Author of various standard works, "Travels in Switzerland," "Historical Memoirs of the House of Austria," "Kings of Spain," &c., &c.

[5] This celebrated wooden bridge of a single arch, 365 feet in span, was burnt by the French in 1799. The architect was a carpenter from Appenzell, named Grubenmann.

curiously constructed across the Rhine, so that the road on which you pass is below the arch which supports it ; it is not pretty to look at, as it is covered on the top and sides, and painted red."

FROM THE SAME.

" Berne, July 27th, 1791.

" We have not been here above an hour, and, whilst waiting for our supper at the *table-d'hôte,* I will begin a letter to you. Since I last wrote we have had a very fine journey. I thought of you, especially at the Falls of the Rhine. The river was more than usually full, and the cascade was therefore in very fine order. In walking to it we first tried our stout shoes, and shall, I am sure, find a great difference in mounting the Montanvert with them, instead of tight boots and leather breeches, the worst walking machinery in the world. From Zurich we took horses, and rode along one side of that singularly pretty lake to Richterschwyll, and from thence, the next morning, to Einsiedeln,[6] the famous Benedictine monastery, containing the *black* image of ' Notre Dame des Ermites.' We met pilgrims in plenty. The convent is very large, and the situation in a deep valley between mountains which are there very high, and backed by *true alps,* is very romantic. The church within is very large, and you would not have expected in these distant parts to have heard a mass performed with instruments of all kinds, and monks singing solos. The music was concealed behind the altar, which has a fine effect, but the performance, the organ excepted, was indifferent. The riches of this convent are astonishing, and the

---

[6] The convent was plundered of nearly all its treasures by the French revolutionary invaders in 1798.

shrine of ' Our Lady ' magnificently rich; her chapel was full of the devout, praying with great fervency. After breakfasting at this place we rode on to Rapperschwyll, on the other side of the lake, crossing it by far the largest bridge I ever saw; it is three-quarters of a mile in length, is made of piles with boards laid across without any railing, and not above twelve feet wide. There are persons always ready to lead your horses, and even that would be an awkward job if they were not well used to it. At the *table-d'hôte* at Zurich we met a young Russian baron, one of the pleasantest men I ever saw, and I am to show him London next spring, when he means to be there. I have not seen an English newspaper, or heard any news for an age, except from an aristocrate this evening, that there has been a riot at Paris, and several people killed, and many more wounded by the National Guard. We have also seen a pleasant Démocrate Frenchman, who left Paris since the 14th of July. He told us nothing was settled yet. The King is in close confinement, and has an officer of the National Guard constantly in the room with him, and when he is gone to bed they come to look within the curtains to see that he is safe. This gentleman was a great Démocrate, and said that the King had drunk fifteen bottles of wine the day he arrived in Paris, and was as drunk as an ape when he got there. You may believe what you please of this story."

I insert here two letters, which I found amongst my other papers, addressed to Dr. Arnold :—

" *Lille, July 6th*, 1791.

" DEAR ARNOLD,—I arrived here on Saturday last. Since the capture of the King, or rather since his flight, they have been more strict about passports than before; that

is all the difference I have yet been able to discover,
except an increased scarcity of money, between the
country as it is now and when I was last here. The day
after my arrival the new oath was tendered and accepted
by those officers of the army who were *democratically*
inclined; those of a contrary opinion were obliged to
make their escape the day before; of the Regiment de
Dillon twelve men were absent; of the Regiment of
Cavalry there were but eight officers out of near forty
that swore. The other three regiments all swore. The
form was, to use the arms put into their hands for the
defence of the New Constitution, to die rather than suffer
foreign invasion, to obey no orders but such as were
given in consequence of decrees of the National Assembly,
and much more to the same purpose, without ever
mentioning the King's name. To the above oath the
Swiss regiment was allowed to add, ' Sans préjudice à
ce que nous devons à notre souverain et à la capitulation.'
The ceremony lasted nearly two hours. Old Rochambeau [7] was the first who took the oath; he is here as
' Commandant des Troupes de Ligne du Département
du Nord.' To give you a specimen of French *oratory*
as it now stands, I will write you at length his speech
made to the municipalité upon his arrival: ' Le Char de
la Constitution,' says he with a voice of thunder, ' s'avance
d'un pied majestieux mais lent. C'est traîné par quatre
branches, la puissance législative, la puissance éxécutive,

---

[7] Jean Baptiste de Vimeur, Comte de Rochambeau, Aide-de-camp du
Duc d'Orléans; Maréchal-de-camp, 1761; envoyé en Amérique, 1780,
avec 6000 hommes, où il réunit ses forces à celles de Washington et de
l'amiral Comte Grasse. Louis XVI. éleva Rochambeau à la dignité de
Maréchal de France, 1791. Il donna sa démission en 1792 et se retira
dans ses terres du Vendômois. La terreur le poursuivit dans sa retraite.
Le comité de salut public le fit arrêté et conduit à la Conciergerie. Le
9 Thermidor le sauva. Rochambeau est mort à Thové, Mai, 1807.

la puissance judicative, et la puissance militaire ; si l'on ne traîne pas ensemble, la machine s'arrêtera—mais si l'on traîne tout droitement—ça ira.'

" This day's post brought no news from Paris ; nothing yet, I should imagine, is settled about the King.   The real history is, I suppose, that they themselves are puzzled what to do with him.   There are two officers in prison here for having endeavoured to fly at the time of the King's escape, but were unfortunate enough to have been stopped by the guard, upon whom they fired, though without mischief ; they will probably be hanged.

" We are obliged here to take a passport for the purpose of taking even a morning ride, so strict are they at present.

" As I do not find any inconvenience that a stranger can experience in his progress through this country, if he does not make a fool of himself by sporting opinions counter to the revolution, I shall set out from hence for Paris on Monday next, from which place, if anything entertaining or interesting arises, you shall hear from me, unless I find that it will be unsafe to write.   Adieu.

" Ever yours,

" KEATING." [8]

THE SAME TO THE SAME.

" Paris, July 18th, 1791.

" I shall write you but a few words, as the post is upon the point of going out, and I can assure you, by

---

[8] I have been unable to discover anything positive respecting the writer of these letters.   I, however, believe him to be the Colonel Keatinge who in 1785 accompanied Mr. Payne, when the latter was sent on a diplomatic mission to the Emperor of Morocco, and who published "Travels in Europe and Africa," a book reviewed and criticized in the <i>Quarterly Review</i> of April, 1816.   The signature is certainly peculiar.— H. G. M.

what I am given to understand, there is some hazard in writing at all upon any public matter. I arrived on Wednesday last, and on Thursday was present at the Confédération,[9] which struck me as magnificent, much more from the multitude of persons and situation of the ground than from any striking ceremony or procession which, though excellently situated, I could be witness of. I pass over the almost nothing which I have seen since my arrival here, to come to the main point of this letter. Saturday and Sunday the whole town was in disturbance, and on the latter of the two days a scene took place in the Champ de Mars, which, I thank God, I was not a spectator of. It seems that the National Assembly, having adopted the ideas of the Comité relative to the inviolability of the King's person (though with exceptions in certain particular cases, and although they suspended him during the fixing of the Constitution), had given great offence to the people, or rather to certain minds doubly discontented, who by money, handbills, and disguised emissaries, had roused the mob to *protest* or *petition* against the proceedings of the Assembly. For this purpose a multitude had assembled on Saturday in the Champ de Mars to sign their names to this protest or petition, but were soon dispersed by a body of the National Guard.

" On Sunday, however, they reassembled, when it was thought necessary finally to put a stop to such tumultuous meetings, and every means having been used for this effect without the desired success, martial law was proclaimed, the *drapeau rouge* displayed, and the national troops were obliged to fire upon their *concitoyens*.

[9] On the 14th of July, 1791, a grand celebration was held on the Champ de Mars, of the anniversary of the " Fédération " which took place the preceding year.

"Various are the accounts of the numbers killed; some, whose reports I hope and trust are exaggerated, say that near a thousand fell; others, between 500 and 600; others, whose multiplying powers are not so great, say about forty or fifty, to this latter opinion I should rather incline, though I fear from the number of persons assembled, and the body of troops, that the last is not an exaggerated statement.

"The cruel thing is that many of those killed had no part in the riot, but were led there merely from curiosity, and among these, women, and those also of the better sort, were of the number.

"I have only to add that the mob had in the morning hung up two unfortunate devils on suspicion of having attempted to blow up the altar upon the Champ de Mars.

"All entrance into the Palais Royal was prevented last night by order of M. de la Fayette for fear of further disturbances. Excuse inaccuracies.

"Ever yours,
"KEATING."

C. B. WOLLASTON TO MISS FAUQUIER.

"Lausanne, August 1st, 1791.
"We saw Lavater,[1] the physiognomist, at Zurich. He is

---

[1] John Caspar Lavater, born at Zurich 1741, minister of the Church of St. Peter at that place for twenty-three years. On the capture of the town by the French army in 1800, Lavater was shot within a few steps of his own door by a French soldier, to whom only a few minutes before he had given wine and offered money, and whilst he was in the act of assisting another soldier who had been wounded. Massena, the French commander, offered a high reward for the discovery of the murderer, but Lavater refused to inform against him, and expired after three months of excruciating agony, January 2nd, 1801. His simple grave is in the churchyard of St. Anne at Zurich.

one of the lions of the place, and it is usual for strangers who go there to send a note, and beg leave to pay their respects to him. He was very civil, and has something uncommonly pleasing and spirited in his countenance, but he did not talk much. He expresses himself with great difficulty in French, and I could not get him to talk on physiognomy. I told him of the English edition of his works. He said it had been undertaken without his knowledge or inspection, and by a man who is not at all acquainted with the science of physiognomy, and therefore it is very imperfect, and he should be obliged to protest against it. Our visit lasted about a quarter of an hour, which is the time people usually stay. M. Lavater then desires you to write your name in a book, which is one great object to him of being visited by strangers, as he fancies he can guess characters by the handwriting as well as by the countenance. Gibbon,[2] we have understood, is not attentive to the English unless they are particularly recommended to him. I do not wonder at it; there are so many here constantly.

"Whether our plans after we quit this place will be such as we proposed I think is very uncertain, owing to the situation of France. I do not much think that the Emperor will march his troops into France, though the last papers seem to make it more probable, owing to the resolutions of the Diet about the possessions of the German princes in Alsace. I believe that you and I agree very well about the Revolution, though not entirely about the *Constitution*. The National Assembly has been governed hitherto by the help of the mob; now the mob

[2] Edward Gibbon, the celebrated author of the " Decline and Fall of the Roman Empire." He resided at Lausanne from about 1783 until the French Revolution obliged him to return to England, where he died in 1794.

has quarrelled with them, and I am anxious for the consequence.

"I met to-day a very sensible Frenchman, a Démocrate, who is come into this country on business, as he says (perhaps an Embassy to kick up a disturbance here), and it is curious how the same facts are differently represented by different parties. He swears that they are all as quiet as lambs at Paris, and says that when the Constitution is finished the King will be set at liberty, and have the choice of his own guards, and then, if he does not give his assent to the Constitution, he will be set aside, and *the Boy*, as he called the Dauphin, put in his place.

"I dined in company with Mounier[3] at Berne, but without knowing it till afterwards. He and Lally-Tollendal, and those who quitted the country at the same time, are shunned by the princes and their party, who are entirely under the direction of Calonne, and seem to look forward to a perfect restoration. This I think they will never see, and I do not believe that all the Powers of Europe could bring it about."

The next sentence alludes to the riots at Birmingham, where the revolutionary principles were unpopular, and "Church and King" at that time the rallying cry of the people.

"Although I should not have been at all sorry to hear of Dr. Priestley's[4] windows being broken and himself

---

[3] Jean Joseph Mounier, un des membres les plus distingués des États Généraux de 1789.

[4] Minister of several Dissenting congregations. Author of the "History of Electricity," and of various philosophical works, which procured him the appointment of librarian to the (second) Earl of Shelburne, with whom he resided some years. He subsequently published several books against Christianity, and especially in favour of the French Revolution.

pelted, I very much regret that the riot at Birmingham was so serious. The Revolutionists must be, however, not a little disappoiuted. People say that the French employ emissaries to spread their Rights of Man and equalizing principles among other countries. If so, I should not feel for any calamity that may befall them. They have been at work *here*, and with effect. There has been a vast disposition to riot in the Pays de Vaud. So much so that the Canton of Berne are now raising 8000 men, who are to be quartered about in these parts."

FROM JAMES FRAMPTON.

" *Lausanne, August* 3*rd*, 1791.

" Since I wrote last we have been to see the Lake of Thun, but the heat was so intense that our brains were almost burnt out; indeed, the heat has lately been far beyond what is usual in this country. Our lodging, which is very tolerable, is just out of the town on the Vevay Road, but the *table-d'hôte* is this year out of repute, and no good company dines there. We therefore have our dinner from a *traiteur*. The French have almost all left, as this place is too hot to hold them, there having appeared many symptoms of unquietness in the neighbourhood, and the song of ' Ça ira ' is very popular. The troops of Berne are got together, and some are encamped to be ready.

" Horses are not very easy things to procure, at least not good ones. As there are so many English here they are all snapped up. We have, however, got two things,

At length, an entertainment given at Birmingham, where Priestley then resided, on July 14th, 1791, to celebrate the destruction of the Bastille, produced a serious riot, and, amongst many others, his house was destroyed. Dr. Priestley died in America, 1804.

such as they are, at the enormous price of a Louis apiece per week, but they are necessaries to ride down to the water's edge to bathe of a morning. There is finer bathing here than I ever saw anywhere else.

FROM C. B. WOLLASTON.

"Lausanne, August 11th, 1791.

" We have had a constant succession of storms of thunder and lightning, but always in the evening. Last night there was a most violent one, the lightning was of a bluish-pink cast which shone bright into the room where we had candles. We saw several balls of fire which appeared to strike perpendicularly on the ground, and these upon the lake and mountains behind had a fine effect. They say that it rarely does damage here on account of the mountains which attract it from these parts, but a large house upon the hill above Vevay was last night set on fire by the lightning and burnt to the ground, as the engines could not come near the place. Trench[5] joined us on Tuesday; he was detained two days at Paris to procure passports, and he found the roads so bad that he was longer on the journey than he expected. We get up early, bathe in the lake before seven o'clock, and ride about the country when the heat will permit. The bathing is delicious, and I have found an excellent place where we can go in head foremost. All this is exceedingly pleasant, but I doubt we shall not meet with so much society here as we hoped for. English there are in plenty, but not many French, or many families in the town where people visit. There is nothing which throws people together as at a public place, and families and parties live very much by themselves.

[5] The Honourable Richard Trench, afterwards second Earl of Clancarty ; Ambassador to the Hague after the Pacification of Paris, 1813.

"The Cerjats (a very old and well-known Swiss family of whom the head married an Englishwoman, and two of the sons were officers in English cavalry regiments) have been exceedingly kind and civil to us. They are extremely pleasant people, and both English and French are spoken in the family. We are going to them to-night to a party, and I hope shall meet some French.

"Most, however, of the French have left this country and have gone to join their friends at Coblentz and on the Rhine, to see what they can do for the royal cause. We spent an exceedingly pleasant day on Sunday with a family living at Morges, about six miles off. The situation of the house is beautiful, on a steep hill with a garden and terrace looking across the lake. It commands Mont Blanc between the opposite mountains, but the day was not clear enough to see distinctly. There was a kind of "Société" in the evening; Monseigneur le Bailli de Morges and *Madame la Baillive*, who leant back in her chair with an air which none of the other ladies ventured to assume. Monseigneur, being a member of the *Souverain*,[6] had a proportionable quantity of dignity annexed to his carriage, but was very civil. He and the rest of the souverain rather shake in their shoes as the people of the Pays de Vaud are very restless.

"There is a 'Club des Jacobins,' as it is called, at a café opposite the Café Littéraire, and they discuss things with great freedom. Most of the Bourgeois are Démocrates, all the great people Aristocrates, of course, but when a spirit of that kind is once excited, it does not easily subside. They would be fools to change, however aristocratical the Government may be, for they have no

---

[6] This was the Superior Court at Berne, when the Pays de Vaud was dependent on Berne. (Information from M. Gustave Perdonnet, 1876.)

taxes, and the Government is equal and by no means oppressive. We mean to row across the lake to-morrow to Meillerie, &c. All the world here wears a long sort of breeches which tie down at the ankles, very cool things, and very convenient for riding, besides they save one's legs from the biting of the flies. *They* are a great torment, I assure you."

THE SAME TO MRS. FRAMPTON.

" *Lausanne, August 23rd,* 1791.

" MY DEAR MOTHER,—I was exceedingly vexed, on receiving your last letter, to find that we had actually passed through Carlsruhe, and slept a night there without having the least idea of Mrs. Gibbs. I thought she had been at Carlscroon, in Sweden. I should have been exceedingly glad to have visited her."

[Mrs. Gibbs was a friend and contemporary of my mother, a daughter of Sir W. Rowley, first married to Admiral Martin, afterwards to Colonel Gibbs. Their eldest son, General Gibbs, was a most agreeable man and good officer; he was killed in the unfortunate attack on New Orleans in 1815.

Mrs. Gibbs was particularly agreeable; circumstances obliged her to reside many years on the Continent, and the capital of Baden-Durlach was her principal residence, where she and her daughters lived in habits of the greatest intimacy with the Court of Baden, and after her return to England a correspondence was kept up with the Princesses of Baden,[7] one of whom became Empress

[7] Daughters of Charles Louis, Hereditary Prince of Baden (who died 1801). The eldest, Elizabeth Louisa, married, 1793 the Emperor Alexander of Russia, and Frédérica Dorothea, her younger sister, became in 1797 the wife of Gustavus IV., King of Sweden. Their mother was Amelia Frédérica, daughter of Louis VI., Landgrave of Hesse-Darmstadt, who died 1832.

of Russia, and another Queen of Sweden. Nothing could be more easy—as I have heard them describe—than the Court society there; an assembly of the best company meeting frequently in an evening at the palace, and with such a variety of games for all ages, that form was banished; the young never without some amusement, *jeux d'esprit, jeux de cartes*, &c., always something going on to prevent silence and formality, though all the dignity of a German Court was kept up with a less revenue than is possessed by many English gentlemen. The daughters were exceedingly amiable and well informed, and most of them handsome.]

" Of the town of Carlsruhe we saw as much as Tristram Shandy did of Calais, though I could not write so good a chapter upon it, for we arrived there after it was dark, and set out again early the next morning.

" I believe the descent upon France will prove to be ' great cry and little wool.' One has not seen that the Emperor has yet declared himself, and I do not think he will be in a hurry to do so. Trench left all the amusements going on at Paris as usual. Provided no disturbances arise there, the situation of the country must make it still more amusing to reside there, but where there is so little of a Government there cannot be much security. I am sorry to say that the language of almost all the English we have met with abroad is extremely absurd. They are for marching into France, cutting the throats of all the National Assembly, and restoring the poor good king, as they are pleased to call him, to *all* he has lost. I should be extremely sorry to see such an unqualified restoration. Had *hè* escaped, a civil war would have been inevitable; as affairs are at present, it is probable, but may be avoided. I think we are pretty safe at home."

FROM THE SAME.

" Lausanne, August 24th, 1791.

" We have fallen in with some of our former *table-d'hôte* friends—amongst others two young Brabançons whom Trench had met, and of whom we have seen a great deal since. They are very pleasant, gentlemanlike men. At an assembly at the Cerjat's, who have been as civil as possible, I one evening played two rubbers of French whist, which lasted as many hours, and I never was more tired in my life.

" On Monday we left Chamouni. Trench and my brother went over the Col de Balme. I chose the *Tête-noire,* and was much delighted. In my opinion glaciers, though they are fine things with accompaniments, do not do any better by themselves than the bass of Handel's music would do without the other parts. We shall not be here many days more. We mean to go to Neufchâtel on Tuesday. Trench, I believe, will not go any further, so we shall part when we start for St. Gothard, Milan, &c.

" I think there is no great probability of being prevented from going to Paris on our return by a counter revolution. I have no idea that it will come to anything. The Emperor keeps off like a wise man. There is much to admire in the principles of the Constitution; but abstract truths, however wise and indisputable, are for the closet and not for the public. Legislators should have them in their minds, but not publish them. I have thought a great deal about these matters, and confess I am sometimes so puzzled between the beauty of theory and the insufficiency of practice that I do not know which way to turn. At present, adieu."

FROM JAMES FRAMPTON.

" *Lausanne, September 4th*, 1791.

" To-morrow we start from hence for good. Our late expedition turned out a very pleasant one, but the Lake of Neufchâtel is not to be compared with the others we have visited. From thence we made an excursion into the watchmakers' country. There are several large villages amongst the mountains inhabited almost entirely by watch and lace-makers. The traffic they carry on is immense, and the country appears like a new creation with neat, well-built houses, interspersed with pines, &c. I bought a watch for a Louis-d'or, the works of which are as neat as any I ever saw. I think it a great curiosity. On our return we saw a camp, which the Bernois keep up at Payerne, as many signs of revolutionary principles have appeared. It was beautifully situated on the side of a hill, having a very fine view, and with walnut and other trees interspersed amongst the tents. The troops, in point of dress and discipline, are not *quite* so fine as the Emperor's ! Trench goes straight to Paris. The presenting the Constitution to the King and his acceptance or refusal is the crisis which must determine much, and they seem to be putting it off from not knowing what to do. It is strange to see so much wisdom and so much folly blended in the proceedings of the same set of men ; it puzzles one to know what to think of them. Their late decree about the titles of the princes is so extremely absurd and so totally inconsistent with their own fundamental principles (if I understand it right) that one would think they were all blockheads, which they certainly are not."

FROM C. B. WOLLASTON.

" Dijon, October 2nd, 1791.

"Nothing could be more fortunate than we were in our last tour, and our Italian travels were most agreeable—the Lake of Como, &c. I dare say James Frampton told you that we met with an old friend, the opera of ' Gli Schiavi per Amore,' at Milan. They do not change their operas in Italy so often as in London, but repeat the same opera and dances *every* night for six weeks together. We went to it the three nights we were there, and I assure you I came away more delighted than ever. The Archduke[8] and his court were there the last night, and the house was very full.

"We heard an *execrable* opera at Turin in a small house, as the large one is never opened, excepting during the Carnival, and which, by the by, is not nearly so fine as that in the Haymarket or at Milan. The King of Sardinia's palace is magnificent, and contains one of the finest collections of pictures in Europe, which, however, we had not half time to look at.

"From Turin to Chambéri was an exceedingly tiresome journey. We took a carriage and horses the whole way (for eight Louis-d'ors), which was certainly the cheapest and best for us, but it occupied three days and a half. We crossed the Mont Cenis on mules, but carriages are carried over without difficulty. On our way to Lyons we saw the famous Grand Chartreuse. This is, I believe, the only convent in France which is not suppressed, and

---

[8] Ferdinand, son of the Empress Maria Theresa (and of the Emperor Francis I.), Governor of Austrian Lombardy, died 1806. He married Maria Beatrice d'Este, Duchess of Massa and Princess of Carrara, daughter and heiress of Hercules Rinaldo, third Duke of Modena, who survived until 1829.

in this the monks have only permission to continue for
their lives upon a pension.   They treated us most civilly,
and, after showing us the whole building, &c., gave us
fish and other things for dinner.

" We had heard nothing of the King's acceptation of the
Constitution till we were on the point of entering France.
The consequences of it *to us* at least are very convenient, for there is a perfect free passage through the
country, without any passport or questioning whatever.
Whether the King is sincere or not time will show, but
it is impossible for any set of men to have acted with
more wisdom and discretion than the National Assembly
have done in everything that has concerned his escape.
He is now at the height of popularity.   At Lyons ' La
Partie de Chasse de Henri Quatre ' was performed, and
at every mention of the King's name the house was
in an uproar of applause.   It is very curious to have been
present at such violent applause on two such different
occasions—I mean at Brussels among the aristocrats
and at Lyons amongst the patriots.   The country seems
as quiet as if they were in the most settled state.   I
sincerely wish they may continue so, and that the com-
bination of kings may not be able to disturb them."

FROM JAMES FRAMPTON.

" *Dijon, October 2nd.*

" We arrived here to-day.   Nothing now gives any
trouble but the assignats, which the people do not care
to take, and you pay an immense discount for money.
You cannot conceive how ridiculous it is to hear the
amazing popularity of the King at present.   I was in the
same state at Lyons as Sterne in " Tristram Shandy,"
for I could neither see the Chinese MSS.—the library

being shut up for a month—nor Lippeus' clock, as they are at work in the church removing an altar from the chapel of the *ci-devant* Carthusians, which was absurd enough.

"The dust here is beyond belief; they have not had one single drop of rain for five months, and they are consequently in great distress about their crops. They say, however, that the vintage has been very fine; but though we are now and have been in the very heart of Burgundy, I do not think that we have found very good wine at the inns. Since we have left Lausanne, the Bernois have had a camp close to the town in the public walk, and they are now about the town and in the churches. They complain much of the officers as being very impertinent to the inhabitants as well as to strangers. If their Excellencies do not take care, by their very precautions they will bring an old house upon their heads. We shall be at Paris on Wednesday, where I shall post this.

"*Hôtel du Palais Royal, Paris, October 5th.*

"After hard travelling for three days, since I last wrote the above, here we are safely arrived. I am just returned from hearing a most excellent Italian comic opera and from supping at the Quatre Nations. We were attacked at the last post before reaching Paris by the Poissardes, who surrounded our carriage and opened the door, calling us friends and shaking hands with us. We were forced to give them a piece of paper worth five livres to get rid of them. We were very nearly being in a scrape from not having money enough to bring us to Paris, partly owing to their giving us at some places Bankers' bits of paper which go here in exchange for assignats, but which they would not take at the posts. We were

reduced to changing our English guineas, and that just
did for us; the colour of money is such a rarity."

C. B. WOLLASTON TO MRS. FRAMPTON.

"*Paris, October* 12*th*, 1791.

"Paris, since our arrival, has been as quiet as any
large city can be, and as amusing as I found it last
year. The King has been to the opera and the play in a
private box, without decorations or ornaments. He is
become extremely popular. The minds of people seem
to be much more settled since the finishing of the constitution, there is not nearly so much of politics talked in
the cafés, nor are there the meetings and mobs in the
Palais Royal. One hears nothing of the army on the
Rhine, and the letters and declarations laughed at and
their authenticity doubted.

"La Fayette has resigned his command, not in disgust,
but in consequence of a decree of the last Assembly, which
enacted that it should be exercised in rotation by the
commanders of the different battalions of National Guards.
He has retired quietly into the country until his services
may be required. A circumstance lately showed the increasing popularity of the King. The old Assembly had
regulated the ceremonial of his reception upon his coming
to make the speeches, and had allowed him a chair ornamented with fleurs-de-lys, and required that the members
should stand uncovered as long as the King should so
continue. The new Assembly on Wednesday last resolved
that the King should have a chair, the same exactly as
that of the President, and placed on the same line, and
that as soon as he should reach his place all the members
should sit covered. This resolution produced much discontent amongst the generality of persons, and the Banker

told us that the Funds sunk 2 per cent. in consequence. In effect the next day the Assembly reversed the decree and restored the former ceremonial.

" The King made his speech on Friday; we were present. When the chair was brought in, *it* was exceedingly applauded, and the King himself received with violent applause, and stopped by it frequently in the midst of his speech.

" He came in attended by a deputation of the Assembly and his ministers, read his speech in a distinct, clear voice, was answered by the President, and then retired.

" The King did not sit down at all, so the Assembly stood likewise.

" On Sunday evening I was at his mass.[9] When it was over a man got upon a bench and cried out very loud, ' Je demande justice à votre majesté, je n'ai pas du pain à manger.' The King looked exceedingly red and alarmed, but collected himself, and bid him hold his tongue and go away. Everybody seemed to be on the King's side, and the man was carried away. He keeps a Court, rides out, and goes hunting without interruption. These circumstances would seem to show that if the King manages well, he may gain popularity and confidence, and, if he was well advised, might in time bring about some changes beneficial to all. Yesterday it was reported that Monsieur was coming back. James is in love with the Queen, and vows he will go every day to see her pass to mass.

[9] The gallery at the Château de Versailles is one of the finest in Europe. In this gallery all the strangers who came from every part of France and elsewhere to see the King took post to await the moment when the whole royal family issued from the King's apartments to go to Mass.

" We dined with our ambassador (Lord Gower[1]) on
Sunday—a very large party entirely English.   He and
Lady Sutherland were extremely civil and easy, and the
party was as agreeable as so large a one consisting of
people almost all strangers to one another could be. Lady
Sutherland is a charming woman, extremely elegant, unaffected, and pleasing in manner.   Their table and attendants are magnificent.   Lord and Lady Hardwicke[2] were
there, and are returning directly to England.   -

" There seem to be fewer carriages and fewer fine
people about this year than there were last.   The fact is
that almost all the nobility have left the country.   Since
the passage has been left open the emigrations have
been amazing.

" The new Assembly consists of very few of the
ancient gentry; but there are several very sensible men
amongst them.   The most of them write their speeches,
and read them, which is wise at first, as they are unused
to speaking, but they are extremely disorderly for want
of rules to preserve regularity and deference to some
authority."

1792.

THIS year the horrors of the revolutionary spirit in
France were increased tenfold by the Proclamation of the
Duke of Brunswick,[3] and the march of his army to the

---

[1] Eldest son of first Marquis of Stafford ; created Duke of Sutherland,
1833.   He married Elizabeth, Countess of Sutherland, in her own right.

[2] Philip, second earl ; married, 1740, Lady Jemima Campbell, only
daughter of third Earl of Breadalbane.

[3] Charles William succeeded 1780.   He married, 1764, Augusta,
daughter of Frederick, Prince of Wales, and was killed at the Battle of
Jena, October 14, 1806.

The famous Declaration or Memorial, published by the Duke of
Brunswick as Commander-in-Chief of the Allied Armies of the Emperor

French territory. In vain poor Louis XVI. denied all participation in it. Whether this on his part was true or false, no doubt could be entertained that the emigrant princes fostered these injudicious measures, and by so doing hastened the miseries of their unhappy brother and his family. England as yet kept aloof from war.

The slave trade discussion was yearly brought on by Mr. Wilberforce,[4] the untiring advocate for its abolition and for every other good work—one of the most fluent of orators, and best of men; very plain, with a bad figure and wretched health, yet doing much more than others of Herculean strength, and always cheerful.

His book produced more sensation, was more universally read, and perhaps did more good than almost any religious publication, and is still a standard work. Whether the whole length to which he goes in regard to amusements be or be not followed, makes no difference as to the real principles of sound religion to be found in the work, clothed in the most beautiful language.

1794.

FROM LADY SUSAN O'BRIEN TO HER NIECE, LADY MARY TALBOT, AT PENRICE.

"*Melbury, February* 18*th*, 1794.

"We mean to return to Stinsford next week, if the French don't disturb us. An invasion is really so much and so universally talked of that one hardly knows what to think; but yet I cannot, for one,

and King of Prussia, was dated from his headquarters at Flans in Champagne, September 28, 1792. The Duchess of Brunswick died in London, 1813.

[4] Born 1759; M.P. 1780—1825, when he retired from active public life. Died 1833; was buried in Westminster Abbey. In 1797 he published "A Practical View of the Present State of Religion."

bring myself to believe it can ever happen. But if they should land at Weymouth, I hope you will give me a retreat in your mountains, should I be obliged to fly, which it will be much against *the grain* if I do from Frenchmen. Even the prisoners at Dorchester cut off the heads of the kings and queens on the cards they played with, which is rather *outré-ing* their dislike of monarchy."

1795.

THE winter of 1794-5 was intensely severe, and the cold greatly increased our losses and disgraces in the campaign in Holland,[5] where the Duke of York commanded the army, and General Harcourt [6] was second in command. The general was a remarkably amiable man in private life, brother to Simon, Earl Harcourt, and succeeded to that title upon the death of the latter without children. His wife accompanied him, and was said to command him better than he commanded his soldiers. General Harcourt married for love a very handsome, very clever, but rather eccentric person, the eldest daughter of a very great friend of my father's, Mrs. Danby of Yorkshire, then a widow. Mrs. Harcourt was a clever, spirited woman, deterred by no difficulties, and made herself

[5] In 1793 the French Republican army entered Holland, when the people declared in their favour,

The Duke of York with 10,000 troops, destined to co-operate with the allies against France, landed at Ostend in April, 1793.

After the loss of Crèvecœur the Duke of York resigned the command to General Walmoden, in January 1795, and returned, to England universally regretted by the army, and on the following April the English troops finally embarked from Bremen.

[6] Field-Marshal, G.C.B., &c., subsequently third Earl Harcourt ; died (s.p.) 1830, when the title became extinct,

The Honourable Mrs. Harcourt attended the Princess Caroline of Brunswick to England previous to her marriage.

useful during the campaign by her attention to wounded and suffering soldiers, but the General was laughed at for his care of his wife, and she was supposed to have had escorts and advantages from headquarters which were found fault with. He had had a paralytic stroke early in life, but it was not discovered until some few years afterwards that good generals were more necessary than rank in the army.

I copy the following interesting letter from Holland :—

"*Deventer, January 25th*, 1795.

"MY DEAR MISS FAUQUIER,—I wrote by different means, different letters these four days past, hoping some will reach their destination and relieve the minds of our friends, who surely must be anxious about us. Our position has been so critical, and the sufferings of the army so far beyond description, that imagination cannot have formed anything beyond it, though it may have distressed you all for the fate of those individuals who most interested you. I hope we shall one day meet again, and that rest and peace of mind will repair what anxiety and fatigue have done to General Harcourt, and indeed to us both; but, except a severe cold (occasioned by such a march for three days and nights as never was made), I hope he is well; and to-day his cold is better. The air is softer, it is only 17 degrees below the freezing point. Yesterday it was 28 degrees below, which is a difference of 11 degrees.

"By the first opportunity I wrote to Lady Elizabeth Lee,[7] and indeed to everybody, but I will beg you again to send her a line to tell her that both of us and William

[7] Daughter of Simon, first Earl Harcourt, wife of Sir William Lee, Bart. She was one of the bridesmaids of Queen Charlotte, 1761.

were well at this date. I have not seen him since our retreat, but I know he is well.

" Our remaining here is very uncertain. We have an immense army opposed to us who will make us their object as soon as their business in Holland is settled, and probably that will be soon, because they meet with no opposition : they are received with open arms, with cockades and with illuminations, and all the ladies at Amsterdam came out dressed, in traineaux and carriages.

" They gave out on their arrival that they acknowledged no States nor magistrates, and the Dutch in consequence dissolved their Constitution and established the popular one.

" We have reason to expect that the Dutch who have never been our friends, will become our enemies; and even already close to our outposts, we know that the peasants are arriving and that meetings for rising *en masse* against us have been called in different towns. This, and other circumstances will make our stay here impossible for any length of time, but ten days' rest would refresh our troops and enable us to get off many of our sick who otherwise must be left behind; moving them in this weather is dreadful, but owing to their having many blankets and all the care General Harcourt could give them, they have not hitherto suffered from their journey as one would expect. Change of air and moving from infectious rooms afreshed many, and on the whole our troops who marched on those horrid nights have suffered more than our sick from being removed.

" Such a dreary country as we have already passed through, and as we shall again encounter, I never saw, and this in the hardest frost and storms of snow.

" I beg you to let Lord and Lady Harcourt also know that we are well this date.

"I wrote to her three times these three days. I hope Lady Vernon is much better, and Mrs. Frampton and all belonging to you. I wish I knew whether Lord St. Helens [8] was got safe to England, and where the poor family of Orange [9] went to—what misery do I see and hear of!

"I send you a ribbon made at a Moravian settlement near Utrecht, which will wash; it is only meant to prove that we do not forget you. General Harcourt joins in best love to you, and hopes to see you some day or other, notwithstanding all. He has the comfort of feeling that he has done all that could be done under the existing circumstances, and that no human power under such circumstances could have saved Holland: had we stayed longer the army would have been sacrificed.

[8] Alleyne Fitz Herbert, brother of Sir William Fitz Herbert of Tissington, Co. Derby; English Plenipotentiary at Brussels, when he concluded a peace between France, Spain, and the States General in 1783, in which year he was appointed Envoy Extraordinary to the Court of St. Petersburg, and in 1787 Mr. Fitz Herbert accompanied the Empress Catherine in her memorable tour to the Crimea. Successively Ambassador Extraordinary to the Hague (1789) and to Madrid (1791). He returned to the Hague in 1794, where he remained until the Government was overthrown by the invasion of the French in the following winter.

The last foreign mission of Lord St. Helens was to St. Petersburg (March 1801), to congratulate the Emperor Alexander on his accession. and he attended his coronation at Moscow the following September. Created an Irish peer, 1791, and Baron St. Helen's in the peerage of England, 1801, G.C.B., G.C.H., F.S.A., and a Privy Councillor; one of the Lords of the Bedchamber to George III. and George IV., June 1803 to 1830. Lord St. Helens died unmarried, 1839.

[9] The Prince of Orange with his son, the Hereditary Prince, were obliged to escape from the Hague after the French had taken some of the more important places in Holland, and this was not effected without great difficulty, owing to the fury of the people against the Stadtholder. They took refuge in England in January 1795.

" Adieu once more.   Believe me ever, my dear friend, most truly and affectionately yours,

" M. HARCOURT."

The event which occupied the public attention was the marriage this year, April 8th, 1795, of the Prince of Wales to the Princess Caroline,[1] daughter of the Duke of Brunswick, his first cousin, a match which brought so much misery to both parties.   He consented to it in order to have his debts paid, and have a large income allowed him.   The Prince was then under the influence of Lady Jersey,[2] a clever, unprincipled, but beautiful and fascinating woman, though with scarcely any retrieving really good quality.   She had lived a good deal in the Harcourt society, being very clever, and there my aunt Elizabeth Fauquier met her and knew her well.   Amongst other freaks she was a very fine lady, but in general

[1] April 5, 1795.   The Princess of Brunswick, accompanied by the Honourable Mrs. Harcourt and Lord Malmesbury, landed at Greenwich Hospital, and was conducted to the house of the Governor, Sir Hugh Palliser.   Lady Jersey arrived from London, bringing with her a white satin gown and turban cap of satin, for which the princess exchanged her previous muslin dress, with blue satin petticoat, and black beaver hat with blue and black feathers ; but H.R.H. travelled in a mantle of green satin trimmed with gold, with loops and tassels à la Brandenburg, and wore a beaver hat.   About two o'clock the Princess proceeded in one of the King's coaches, drawn by six horses, and escorted by a party of the Prince of Wales' own regiment of Light Dragoons to St. James's Palace, where apartments had been prepared for H.R.H.'s reception.   After a short time the Prince arrived from Carlton House, and about five o'clock the Prince and Princess sat down to dinner.   The marriage was solemnized on the evening of April 8 in the Chapel Royal by the Archbishop of Canterbury.   The bride, who wore a coronet, was led by H.R.H. the Duke of Clarence, her train supported by four unmarried daughters of dukes and earls.

[2] Frances Twysden, daughter and heiress of the Bishop of Raphoe, wife of fourth Earl of Jersey.   Lord Jersey was successively Lord Chamberlain and Master of the Buckhounds ; he died 1805.

respected my aunt. One day, however, Lady Jersey went up to her at an assembly in a very insolent manner, saying, " Oh, Miss Fauquier, you are just the person to have a pincushion about you ; I want a pin." Upon which my aunt, opening her large eyes at her, replied, " Yes, I always have a pincushion and plenty of pins, but I am just the person *not* to give you one of them." Lady Jersey walked away, but did not quarrel with my aunt.

Lady Jersey by her intrigues persuaded the Prince to appoint her to go to meet the Princess. The Princess was in the highest spirits on the voyage. Some of the attendants, knowing the discomforts she would have to contend with, were sorry to see her so, and one of them making some remark to her on her apparent happiness, the Princess answered, " How can I be otherwise ? am I not going to be married to the finest and handsomest prince in the world, and to live in the most desirable country in Europe ? "

There were, however, even at that time, some rumours against her character, and an officer of the King's German Legion,[3] Major Töebingen, whom I knew very well,

---

[3] Raised in Hanover by George III. in 1803, and disbanded in 1816. The Duke of Cambridge was colonel, and the other officers all Hanoverians of the very best families. They were principally quartered at Dorchester, and at least one regiment was always there during the early part of the year.

I remember my father and mother mentioning as a curious and melancholy circumstance that *more than once* several of these most agreeable and gentlemanlike Hanoverian officers were dining at Moreton— eight miles only from Dorchester—when a message arrived with orders for them instantly to embark and to join the army in Spain ; and *each time every one* of those officers was killed in the first engagement !

I can just recollect once seeing General Alten, who was a very great friend and favourite at Moreton, when I was very young, not more than three or four years old. He was a very fine, tall man.—H. G. M.

an immense man, was said to have been a person admired
by her, and I have seen him wear a very large amethyst
stud or pin, reported to have been presented to him by
the Princess Caroline.

The King her uncle, George III., was much attached
to his niece—the Queen never liked the Prince to marry
her, and was said to have been prejudiced against her.
The *on dit* of the time reported that the Prince was
pleased with the Princess at the first sight, but that Lady
Jersey contrived to speak to him alone, and set him
against her before the ceremony.

EXTRACT FROM THE JOURNAL OF MISS ANN AGNES PORTER,
  FOR MANY YEARS THE MUCH-VALUED PRECEPTRESS AND
  FRIEND IN LORD ILCHESTER'S FAMILY.

1796.

" *Sunday, Oct. 30th.*—In the evening set out from
London for Sarum.

" *Oct. 31st.*—Arrived at dear Mrs. Peniston's at Sarum.

" *Nov. 2nd.*—Monsieur Panzer, Chaplain to the nuns at
Amesbury, dined at Mrs. Peniston's. A Mr. Edgeworth,
confessor to the late King of France, had been to visit
Monsieur Panzer, and gave him the following affecting
particulars, which he repeated to me with tears.

" Mr. Edgeworth had been dismissed by the King when
every other comfort was taken from him, and no mass
allowed to be celebrated. He remained in retirement
and disguise for some time, only the King knowing of his
retreat, when at last, after some months, he received an
order from the Convention to attend their summons.
When he appeared at their tribunal, he perceived about
ten or twelve in close consultation who had the air of
self-condemned criminals. He was asked if his name

was Edgeworth?   Upon answering that it was, they told him they had given Louis Capet permission to see him, and he might then depart with the deputy who was going to carry his Arrêt of death for the next day.   A fiacre was in waiting which carried them to the prison.   During the way the deputy wept and deplored his unhappy fate in being the 'fatal messenger of death to the best of kings.' When they reached the prison the deputy went to the King alone to announce the fatal sentence.   Mr. Edgeworth looked round him with terror and dismay—the monsters he beheld looked like demons from hell, ready to execute all evil with greediness : in a few minutes the messenger returned, and told him to go up to the prison.   When he saw his royal but unfortunate master, he lost all command of himself, and embracing the King's knees he exclaimed, ' O Sire, I ought to comfort you, but, alas ! I have none for myself.'   The King raised and embraced him. ' I am accustomed to calamity,' he said, ' and prepared for the worst that can befall me—but to see a faithful subject is too, *too* much.'   He then leaned his head upon Mr. Edgeworth's breast, and burst into tears.   In a few minutes he recovered his composure, and said his most ardent desire was to have mass performed the next morning, that he might have the comfort to leave the world with decency and composure by the confession of his faith and a communion with his God.

"Mr. Edgeworth offered to procure him this consolation.   He flew back to the Convention, and told them the *King* wished to hear mass before he died.   They demurred upon this request, and said it would not be convenient : there was no priest, there were no requisites ; besides, their number then present was insufficient to form a Convention.

"Mr. Edgeworth replied that he summoned them in the

King's name to call a Convention, and to give an answer
to his request. This was done, and they all repeated it
would be inconvenient, as there was no priest. Mr.
Edgeworth then said that he himself was a priest, and
would undertake the office. A reluctant consent was at
last given, and Mr. Edgeworth returned to the King, who
expressed the utmost satisfaction on finding his request
granted. Six long weeks, he said, since he had been
withheld from the altar, but I shall now, said he, depart
this life with decorum and with peace. ' God,' he added,
' is my Comforter; my enemies cannot take His peace
from me.' Just then a soldier, or rather gaoler, entered
and said, ' Louis Capet, the Convention have given your
wife and family permission to take leave of you.' Such
a scene then followed as surpassed the power of description. Mr. Edgeworth did not attempt it, but leant his
head on the table and wept. The same guard came and
told the royal mourners they must part immediately.
The King was quite overcome for some time, and repeatedly said, ' Ah, quel malheur d'être tant aimé—
bénisse-les, mon Dieu—bénisse-les à jamais."

" He then wiped his tears and recovered his serenity.
Mr. Edgeworth no more saw him either depressed or
agitated, he was all calmness and fortitude. He read his
last will to Mr. Edgeworth twice over; his voice never
faltered. He laid down on his paillasse and slept most
profoundly for six hours. He rose at eight and went
through the Service of the Mass with the utmost alacrity
and satisfaction. ' I die innocent,' he said; ' my just
Judge and Heavenly Father will make me happy.' At
ten o'clock a gaoler entered abruptly. ' I understand
you,' said the King; ' I come—will you, my friend,
accompany me?' he said to Edgeworth. ' O Sire, I am
ready to die with you.' The King went out with his hat

in his hand, but perceiving all those without the apartment had their hats on, he put his own on, and passed them with an air of firmness and dignity. At the door a fiacre was ready with a messenger from the Convention, who was stepping in first, when the King stopped him and said, 'Que je passe le premier; Moi.' The messenger was seating himself on the King's side in the fiacre, but the King placed Mr. Edgeworth, saying, 'C'est lui qui est ma partie.' They were *two hours* in arriving. The King read in his Prayer-book alternately with Mr. Edgeworth in a firm voice. When they reached the place and they offered to tie his hands, he resisted and said, 'C'est trop,' but on Mr. Edgeworth's reminding him how acceptable the humiliation would be in the eyes of God, and cited his Saviour's example, he held both his hands out, and suffered them to be tied. When on the scaffold the trumpets and drums sounded according to their orders, the King bowed, as desiring leave to speak. Every instrument ceased; all was silence and attention. The King said, 'I die innocent; I forgive my enemies, and pray God to avert His vengeance for my blood, and to bless my people.' He took two turns on the scaffold, and then prepared himself for death. Mr. Edgeworth was kneeling by him, and in the excess of feeling had lost all recollection, till he was roused by the words '*the head of a traitor*,' and looking up saw his sovereign's head streaming over him in the monster's hands. Mr. Edgeworth instinctively fled, and got safe to England, where he is known for his talents and admired for his fidelity. When he told his master that the clergy had been received and sheltered in England, 'Ah! la généreuse nation,' said the King, 'la généreuse nation.'

"Mons. Panzer spent the day with us, and invited us to see the Convent at Amesbury.

" *Thursday*, 3*rd Nov.*—Mons. Boisvy read me an hour in Bossuet. Mons. Marêt gave me the Pope's Oration of Louis XVI. to read. I did not like it.

" *An agreeable Evening.*—Travelled all night, and reached Melbury at 8 a.m.

" *November 7th.*—Very polite letters from both my French priests in return for my compliments. They, with Mons. Panzer, were as agreeable men as I ever knew—all of them insinuating to a degree : very different, yet all pleasing. Boisvy was pensive and profound. Mons. Marêt was gay and sweet-tempered, extremely handsome and full of vivacity. Mons. Panzer was benevolent and courteous, with a flow of words.

" They were all interesting. Mr. Edgeworth received a letter of thanks from Louis XVIII., written by his own hand."

1797.

LADY MARY TALBOT [4] TO HER SISTER, LADY HARRIOT FOX STRANGWAYS.

"*Penrice Castle, Feb.* 26*th,* 1797.—MY DEAR HARRIOT,— Only think what a fright we have been in ! [5] There have

[4] Second daughter of Henry Thomas, second Earl of Ilchester ; married, 1794, Thomas Mansel Talbot, Esq., of Margam and Penrice Castle, Co. Glamorgan.

Penrice Castle is situated on the coast, about twelve miles from Swansea.

[5] "London Gazette Extraordinary, February 27, 1797." The following letter has this day been received at Whitehall by his Majesty's Principal Secretary of State for the Home Department :—

"The Right Honourable Lord Cawdor to his Grace the Duke of Portland.

"Fishguard, Friday, February 24th.

"MY LORD,—In consequence of having received information Wednesday night at eleven o'clock, that three large ships of war and a lugger had anchored in a small roadstead upon the coast, in the neighbourhood of

been three French frigates and a lugger cruising off
Lundy Island, and their lights were seen two nights

this town, I proceeded immediately with a detachment of the Cardigan
Militia, and all the provincial force I could collect, to the place. I soon
gained positive intelligence they had disembarked about 1200 men, but
no cannon. Upon the night's setting in, a French officer, whom I found
the Second in command, came in with a letter, a copy of which I have
the honour to enclose, &c., together with my answer: in consequence of
which they determined to surrender themselves prisoners of war, and
accordingly laid down their arms this day. . . .

"It is my intention to march them this night to Haverfordwest, where
I shall make the best distribution in my power. The frigates, corvette,
and lugger got under weigh yesterday evening, and were this morning
entirely out of sight.

"The fatigue we have experienced will, I trust, excuse me to your
Grace for not giving a more particular detail. . . The spirit of loyalty
which has pervaded all ranks throughout this country is infinitely beyond
what I can express.

"I am, &c., &c., &c.,

"CAWDOR."

"Cardigan Bay, 5th of Ventose,

"5th year of the Republic.

"SIR,—The circumstances under which the body of the French troops
under my command were landed at this place render it unnecessary to
attempt any military operations, as they would tend only to bloodshed
and pillage. The officers of the whole corps have therefore intimated
their desire of entering into a negotiation, upon principles of humanity,
for a surrender. If you are influenced by similar considerations, you
may signify the same by the bearer, and in the meantime hostilities
shall cease. Health and respect,

"TATE, Chef de Brigade.

"To the Officer commanding his Britannic Majesty's troops."

"To the Officer commanding the French troops.

"Fishguard, February 25th.

"SIR,—The superiority of the force under my command, which is
hourly increasing, must prevent my treating upon any terms short of
your surrendering your whole force prisoners of war. I enter fully into
your wish of preventing an unnecessary effusion of blood, which your
speedy surrender can alone prevent, and which will entitle you to
that consideration it is ever the wish of British troops to show to an

running as high up the Channel as this. They took a vessel laden with timber in sight of Ilfracombe and scuttled her, but she floated and came ashore near Port Eynon, where the ground sea knocked her all to pieces before half the cargo could be saved. A gentleman from Swansea dined here the other day and brought us certain intelligence of the French—out of these very frigates—having landed, but in what force was uncertain, as the lady who brought the intelligence came away with her children in too great a hurry to know.

"Yesterday Mr. Talbot went to Swansea to a meeting, where they agreed to form themselves into bodies of horse and foot to defend this part of the country in case of a similar attempt; he heard there that the frigates—I do not know why—sheared off, and of course all those who had landed were obliged to surrender. Two thousand people collected in a very short time, and Lord Cawdor's troops of Fencibles had several skirmishes with the people, who endeavoured to drive off the poor farmers' cattle; it is said that four or five of them have been killed. The French burnt several farmhouses, and plundered some gentlemen's houses in the neighbourhood.

"There are different accounts of the number taken prisoners; some say fourteen hundred, and some say three hundred, but I think the latter most probable. Everybody complains how badly *this* county is secured, and the people at Swansea have petitioned Government for some cannon.

"The French were expected to land at Milford Haven,

enemy whose numbers are inferior. My major will deliver you this letter, and I shall expect your determination by ten o'clock, by your officer, whom I have furnished with an escort that will conduct him to me without molestation.

"I am, &c., CAWDOR."

where there is only one old ship to take care of the whole
trade of these parts, and they might have burnt two
hundred sail of merchantmen that are now there without
any opposition.

"Do not you think we had reason to be in a fright, for
although they landed in Fishguard Bay in Pembroke-
shire, as we did not know how many there were of them,
we thought we should have their company soon.

"Write to me soon and tell me how you all are at
Melbury. This fine weather is just the thing to recover
all invalids.

"The French have unsettled all our plans, Mr. Talbot
being engaged as a volunteer in case we hear any more
of them.

"Give my best love to my father, Lady Ilchester and all.
"Yours affectionately,
"M. L. TALBOT."

LADY ELIZABETH TALBOT[6] TO LADY HARRIOT FOX
STRANGWAYS.

"*Grosvenor Street, March 3rd,* 1797.

"MY DEAR HARRIOT,—You are quite mistaken in supposing we are all *in confusion* here. Everything *appears*
to go on just as quietly and as merrily as if nothing had
happened, though God knows how long this calm may
last, as *knowing* people predict all sorts of horrors, and
say that London is to be set on fire in seventy places at

---

[6] Eldest daughter of Henry Thomas, second Earl of Ilchester; married, 1796, W. Davenport Talbot, Esq., of Lacock Abbey, Wilts. Their
only son, Henry Fox Talbot—who died 1877—is well known as the
discoverer of the art of Photography.

Lady Elizabeth married secondly, 1804, Captain, afterwards Rear-
Admiral Charles Feilding. Their eldest daughter married Ernest, third
Earl of Mount Edgcumbe.

once, and that there are quantities of Arms concealed in night cellars, and many other things that make one quite nervous sometimes. However, it is perfectly certain that there are forty thousand *émigrés* in this town at present; a greater number than have ever been known at any one time since the Revolution; and if Government do not send them all away *with a flea in their ear*, they undoubtedly deserve the consequences. One of the Directory was seen a few days ago in the Strand, and recognized by a French lady whose father, mother, and brother he had murdered. She fainted away in the street, and before she recovered enough to speak he had escaped in the crowd.

" I hope you do not intend remaining at Abbotsbury. I think it is highly imprudent. It is a great comfort to me to think that my father is so beloved by all his poor neighbours and dependents that if any tumult or in-, surrection were to happen in Dorsetshire, he would be as safe as anybody can hope to be.

" I hear Mr. Fox's speech last night was a blaze of eloquence.

" Ever yours,

" E. T. T."

" The Tower guns are firing for Sir John Jervis's having beat the Spanish fleet;[7] tell my father this to raise his spirits."

FROM MISS PORTER TO LADY HARRIOT STRANGWAYS.[8]

" *Yarmouth, October 15th,* 1797.

" MY DEAR LADY HARRIOT,—Yarmouth is very gay at present. Admiral Duncan's victory [9] has made a display

---

[7] The Battle of St. Vincent, February 14, 1797.

[8] Third daughter of Henry Thomas, Earl of Ilchester.

[9] The Battle of Camperdown, October 11, 1797.

of red flags and jolly faces. The Duke of Gloucester [1]
and Prince William were some days at Lowestoft, a
bathing village in our neighbourhood. He was at a Mr.
Jacks's, whose father received George II. in the year 1737.
His Majesty was returning from Hanover and forced to
land there. Mr. Jacks took him up in his carriage, but
to do his Majesty more honour chose to be *coachman
himself*. The horses, unused to his holding the reins,
set off at full gallop up a hill, and, to the utter dismay
of Mr. Jacks, they never stopped till they reached his
own door, where fortunately they terminated their wild
career.

"The King said to him, 'Mr. Jacks, you *excellent
driver*,' and invited him to Court. He took Mr. Jacks's
carriage to London, who never heard more either of the
equipage or King for several months. At last he went to
Court, where his Majesty spoke kindly to him, which was
all the recompense done him for the loss of his carriage
and the hazard of his neck.

　　　　　　　　"Your affectionate,
　　　　　　　　　　　　"ANN AGNES PORTER."

JOHN NEWBOLT,[2] ESQ., TO LADY HARRIOT STRANGWAYS.

　　　　　　　　"*London, December 20th*, 1797.

"MY DEAR LADY HARRIOT,—Though my account of the
procession will come what you call a day after the fair,

---

[1] H.R.H. Prince William Henry, third son of Frederick, Prince of
Wales. His son, Prince William Frederic, was quartered at Norwich,
1797.

[2] Subsequently Sir John Newbolt, Knight, a barrister, &c., Recorder
of Bombay and afterwards Chief Justice of Madras, "situations which
he filled with great honour to himself and advantage to his country!"
Died 1823. He married Juliana, daughter of the Hon. and Very Rev.
W. Digby, Dean of Durham (sister of Maria, Countess of Ilchester).
Previous to her marriage, in 1794, Mrs. Newbolt had been one of the

yet as I promised I should give a little account of our
own, you shall have it upon the maxim of 'better late
than never,' for I was so thoroughly jaded yesterday
upon my return, it was out of my power to do any one
thing; and I feel it so much to-day I am not much
better, but I can with truth assure you that it was in my
opinion one of the finest spectacles ever seen in this
country.[3]   The day was beautiful, and from the doors of
St. Paul's to the House of Lords the streets and houses
were so completely filled that the only manner of com-
puting the numbers present on the occasion would be to
calculate how many men could stand in the streets, and
how many people the houses—taking in the tops—could
contain.   The very steeples of the churches were so completely filled that they looked like bee-hives, the people
swarming round the sides like bees; but notwithstanding

Maids of Honour to Queen Charlotte, and in 1805 was appointed Woman
of the Bedchamber to her Majesty.   Their only daughter married Sir
Robert Sheffield, Bart.

JULIA, LADY SHEFFIELD, TO MRS. MUNDY.

[Extract.]   "Normanby Park, September 21st, 1868.

". . . My mother died in the spring of 1809, and I went to my Aunt
Ilchester in the autumn.   She was then about the Queen and had a house
at Windsor.   She was also at Weymouth with Queen Charlotte, for I
have often heard my aunt talk of this, and of having been obliged to cut
off her hair and wear a wig, in order to be ready for dinner on returning
from the royal yacht. . . ."

[3] The 19th of December, 1797, was appointed for a General Thanksgiving at St. Paul's for the three great naval victories by her Majesty's
fleets under the command of Lords Howe, St. Vincent, and Duncan.   A
grand procession of the Royal Family and the two Houses of Parliament
took place.   In the royal cavalcade were the Duke of York, the Duke of
Clarence, Prince Ernest, the Duke of Gloucester, and Princess Sophia of
Gloucester, and immediately following their Majesties were the Princesses
Augusta, Elizabeth, Sophia, and Mary.   On entering the choir their
Majesties were seated under a crimson canopy of state, the Princesses in
a compartment on the left.

the immensity of the crowd I describe, such was the excellence of the arrangement upon the occasion that it would be impossible for you to walk from Melbury Church to the House in better order than the Lords and Commons *went* from their respective Parliament Houses to church.

"I say 'as they *went*' because the same good order, I heard, was not observed on the return; the Chancellor, however, got home as quietly as he left it.

"The streets the whole way were lined with soldiers of different regiments of Guards till you got to Temple Bar, and within the City were guarded by the different Volunteer Companies; and the different dresses, manners, &c., of these various corps I assure you afforded a very complete military spectacle, and tended to enliven the scene very much, particularly from their having divided their bands so as to have music at an interval of every five minutes in the procession, who played all sorts of loyal and military tunes.

"The streets themselves seemed almost alive, and the display of beauty in the windows with a considerable intermixture of quizzes rendered our drive very interesting. The only sulky face I saw was that of an old woman who sat alone at the windows of her house, and let no person share the pleasure of the sight with her. We all agreed that she must have outstood her market by asking too high a price for an admission, and was in the act of lamenting having been too sharp for herself, which is not an uncommon thing in this world. I confess I longed to be mobbing it, as I should have seen much more of the fun of the thing in that situation. A person I knew went in a sailor's dress as one of the seamen of Lord Duncan's ship, and very curious adventures he met with in that character. But to return to what I did see,

H

from what I wished to see. The inside of St. Paul's presented so magnificent a *coup-d'œil* that upon my entrance—to compare small things with great—I was affected in the same manner as Lord Somerville described himself to have been affected when he first saw his famous Lincolnshire bull, that is, I could scarce draw my breath from admiration and surprise.

" We entered at the west door, and commanded the whole length of the aisle, which was at that time so completely filled we could scarcely make our way along; the sides were lined with detachments from several regiments of Guards, and between their line we saw the procession of the Peers in their fine robes, judges in their great wigs, and in short all the magistracy of the realm. In the centre of the dome there was a circular scaffolding above completely filled with well-dressed ladies, and below were the sailors with Admiral Duncan and his officers holding the colours taken at the three great victories.

" The moment the King's carriage arrived at the west door the commanding officer ordered the troops in the church to rest arms, and instantly three or four bands of martial music struck up ' God save the King.'

" The effect produced by this I shall remember the longest day I have to live.

" The applauses and huzzas of the ill-dressed mob without and well-dressed mob within, mixed with the sound of the ' spirit-stirring drum and ear-piercing fife," and the greatness of the space in which this scene was passing, was in character with the magnificence of the whole thing.

" The King stopped under the dome and conversed for some time with Lord Duncan and the sailors, and to the great scandal of good church-goers, did not hold his tongue for any considerable time together during the Service. The Consecration of the Colours was a ceremony very well calculated to produce a fine effect. The Colours were laid lengthways, and carried to the Altar by the different officers who had signalized themselves in the respective engagements. Admiral Duncan was so much affected that he could not conceal his tears, and the Queen showed considerable feeling upon the occasion.

" The Bishop of Lincoln paid Lord Duncan a very neat and appropriate compliment in the course of his sermon. After speaking of the blessings which the piety of individuals might acquire for a whole nation, he said he hoped that when historians recorded the gallant event which they were that day assembled to celebrate, they would not forget to mention that one of the principal actors in the last gallant action had contributed to the success of his country as well by the punctual discharge of his religious duties, as he had done by his valour and skill in his profession. I believe the Bishop intended to have given the King a similar compliment, but as he saw him talking during his sermon he scratched it out !

" Pitt was attacked at Temple Bar by three ruffians, who rushed from the mob and seized upon the door of his carriage, undoubtedly with an intent to drag him out, but three of the Light Horse Volunteers rode up, and backing their horses against them, sent them head over heels to the place from whence they came, rather faster than they ventured out.

" What you see in the papers respecting the throwing the *cats* to injure the cavalry is strictly true.

" I will now leave off, only adding that Julia sends her best remembrances.

" Your affectionate friend,

" J. NEWBOLT."

1798.

JOHN NEWBOLT, ESQ., TO LADY H. STRANGWAYS.

" 1798.

" MY DEAR LADY HARRIOT,—I know you are so good a wisher to Government that my present scrawl will be very welcome, unless you have heard the news before, and if ever a tale twice told could please, it would be in the present instance, as it is neither more nor less than an account of Buonaparte and his whole army being cut to pieces by the Arabs.   The news comes from Hamburg— that is the express to Government; but there is also an express come to the East India Company, but whether that comes overland from India or by the same mode of conveyance that Government have received their intelligence, is more than I can say.   The story is very particular, and mentions Buonaparte himself having been killed by one of his own men.   I allow Buonaparte was a great man, but he had very much sullied his greatness, in my opinion, by his cruelties at Alexandria, and the infamous lie he told of the poor admiral who was killed in the Battle of the Nile.   Julia's love.   She continues quite well.

" Very sincerely yours ever,

" J. NEWBOLT.

" I can only say that the Chancellor[4] believes the report I have sent you."

MISS PORTER TO LADY H. STRANGWAYS.

" *Yarmouth, October 2nd,* 1798.

" MY DEAR LADY HARRIOT,—Sir Horatio Nelson's first

---

[4] Baron Loughborough, created Earl Rosslyn, 1801.

lieutenant passed here yesterday on his way to London.[5] They have taken nine ships, burnt two, and sunk two frigates of the French fleet.

"Most affectionately yours,
"Ann Agnes Porter."

CHARLES DIGBY[6] TO HIS COUSIN, LADY HARRIOT STRANGWAYS.

" Hamburg, December 23rd, 1798.

"Dear Harriot,—I have but one fault to find with your letters, which is that they are so tortoise-footed that they can only overtake me in Germany, where going and standing are nearly synonymous terms.   We propose leaving this place for Berlin on Monday next, where we shall probably stay a month or six weeks, and where I hope to receive from you as stupid a letter as the one I received yesterday !   As I have spent near a fortnight at Hamburg, you will now expect I should give you some account of it.   I will.   Tweddell asking his *lacquey de louage* what there was worth seeing in Hamburg, was answered, ' Monsieur, exactement—rien ! '   From personal acquaintance with the inhabitants I am not qualified to give you any account of their character.   I know not even one of them.   We see scarcely anything but *émigrés*, who are very cheerful and pleasant.   From all that I have seen and all the accounts I have received, I should think that if you took one-third of Judaism, of ugliness, and of dirt, and mix them well together, you will stand some chance of forming a Hamburg hodge-podge.

---

[5] The Battle of the Nile was fought on August 1, 1798.

[6] Son of the Honourable Stephen Digby [brother of Henry, first Earl Digby], Vice-Chamberlain to Queen Charlotte ; and of Lady Lucy Strangways, daughter of first Earl of Ilchester.   Subsequently Canon of Windsor and Rector of Bishop's Caundle, Dorset.

" The summer we intend to spend in Switzerland, and, as you rightly suppose, the winter at Naples.

" *Brunswick, Jan.* 11*th.*—When I laid down my pen I did not expect to have resumed it till my arrival at Berlin ; but as Heaven alone knows whether we shall ever arrive there through such roads, I intend to finish my letter and send it from this place. It is impossible for an English person to form any idea of the roads at this season in this part of the world. You may form some notion of the expeditious manner in which we travel when I tell you that we were five days from Hamburg to this place, travelling from daybreak till often near midnight, the distance about 100 English miles. We have now 150 to Berlin. This morning we have been to Wolfenbuttel, where there is a magnificent library of ancient books and manuscripts. There we saw wonders upon wonders—MSS. of the fourth century, the laws of Confucius, the Metamorphoses of Ovid, interspersed with prints, a book written by a man with his foot, another by his mouth, all inimitable in their way, and many worth the many narrow escapes we had of being overset.

" At Saltzdalum, a place not far off, we saw a gallery of pictures, amongst which there are some very fine. I could choose about twenty which would assist in furnishing the rooms at Melbury very well.

" We paid our respects to the court yesterday, for which we were rewarded with a magnificent dinner and supper —I will not say a good one, for the only thing I could get to my taste was the leg of a fowl.

" The Duke of Brunswick is a fine-looking man, and much liked both in his private and public character. I wish he had not published that manifesto ; they say he is much concerned at having done it.

" To-morrow we are to see a superb onyx.   O fortunati nimium !

" Your affectionate cousin,

" C. DIGBY."

1799.

FROM MRS. GUMBLETON [7] TO HER NIECE, LADY HARRIOT STRANGWAYS.

" *Cappercullen, January 29th,* 1799.

" MY DEAREST HARRIOT,—I should have answered yours directly, but had written a few days before to your father.   I wish I could find words to express how grateful I am for the kind anxiety you all feel for us poor mortals, doomed to live in this ill-fated country.   However, our prospects, thank God, at present seem to brighten.

" The rebellion in the County Clare is almost got under, and in other parts they lay dormant to try the effect of the proposed union, for they took every method to say, and make *persons feel*, that Government was assisting them in their plans, for hundreds that were at present loyal would, in the case of an union with England, join the rebels hand in hand.

" Thanks to Providence, we have still some left in the House of Commons who love their country, and the measure of an Union is for the present given up, and we may now hope that Lord C.[8] will endeavour to protect

[7] Catherine, fourth daughter of Standish Grady, Esq., of Cappercullen and Elton, Co. Limerick, sister of Mary Theresa, Countess of Ilchester. Married first, John Quin, Esq., of Adare, brother of the first Earl of Dunraven, and secondly, George Gumbleton, Esq., of Castle Richards, Co, Cork.

[8] Charles, first Marquis Cornwallis.   In 1798 Lord-Lieutenant of Ireland and commander of the forces there.   Governor-General of India —for the second time—1804, where he died 1805.

the Protestants and our mail coaches, which are almost daily robbed in some part or other, though they travel with what is called a guard of two or three.

" Now I do not expect to see a soul here, or to leave this until May, when (if I can) I will go home. Perhaps by that time it may be safe for the Grady's to come in my place. I long to hear how pumping has agreed with your father. I trust in God he will get strong with every exertion he is making. You and I agree perfectly about our ideas of Bath, for I never was in a place I disliked more, though it always did me so much good. You need not tell me how full of Irish the town is at present: I am told that there are two thousand families, and I believe I know forty at least.

" I hope Lady Ilchester is in good health and spirits. Pray remember me very particularly to her, and tell her that had I only consulted my own peace and security as well as pleasure, she should have been tormented with much of my company this winter. Austen Fitz Gerald[9] is on severe duty, endeavouring to quell the rebellion in the part of the County Clare where his father has some property in the town and on the coast. His wife is in Ennis, afraid to stir from it. The Grady's very gay in Limerick—your uncle, Standish Grady, keeping garrison at Elton, and I can assure you all the doors and windows here are planked up with ball-proof planks and fastened, so that no sledge can burst them in ; and we have two servants that we think would protect us, one of mine, and one of my mother's. Two people would keep off a host of foes. My mother desires to be remembered to your father, Lady Ilchester, and all the young people.

---

[9] Subsequently Sir Augustine Fitz Gerald. Son of Edward Fitz Gerald, Esq., of Moy Castle, Co. Clare, and of Rachel Grady.

With every sincere wish for health and happiness to all your dear family,

"Believe me ever yours,

"C. GUMBLETON."

In September this year Mr. Frampton married Lady Harriot Strangways,[1] daughter of Lord Ilchester—a union which gave the liveliest satisfaction to my mother and myself, and was indeed productive of the greatest happiness to us all. My sister-in-law was a woman of the highest principles and most superior understanding, extremely clever, and in the greatest degree cultivated and well informed. She was a devoted wife and mother, but at the same time the delight of society from her agreeable manners and conversational powers.

All the five sisters were charming in their different ways, and very much admired, and three of them, Lady Mary Talbot, Lady Charlotte, and the youngest, who became Lady Lansdowne, were extremely handsome.

MRS. FRAMPTON TO HER SISTER-IN-LAW, MRS. HEBERDEN,[2] AT WINDSOR.

Dorchester, Thursday, Sept. 12th, 1799.

"DEAR SISTER,—You will be glad to hear that our wedding[3] is over. They were married on Monday last at Melbury

---

[1] Third daughter of Henry Thomas, second Earl of Ilchester, born 1778, died 1845. She was great-granddaughter to Sir Stephen Fox.

"It was said of my mother by her husband's family, that whenever there was sickness or sorrow, or on the other hand, any great joy or happiness, the first person thought of was Lady Harriot Frampton. Her sympathy was certain on every occasion, and her advice, help, and comfort never-failing."—H. G. M.

[2] Mary, sister of Dr. Wollaston, the first husband of Mrs. Frampton ; and wife of William Heberden, Esq., M.D., Physician to his Majesty George III., who died 1801.

[3] The marriage of her son, James Frampton, Esq., of Moreton.

Church, by Mr. Strangways, Lord Ilchester's brother.
We went to Melbury the day before, and numbers of
relations and near connections joined us, so that we were
a numerous party. It poured with rain, which prevented
the *procession* to church, for it is not approachable with
a carriage, and though near the house, is distant enough
to get wet in such a heavy rain. Some of us went in a
sedan chair which Lord Ilchester uses in the gout, others
ran on in cloaks, with umbrellas, &c. On our return a
fine cake, fruits, &c., &c., were placed for us, and after
salutations and congratulations were over, the bride
retired to disrobe. Her bridal dress of embroidered
India muslin, the finest possible, with veil of Brussels
Honiton lace, was changed for a riding-habit, and about
two o'clock the bride and bridegroom set out for Redlynch, another seat of Lord Ilchester's, which Lady
Harriot preferred going to, rather than Moreton just at
first. *We* had a very magnificent dinner, and everything that could show the joy of the family on the
occasion, but the day appeared a week to us, being
dressed before breakfast, and the weather so bad, we
could not amuse ourselves out of doors. We returned
home on Tuesday, and yesterday the happy pair called
on me in their way to Moreton—they had most sad
weather for their reception, and for the treat of the poor
people.

"You will have seen by the newspapers that I have
had a hurry of a different kind, and more embarrassing,
the visit of their Majesties, most unexpected, and totally
without any preparation. We were sitting at work in
my little room with Mrs. Drax,[4] I happened to look out,

---

[4] Sarah Frances, daughter and heiress of Edward Drax, Esq., of Char-
borough Park, Co. Dorset. She married, 1788, Richard Grosvenor, Esq.,
nephew of Richard, Earl Grosvenor, who took the name of Drax.

and actually saw the King and Princess Sophia with their attendants, at my garden gate. I screamed out, threw down everything about me, and flew out to them. Mr. Damer [5] met me, and told me the Queen and three other Princesses and their suite were following.

He bid *me* attend to *them*, and then kindly went in to Mary and told what was necessary to be done, helped to put the drawing-room in order, and bespoke mutton-chops. By this time they all arrived, and I ran through the house to meet them at the front door. The King called out, ' Well run, Mrs. Frampton.' Into the drawing-room they went, asked for Mary, talked very easily, and asked for her cuttings-out, which of course they admired. They then proposed walking, and we all went through my fields to the walks round great part of the town, and returned the same way, and they seemed much pleased.

I conducted them into my eating-room, trembling lest the Collation should not be as it ought, but really it was as well prepared as could be expected on so short a notice—cold partridges, cold meat of different sorts, and removes of mutton-chops and fruit—tea at the side-table.

" Mary made tea, Mr. Damer carried it to them, and I waited on their Majesties as they ate, and Mary on the princesses.

" The ladies they asked to sit down were, Lady Poulett,[6] Lady Radnor,[7] Lady Charles Somerset,[8] Lady

---

[5] The Honourable Lionel Damer, youngest son of the first Earl of Dorchester, M.P. for Peterborough, died 1807.

[6] Sophia, daughter and heiress of Admiral Sir George Pocock, K.B., wife of John, fourth Earl Poulett, one of his Majesty's Lords of the Bedchamber.

[7] The Honourable Anne Duncombe, daughter and co-heir of Anthony, Lord Feversham. She married Jacob, second Earl of Radnor.

[8] Elizabeth, daughter of William, second Viscount Courtenay; married General Lord Charles Somerset, son of fifth Duke of Beaufort. He was

Matilda Wynyard,[9] and Lady Pitt.[1] Miss Townshend stood with Mrs. Drax. After the repast the female part went into all the bedrooms, and approved and looked at everything everywhere. In short, they were all good-humoured and easy. They stayed about two hours, and I hear from various hands that they were pleased with the day's amusement and thought all was so well conducted. This gives us comfort after our bustle.

" We went yesterday to Weymouth and stayed to the Play, which is the right etiquette, and they graciously noticed us directly. We are to go on Sunday evening to the Rooms again.

" My garden and field were full of people to view the Royal Family.

" The King goes away on Monday se'night to meet the Parliament, but returns the following Thursday. Adieu. Love to all.

" Yours ever,

" PHILLIS FRAMPTON."

1800.

September 16*th*.—The Dorset Yeomanry were reviewed by the King in person.

Friday, September 26*th*.—The King, Queen, five Princesses, Princess Sophia of Gloucester, Duke of Cumberland and suite drove over from Weymouth to Moreton and spent some hours there.

at this time Comptroller of the Household to the King. Subsequently Governor of the Cape of Good Hope, &c.

[9] Second daughter of John, second Earl Delawarr, and wife of General Henry Wynyard.

[1] The Honourable Mary Scrope, daughter of Emmanuel, second Viscount Howe of Ireland ; wife of General Sir William Augustus Pitt, K.B., brother of George, first Lord Rivers ; died 1819. Lord Rivers was in 1799 one of His Majesty's Lords of the Bedchamber.

1802.

IN this year all the most valuable Deeds and family Documents at Moreton had been sent for safety to Mr. Shirley's house at Ettington in Warwickshire.

Beacons were prepared on all the most prominent hills along the coast of Dorset, ready to be fired the instant the French fleet should appear. The yeomanry, commanded by Lord Dorchester, and in which my brother was a captain, were also on the alert, to be available at a moment's notice.

C. BURRELL MASSINGBERD, ESQ., OF ORMSBY, CO. LINCOLN, TO F. N. C. MUNDY, ESQ., OF MARKEATON.

"*Paris, April 30th*, 1802.

"MY DEAR SIR,—It is astonishing to hear almost every person I speak to regret the Revolution and the loss of the best of kings and men, which they now say Louis XVI. certainly was. The present Government is returning as fast as possible to its ancient show of royalty, and with such a military force in Paris and such popularity as the first Consul now seems to enjoy, I think he may in everything follow his own inclinations, which, however, seem to be entirely bent on doing essential service to this country.

" The introduction of public worship and re-establishment of bishops, &c., was a most popular act, and was executed on Easter Sunday, in such parade as has never for many years been seen in Paris. Buonaparte, with the two other Consuls, was in a state coach drawn by eight very fine horses, and there were many coaches and six for the other members of the council and for the ladies of Buonaparte's family, and about 10,000 troops,

with such magnificent dresses and such exact discipline
as made the procession very well worth seeing. To be
sure, the members of the different legislative bodies did
not show much taste or grandeur, but you must consider
that they are (many of them) of the lowest extraction,
and not made so rich by plunder as the great generals are.
Most of the senators and legislators were in hackney-
coaches, with the numbers taken off. It is, however,
sufficient for the people of this country if they have one
grand object to look up to, and whether it happens to be
a king or a consul they will be equally servile to either.
The decree passed a few days since in favour of the
emigrants has the appearance of great generosity, but
it is so cautiously worded as not to risk any claims of
their property being restored to the great princes or
clergy.

"I find grain of all sorts dearer at Paris than in
London. Good wheat sells for 4l. a quarter, and oats
and barley in about the same proportion. I think it
must be some length of time before any improvements
in agriculture can produce any sensible advantages in
this country. The reduced state of individual fortunes
and of population is most felt in the country, as all the
rich and powerful have been drawn to Paris, and we well
know that no improvements in agriculture can take place
without great exertions among the individual persons
who have hopes of increasing their fortunes by those
exertions.

"I do believe that the public will make every possible
exertion to encourage commerce and agriculture, but
their military government must require so large a proportion of the property they call national, and to restore
their navy must be such another heavy demand, that I
conceive they will make a very slow progress in the other

important objects of their wish. The members of the
Institut are many of them men of good knowledge, and
their theory will, I have no doubt, be wisely debated;
but I do not see how any general benefit can arise
till several great impediments to single adventurers in
trade and agriculture are removed. But time will show
more, and when I have the pleasure of seeing you,
which is always a very great one, I shall be glad to tell
you more fully the remarks I have been able to make in
these extraordinary times at Paris.

"My dear sir, with true regard and respect,
"Your faithful servant,
"C. BURRELL MASSINGBERD."

1803.

ANECDOTES OF PARIS FROM MR. W. CHURCHILL,[2] ARRESTED
IN MAY, 1803, AND KEPT THERE UNTIL JANUARY, 1804.

MR. CHURCHILL had proceeded four posts on the road to
Lyons when he was stopped and ordered back to Paris.
When he returned thither he was conveyed to the office
for examining the English; he produced his passport
from General Andreossi, as well as his certificate from
Mr. Talbot, Lord Whitworth's[3] secretary, purporting him

[2] The Rev. William Hallett Churchill, of Colliton, Co. Dorset; died
1847. He was descended from John Churchill, who was seated at
Dorchester *temp.* Henry VIII. This family and that of the Duke of
Marlborough derive from a common ancestor, Roger Churchill, of Cathers-
ton, Co. Dorset.

[3] Charles, son of Sir Charles Whitworth, Knight. From 1788 to 1800
Envoy Extraordinary and Plenipotentiary to the Court of Russia;
created Baron Whitworth, 1800, and in 1816 Earl Whitworth. Ambassador to the Consular Court of France, 1802. The conference
which took place between the First Consul and Lord Whitworth, relative
to the retention of Malta by the British Government, in which the
prompt and dignified repression of Napoleon's intemperate address by

to be an English clergyman, not liable to serve in any way in the English army, and consequently by Buonaparte's own rule, exempt from arrestation. The certificate availed him nothing. General Junot (formerly a baker), before whom he was brought, after reading the certificate, sternly asked whether Mr. Talbot had left Paris, and being answered by Mr. C. in the affirmative, said, " Tant mieux pour lui," and immediately tore the certificate into a hundred pieces and threw it on the ground. Thus ended his hopes from this quarter.

The government is military in the strictest sense of the word, a military police, as sentinels, are placed at the corners of every street, who have the power to stop people and oblige them to produce their " Cartes de Sureté."

These *Cartes de Sureté* every one is obliged to have, or they are liable to be drawn to serve as conscripts, and it is in the power of the Government to give or refuse them. In consequence, some of the most respectable trademen in Paris were enrolled, and amongst them was the chief clerk of M. Perigeaux, the banker for the English.

The conscripts are marched off handcuffed, and go to serve as common soldiers. Four children are allowed as

the English Ambassador, in presence of all the other foreign ambassadors, has been celebrated throughout Europe. Viceroy of Ireland, 1813-17, and Lord of the Bedchamber. Lord Whitworth married, 1801, Arabella, daughter and co-heir of Sir C. Cope, Bart., and widow of John, third Duke of Dorset. They both died (s.p.) 1825, when the title became extinct.

The retention of her title by the Duchess of Dorset, although she was the wife of another man, caused considerable embarrassment to the society of Paris during Lord Whitworth's residence there. In fact, the French could not comprehend the state of the case at all, and I believe many persisted in doubting whether they were really married !—w. M.

an exemption.   After twelve o'clock at night every one
is liable to be stopped and carried to the guard-house and
detained there until it is the pleasure of the general who
happens to be on guard to examine your passport.   An
immense force is in Paris and the environs.

The English arrested in Paris had no communication
with officers, they having been prohibited from associating
with them, and they received every sort of insult and
incivility from those belonging to the Government, but
not from the people in general.   The latter part of the
time that Mr. Churchill was in France, Buonaparte
resided entirely at the Tuileries, having taken a disgust to
St. Cloud, which before had been his principal residence,
from an attempt having there been made to assassinate
him.   At the end of a long passage at St. Cloud he
espied a man who did not belong either to himself or his
guard.   Buonaparte called a sentinel, who seized the
man and found a large knife concealed under his coat.
The man, of course, was put under confinement, but is
said to be mad.

The other two Consuls (Cambacérès and Lebrun) are
mere cyphers ; one of them, in the absence of Buonaparte
on one of his visits to inspect the army of England,[4]
thinking to pay Buonaparte a compliment on the placing
of the statue of the Venus of Medicis in the Museum,
ventured to make an *arrêté,* naming it the "Musée
Napoleon."   On the return of Buonaparte to Paris,
he sent for the Consul, and said, "Know, sir, that
wherever *I* am is the seat of government, consequently
no *arrêté* can be made in my absence."

Buonaparte himself is decidedly unpopular, and his
passions at times are dreadful.   He shows himself but

4 The French army intended for the invasion of England, encamped
in the neighbourhood of Boulogne, was so denominated.

little, and when he goes to the opera sits so far back in
his "loge" that he cannot be distinguished.   On the
4th of July—the day of the Federation—the Tuileries
gardens were superbly illuminated.   His box alone was
dark, and so dark that in the momentary appearance he
made there, Mr. Churchill says he should not have known
whether it had been he or not.   There was a slight
attempt at applause when he entered, but he disappeared
before it could have become general, even if the voice of
the people had been for him.   The real Frenchmen dislike
the reputation of a foreigner reigning over them, and
you cannot offend them more than by reminding them
that their Governor is a Corsican.   Many of the old
nobility reside in Paris on the débris of their fortune,
saying they prefer Paris, even as it is, to any other
country.   A Monsieur Dillon, one of that class, said,
"Car je puis avoir mon dîner et ma dissipation pour six
francs, and where can I get that in any other country?"

   The taxes paid to Government are very great; every
ox that is brought into Paris pays quinze sous toll,
and other things in proportion.   The revenue of the
Government is said to amount to thirty-one or thirty-
two millions more than in the most flourishing state of
the monarchy.

   Buonaparte has established a sort of bank, into which
every person, on taking any office under Government,
deposits a certain sum of money in proportion to the
annual value of the place they have got; for this money
they receive three per cent. interest, but should any
improper conduct be discovered whilst they are in office,
or should they displease Buonaparte, he takes from the
money *so* deposited such a portion as he thinks adequate
to compensate for their crime.   By this means he has a
bank from which he - can always borrow money, and

besides has the advantage of keeping a large body of people at his command.

His policy in regard to opening *to all*, entirely free of expense, all the fine galleries of pictures, statues, and other monuments of the arts, is admirable; it attracts multitudes of foreigners who spend money in Paris, and is certainly worthy of a great nation.

The arrestation of the English, on the contrary, was the measure of a little mind swayed by passion, and could not in any light conduce to the glory or advantage of the nation he governs. It was represented to Buonaparte that the arresting the English artisans, and those who came for the purposes of trading was an essential disadvantage to him, but all that could be obtained was leave from him to have a month in which they might settle their affairs, after which time they were to be in the same situation with the other English. In whatever parts of France the English were, there they were stopped.

Those at Paris were considered the best off; some were sent from thence to Fontainebleau, and some who had used indiscrete language against the Government were put in confinement there.

In the month of December, 1803, a decree passed ordering all the English in Paris to repair before a certain day to Verdun in Lorraine. Mr. Churchill had, before that decree was issued, obtained a passport for his unfortunate brother, a helpless invalid, but as no one he could trust was permitted to be with him on his journey, Mr. C. had hoped that humanity could not be so entirely banished even from France as to make the chief consul refuse him a passport to accompany his brother. Trusting to this hope, he remained in Paris beyond the day limited for his arrival at Verdun; but before that day arrived Mr. Churchill waited upon General Junot, representing his singular case. The general heard him with perfect *sang-froid*, and said to him, " C'est votre affaire ; if you do not go to Verdun, you will be arrested and sent to the Temple." With this answer Mr. Churchill retired and determined to await his fate. A gendarme arrived in a day or two with an order to arrest and conduct him to the Temple, but luckily the name was spelt wrong ; the gendarme confessed his mistake, retired with a douceur, and promised not to inform against him. After this Mr. Churchill thought it might be prudent to feign sickness, which he accordingly did, and sent for a French physician, who very conveniently declared that his throat was ulcerated, and retired ordering him various remedies. In the meantime the remainder of the English were on their journey, or arrived at Verdun.

Mr. Churchill remained a considerable time in confinement at Paris, but at length—by bribery, I believe, but he was bound to secrecy—procured a permission to get out of the country with his brother.

A friend who had accompanied him there was still detained, and died in captivity a year or two afterwards.

1804.

EXTRACT FROM A LETTER FROM MR. FOX [5] TO MR. O'BRIEN, IN REPLY TO AN APPLICATION FOR HIS INTERCESSION ON BEHALF OF MR. W. CHURCHILL WHEN A " DÉTENU " AT PARIS.

" *January 2nd*, 1804.

" As you desire an answer by the return of the post, I

---

[5] The Right Honourable Charles James Fox was first cousin to Lady Susan O'Brien. Mr. O'Brien was a near neighbour and friend of the Churchill family.

will not delay sending it to you, though I found every application made by me to France at the beginning of the war useless, and therefore I say to you, as I am obliged to do to all others, and the applications have been numerous—that I have no communication whatever with any one in France.

"If I could have done any good (although fully aware of the misinterpretations such a conduct might have given rise to), I am not sure that I should not have attempted it."

THE QUEEN TO MARIA, COUNTESS OF ILCHESTER.[6]

"MY DEAR LADY ILCHESTER,—If it is not inconvenient to your arrangements, I should wish you to come to Kew to-morrow by four o'clock, which is our dinner-hour, to pass the day with us and stay the night; and on Wednesday my daughters will have the pleasure of carrying you back to town.

"You may dress in a muslin gown with a hat on, and shall be presented to the King after dinner.

"CHARLOTTE.

"*Kew, June 25th*, 1804."

---

[6] Maria, third daughter of the Honourable and Very Rev. William Digby, Dean of Durham, became in 1794 second wife of Henry Thomas, second Earl of Ilchester. Lord Ilchester died 1802; and in June, 1804, his widow was selected by Queen Charlotte to be an extra and supernumerary Lady of the Bedchamber to her Majesty. The appointment was made by the Queen herself, and being, so to speak, a private arrangement, and the salary paid from the Queen's private purse, Lady Ilchester's name does not appear in the published lists of the Royal Household. In the year 1814, by an arrangement between the Queen and H.R.H. the Prince Regent, Lady Ilchester was *lent*—very much against her inclination—to assist in forming the establishment of the Princess Charlotte, with whom she remained until the marriage of the Princess in 1816. Lady Ilchester then returned to her former duties, and was in attendance on Queen Charlotte at the time of her death. Lady Ilchester died at Abbotsbury, 1842.

In the latter part of the summer the royal family were again staying at Weymouth. During September and October the King and Queen gave several fêtes there, and on the 20th of October the King reviewed the Yeomanry in person.

The following letters were written by my niece, Mary Shirley,[7] who was then with her parents and elder sister Selina on a visit to my mother at Dorchester. She was only thirteen years of age.

FROM MARY SHIRLEY TO HER GREAT-AUNT, MRS. E. FAUQUIER, AT SUDBURY.

"*Dorchester, October 18th,* 1804.

"MY DEAR AUNT,—*Dorsetshire* is certainly the gayest county in England: I will now go on with the account of our daily proceedings. Last Sunday at half-past four, mamma, Aunt Harriot Frampton, Aunt Frampton, Miss Lyte,[8] Selina, and I, all went in the coach, and the two gentlemen, Uncle Frampton and Uncle Wollaston, in the chaise to Weymouth Rooms. We first of all went to Lady Charlotte and Lady Louisa Strangways, to their house and drank tea there, where we heard that the royal family was not to be at the rooms because of the rain. Then Lady Ilchester came in with an invitation for mamma and Aunt Harriot to go with her to the Lodge,[1]

[7] Mary, third daughter of Evelyn Shirley, Esq., of Ettington, Co. Warwick, born 1791. She married, 1813, George Morant, Esq.

[8] Relative of Henry Lyte, Esq., Sub-Preceptor to the Prince of Wales (afterwards George IV.), and subsequently Master of the Robes, Treasurer and Auditor of the Duchy of Cornwall to H.R.H. He died, 1791. Mr. Lyte was guardian to Mr. Frampton and his sister Mary, conjointly with Admiral Houlton.

[1] Originally belonging to the Duke of Gloucester, who lent it to his brother, King George III., and then called Gloucester Lodge. The King subsequently purchased that with several adjoining houses, after

which they did.   Aunt Frampton and Miss Lyte took the
care of Selina and me, and we went to the rooms, but were
much disappointed in not seeing the royal family, but we
saw a great many ladies and gentlemen and German
officers, and Mr. Pitt.   We stood close by him and heard
him *talk*.   After we had stayed there till half-past ten,
we went to the Lady Strangways' again and sat there
till mamma and Aunt Harriot came, and then went away
with Lady Louisa also.   When we got home we ate a very
good supper at half-past one, and then went to bed.
The next morning mamma told Selina and me the conversation she had with the Queen, Princesses, and Duke
of Cambridge.   On Monday, Lord Ilchester and Mr.
Haines [2] came to Moreton for the christening.   At half-
past three little Henry was christened at the church, and
all of us were present at it.   Of course we were all
dressed in our best clothes, and when we came home we
dined.   After dinner and tea we had a most delightful
dance.   There were four reels with Lady Louisa Strangways, Selina, Lord Ilchester, and myself.   We ended
with the Boulanger, and a very pleasant dance we had.
We went to bed at two.   The next day all the gentlemen
went away before breakfast, and at one o'clock we went
to Dorchester and left Aunt Harriot by herself.   We
brought Lady Louisa here where her carriage came for
her.   Yesterday morning Aunt Frampton took Selina
and me in her open carriage to Weymouth, and there we
saw the King just before he got upon his horse, and
Mr. Pitt and a great many other gentlemen with him.

which it was denominated the King's Lodge, or the Royal Lodge.   It
was sold with the other Crown property in 1820.

   [2] Nephew of Sir J. Chudleigh, Bart., to whose estates at Chalmington
he eventually succeeded.   His sister Jane married the Honourable and
Rev. Charles Strangways, brother of second Earl of Ilchester.

He came and spoke to Aunt Frampton, and then both she
and Dr. Heberden whispered who we were, then his
Majesty came and spoke to me a great deal and said,
'Do not you think your sister Fanny very much improved?' I said, 'Yes, sir,' and curtseyed. Then he
said, 'What, what, what!' which Aunt Frampton said
made me look quite pale, but I said, 'Yes, sir, yes,
sir,' over again. Adieu, dear aunt.

"Believe me ever yours,

"MARY SHIRLEY.

"Yesterday, Granny had her rooms full of Yeomanry,
and so she will every night till the Yeomanry meeting
is over."

FROM THE SAME TO THE SAME.

"Dorchester, October 21st.

"MY DEAR AUNT,—Many thanks for your letter, which
I am now going to answer. Last Thursday we all went to
Lord Poulett's ball, and very much delighted we were;
that is, Selina and I. At seven we got to the Weymouth
Rooms, where we only found three little girls, which I
was very glad to see; but very soon after Lord and Lady
Poulett, with their two eldest daughters, Lady Sophia
and Lady Mary, came, with all the royal family. The
King went to one part of the company and her Majesty to
the other, and the Princesses dispersed about as they
liked. After they (the King and Queen) had spoken to
everybody in the room—Selina and me amongst the
rest—the dancing began. Three of the Princesses began
the ball. Mr. Verney came and asked Selina to dance,
so they went to the bottom of the room immediately.
Then mamma and my aunts advised me to stand up that
the King might see that I had no partner. The King
came up to me and said, 'Have not you got a partner?'

I curtseyed and said, ' No, sir,' so away he went and
fetched me Lord Poulett's second son, about twelve
years old, and he made excuses to me for bringing so
young a one, so I am afraid he must think me older than
I am.   Then he took hold of my arm and gave me to
my partner, and we went of course to the bottom, but
Lady Mary Poulett (whom we got a little acquainted with
in London) was so good as to take us up to the top, for
she said otherwise we should be a long time before we
got there, as there were fifty couples, and I was not sorry
to get down again, for it was so *very very* hot, and
crowded to a great degree.   I danced four dances with
my partner, for it was the King's desire we should dance
together all night, and there were only four dances in
all, three of which were danced before the royal family
went, and three little girls, Miss Gunns, danced a figure
dance besides.   We did not leave the rooms till one,
and we arrived here to supper at half-past two.   The
Duke of Cambridge talked to Selina and me once when
we were dancing.   Yesterday we had a grand ball here,
which Selina has given Cousin Georgiana an account of,
but I will tell you my partners.   I began with Mr.
Haines, then a German officer, then Mr. James Weld,[3]
then with his elder brother, and I ended with Captain
Bock, another German.   We had reels, and ended with
the Boulanger.   Next Friday the King has invited all of
us to go to his ball.   The children are to dance first, then
the grown-up ladies and gentlemen.

" Friday is the Dorchester ball, and all except Granny
and I are to go to it; the Duke of Cambridge[4] is to be

[3] Son of Thomas Weld, Esq., of Lulworth Castle, Dorset, who was
the founder of the Roman Catholic College at Stoneyhurst.

[4] The Duke was on the most friendly and intimate terms with my
father and mother, and was a frequent visitor at Moreton, sometimes

there, and is to begin with Aunt Harriot. Papa does not go there, I believe, but he does and *must* to the Friday ball, because the King invited him. We were going on that day, but now it must be put off till Monday or Tuesday, as on Sunday they must go to the rooms, as it is the last. Pray give my love to my aunt, cousin, &c.

"Believe me, dear aunt, ever yours,

"MARY SHIRLEY."

FROM THE SAME TO THE SAME.

"*Dorchester, October* 28*th*, 1804.

"MY DEAR AUNT FAUQUIER,—I must write again to tell you of the King's ball. On last Friday, at five o'clock, mamma, grandmamma, Aunt Frampton, Selina and myself, all went to *the* ball, and papa and Uncle Wollaston went at two o'clock to dine at Weymouth and then go to it ; Uncle Frampton and Aunt Harriot went there from Moreton. The ball began at seven, and the Royal Family were quite exact to the time. There were three sets, the children at one end of the room, where there was a rail put across, and then the other ladies and gentlemen divided into sets, which made it very pleasant. I was between both (that is, most of the children were mere babies ; the eldest was not older than eight, and the youngest of the little Pouletts was about two); but, however, mamma said if I could get in with the children she should like it the best, so my grandmamma spoke to the Queen, and Princess Elizabeth came up to me directly and told me to take her arm and that she would get me

passing a night or two there when staying in Dorsetshire ; and H.R.H. never failed in showing them every attention in his power whenever they happened to be in London.—H. G. M.   In 1816 H.R.H. was appointed Viceroy of Hanover.

a partner, so away we went together through all the crowd to the King, and she said that the youngest Miss Shirley wanted a partner to dance with the children, so the King said he would try to get me one; but, however, he forgot it.   Then the Princess left me under Lady Sheffield's [5] care, and told her to get me a partner; but presently afterwards the Queen sent Aunt Harriot to me, desiring her to get me one for the grown-up ball; so Lady Sheffield, Aunt Harriot, and Princess Elizabeth were all three telling everybody that it was the Queen's desire for them to try to get me a partner, and at last General Garth [6] got me Captain Jolliffe, with whom I danced two dances.   Selina had got a partner, of course. Then Captain Ingram got me a very famous German, with whom I danced two dances; then somebody got me an immense, large, tall officer, whose name I do not recollect, but I danced one dance with him, and that was the end of the ball, as there were only five dances, and the royal family went away at that time, which was about twelve o'clock.   Four of the Princesses danced—Princess Sophia of Gloucester, Princess Sophia, who danced beautifully, Princess Augusta, and Princess Mary. Lady Sophia and Lady Mary Poulett were both there, and they are both very nice girls.   Lady Mary is not out.   There were fireworks for the children, and before I began to dance I went to see them, and the Duke of Cambridge was so good as to help me up on a

---

[5] Lady Anne North, daughter of second Earl of Guilford (as Lord North, the celebrated Minister of George III.), Lady of the Bedchamber to the Princess of Wales, 1799—1810.   Wife of John Holroyd, Lord Sheffield.

[6] Thomas Garth, Esq., son of John Garth, Esq., M.P. for Devizes. One of his Majesty's Equerries, 1791—1808.   He died 1829, aged eighty-five.

bench to see them, and told Aunt Harriot, ' I will take care of her,' and so he did, and then I jumped down and began dancing. The King stood between the sets part of the time, so that we could not help turning our backs on him. He was the greatest part of the time playing with all the children, who made such a riot with the Duke of Cambridge. The King stood the whole evening, and carried about the little children and danced with them. There were four of Lord Spencer's children and four little Miss Gunns,[7] and there was one of Lady Ilchester's little boys. Lady Louisa Strangways was as good-natured as usual, and looked extremely pretty. To-day, all but grandmamma and I are going to the Rooms, as it is the last Sunday, *alias Sob Sunday*. The King has had a passage made from his Lodge to the hotel through Dr. Heberden's [8] house, so that the weather will not now hinder him from going to the Rooms. My next letter shall be from Eatington, as we go home on Wednesday.

" Believe me, ever yours,
" MARY SHIRLEY."

1805.

AT the beginning of this year the question of forming a household for the Princess Charlotte was first agitated. She was then just nine years of age, having been born January 7th, 1796. But the arrangement was difficult

[7] Daughters of George Gunn, Esq., of Mount Kennedy, Co. Wicklow. Miss Jane Gunn married (1814) Viscount Newry, afterwards Earl of Kilmorey.

[8] William Heberden, Esq., M.D., son of the Dr. Heberden mentioned before. He was one of his Majesty's physicians, and used to attend the King at Weymouth, usually in turn with the other physicians, and George III. was always particularly glad when it was Dr. Heberden's period of service.

on account of the antagonism of the Prince of Wales to
any measure proposed by the King.   Mrs. Campbell[9] was
offered the appointment of sub-governess to the Princess,
which she at first positively declined, as appears from
the following letter, but was after much solicitation ultimately induced to accept ; and a letter from the King to
Lord Chancellor Eldon, on the 18th of February, an-
nounces his Majesty's satisfaction at the successful
termination of this affair.

From Mrs. Campbell to Lady H. Frampton.

> " 31, *Old Burlington Street,*
> " *January,* 1805.

" My dear Lady Harriot,—Do not think me ungrateful
for not having given you the first intelligence of the very
flattering mark of his Majesty's good opinion and favour

[9] Alicia, daughter of Thomas Kelly, Esq., of Dawson's Grove, Co.
Armagh, and widow of Colonel William Campbell, Governor of Bermuda,
at which place he died in December, 1796.   Colonel Campbell was a
great friend of the Honourable Colonel S. Strangways, brother of Lord
Ilchester ; and, after the death of her husband and return to England,
Mrs. Campbell resided entirely with Lord Ilchester's family, or at his
house in London.   The King and Queen had the highest possible
opinion of Mrs. Campbell, of whom they had personal opportunities of
judging, from her intimacy and residence with Lady Ilchester, of whose
step-daughters Mrs. Campbell always took charge when circumstances or
her attendance on the Queen prevented Lady Ilchester from herself
accompanying them into society.   Mrs. Campbell, however, resigned the
office in 1809, in consequence of the *tracasseries* respecting the childish
Will made by the Princess.

It was on one occasion about this time when Mrs. Campbell said to
the King that she was not a suitable person for such an appointment, on
account of her total want of accomplishments, so necessary to one in the
Princess Charlotte's position, that his Majesty paid her this high compliment : " Madam, I hope we can afford to purchase accomplishments, but
we cannot *buy* principles."   This Mrs. Campbell told my mother (Lady
Harriot Frampton).—h. g. m.

that I have had the honour to receive. The truth is that
surprise, gratitude, and the various feelings excited in
my breast, put it out of my power to write. Nor am I
much more composed at this moment. Never having
presumed to aspire to the situation of sub-governess to
the Princess Charlotte, you may judge of my astonishment at being commanded to accept it. Perhaps your
surprise will be as great to hear that I have declined it;
but do not, my dear friend, be hasty to condemn me.
Never did I pray more fervently to be directed in my
conduct, but the more I reflected the stronger was the
impression upon my mind that I was not equal to this
awful trust, and the idea of failing in such a duty made
all worldly considerations appear to me as nothing. I am
now suffering under the full conviction that I have
offended his Majesty and the royal family, and disappointed all the kind and anxious hopes of my friends.
Yet all this I can bear, for my conscience approves of
what I have done.

"I stated as my chief objection that misfortune had
subdued my spirits and destroyed my constitution. This
you know to be true, for though my disposition is naturally cheerful when surrounded by kind friends, yet I
should ill bear up against pride or the coldness of
strangers, who probably would seek more for my defects
than anything else, and be but too ready to magnify
them. You know that I should have gone into Carlton
House as the person chosen by the King in opposition
to the Prince. My *feelings* are still too much alive for
such a charge, and how very soon my weak frame gives
way when they are affected!—then, my dear Lady
Harriot, upon what would rest my support under these
impressions?

"It is not a duty that Providence has laid upon me.

All that any one has yet suggested is ambition, and that is a spark which Heaven has seen fit to extinguish in my breast by the most awful and impressive scenes.   I am like the old man in 'Rasselas,' I have no husband to participate my honours, no children to inherit them. The best of life is past.   I am satisfied that I could not perform the duties of so important a situation.   At the same time I feel for the disappointment to the dear good King and to my friends.   My mind is too unhinged to say more, but I will write again when I can.

"With kind wishes to Mr. Frampton,

"Believe me ever your very affectionate

"A. CAMPBELL."

EXTRACT FROM THE DIARY OF LADY SUSAN O'BRIEN.

"*February 9th*, 1805.—Lady Harriot Frampton called here (Stinsford) and told me that Mrs. Campbell was chosen for sub-governess to the Princess Charlotte and had refused it.   Both very surprising.   I think she has judged for her own happiness if friends do not persuade her otherwise."

"*February 11th.*—Lady Harriot called on her return from Melbury.   The Princesses have written to Lady Harriot to prevail with Mrs. Campbell to accept the place offered to her, all expressing the anxiety of the King that she should—all so pressing she could not refuse; the King's *most* pressing.   No instruction required, only to form the heart and morals of that most interesting child.

"No one can be better principled, or more likely to give example and precept."

THE KING TO LORD ELDON.

"*Windsor Castle, February 18th*, 1805.

"The King authorizes the Lord Chancellor to acquaint

the Prince of Wales that his Majesty has this morning received notice of Mrs. Campbell's acceptance of her nomination as sub-governess to his dearly-beloved grand-daughter, the Princess Charlotte, thus completing the most necessary attendants on the young Princess.

" The King approves of the Baroness de Clifford taking the charge of the Princess, whenever it shall be most agreeable to the Prince of Wales. She will then be a better judge of the requisites necessary in the lady she may recommend as assistant sub-governess, who must be of sufficient birth to appear with the young Princess in the absence of Mrs. Campbell.

" The Earl of Dartmouth has very handsomely con-sented to regulate the expenses of the young Princess's establishment.

" GEORGE R."

FROM H.R.H. PRINCESS SOPHIA TO MARIA, COUNTESS OF ILCHESTER.

" *February*, 1805.

" MY DEAR LADY ILCHESTER,—I have received the King's commands to inform you that it had been his intention to have written to you this morning had he had time; but that being out of his power, he orders me to act as his secretary, and to express for him his satisfaction at Mrs. Campbell's having accepted her present situation about Charlotte, and to thank you for all the trouble you have so kindly taken to urge her to it. These are, I hope, exactly the King's words, for he charged me not to forget them, and to add how sorry he is to hear you are so far from well.

" Ever, dear Lady Ilchester,
" Your affectionate friend,
" SOPHY."

FROM LADY LOUISA STRANGWAYS TO HER SISTER, LADY
HARRIOT FRAMPTON.

" *Windsor, April 24th*, 1805.

" MY DEAR HARRIOT,—I must begin by stating that I am
cross and stupid—cross because I cannot get anybody to
go and gather cowslips with, which I have set my heart
upon doing, and stupid because I am very tired. I was full
dressed for seventeen hours yesterday,[1] and sat in one spot
for seven, which is enough to tire any one who enjoyed
what was going on, which I did not. I saw them walk to
St. George's Chapel, which was the best part, as it did
not last long. The Queen and all her ladies walked in
the procession. Lady Ilchester looked remarkably well.
Harry[2] and I had tickets for the under-gallery in St.
George's Hall, and we went with Lady Vernon.

" We saw them dine, which did not at all answer
my expectations, and I was so tired that I had scarce
strength to look at them. Their dresses were very
magnificent. The knights before they were installed were
in white and silver, like the old pictures of Henry VIII.,
and afterwards they had a purple velvet mantle put on.
They had immense plumes of ostrich feathers, with a
heron's feather in the middle. St. George's Hall would
have disappointed you very much, as the galleries stuffed
it up, which took off the grandness.

" The King and the royal party dined at the upper end
of the room on a raised place ; they had magnificent gold
plate.

" The drawing-room was very full. Harry was pre-

[1] 1805, April 23rd.—The magnificent ceremony of the installation of
the Knights of the Garter by George III., at Windsor Castle, took place.
On this occasion all the ancient customs were as much as possible kept
up, by desire of the King.

[2] Her brother, the Earl of Ilchester, then in his nineteenth year.

K

sented to the Queen, and was invited to Frogmore.   The
ball in the evening was very pleasant; we had a cold
supper afterwards, and were home about three o'clock.
The dresses in general were more magnificent than last
time.   Lady I. wore your gold muslin, and it looked very
well indeed.   We left Charlotte at Fulham with Mrs.
Newbolt ; she is very much better.   I believe now I have
told you all I can think of.

" Yours affectionately,
" L. S."

In the early part of 1805 a French squadron consisting
of six sail-of-the-line and two frigates managed to elude
the vigilance of Lord Nelson's blockading squadron, and
leaving Rochefort (France), where they had been hemmed
in for the last two years, proceeded to the West Indies.
After having made a descent upon Dominica and levied a
heavy contribution upon the inhabitants, obliging the town
of Roseau to surrender on certain terms, the squadron
proceeded for Antigua.   Great were the fears of the
Antiguans when this intelligence reached them ; the
militia were called out, and the island put into a posture
of defence.

The French squadron, however, passed Antigua, and
landed upon Nevis ; and after laying the inhabitants
under contribution, proceeded to St. Kitts, and lightened
the pockets of the Kittifonians.   The alarm had scarcely
subsided when news of the arrival of the Toulon fleet
under Admiral Villeneuve in these seas was received.
Again Antigua prepared for war, but Lord Nelson
quickly followed the enemy, and upon his arrival at Bar-
bados, on June 4th, heard that Villeneuve had only
reached Martinique.   The name of Nelson so intimidated
the French admiral that he immediately quitted the West

Indies, and was followed by Nelson in the hope of overtaking him and of chastising the French for their audacity.

MRS. KERBY[3] TO MRS. E. FAUQUIER, FROM ANTIGUA.

"*Antonia Place, August 2nd*, 1805.

" Your kind letter, my dear and valued friend, of June 19th, received a few days since by our anxiously-expected Packet, claims the immediate and grateful acknowledgment of an affectionate heart, and glad am I, after all our captures of fleet, Packets, &c., and our hairbreadth escapes from squadrons, combined fleets, death, fright, and fatigue to greet you once again as a British subject *unsullied* by *tribute*, unconquered (nearly ruined *à la vérité*), but all in good health, spirits, and loyal even unto death.

" You will have heard, no doubt, how the combined fleet escaped by magic; how in reality (for I counted them myself—twenty-four of the line) they rode triumphant on *our element* for some weeks; how the gallant hero of the Nile followed them; how *he*, misled, could not catch them; and how they, afraid of *him*, gave up the attack of the little England of the archipelago (Antigua), whose bulwarks are rocks instead of oak. How they peeped into the beautiful harbour of St. John's, missed the rich sugar-loaded ships, received intelligence of their departure the night before; how they tried to look warlike and form a line of battle,

---

[3] Jane Byam, only child and heir of Edward Byam, Esq., Judge of the Vice-Admiralty Court of Antigua, and President of the Council of Antigua for nearly half a century. She married, in 1784, Thomas Norbury Kerby, Esq., of Antigua, and died at Hampton Court Palace in 1837. Their only child, Anne (mentioned in the following letter), became, in 1820, the wife of the Hon. and Rev. Miles Stapleton, third son of Lord De Despencer, and died in 1842.

but they could not; but how, alas! they scampered after our sugar, took fourteen ships full of that and various good things going to our friends; and how to our great joy they burnt this treasure on its way to some of these islands by the manœuvres of a sloop of war, who, afraid of being taken, threw out signals as for approaching friends, and they, *toujours Nelson en tête*, saw his ghost, and destroyed their prizes in the most premature and shameful hurry.

"I cannot attempt to describe our terrors, movings, *removings*, packings, and unpackings. I consider myself *now* quite as a heroine, having *commanded myself*, and though frightened most completely, having quietly parted with my husband and father on the point of going into action (the enemy being then off Five Islands Harbour, and expected there to land), kept up my mother's spirits, set a good example to my child, and left my home for the country, never expecting to see it again, but under some heavy calamity and occupied by French officers.

"But as you justly observe, my nerves have not suffered *less* from this exertion and my severe headaches, &c., remind me *de tems en tems* of my past heroism. However, I shall always feel as I then did, that men in the moment of honourable danger become so sacred, and so precious, that to distress or annoy them by any foolish selfish feelings is sacrilege: thus am I awed into an appearance of courage, when I am at heart a very woman.

"Since Lord Nelson left us, which was on the 12th or 14th June (the French fleet having been with us on the 8th), we have been quiet, but we have expectations of a return of the Rochefort squadron, and six sail of the Spanish from Cadiz; and as the mother country appears to be in a state of confusion and falsehoods, and has not yet sent us a naval superiority, we shall be again harassed and kept on the alert, for as to being taken, *we Antigonians admit it not.*

" My dear father is the wonder of the country, enjoying better health than in his younger days'; his most affectionate love ever attends you, and your kind messages always make his fine eyes glisten. My poor mother is in sad attendance on my aunt, whose situation from an incurable complaint makes us all very unhappy, and again throws my return for Anne's education into uncertainty, as I cannot reconcile myself to the cruelty of quitting my friends and parents, when approaching trials and affliction is their perspective.

" My darling continues well ; I devote myself as much as possible to her education, and I will hope that my adherence to affectionate duties may not prove materially injurious to her hereafter. I can enter into the pleasure of Lady Vernon [4] on her amiable daughter's *entrée* into life ; it must be quite a Da Capo, though with less of the Allegro, than one's own, from those two disquieting companions, experience and knowledge of the world.

" I think it very probable that you will meet, or perhaps are already acquainted with Lady Hood [5] (Miss Mackenzie that was). Her conduct and manners have gained her friends and admirers in Antigua, and amongst the warmest am I ; and should you have the opportunity, bring me to her recollection by my best wishes for her and Sir Samuel, whose bravery and uncommon humanity in a business that happened at Jamaica, and of which I have

---

[4] Georgiana, Lady Vernon, and her sister, Mrs. Elizabeth Fauquier, were related on their mother's side to Mr. and Mrs. Byam, and consequently to Mrs. Kerby.

[5] Hon. Frederica Mackenzie, daughter of the first Baron Seaforth. She married, in 1804, Vice-Admiral Sir Samuel Hood, K.B., subsequently created a baronet for his signal services.

been reading in an old magazine, have entirely made a conquest of *me*. Your souvenir to Mynheer is most gratefully received by Anne, whose attentions are now divided by a tame Marguerite (small parrot) and turtle-doves.

"My spirits are much depressed on hearing that the dreadful fever has broken out at English Harbour in the *Amelia*—poor Lord Proby's [6] ship when he convoyed us out—and as this is our hot season, I dread its becoming contagious and prevalent. This is a country of unceasing terror, without any pleasing circumstances to rejoice the heart or gratify the eyes, worn out by scorching sun and want of verdure, shade, or water.

"*August 4th.*—We were visited yesterday by one of our numerous evils, a smart shock of an earthquake; I felt only one, but there were three in the course of the day. The awful horror of this convulsion of nature is not to be described, and as our archipelago has every appearance of having been disunited and shook into *atoms* (of which we are one) by volcanic causes, these *remembrancers* are as you will allow, rather disquieting. Mr. Kerby seems determined on my return to England next summer, and regrets what he had not resolution enough to prevent—Anne's loss of those advantages she might have had by remaining. Unavailing retrospection is always to be avoided if possible, and I will hope that what was so good in its principal motives may prove a source of comfort and benefit; and I assure you that from many disagreeable local circumstances, and my unfortunate aversion to this climate, property, &c., it requires my utmost efforts and exertions to keep myself in a tolerable state of resignation, especially, too, as I am becoming daily

[6] William, eldest son of the first Earl of Carysfort, born 1773, died unmarried, 1804.

more nervous and out of health.   My father, Mr. Kerby, my mother, Dr. Byam, Anne, and myself unite in all that is kind and affectionate in our different characters, and pray so present us to our friends, believing me ever,

" Your obliged and truly attached
" J. B. KERBY."

In connection with Antigua, a curious anecdote is mentioned by Mr. Byam in his interesting History of that Island, relating to the famous ring given by Queen Elizabeth to the Earl of Essex.[7]

" After the demise of Queen Elizabeth, this ring passed with the other crown jewels to her successor, James I., from whom it was handed down to his son, Charles I., who, at the instigation of his Queen, Henrietta Maria, presented it to Sir Thomas Warner, the first English Governor and colonizer of many of the West India Islands, and who, for his energetic exertions in extending his Majesty's dominions in the American seas, was complimented, and had the honours of knighthood conferred upon him by King Charles I., at Hampton Court Palace, September 21st, 1629.   He died 1648.

" From Sir Thomas the ring passed " [*in a direct line*] "to his great-grandson, Colonel Edward Warner" [grandfather of Mrs. Frampton], "who bequeathed it by will to his brother, Ashton Warner, as ' a diamond-ring in the shape of a heart, given by Queen Elizabeth to the Earl of Essex.'   From the Hon. Ashton Warner it descended as an heir-loom, and is now in the possession of Charles Warner, Esq., Solicitor-General of Trinidad, 1844."

[7] Vide " Hume's History of England."

EXTRACTS FROM LETTERS FROM THE COUNTESS OF ILCHESTER
    TO LADY HARRIOT FRAMPTON, WRITTEN FROM WINDSOR
    IN THIS YEAR, 1805.

" I saw a letter from the Princess Royal [8] the other
day, naming Buonaparte as her guest. She says he is
extremely polite, and particularly so to her. Her letter
is prudent, sensible and religious, and she seems bent
upon meeting her trials with firmness and never leaving
the Elector.

" I cannot say I think the King's eyes better, but he
still plays at cards and never makes any mistake ; his
general health is wonderfully good apparently, and his
spirits, though not so good as they used to be, yet
cheerful and calm. I am sorry to have left Kew, but
that is not the general feeling. Princess Mary has
been ill, and also poor Princess Amelia too ill to come
here yesterday with us. She is, however, to come on
Monday; it seemed so odd no sister remaining behind
with her."

" *Tuesday and Wednesday, November*, 1805.

" What terrible accounts from the Continent. It is
by some believed that General Mack [9] was *bought* by the
diabolical intrigues of Buonaparte—only think of the
Elector of Wurtemberg being presented with the cannon
of the Austrians to turn them upon the friends of
England. Poor Princess Royal, how much she is to be
pitied !

[8] The Princess Royal, Charlotte Augusta Matilda, had, in 1797, married
Frederic William, Hereditary Prince of Wurtemberg Stutgardt ; suc-
ceeded his father the same year. In 1806 he took the title of King of
Wurtemberg.

[9] The Austrian army, under Mack, capitulated at Ulm, October 20th,
1805.

" The defeat of the Austrians lowers every one's spirits, and the poor dear King says he cannot get the Austrian army out of his mind.

" Princess Sophia mentions having a very indifferent account of Mr. Damer to-day, but as you say nothing about him, I hope he is not very ill.

" What glorious news is just arrived! I quite envy Lord Nelson his death.[10]

" We are all spirits now, and the dear King since yesterday is much revived."

1806.

LADY ELIZABETH FEILDING TO LADY MARY TALBOT.

" Portsmouth, August 24th, 1806.

" What do you think of the Prince of Wales at the Duke of Clarence's fête—handing out Mrs. Jordan *before* the *Countess* of Athlone and the *Duchess* of Bolton? *I* say that the Duchess and Countess were very well served for putting themselves in such company."

1807.

FROM H.R.H. PRINCESS ELIZABETH TO MARY FRAMPTON.

Windsor Castle, June 10th, 1807.

" I fear you will think me very ungrateful, my dear Miss Frampton, in not thanking you immediately for your very kind attention in sending me Mrs. England's letter. Interested as I am about Mrs. Damer [1] you know not the

---

[10] Battle of Trafalgar, and death of Nelson, October 21st, 1805.

[1] Williamsa, niece of Sir Theodore Janssen, Bart., married, 1778, the Hon. Lionel Damer. They resided at Came, near Dorchester, and Mr. Damer was much with the King and Queen during their visits to Weymouth. The Royal Family were very intimate with, and partial to, all Lord Dorchester's family.

comfort that that letter was to us all, and you were
thanked all round for your good nature; but the hurry I
have lived in since Sunday must plead my excuse.

"Pray tell dear Mrs. Frampton how happy I am she
has not suffered from the length of her journey and the
shock, which, though we must with humility bear our loss,
we must ever mourn for him; for Mr. Damer was not
an indifferent person to any one, for all who knew him
could not help loving and now lamenting him. One is
sure he is happy and at peace, and that must be our
comfort.

"I hope to see dear Mrs. Drax in a few days.

"Yours very sincerely,

"ELIZA."

FROM H.R.H. THE PRINCESS ELIZABETH TO MARY
FRAMPTON.

"*June 23rd*, 1807.

"You will, I fear, find me very tiresome, but your
good heart will, I trust, forgive me, for, loving our sweet,
angelic Lady C. Damer as I do, I cannot help troubling
you again to tell me how you really think her—how
the meeting went off, and what your opinion is of both
her and Mrs. Damer?

"I know that if she can in any way take comfort,
that your being so near her will be a real cordial to her
heart, as I know she has often said to me (pardon the
expression from me), 'Mary is a perfect angel.'

"I will not take up more of your time excepting to
tell you Mary is much better—she has been very
unwell with one of the fashionable colds.

"My kind compliments to Mrs. Frampton, and believe
me,

"Yours affectionately,

"ELIZA."

1809.

FROM H.R.H. PRINCESS ELIZABETH TO THE COUNTESS OF
ILCHESTER.

"*May* 18*th*, 1809.

" MY DEAR LADY ILCHESTER,—I put off writing until I
got the account of what the girl wanted for the school;
besides which I was not in spirits to write.

" *Now*, thank God, we are too happy with everything
last night, and our minds are quieted.   The dear King's
joy would have done your heart good.

" I am too happy to find that Lord Ilchester [2] is going
on so well; I heard of him from Lady George Murray.[3]

" How good you are in all you say of me! but I
trust you will never find me forgetful when I know
your wishes—it is seldom I can do any good, but
when I can I am delighted.

" My younger sisters have all had colds.   Amelia is
still in her bed, but better.   God bless you.   I hope your
cold is now better.   Excuse great haste, and believe me,

" Yours affectionately,

" ELIZA."

EXTRACT FROM THE JOURNAL OF LADY SUSAN O'BRIEN.

" *May* 30*th*, 1809.—While I was in town I was
informed of a curious transaction going on at Carl-

---

[2] Lord Ilchester had broken his leg from a fall when out hunting.

[3] The widow of Lord George Murray, Bishop of St. David's, second
son of the third Duke of Athol, who died 1803.   She married in 1780,
at the age of fifteen !   In 1808 the King appointed Lady George Murray
Lady-in-Waiting to the Princesses Augusta and Elizabeth, which post she
resigned in 1813; but she was again in attendance in 1817, and died in
1844.   The eldest son of the Bishop and Lady George Murray became
Bishop of Rochester; their second daughter, Countess of Ilchester, and
the youngest, Amelia, was Maid-of-Honour, &c., to Queen Victoria, and
survived until June, 1884.

ton House, on account of a childish Will the Princess Charlotte had made, in which she left half her jewels to Lady De Clifford, and half to Mrs. Campbell, and all her *valuable* jewels to her papa and mamma. They suppose Mrs. Campbell concerned in making it, and told the Bishop of it,[4] *who smiled.*

" The Prince was displeased, and said it was high treason, and called Mr. Adam and told him what he had said, who answered, ' Your Royal Highness has a just conception of the matter.' How can a lawyer hold such language, or how can a prince hear a word of truth ? All this nonsense has been before the Privy Council, whose time might be better employed.

" The Will expresses a wish that Mr. Nott, sub-preceptor, might be made a Bishop."

1810.

FROM LADY ELIZABETH FEILDING TO LADY HARRIOT FRAMPTON.

31, *Sackville St.*, *February 3rd*, 1810.

" MY DEAR HARRIOT,—As you desire, I write to let you know that the children arrived very safe yesterday, and do great credit by their looks to Moreton air and *care.* If I had a moment's time I would describe the Persian Ambassador to you, who I fell in love with last night at Lady Sidney Smith's.[5] His black eyes and white teeth, and long curly *clean* beard made a great impression

---

[4] John Fisher, D.D., tutor to H.R.H. Prince Edward (subsequently Duke of Kent) from 1780 to 1785, when the Prince was sent to Germany to finish his education ; Chaplain to the King, &c. ; Bishop of Exeter 1803, in which year he was appointed Preceptor to the Princess Charlotte. He was translated to Salisbury 1807, died 1825.

[5] Widow of Sir G. B. Rumbold, Bart., Minister Resident at Hamburg.

on me, and he has learnt a great deal of English, considering.

"Sir Gore Ouseley, his interpreter, is a very agreeable man, and I daresay you have heard of Mr. Morier the Greek, who has been everywhere and speaks all languages.

"The Persian took a fancy to Lady Ponsonby's [6] pretty face, and desired Sir Sidney [7] to *send* her to him. She was much flattered, and reclined by him on an ottoman while he fanned himself. I asked him whether he was tired; he said, 'No, not tired—very long evening (and putting his hand on his embroidered breast)—patience, patience.' This answer, which he meant to be very civil, conveyed quite another idea to the company, who were all much diverted.

"He must think us a nation of starers, for all London has collected to gaze at him.,

"Your affectionate

"E. T. F."

FROM THE SAME.

"*March*, 1810.

"I am just returned from chaperoning Mary to Mdlle. le Noir's French Readings, as Louisa Lansdowne could not go with her, being commanded to the Princess of Wales. It was a tragedy of Racine's."

---

[6] Lady Elizabeth Villiers, daughter of the fourth Earl of Jersey.

[7] Admiral Sir Sidney Smith, G.C.B., &c., so well known from his distinguished services and splendid relief of St. Jean d'Acre, besieged by Buonaparte in 1799. He entered the navy at twelve years of age, under Lord Rodney, and at nineteen was a post-captain! Soon after he entered the service of Sweden, and having received the "Order of the Sword" from Gustavus III., was from that time called Sir S. Smith. In 1830 he succeeded H.M. William IV. as Lieut.-General of Marines. He died at Paris, 1840.

MARIA, COUNTESS OF ILCHESTER, TO LADY HARRIOT
FRAMPTON.

" *Windsor, March 4th or 5th*, 1810.

" MY DEAR HARRIOT,—Last night I thought all in good spirits, and the scene much changed for the better. To-day all look sadly down, and as the dear King slept well, and has been taking his daily walk with a firm step, and looking as erect as ever I saw him, it is not on his account they are low.

There is a surmise that the Prince is very ill, but if you do not see it in the Paper, do not know it from me.

" The Queen is grown very thin, and all the Princesses much altered. The Queen told me that she took her own letter to the Prince, with his answer, to show to the King in case she judged it prudent, which she found might be done, and when she had finished the King said, " Who knows that from my very severe trial Providence may not intend to recall many to their duty ? I have nothing now to do but to take care of my health."

" The Prince's message through Mr. Perceval was very handsome indeed, and the King acknowledges it so with great satisfaction.

" The King conceives himself quite well, but acknowledges the propriety of his not coming forward now as a prudent measure.

" I have not time for more by this night's post. Pray give my love to your aunt and Mrs. Frampton. I was wet through before I got to Andover, and frozen by the time I got here.

" Pray write to
" Your very affectionate,
" M. ILCHESTER."

LADY SUSAN O'BRIEN TO HER NIECE, LADY HARRIOT FRAMPTON.

" *London, April* 16*th*, 1810.

" MY DEAR HARRIOT,—As you will perceive I have not been in a hurry to answer your letter, but I think it will not have disturbed you very much, as we are none of us very regular correspondents. We have stayed here longer than Mr. O'Brien first intended ; the weather has been such as to give us no wish for the country, at least for its own sake, and London has been altogether pleasanter than the last time I was here.

" The last week, however, was very disagreeable from the noise and riots in our neighbourhood, and even my humble carriage did not escape, as Sir Francis'[8] worthy friends broke my glass, and gave me and Lily, who was with me, a specimen of the pleasures of a mob government. To-morrow the Westminster electors meet, but I hope it will all pass quietly—but that is very uncertain.

" I hear you have written to inquire if the future Mrs. S. is as plain as is reported. Don't flatter yourself on that subject—her merits no doubt are great, but her beauty is small ; who can add one cubit to his stature, or one shade to his complexion?

" I was at the Play Saturday ; the new theatre is very handsome. The O.P.'s need not grudge the ladies the private boxes, as they can neither hear nor see in them, two things requisite, or at least used to be so—the only good thing is getting out easily.

" Our way is dining out almost daily, which for old folks is the only London society to be enjoyed with early hours.

8 Sir Francis Burdett was committed to the Tower, April 7th, 1810. He was first cousin to my father-in-law, the late Francis Mundy, Esq., of Markeaton, Co. Derby.—H. G. M.

"Louisa Lansdowne is to go to Bowood, or rather to Calne, to see it during the recess. It is desolate to the greatest degree, not a nail or screw that could be moved is left. I went to see it and Laycock Abbey in my way from Bath. I have seen Mrs. Damer very lately, she looks well, and is in good spirits, but seems quite determined not to come to Came.

"Mr. O'Brien desires his love to you and Mr. Frampton—mine also.

"I am, dear Harriot,

"Your affectionate aunt,

"S. L. O'BRIEN."

THE SAME TO THE SAME.

" Sir John Hippesley [9] gave me letters from all parts of Europe to amuse me. He really has been a very useful and friendly man to many very great personages. He showed me what I really think a very great curiosity—the Veil that Mary Queen of Scots wore when she went to the scaffold. It is of gauze. One of the ladies had it, and gave it to the Jesuits' College, where it was revered as a relic.

" Afterwards the Cardinal of York [10] had it, and by Will

[9] Sir John Coxe Hippesley, Bart., F.R.S., F.S.A., one of the managers of the Royal Institution, &c. He was engaged in various diplomatic negotiations, and from having been employed in arranging the marriage between the Princess Royal of England and the King of Wurtemberg, Sir John obtained letters-patent from that Prince, granting to himself and his descendants the right of bearing the arms of the House of Wurtemberg, &c. Sir John Hippesley died 1825.

[10] Henry Benedict, youngest son of "The Pretender." Born at Rome, 1725; cardinal, 1747; died at Frascati, 1807. He was buried in the crypt of St. Peter's at Rome. A monument in memory of himself and his brother, Prince Charles Edward (called the Young Pretender), was placed by George IV. in St. Peter's at Rome. In 1806 the cardinal was allowed a pension of £4000 by the English Government, chiefly through the good offices of Sir John Hippesley.

bequeathed it to Sir John, with great testimonies of friendship.

" Sir John showed it to the Pope, who kissed it twice and blessed it. It is a singular history.

"I assure you I looked at it with great reverence and pity for its unhappy mistress.[1]

" Yours affectionately,
" S. L. O'BRIEN."

FROM LADY HARRIOT ACLAND [2] TO LADY HARRIOT FRAMPTON.

" Tetton, near Dulverton, August 8th, 1810.

" MY DEAR HARRIOT,—I have just received yours. The ' Blue Anchor ' is on the coast (of what is here called) the North Sea, near Dunster and Minehead, a wretched little inn with one tolerable parlour and dining-room; but Kitty is so fond of the sea that she puts up with all sorts of inconveniences, but only goes for a week or ten days at a time. She joins in kind love to you, and good wishes for the speedy recovery of my little goddaughter. I expect a visit from you all before the winter. I fear

---

[1] I had the satisfaction of seeing this curious veil, together with a collection of portraits and relics of Mary Queen of Scots, collected by the Society of Arts, and exhibited at their rooms at the Adelphi (about 1853-58.) It was very yellow, from age apparently, but seemed otherwise in good condition. It was shaped, as far as I recollect, like a scarf. —H. G. M.

[2] Lady Christiana Henrietta Strangways, daughter of Stephen, first Earl of Ilchester; born 1750; married, 1771, John Dyke Acland, Esq., of Pixton, Co. Somerset, eldest son of Sir Thomas Acland, Bart., Major 20th Regiment of Foot, British Grenadiers, M.P. for Callington, Co. Cornwall; died 1778. Lady H. Acland died 1815. "Kitty" mentioned below, was their only surviving child, and inherited a large portion of the estates. Miss Acland married Henry George, Lord Porchester, who succeeded, 1811, as second Earl of Carnarvon. She died 1813.

the death of Mr. Weld will be a great loss to you and your neighbourhood.

" Remember me very kindly to Mr. Frampton.
" Believe me affectionately yours,
" H. ACLAND."

STATE OF THE EXPEDITION FROM CANADA AS LAID BEFORE THE HOUSE OF COMMONS BY LIEUT.-GENERAL BURGOYNE,[3] 1780.

(*Extracted and communicated by N. S. Maskelyne, Esq., from the British Museum Library,* 1875.)

Lady Harriot Acland had accompanied her husband to Canada in the beginning of the year 1776. In the course of that campaign she had traversed a vast space of country in different extremities of seasons, and with difficulties that an European traveller will not easily conceive, to attend her husband, in a poor hut at Chamblée, upon his sick-bed.

In the opening of the campaign of 1777, she was restrained from offering herself to a share of the hazard expected before Ticonderoga, by the positive injunction of her husband. The day after the conquest of that place he was badly wounded, and she crossed the Lake Champlain to join him. Upon his recovery Lady Harriot proceeded to follow his fortunes through the

[3] General John Burgoyne. An illegitimate son of Lord Bingley. He entered the army at an early age. In 1775 he was sent as Governor to Canada, and in 1777 received orders to march against the American Congress. Burgoyne was successful at Ticonderoga, but at Saratoga, October 17th, 1777, was obliged to capitulate to General Gates, with the condition that neither himself nor his army should again serve against America. He had already lost 4300 men since the opening of the campaign. He became a Member of Parliament 1781, but never again had any military employment. General Burgoyne died 1792. His son was the late Field-Marshal John Burgoyne, who died 1871.

campaign, and at Fort Edward, or at the next camp she procured a two-wheel tombril, which had been constructed by the artillery artificers, and something similar to the carriage used for the mail in England. Major Acland commanded the British Grenadiers, which were attached to General Fraser's corps, who were always the most advanced post of the army. Their situation required extraordinary vigilance, and was frequently such that no persons slept out of their clothes. On one of these occasions, the tent in which the major and Lady Harriot were asleep, by some accident suddenly took fire. An orderly-sergeant of Grenadiers, with great hazard of suffocation, dragged out the first person he caught hold of. It proved to be the major. It happened that in the same instant Lady Harriot had almost unconsciously providentially made her escape by creeping from under the back part of the tent. The first object she beheld upon the recovery of her senses was the major on the opposite side rushing again into the fire in search of her. The sergeant once more saved him, but not without the major being very severely burned. Everything they had with them in the tent was consumed, a circumstance which, in such a situation, was in itself sufficiently distressing. This accident, however, which took place a short time before the army passed Hudson's River, produced no alteration in the resolution and cheerfulness of Lady Harriot, who continued her progress, a partaker of the fatigues of the advanced corps. On the march of the 19th, the Grenadiers being liable to action at every step, the major directed his wife to follow the route of the artillery and baggage, in which situation she would be less exposed.

At the commencement of the action which now took place she found herself near a small uninhabited hut, where she alighted. Of this hut, when the engagement became general and bloody, the hospital surgeons took possession, finding it convenient for the first care of the wounded. In this dreadful situation Lady Harriot remained for some hours, within hearing of one continued fire of cannon and musketry, to which her husband at the head of the Grenadiers was particularly exposed. Three other ladies were her companions in this scene of alarm and distress, the Baroness von Reidesel, wife of General Reidesel, and the wives of Major Harnage and Lieutenant Reynell, two British officers. Major Harnage was soon brought in dangerously wounded, and shortly after intelligence arrived that Lieut. Reynell was shot dead. From the date of that action to the 7th October, Lady Harriot with her usual fortitude stood prepared for new trials, the severity of which continued to increase. She was again exposed, during an engagement, to the hearing of the cannon, and at length received, with news of the defeat of the troops, intelligence that Major Acland, desperately wounded, had fallen into the hands of the enemy. The ensuing day was passed by Lady Harriot and her companions in one common anxiety ; not a tent or shed was standing excepting what belonged to the hospital, and these were crowded with the wounded and the dying.

When the army was on the point of moving, I received a message from Lady Harriot, submitting to my decision a proposal (and expressing an earnest solicitude to execute it, if not interfering with my designs) of passing to the camp of the enemy and requesting General Gates' permission to attend her husband. Though I was ready to believe (for I had experienced) that patience and fortitude in a supreme degree were to be found, as well as every other virtue, under the most tender form, I was

astonished at this proposal.   After so long an agitation
of the spirits, exhausted not only from want of rest, but
absolutely from want of food, drenched in rain for
twelve hours together, that a woman should be capable
of such an undertaking as delivering herself to the
enemy, probably in the night, and uncertain of what
hands she might first fall into, appeared an effort above
human nature.   The assistance I was enabled to give
was small indeed, I had not even a cup of wine to offer
her, but I was told she had found, from some kind and
fortunate hand, a little rum and dirty water.   All I
could furnish to her was an open boat and a few lines
written upon dirty wet paper to General Gates,[4] recom-

---

[4] General Horatio Gates was by birth an Englishman, and when very
young entered the British Army.   He went to America as a captain of
infantry, under General Braddock, and continued in that service until the
peace of 1763 ; subsequently he sold his commission, and purchased an
estate in the colony of Virginia, where he resided until the breaking out
of the war, when he joined the standard of his adopted country.   His
qualifications obtained him so rapid a promotion that he was appointed
Commander-in-Chief of the North American Army, when he obtained
distinguished celebrity by the capture of General Burgoyne and the
English army under his command.   His humanity to his captives was
equal to his success, and after the surrender of General Burgoyne at
Saratoga, the British officers bore testimony to General Gates' moderation
and endeavours to mitigate the distress of mind in which the fortunes of
war had involved his adverse commander, and by every means to render
his situation and that of his officers less irksome.   The attention he
showed to Lady Harriot Acland will ever render his name respected in
England.   The complicated distresses, the extraordinary fatigues, and the
heroic resolution of that lady were subjects of astonishment to the contending armies.   General Gates was then given by the Congress the
command of the Southern Army, but here he was in his turn defeated by
Lord Cornwallis, who thus for a time subdued the Carolinas, and being
superseded by General Green, he quitted the army and retired to his
estate in Virginia, where he died in 1806, universally esteemed and
lamented.

General Gates, in a letter to his wife, written from Albany three days

mending her to his protection. Mr. Brudenell, the
chaplain to the artillery (the same gentleman who
had officiated so signally at General Fraser's funeral),
readily undertook to accompany her, and with one female
servant and the major's *valet de chambre* (who had a
ball which he had received in the late action then in his
shoulder), she rowed down the river to meet the enemy.
But her distresses were not yet to end. The night was
advanced before the boat reached the enemy's outpost,
and the sentinel would not let it pass, not even once on
shore. In vain Mr. Brudenell offered the flag of truce
and represented the state of the extraordinary passenger.
The guard, apprehensive of treachery and punctilious to
their orders, threatened to fire into the boat if it stirred
before daylight. Her anxiety and suffering were thus
protracted through seven or eight dark and cold hours,
and her reflections upon that first reception could not
give her very encouraging ideas of the treatment she
was afterwards to expect. But it is due to justice at
the close of this adventure to say that she was received
and accommodated by General Gates with all the
humanity and respect that her rank and merits and her
fortune deserved." [5]

after Burgoyne's surrender (October 16th, 1777), makes some rather
interesting allusions to his prisoners :—"I got here the night before last.
. . . Amongst my prisoners are Lord Petersham, Major Acland—son of
Sir Thomas—and his lady, daughter of Lord Ilchester. I hope Lady
Harriot Acland will be here when you arrive. She is the most
amiable, delicate piece of quality you ever beheld. Her husband is
learned, sensible, and an Englishman to all intents and purposes."

[5] General Burgoyne adds : "I consider this story as so far connected
with my immediate business of pursuing the evidence upon the retreat to
Saratoga as to give it in the margin. It may well stand by itself ; and I
venture to think this example of patience, suffering, and fortitude will
be permitted to pass without censure or obloquy."

HON. GEORGE EDEN [6] TO LADY HARRIOT FRAMPTON.

"*Lancaster, September* 13*th*, 1810.

"MY DEAR LADY HARRIOT,—I hardly know how to reproach you for idleness without at the same time reproaching myself, which I am very unwilling to do, so will leave them both alone. What a tremendous time has elapsed since I have heard anything of or from you, or any of your family, yet my mind and memory often travel to my old haunts in Dorsetshire. I am now writing my second letter to your none, which is the greatest proof of faithful attachment ever recorded—at least since the time of Ulysses' dog. My circuit is now drawing very near to a conclusion, but as the time of the Sessions is not far distant I shall not yet return to the south. I think you had better direct all your letters to Eden Farm, from whence they will be forwarded to me wherever I am. My circuiteering has been very pleasant. I have lived a great deal with the George Lambs;[7] he is an old friend of mine, and I hope that she

[6] Succeeded as second Baron Auckland, 1814; subsequently created Earl of Auckland, Governor-General of India, &c.; died, unmarried, 1849.

[7] Son of the first Viscount Melbourne, Under Secretary of State for the Home Department, &c. He married, 1809, Mademoiselle Caroline Rosalie de St. Jules.

Mrs. Lamb was brought up at Devonshire House. Her brother, Sir Augustus Foster, Bart. (Envoy Extraordinary, &c., to Sardinia, &c.), being the son of Lady Elizabeth Foster, afterwards Duchess of Devonshire. She was a charming person, and survived her husband many years.

Mr. and Mrs. Lamb resided, when in the country, at Melbourne Hall, Lord Melbourne's place in Derbyshire, and, subsequently to our marriage, Mr. Mundy and I frequently spent some days at a time with them. Mr. Lamb, too, was most agreeable; and nothing could be more pleasant than the small society there collected, of which Sir Augustus Foster usually formed one, and we were sadly grieved when the death of Mr. Lamb, in 1834, broke up our visits to Melbourne.—H. G. M.

will become so, for I like her of all things.   She has gone
regularly through the Circuit, and has exposed herself to
its hardships as gallantly as a soldier's wife to those
of a camp.   She makes the best of her dirty lodgings,
attends the assize balls, sits half the day in court, makes
up to all the lawyers, and appears as happy withal as if
she were still living in Devonshire House.   She has a
fine lady of a maid travelling with her, whose remarks
are highly amusing and who is leaving the north with
very little respect for its inhabitants.   She says they are
a sad set of people.   She has not been to a single town
yet where they were not trying a parcel of thieves and
murderers, and that nothing of the kind ever happens
in London.   As for me, I have certainly had more
bugs than briefs, more fleas than fees, &c. (for you
must hate alliterations); but as I made nothing at all
last year the little I have made this year is not discou-
raging.

"I went for two or three days to the lakes, and paid
a visit to Mary of Buttermere.[8]   I found her a coarse,
dirty, fat, rather old mother of two or three children—
not at all like a lady of a lake.   I can't say that I ever,
had much pity for her, and perhaps other people would

---

[8] Immortalized by some rather too flattering lines of Wordsworth in
his "Prelude."   She was the daughter of a small innkeeper in that
district, and obtained an unenviable notoriety from having been
inveigled into a false marriage by a villain calling himself the Honourable Colonel Hope ; in reality, of the name of Hatfield.   It was afterwards discovered that he had not only deserted a wife and family, but
had defrauded many persons of large sums of money, &c.   Ultimately,
Hatfield was tried and convicted of forgery, and was executed at Carlisle
in August, 1803.

All this publicity caused Mary to be for some years an object of
curiosity to the numerous visitors to the Lakes.   She subsequently married a farmer in Caldbeck.   The "Beauty of Buttermere" is also
mentioned at some length in De Quincy's "Autobiographic Sketches."

not have had more if they had known how little handsome she was. I have no more room, so adieu.

"G. EDEN."

1811.

FROM MARIA, COUNTESS OF ILCHESTER, TO LADY HARRIOT FRAMPTON.

"Windsor Castle, June, 1811.

"MY DEAR HARRIOT,—I want to hear all about you and yours. I wish I could give you much comfort from hence, but we stand still, I fear, rather than advance, though the King seems to walk stoutly. The patient and cheerful resignation of all here under so much anxiety is really admirable, for their earnest anxiety is *unabated,* but neither murmur nor discontent at any time is uttered, but the most steady reliance on the goodness of Providence.

"Indeed all the females evince in the most striking manner the invaluable blessing of thoroughly religious minds. They are all very considerably thinner, and Princess Sophia looks ill.

"Pray tell Miss Mason that I like all the work she has done for me very much. Princess Augusta has desired me to order for her a chemisette of the pattern of mine.

"Ever yours affectionately,

"M. I."

C. B. WOLLASTON TO MARY FRAMPTON.

"Downing Street, November 1811.

"MY DEAR MARY,—There have been strange rumours about the Regent,[9] but I verily believe without founda-

[9] February 5, 1811.—The Prince of Wales was sworn in before the Privy Council as Regent of the Kingdom, he going in great state.

tion.   The fact is, as Ryder[1] told me this morning, that
he is still in considerable pain from his legs and obliged
to keep almost entirely in a horizontal posture, which
is an inconvenient one for writing; but certainly much
distress and inconvenience has arisen in all public offices
from the want of his signature.   It has been said that a
report of his being in the same state as his father was
traced to the Duke of Cumberland, and that in consequence the Prince has broken off all intercourse with
the Duke, but Ryder tells me that he saw the Duke at
Oatlands[2] two mornings ago, and that he and the Duke
of Kent had been breakfasting in the Prince's room.

"As to the poor King, it is said that he does not
suffer bodily or mental pain or distress, but that he is
perfectly contented.   All hope of recovery is, I believe,
abandoned.

"The great business which Parliament will sit upon
is the arrangement of the households of the King and
Regent.   Nobody knows what the latter means to do
when the restrictions entirely cease, but it is still thought
by those in office that a change will take place.

"I met the Lansdownes walking together very com-

---

[1] The Right Honourable Richard Ryder, at this time Secretary of State
for the Home Department.

[2] The residence of the Duke and Duchess of York.   It was a royal
demesne and seat of a palace during the Tudor and Stuart eras.   In the
park was a standing where Queen Elizabeth used to shoot with a cross-
bow, and Queen Anne of Denmark resided at Oatlands for some time.
Charles I. bestowed the palace upon Henrietta Maria, and here was
born Henry of Oatlands, Duke of Gloucester, in 1640.

During the Civil Wars the palace was dismantled and the park
disparked.   It subsequently came into the possession of Henry Clinton,
and was sold by his descendant, the Duke of Newcastle, in 1774, to
Frederic, Duke of York, and became the favourite residence of the
Duchess until her death in 1820.   On the death of the Duke of York,
in 1827, the Oatlands property was sold.

fortably yesterday, and communed with them and con-
gratulated her on her brother's [3] intended marriage.
Lord L. expressed a wish that I should meet him at
Moreton, but it is unfortunately out of the question."

1812.

EXTRACTS FROM VARIOUS LETTERS WRITTEN TO ME BY MY BROTHERS IN THIS YEAR.

FROM CHARLTON B. WOLLASTON.

" *Friday, February* 14*th.*

" I dined at Lansdowne House, and went to the play
with the party on Tuesday last. Lord Lansdowne appears very amiable and pleasing upon further acquaintance, and I am glad to have had an opportunity of seeing
more of him. He is full of information and has not the
slightest tinge of vanity or pride, and his only fault in
society seems to be a reserve or shyness, which to those
who are also reserved or shy, checks intimacy.

" I never saw man and wife who seem to be more
happy in each other, and on Tuesday I saw their boy, who
appears to be a fine child."

FROM JAMES FRAMPTON.

" *April*, 1812.

" I was at the Opera—'La Clemenza di Tito'—the best
singer, Catalani, did not appear, owing to the death of her
brother, but the music was good, and the ballet ' Zephyr
et Flore' very pretty. I left my name with the Duke of

---

[3] Henry Stephen, Earl of Ilchester, married, February, 1812, Caroline,
second daughter of Lord George Murray, late Bishop of St. David's.
She died universally lamented in 1819.

Cambridge, asking him for a ticket for the Ancient [4] Music, which he immediately sent me in the civilest manner. Mr. Ralph Leycester (as you know, a strong Whig) sat by me at the Opera; his troop of Yeomanry are out on very unpleasant service in Cheshire, quelling rioters. He says that many men are obliged to work at reduced wages from want of trade and reduced prices, combined with high price of provisions : these calamities are the cause of the riots. He did not seem to make the worst of the riots, notwithstanding his politics. He told me that his father had some ground-rents in Manchester of the value of about £300 per annum. Houses had been built upon it four years ago to the value of at least £10,000, which now are as perfectly desolate as Babylon, and you may now have the buildings for the ground-rents."

" Provisions are very scarce in France, and the Emperor cannot put his last conscription in force, and cannot get sufficient provisions to one spot in Spain to feed an army that might relieve Badajos,[5] so that will fall.

" He has 350,000 men in Poland, 200,000 of which are French, the rest the contingent troops, ready to fall on Russia when it suits him."

[4] The " Concerts of Ancient Music" were originally suggested by the Earl of Sandwich in the year 1776, for the performance of solid and valuable productions of the old masters—Purcell, Handel, &c.—and were supported with much spirit by the concurrent zeal and activity of other noblemen and gentlemen. They were managed by a Committee of Directors, who in turn selected the music to be performed at these concerts. H.R.H. the Duke of Cambridge was one of them, and no one could be admitted without a ticket either from a Director or subscriber. The King and Queen constantly attended the concerts at the end of the last century.

[5] Invested by Lord Wellington, March 16; stormed and taken, April 6, 1812.

FROM C. B. WOLLASTON.

"Downing Street, May 1st, 1812.

" We were at the Opera last night, and Lord Vernon went for the first time in my Lady's place, she being invited to Carlton House, where there was a concert and everybody much dressed, and all standing except the Royal Family. Manners Sutton was there. As is usually the case on such occasions, there are considerable heart-burnings in consequence of omissions and admissions.

" The Princess of Wales was at the Drawing-room and so was the Regent, who seems to have gone, not in that character, but in compliment to the Queen. He had, however, his proper household attendants, and went in state. He and the Princess were in the same room, but not near each other.

" The Queen seems to have gone through her fatigues very well. James Frampton was presented on his rank of Lieutenant-Colonel, and was duly noticed.

" May has brought a little more warmth, and there has now been enough rain to ensure crops of grass, so I trust there will soon be some appearance of Spring. I scarcely ever remember everything so backward.

" There is a work called ' Anecdotes of Literature and Scarce Books ' by Beloe, which has been much recommended, and which I think my mother and you would like much.

" I have not got the Greek Tragedies from the binders, but I send one of Woodhull's translations which I borrowed, and did not think it much better than Potter's. I have bought Lord Byron's poem, ' Childe Harold's Pilgrimage,' and will take an opportunity of sending it hereafter.

" I have understood that the Roman Catholics do *not*

mean to stir any more this year. If they play their cards wisely and concede their veto and some other points, I think they will succeed in their application another session."

FROM THE SAME.

" Downing Street, Saturday (May).

" I am very busy, and have but little to say. As to politics, everybody is talking of the Prince's exposure of himself and the dignity of the Sovereign at his party on Saturday. What passed is represented in different ways, as will always be the case, but there is no doubt of a very discreditable scene having taken place. Lord Castlereagh is now again in office, and Canning *of course* in opposition. As to our friend Ryder, I do not believe he has any thoughts of retiring, though he is apt amongst his friends to express his desire to do so."

1813.

FROM LADY ELIZABETH FEILDING TO HER SISTER.

" Sackville Street, February 10th, 1813.

" I am afraid all my powers of description would fail to give you an idea of the oriental air of everything in that Mahomet's Paradise, Carlton House. I do not know whether *we* all looked like *Houris*, but I for one was certainly in the seventy-seventh heaven.

" Of course I need not say that I was beautifully attired, for that is always part of a woman's happiness, if she is of a true feminine gender.

" Imagine yourself ascending a flight of steps into an immense saloon lighted up to the ceiling with a profusion of candles and a display of gold plate on either hand that dazzled the eye, with a *sonorous* band of turbaned slaves playing ' God save the King.'

" The sight and sound were both animating, the kettle-drums and cymbals, the glitter of spangles and finery, of dress and furniture that burst upon you were quite *éblouissant*.

" Then you turned to the right through a suite of rooms, some hung with scarlet and gold, others with blue and gold, and some decorated with portraits of all our great commanders.   At last you arrived at the ball-room, where sat the Queen at the upper end, with the Princesse de Condé on her right hand, and the Russian Ambassadress [6] on her left.   This last was a most singular figure; she was in black velvet up to her chin, with a huge ruff like Queen Elizabeth, or rather more like Mary Queen of Scots, for she is very handsome.   She had no ornaments whatever but a long chain of *very* large diamonds, and a picture that hung *on her back*.   Her head was dressed quite flat, and she looked exactly like something walked out of its frame in an old picture gallery.   Her manners are extremely polished, and she is much shocked at the abruptness and want of grace of

[6] Comtesse de Lieven, sister of the Comte de Beckendorf, Minister of Police under the Emperor Nicholas.   She was married in 1810, at the age of sixteen, to the Comte de Lieven, then Minister Plenipotentiary from Russia to Berlin.   In 1812 he was moved to the Embassy in London, where he remained twenty-two years.   In 1828 Madame de Lieven was appointed dame d'honneur to the Empress of Russia and created " Princesse."   She was celebrated in the diplomatic world by her talents and knowledge of public affairs, and during her residence in London no society was more sought after ; and from the intelligence and impartiality of her character, the most noted persons of opposite parties met at her house, as upon neutral ground, where all opinions might be discussed.

In 1834 the Prince Lieven was recalled, and subsequently appointed Governor to the Hereditary Prince Alexander, whom he accompanied in his travels, and died at Rome, 1839.   The Princess returned to Russia with her husband, but eventually settled at Paris, where she died in 1857.

the English ladies. She sat very demurely by the Queen, and spoke very little, for I suppose she had nothing to say. She was horrified at the crowding and squeezing at Court, and says that these things are 'mieux arrangés at St. Petersburg.' Mrs. Feilding was rather shocked at her giving her opinion of everything here with so much *sincerity*."

FROM JAMES FRAMPTON.

" *Park Place*,[7] *May 3rd*, 1813.

" I have decided on staying till Wednesday, on which day I shall certainly set out, and get home the next day. My dinner in Burlington Street[8] passed off very agreeably, and Lord Lansdowne was very pleasant. I like Sir William Lemon; he seems a quiet and gentlemanly old man. My Lady not fascinating.

" To-night is the fandango here; the Glees will be very good, and such as you would like to hear. I will get a card of them, and bring it down.

" The squadron of the 13th which was surprised in Spain and taken prisoners were dismounted, not thinking an enemy was near. The horses have since been retaken.

" I mean, if possible, to see this fine show of ' Timour the Tartar ' on Monday. Lord Lansdowne told me it was by much the finest thing of the sort we had ever had here. Kemble is very anxious for its success, as, if this fills his house, he means to bring forward the play of ' Julius Cæsar,' which he wishes very much to do, but knows his house would be empty, as no one would

---

[7] The residence of Lord and Lady Vernon, where Mr. Frampton was on a visit; afterwards the Dower House of Lady Vernon. It was subsequently purchased by Lord Redesdale, and is still called Vernon House.

[8] 31, Old Burlington Street, the old family house of Lord Ilchester.

go to hear that unless in the hope of seeing this show. This is a proof of the taste of these times.

"There is now a man in London who teaches people to have a memory. Lord Lansdowne is taking a lesson, so are Lord Spencer and his children. He manages it by supposing rooms with compartments, for Sir George Paul has got to the seventeenth room, each of which has fifty compartments. I should like to ask him what was in the forty-seventh compartment of the fifteenth room. I think it would puzzle him. Lady Lansdowne is learning on the harp, by Lord L.'s desire."

FROM THE SAME.

"*Park Place, May* 11*th*, 1813.

"A party at Lansdowne House yesterday had a very narrow escape. During the dessert the ceiling of the dining-room fell down. Some of the party were bruised a little, but not materially, and neither Lord nor Lady Lansdowne hurt. The latter happened to have moved a little, or might have been much so."

THE MARCHIONESS OF LANSDOWNE TO LADY HARRIOT FRAMPTON.

"*Castle Wellan*,[9] *August* 25*th*, 1813.

"MY DEAR HARRIOT,—Many thanks for your two letters and good accounts of my babes. It will do William so much good to have so many playfellows, if he does not miss them too much on his return home.

"Your commission letter has just arrived in time, as we are on the verge of the linen country, and already can see the benefit of it in the increased tidiness of the people and comparative fewness of beggars.

---

[9] The seat of Earl Annesley in Co. Down.

"We have been passing a delightful four days at Edgeworth town.[1] The country round it is ugly to excess, but that never came into my head to think of, for it is impossible to imagine anything so delightful as Miss Edgeworth's conversation. Such feast of reason I never enjoyed before in my life, and she has the happy art of unlocking one's heart, so that I felt as much at my ease with her as I should have felt with you or any *ordinary* person.

"She has a great deal of imagination, which you would not, I think, expect from her works, and the happiest facility of seizing remote analogies, joined to the strongest perception of humour and wit, whenever it is to be found. The children, five of whom are quite young, do ample justice to their scheme of education. They live entirely with their parents, and consequently with whoever may be in the house, but they are always happy, employed, and never in anybody's way, entering into what is going on in conversation without asking troublesome questions, or being ashamed of giving their opinions if asked. Mrs. Edgeworth is a very agreeable and sensible woman, and seems to admire and love Miss Edgeworth as she ought. Mr. Edgeworth is tiresome sometimes, but he has so much information to impart, which he does so clearly, that he did not plague me at all, and I enjoyed all his mechanical contrivances, of which he has many in various parts of the house, so much that I was a great favourite. In short, I enjoyed myself very much. Mr. E. gave me a lesson in his method of teaching to read, and a Rational Primer, but I fear it will require a better ear than mine to catch the difference of sound.

[1] The residence of Richard Lovell Edgeworth, Esq. Maria Edgeworth, so well known by her writings, was the eldest daughter by his first wife. She died unmarried, 1849, aged 82.

"At Edgeworth-town we met Sir George Staunton,[2] who wrote Chinese for our amusement, which I was surprised to find is a sort of hieroglyphic language. We have been seeing some very beautiful places in this neighbourhood, and go to-morrow to Antrim.

"We leave my brother William[3] at Hillsborough, as he is going to Dr. Macdonnell's at Belfast. George Eden is to meet us at Antrim, and goes with us to the Giant's Causeway.

"I hope we shall not be much more than a week longer in Ireland, as I am in a fever of impatience.

"I hope Mr. Frampton does not repent his kindness in letting my babes add to the noise at Moreton.

"Ever yours affectionately,
"L. LANSDOWNE."

MARIA DOWAGER COUNTESS OF ILCHESTER TO HER SON, THE HONOURABLE GILES FOX STRANGWAYS.

"*Windsor, November* 26th, 1813.

"MY DEAREST GILES,—I am indeed sorry and disappointed in the pleasure I proposed to myself in your company and your meeting dear William with me, but I

---

[2] The celebrated Chinese scholar (Sinologue), President of the Select Committee at Canton. In 1816 he was attached to the Embassy of Lord Amherst as Commissioner to Pekin, M.P., &c.

[3] The Honourable William Strangways. He entered the Diplomatic Service in 1816, from which time he was successively attached to the Embassies of St. Petersburg, Constantinople, the Hague, Florence, Naples, and Vienna. In August, 1835, Mr. Strangways was appointed Under Secretary of State for Foreign Affairs, when Lord Palmerston was Foreign Secretary, with whom he was always on the most confidential terms; and, in 1840, Envoy Extraordinary and Minister Plenipotentiary at the Diet of the Germanic Confederation, from which post he retired in 1849. Mr. Fox Strangways succeeded as fourth Earl of Ilchester, 1858. He married, 1857, Sophia daughter of Sir Robert Sheffield, Bart., and died 1865 (s.p.)

trust it is a happiness only delayed. I am sure you will like to see William's sketches, &c. ; he seems to have enjoyed his Irish tour very much.

"What glorious news!" [4] How thankful should we be for the blessings showered down upon us ; it is impossible to reflect at all and not to feel sensibly what we owe to the steady principles of our dear good King, and the Prince, by taking them up and acting on them as for the King, has been most signally blessed with success. You may imagine the happiness of the Hanoverians here and at Cumberland Lodge. The Duke of Cambridge comes to take leave on Monday ; I hope he may find Tom [5] at Hanover ; I shall not forget to remind him who he is.

[4] 1813. After the battle of Leipzig, October 18, the Crown Prince of Sweden entered Hanover on November 6, when he issued a proclamation announcing the resumption of the Government by the King of Great Britain. The inhabitants gladly embraced the opportunity of shaking off the French yoke, which they detested, and the authority of the Elector and King of England was restored with universal assent. The electorate of Hanover was erected into a kingdom, 1814.

[5] Thomas Fox Strangways, born 1790, second son of the Honourable and Rev. Charles Redlynch Fox Strangways, and grandson of Stephen, first Earl of Ilchester. He entered the Royal Horse Artillery at an early age, and in 1813 he embarked for the North of Germany with the Rocket Brigade under Colonel Bogue, sent from this country to be attached, during the campaign, to the Swedish force in the Allied Army, commanded by the Crown Prince of Sweden in person. Part of the brigade was detached under the command of Lieutenant Fox Strangways, and assisted in the successful issue of two actions, and in the siege and reduction of a fortress in Northern Germany, previous to rejoining Colonel Bogue, then under the walls of Leipzig. One of the first casualties which occurred in the engagement—October 18th—was the death of Colonel Bogue, when the command fell to Lieutenant Strangways, and so distinguished was his conduct in this most important position, and so essentially did the services of his brigade contribute to the victory at Leipzig, that on the field of battle, and at the head of his troops, the gallant young officer received the thanks of . the Allied Sovereigns. He also received from the Crown Prince the Gold Medal of

The circumstance of our dear good King's Bust remaining untouched in the midst of desolation is quite affecting,

Sweden, "for bravery and good conduct," and the Swedish Order of the Sword. The Emperor Alexander I. at the same time presented Lieutenant Fox Strangways with the Order of St. Anne of Russia, which he took from his own great coat, and these decorations were accompanied by the most flattering testimonials from the military commanders of the Allied Sovereigns. At the Battle of Waterloo Lieutenant Strangways was dangerously wounded in the hotly-contested position behind La Haye Sainte, and it was some days before he could be removed from the village of Waterloo to Brussels, where the ball was extracted ; and upon recovering from his wounds he returned to England with the Army of Occupation. After forty years of active service, Lieutenant-Colonel Fox Strangways was sent with the Royal Artillery to Dublin, where during the period of his command he was on all occasions distinguished by H.R.H. the Duke of Cambridge in the most marked and gracious manner. In September, 1853, he formed one of those who accompanied the Earl of Lucan to assist in the reception of the Emperor Napoleon III. during his progress through the Northern Departments of France. The deputation of English officers experienced the most distinguished reception from the Emperor, and were honoured by being kept in immediate attendance upon himself. In taking leave of them, the Emperor expressed his desire that they might be able to visit Paris in the ensuing spring. Lieutenant-Colonel Strangways had the gratification of doing so, when he received many tokens of imperial kindness.

War having been declared by England and France against Russia in March, 1854, and the expedition to the Crimea determined upon, Lieutenant-Colonel Fox Strangways embarked for the East in command of the Royal Horse Artillery attached to the army, with the rank of Brigadier-General. General Strangways was on Lord Raglan's Staff at the Battle of Inkerman, November 5th, 1854, when a splinter from a Russian shell almost cut off his leg. As he was carried as carefully as possible to the rear by his devoted friends and soldiers, his fast-failing eye caught sight of a Battery of his own Division. The General begged his bearers to stop, sent for the officer in command, and after asking a few questions on military points, he added, "God bless you, and good-bye, my brave fellows ! Keep well in front as you always have done." Exhaustion ensued, and he expired in less than two hours from the time he received his mortal wound. His death was universally lamented and deplored, not only by his own regiment, but by the whole British army. General Fox Strangways was buried the following day, side by side with

and I hear that Bernadotte, who, under the French Government, commanded at Hanover, was known to say, that whenever peace should be made he hoped it might be *his* lot to return Hanover into the hands of its own monarch, he was so charmed with the loyalty of the Hanoverians, and with what he heard of the character of the Duke of Cambridge, and *now*, as Crown Prince, how instrumental has he been towards its restoration !

" I hear that Bernadotte says that he will do everything short of carrying arms into France.

" Ever your affectionate mother,
M. ILCHESTER."

LETTER FROM THE CROWN PRINCE OF SWEDEN[6] TO MRS. BOGUE, WHOSE HUSBAND COMMANDED THE ROCKET BRIGADE, AND WAS KILLED AT THE BATTLE OF LEIPZIG, OCT. 16TH AND 18TH, 1813.

(Communicated to Lady H. Frampton by Lieut. Thomas Strangways.)

" MADAME DE BOGUE,—Le Roi mon Souverain a daigné m'autoriser à conférer la Croix de son Ordre Militaire de

General Cathcart and General Goldie, on Cathcart's Hill. The Duke of Cambridge, Lord Raglan, &c., assisted at the double funeral, one of the most impressive scenes ever witnessed. A marble slab was erected over the grave of General Fox Strangways by his family, with an inscription in Russian and English, and a memorial window put in the Garrison Church at Woolwich by his widow. A handsome brass tablet in memory of General Strangways has also been placed in the Church at Melbury by his cousin, Henry Stephen, Earl of Ilchester.

[6] Charles Jean Bernadotte, born at Pau, 1763 ; elected Crown Prince of Sweden, 1810 ; succeeded as [Charles XIV.] King of Sweden, 1818 [on the death of Charles XIII.] He married, 1788, Eugénie Désirée, *née* Mademoiselle Clary, and died 1844.

When we were at Pau, in 1847, we remarked the name of " Bernadotte " over the door of a shop near the entrance of the town, and were told that there was also a rich family of the same name then residing at Pau.—H. G. M.

l'Epée, tant aux Officiers Suédois qu'aux Officiers des troupes Alliées qui se distinguaient en combattant pour la Cause commune.

" La manière dont votre époux s'est conduit durant la Campagne lui avait mérité cette récompense des braves. Il est mort au Champ d'honneur, et les plaines de Leipzig, derniers témoins de son courage et de son intrepidité, l'ont vu périr avant que je puisse le nommer Chevalier.

" Je me conforme, madame, aux usages d'Angleterre, dont la Suède est la fidèle Alliée, et je vous transmets la Décoration de l'Ordre dont votre époux s'est rendu digne.

" Puisse-t-elle être dans vos mains un Souvenir consolateur de sa perte, comme elle est un témoignage de sa valeur et de l'estime particulière qu'il m'avait inspirée.

" Sur ce je prie Dieu qu'il vous ait, Madame de Bogue, en sa sainte et digne garde.

" Charles Jean."

C. B. Wollaston to Mary Frampton.

"*Downing Street, Friday, November,* 1813.

"My dear Mary,—Our ears are now so accustomed to the sound of the Park and Tower guns that they scarcely startle us. On Wednesday evening they fired for the restoration of the King's Government in Hanover, and once yesterday morning for Lord Wellington's victory,[7] and again for the surrender of Dresden,[8] and other important events. Our warmest expectations or .even hopes could scarcely have looked forward to so rapid a succession of happy events, which promise, and one may almost say secure, to us a return of quiet days and a

---

[7] The surrender of Pampeluna took place on October 31, 1813.

[8] Marshal St. Cyr and 25,000 French troops surrendered to the Allies, November 6, 1813.

cessation of irritations and alarms. I cannot, however, help a little regretting the loss of life under Lord Wellington, as the business seems so likely to be settled elsewhere. But it is said that he could not stay where he was, being too much within the cold and mountainous country, and therefore that he was obliged either to advance or retire, and, besides, he probably did not know all that had happened in Germany, by which his conduct might have been regulated. I hope and trust he will *not* attack the entrenched camp before Bayonne. I believe he is not likely to do so for the *éclat* only, and lives are still precious, as we are sending at this time every soldier that can be mustered to Holland, the Militia regiments being for the first time doing the duty of the Guards, to the no small offence, as I hear, of that body, who, men as well as officers, think themselves of more importance than all the rest of the army. They were quite clamorous the first day that the King's Guard was relieved by the Nottingham Militia, but I do not know how it has happened lately that they seem to be less estimated by Lord Wellington, as even in this last engagement I see no mention of the first Division, to which they belong, though one officer of the Coldstream is mentioned as severely wounded. So much at present for public matters.

" My court-martial [9] concluded its sittings on Wednesday, after three days' reading of evidence and deliberations. These were the most fatiguing days to me, as I

---

[9] Mr. Wollaston was at this time Assistant Judge Advocate under Mr. Manners Sutton (subsequently Speaker of the House of Commons, &c.) and the Right Honourable Sir John Beckett, which post he held until after the accession of George IV., but retired from office some years before his death in 1840. He was for many years Chairman of the Quarter Sessions for the county of Dorset.

was either reading or discussing almost the whole five
hours of our Sittings.   With regard to myself, I must
say that it ended very satisfactorily from the handsome
and flattering things that were said to me at the conclusion by the members, with all of whom, even with one
who had given much trouble and with whom I had very
strong differences at first, I parted very good friends.
I have still many hours' work in getting the voluminous
evidence ready for the Report, but I feel much lightened
by having done with the public duty.   Colonel Newdigate[1] was not less happy to be released than myself.
The Stafford have now marched into London to take the
duty, and I suppose will not be spared immediately, even
should they all volunteer for service.   Circumstanced as
we are at present, and as, instead of having to fight
their way at the Helder, they will all be received with
open, not loaded arms, it will be considered no unpleasant
expedition, and I daresay most of the Militia officers
would like it and the men make no objections.

"By the way, I may add, as another consequence
of the change of affairs in Holland, that Dr. A. has
suspended his sending you the roots, a supply from that
country being now expected.

"Yours very affectionately,
"C. B. Wollaston."

1814.

The Marchioness of Lansdowne to Lady Harriot
Frampton.

"Lansdowne House, January 31st, 1814.
"My dear Harriot,—It will make no difference to us

---

[1] Francis Newdigate, Esq., Lieutenant-Colonel of the King's Own
Regiment of Staffordshire Militia.   He married, 1820, Lady Barbara
Legge, daughter of third Earl of Dartmouth, K.G.

your coming later in the spring, and we depend upon you whenever you do come up. I think you will find it pleasanter then than now, as more people will be in town and the weather finer.

"The streets are now in the most horrible state; carriages overturning at every corner, and no one venturing to go out of a foot's pace. I have only been out once, and then I was so frightened that I do not think I shall venture again, though the alternations of thaw and frost seem as if they intended it to be always in the same state.

"I have been reading 'Patronage,' [2] which has disappointed me, though I do not go the lengths which people here do in saying that it gives the idea of having been written by a foolish person, and that it is impossible to read it through. I do not think the romance part and the rest fit well; one is too much ordinary life and the other too extraordinary.

"We had all manner of adventures in the snow coming from Ampthill.[3] I have not time to tell them now. When we meet that will do. I know nothing of anybody to tell you.

"Yours ever affectionately,

"L. L."

FRAGMENT OF A LETTER FROM LORD HARCOURT TO LADY VERNON.

"As to politics, the present moment is indeed most truly critical and anxious, it being but too probable that

[2] A novel by Miss Edgeworth.

[3] In Bedfordshire, built by Sir Philip Sidney. Here the Earl of Elgin resided with his Lady the Countess Dowager of Oxford when Robert Frampton, subsequently Bishop of Gloucester, was Domestic Chaplain, "where he had free use of the Liturgy, and met eminent

before the middle of the present month of February the
fate of the European continent, if not of the world, will
be decided by the issue of a tremendous shock between
the two main contending armies on the plains watered
by the Seine and Marne, an event to which people in
general seem to look forward with the most assured hope
of success.

"But for my own part, besides my old-fashioned
regard for the interest of humanity, I must here confess
I have no great relish for so desperate a *va-tout*, in which
opinion I rather think your Ladyship will be disposed to
agree with me, and therefore not sorry to learn that,
notwithstanding the advantage of the Allied Army, the
negotiation for peace is still kept alive, and will in all
likelihood have been brought to a decision, " Yes " or
" No," on Lord Castlereagh's [4] arrival at the Imperial
Headquarters, which he was expected to reach about the
20th of January.

"I receive constant and good accounts of our excellent and venerable ex-monarch, who is uninterruptedly
well and cheerful, and his constitution so unbroken
that there is no saying how long his life may last.
The ladies of the castle also in pretty good health
with the exception of poor Princess Sophia, who has
been absolutely confined for more than two months with
what is called a slow bilious fever, but it has reduced
her to what I should consider as a most alarming state

divines since remarkable for their sufferings for their King and Church."
Ampthill was bequeathed by the last Earl of Upper Ossory in 1818 to
his nephew, Henry Richard Lord Holland. The place was afterwards
sold to the Duke of Bedford.

[4] Robert Viscount Castlereagh, succeeded as second Marquis of Londonderry, 1821 ; the celebrated statesman and diplomatist. He assisted at
the Conferences of Châtillon, the Peace of Paris, and at the Congress of
Vienna.

of weakness, but for the confidence of the physicians, who do not see any symptoms of danger."

FROM MR. WOLLASTON.
"*Downing Street, February 25th,* 1814.

"I have seen Mrs. Shirley, who had received yesterday a letter from her son Charles, and I was sorry that it held out the probability of the Guards advancing very soon with the army, but whither or for what purpose he did not know, as it was very fit he should not, though he says that Lord Wellington does communicate confidentially with Sir John Hope, and consult him on all occasions, which is a circumstance very creditable to both, as Sir J. Hope was senior to Lord Wellington until the promotion of the latter to be Field-Marshal.

"I do not like the bulletin of last night from France. Though the French have grossly exaggerated the advantages gained over Blucher and his loss, yet it is clear that the schemes of the allies have been checked by the vigorous opposition of Bonaparte and the force he has been able to bring against them, and I fear lest the people who have been in a state of apathy should rise for him if they think he is likely to be successful, in which case the army of the Allies might, notwithstanding their numbers, be in an awkward predicament.

"The forcing the bridge at Montereau[5] and crossing the Seine, which is stated to have taken place on the 19th, may prove a very material stroke. The Corps which had got on to Fontainebleau with old Platow amongst them must look to themselves. All this is *too* interesting. It keeps one in a fever.

---

[5] Battle of Montereau, February 18th, 1814, between the Allied Army and the French, the latter commanded by Napoleon in person. The Allies were defeated with great loss, but it was one of the last triumphs of Bonaparte.

From the Same to Mary Frampton.

"*Temple, March 11th*, 1814.

"My dear Mary,—I am much pleased with the comfortable account you give of my mother. We have had in the course of the night another very heavy fall of snow. It is now melting, but the wind is still at N.E. How happy the people of Dorchester may be considered in having had an opportunity of seeing the great Mr. Kean at their theatre, for there is quite a rage for him at present, and as much difficulty in getting a place in the house as in the early days of Betty.[6]

"I have twice missed opportunities of seeing him with comfort. The Harbords, however, are promised another box, and I shall wait with patience for such a chance without putting myself into a crowd, or getting over spikes, as I was obliged to do on a former occasion.

"I doubt his being a perfect actor by the accounts I hear of him, though some people are in ecstasies; but he must have considerable merit, and promise still better things. The two parts he has as yet been acting are disagreeable ones, 'Richard III.' and 'Shylock,' and not so well suited to so young a man as Kean; but he comes out next in 'Hamlet,' which I shall have more satisfaction in seeing.

"I dined with Mrs. Richards on Tuesday, being invited to meet, amongst others, Browne of Frampton.

"Colonel Grant[7] is still in town, but is going to join

---

[6] Master Betty, the Infant Roscius. He was born in Ireland, 1791. At eleven years of age made his first appearance on the stage at Belfast, and in 1804 appeared at Drury Lane in the tragedy of "Barbarossa." He died 1874, aged 82.

[7] He was present at the capture of Seringapatam and at that of the Cape of Good Hope in 1806. Commanded the 15th Hussars during Sir John Moore's campaign in Spain, and was wounded at the Battle of

the army immediately under very peculiar circumstances, being *ordered to join*—the parole he gave not being admitted as valid. I see a General Order from the Horse Guards on the subject of paroles given at sea issued *now*. Surely it ought to have been notified before, and those who were not aware of the objection ought not to be forced into so awkward a predicament.

"*Downing Street, two o'clock.*—I have just seen a hack chaise and four from Rochester at the office of the Foreign Secretary, so that there will be some news in the papers of to-night. If I learn anything before I close this, you shall have it. Though the face of things has changed again for the better, yet I am not sanguine enough to march to Paris. I do not understand how Bonaparte has got between Laon and Rheims, leaving Blucher at Soissons. This appears by the French papers, but it seems admitted that Blucher, Bulow, and Winzéngerode have united their forces. I do not like Augereau's army in the rear coming up from Lyons. I have just heard that Schwartzenburg had driven the French again out of Troyes with considerable loss, and that he then turned towards Sezanne in the rear of Bonaparte, so as to co-operate with Blucher, and that Monsieur had been joined by a very considerable body of French, and that the general complexion of things was good.

"Yours very affectionately,

"C. B. W."

Sahagun. Aide-de-Camp to the Prince Regent, 1811. At Waterloo Major-General Grant had five horses shot or killed during the battle. K.C.B. &c.; died 1834. Sir Colquhoun Grant married Marcia, sister-in-law of F. J. Browne, Esq., of Frampton, Dorset, to whom he bequeathed the Frampton estates, and their only surviving daughter and heiress became the wife of R. Brinsley Sheridan, Esq.

FROM THE SAME TO THE SAME.

"*Temple, March* 18*th*, 1814.

MY DEAR MARY,—I begin writing before breakfast (though I have already looked forward to the brown bread, which was excellent yesterday), as I am going to dine and sleep at Barnard's,[8] having put off doing so from time to time in expectation of better weather, till it seems useless to wait any longer. The wind still continues in the east, and not a gleam of sun ever shines.

" We are now all in high exultation here at the news of the last two days. That Bonaparte has met with another serious defeat cannot be doubted, and the time and place make it necessarily of great importance, and give rise to the strongest hopes; but I wish Ministers would not send letters to the Lord Mayor containing intelligence founded on the verbal reports of messengers, as they raise expectations beyond what the authentic details will justify, and thus create disappointment. By the second *Extraordinary Gazette* of yesterday, you will see that the fighting was very severe, and the defeat of the French on the 9th[9] and 10th past all question; but the complete rout of the enemy, the subsequent operations, and the death of Macdonald rest on no authority. I own, however, that I am so far *up* again as to hope that Bonaparte will *not* accede to the ultimatum which has been said to be offered to him, and that he may yet have the satisfaction to live to see his annihilation.

"I dined at Lord Harrowby's[1] on Monday—a set

[8] Andrew Barnard, son of Dr. Barnard, Bishop of Limerick, Secretary to the Colony of the Cape of Good Hope in 1800. He married Lady Anne Lindsay, daughter of fifth Earl of Balcarras. She was the authoress of " Auld Robin Gray."

[9] The Battle of Laon, March 9, 1814.

[1] Lord Harrowby, the first earl, married Lady Susan Leveson Gower,

dinner, principally for men.   Lady Harrowby had on her
head as a turban a kind of Indian shawl embroidered
with gold and silver and all sorts of gay colours and
grotesque figures, which had a strange effect with mourning and black ornaments.   Lady Susan is now a very
pretty and very pleasing-looking girl."

FROM THE SAME TO THE SAME.

" Downing Street, 1814.

" You may perhaps observe the difference in the handwriting of the Frank enclosing this, which makes me
almost doubt whether it will pass at the Post Office, but
Sutton's [2] little boy was sitting on his knee when he wrote
it, and assisted in holding the pen !

" After calling on Lady Vernon, I went on to visit
the O'Briens, and found them in their former apartment, which is as much out of the way of sights as if
they were at Stinsford.   He looks better than when I
saw him last, and seemed cheerful and pleasant; but
Lady Susan had evidently begun to anticipate the probability of not getting to any of the sights and gay things
which have been her principal object.   The Lansdownes
are gone, and Lord Ilchester also.   Mrs. Lionel Damer
goes out of town for a fortnight on Monday or Tuesday,
so I cannot help fearing they may be disappointed and
want society.

" I mentioned in my letter to Mrs. Shirley a few days
ago that the Music is to be at Whitehall Chapel, and not
at the Abbey.   The difference is almost everything.   It

daughter of first Marquis of Stafford.   Their eldest daughter, Lady Susan
Ryder, became in 1817 the wife of Earl Fortescue, and was then much
admired.

[2] Charles Manners Sutton, G.C.B., eldest son of Archbishop of Canterbury.   Judge-Advocate, P.C., and M.P. ; subsequently Speaker of the
House of Commons.   Created Viscount Canterbury, 1835.

seems still uncertain when the great foreigners are to come, and *who* will come.

" There are odd stories about the Princess Charlotte—that she has become cool to the young Prince of Orange, and set her mind upon a Russian Grand Duke. I am inclined to think that there is some hitch, as there has been no communication on the subject to Parliament, and that somebody has encouraged her in objections to going to Holland.   The principle of Opposition in this country would, of course lead to fomenting this or any other obstacle to any arrangement which is desirable when brought about by others.

" I wish they had not so much to say on the Norway question.   It always seemed probable that the treaty with Sweden[3] was likely to lead to difficulties and to involve the country in a very awkward guarantee ; but the Crown Prince was to be bought at any price, and certainly at *that time* his co-operation was very important. The consequences of doing evil that good may come are now felt, and must be got over as well as they can be, but not without much inconsistency in supporting a bad cause after having been fighting so manfully for a good one.

" I am going to-morrow into the country, and am to drive Bowles,[4] who is in town and living in this neigh-

[3] January 14th, 1814.

[4] Rev. W. Lisle Bowles, the poet, Vicar of Bremhill, Wilts, author of " Columbus," " History of Lacock Abbey," &c.   The following lines were addressed by Mr. Bowles to Mrs. Talbot, Constance, the beautiful daughter of Francis Mundy, Esq., of Markeaton, and wife of Henry Fox Talbot, Esq., of Lacock Abbey.   She was then in mourning for her father :—

LACOCK NUNNERY.

I stood upon the stone where Ela lay,
The widow'd founder of these ancient walls,
Where fancy still on meek devotion calls ;

N

bourhood. We are going to see an old schoolfellow who lives about fourteen miles off. I hope the weather may mend. For the last four days we have had the worst of all—namely, very cold, drying, and high east winds. I cannot wish my mother to move from home unless it mends.

" Yours affectionately,
" C. B. WOLLASTON."

FRAGMENT OF A LETTER TO THE SAME.

" Downing Street, March, 1814.

" Two o'clock.—I am told that Lord Castlereagh's Despatch is dated the 13th, and it brings an account of another victory gained by Blucher over Mortier between Laon and Rheims.[5] This is all I can pick up.

" Nothing is said about the progress of negotiation, but it does not appear to have been broken off.

" Yours in haste,
" C. B. WOLLASTON."

C. B. WOLLASTON TO THE SAME.

" Downing Street, March, 1814.

" I will beg of you to tell Mrs. Shirley I am very glad

> Marking the ivied arch and turret grey,
> For her soul's rest—*eternal rest*—to pray ;
> Where visionary nuns yet seem to tread,
> A pale dim troop, the cloisters of the dead,
> Tho' twice three hundred years have flown away !
> But when, with silent step and pensive mien,
> In weeds as mourning for her sisters gone,
> The mistress of this lone monastic scene,
> Came, and I heard her voice's pensive tone,
> I said, "Tho' centuries have roll'd between,
> One *gentle, beauteous Nun* is left on earth alone."

W. L. B.

June 24th, 1837.

---

[5] March 13th, 1814.

she has had good accounts from her two sons in France.
I hope things will go on favourably in the neighbourhood
of Bordeaux—much depends upon this.   It is generally
believed that the Conferences of Châtillon have come to
an end, but I believe as yet there is no official intelligence
to that effect.   As it is not probable that my mother will
be well enough to go to Moreton as has been usual during
my Easter holidays, I hope that the Framptons will be
able to pay us a visit from thence.   I hear nothing new
except that the Stocks are as low as 60 and Omnium at
8.   This shows how much the high prices were the effect
of speculation.

"Before we meet great things may have happened.
Every day they may be looked for.   At present I
understand there are multitudes of speculations respecting the arrival of the Duchess of Oldenburg,[6] who is
said to be coming to England for the purpose of marrying the Duke of Clarence."

FROM GEORGIANA LADY VERNON TO THE SAME.

"*April 10th,* 1814 (*Easter Sunday*).

"MY DEAR MARY,—As I went to the Chapel Royal at
eight o'clock to-day for quiet, the Princess going in the
mid-day, I have liberty this morning, and will employ it
in telling you all I know, more than you would have by
your newspaper of last night.   A *Gazette* came out at
five o'clock, that you got, I suppose, in the papers.
After ten   there   came   out   another 'Extraordinary,'

---

[6] The Grand Duchess Catherine Paulowna, daughter of the Emperor
Paul of Russia, married 1809, Prince Peter Frederic, second son of Peter
Frederic, Duke of Holstein Oldenburg, who died 1812, leaving two sons.
The duchess remarried in January, 1816, Frederic William, Prince Royal
of Wurtemberg [succeeded as King of Wurtemberg the same year].   He
was step-son to the Princess Royal of England.

stating that Bonaparte had abdicated[7] the thrones of France and Italy for himself and his heirs, and that there is no personal sacrifice, even that of life, which he is not ready to make to the interest of France. Done at the Palace of Fontainebleau.

" Then comes Lord Bathurst to the Lord Mayor, ordering the public offices to be illuminated in the grandest manner to-morrow night. I suppose, being holiday time, the show will be amazing, and the poor Mayor's Feast of all others the greatest. It makes one feel as if one was scarce alive—so sudden and extraordinary.

" I do not quite like Talleyrand,[8] &c., to have the care of all these great people, for they literally lodge in their houses.

" The place Bonaparte has fixed on for his Asylum, is, I understand, the first place he conquered, and is, though small, strictly fortified. I cannot but think he has great favour shown him, and were he any but what he is one might rejoice at this, but whilst he is on this earth I shall always tremble in fear of some of his machinations which are next to *diablerie*. The strong anxiety upon my mind now is to hear that Lord Wellington is alive, and I have a feeling that I cannot but wish he had been at Paris with the rest of the great men.

" In answer to your question about the Russian Princess, I hear a most amiable character of her in every respect. She married this Duke of Holstein to avoid

[7] Bonaparte abdicated April 5th, 1814.

[8] Charles Maurice de Talleyrand Périgord, Prince de Benevento, &c., born 1754, died at Paris 1838. He was Ambassador from Louis Philippe to the Court of St. James's, 1830-34. The Duchesse de Dino, who resided with Talleyrand in London, was the Princesse Dorothée, daughter of the Duchesse de Courland, wife of Edmond, Comte de Périgord, Duc de Dino, the nephew of Talleyrand.

being pressed to marry Bonaparte, behaved most admirably the whole of his life, nursed him in a putrid fever, and was sincerely attached to him. Her nerves have been so much shook by this and the loss of him that she is travelling to tranquillize her mind and nerves. She does not mean to stay long in London; intends to see everything worth seeing both in the metropolis and all over the kingdom—the Universities in particular—Bath, and all the great Houses, &c. She is very well read and sensible, her conversation interesting, and her manners peculiarly pleasing. Not handsome, but interesting looking. No sort of intention of marrying, is still in slight mourning for her husband, has two children, the eldest with her.

" The guns are now firing—what that can be for I have no guess, but hope to find out before I send this.

" I must not forget to mention one thing for Lady Harriot's information. I believe there is certainly to be a Drawing-room, and if possible it is to be next week. It is to be at the Queen's house,[9] which is preparing, and if finished, and nothing arises, I fancy it will be on Thursday sennight.

" I thought it might be of use to Lady H. to know this if she is to be in town before that time. The Queen is to stand in the second room. Persons to come through and be spoke to and pass on ; go through other rooms ; and the stairs so managed as to get out without any return. This will make an amazing difference in

[9] Originally Buckingham House, bought 1761, of Sir Charles Sheffield by George III., and settled on Queen Charlotte in lieu of Somerset House. All the king's children were born here excepting George IV., who was born at St. James's Palace. Buckingham House was taken down by George IV. in 1825, when the present palace was commenced on the same site.

comfort to those that attend, and infinite to her Majesty. It will be quite an open Drawing-room, at St. James's, and I suppose the Princess of Wales will be there.

"The Dowager Harcourt never gives me any useful information—I got it from an old courtier, or at least who is so to me (Lord St. Helens), and who I have always found in all situations kind and obliging.

"My very kind love to your mother, this fine news will enliven her. I am sure it gives one much to think of.

"Yours ever,

"G. VERNON."

FROM THE SAME TO THE SAME.

"*April 14th*, 1814.

"MY DEAR MARY,—I have got a Frank for to-morrow, but will not let this day slip through without beginning my letter.

"The report yesterday evening was—but it came in a private letter—that Bonaparte had secreted an immense sum of the public money when he was in possession of that, and an immensity of jewels, and that he had intended taking the money, gold, &c., on his retirement—for good use, no doubt! That he would not deliver up these valuables, that the people were ready to pull him to pieces, and that the Cossacks saved him from their fury, that the Emperor of Russia had trebled the guard to save him, but that he was at a loss how to proceed upon Bonaparte's absolute refusal to give up the money, —whether to give him up to the people—whether to guard him to Elba—or, in short, how to proceed on so unexpected an event, he (the Emperor of Russia) having pledged himself to protect him.

"The Archbishop of York came here yesterday evening to give me an account of Miss Acklom's and Lord

Althorp's wedding. He performed the ceremony at her mother's—all went off well. Lady Georgiana Spencer[1] is to be married to-day privately, as they are in black gloves. Lady Caroline Damer and Mrs. Drax called here yesterday morning, the former very gay and good-humoured. She spoke most highly of you, as she always does.

" Yours most affectionately,

" G. VERNON."

C. B. WOLLASTON TO MARY FRAMPTON.

" *Temple, April 23rd*, 1814.

" MY DEAR MARY,—You will be glad to hear of my safe arrival. I went immediately to Downing Street, in hopes of learning something authentic respecting these unpleasant reports of the last efforts of Bonaparte's generals, but nothing is come. They are disposed at the Horse Guards to doubt the Bayonne story ; but it is too circumstantial, I fear, to be entirely discredited. If anything should come to-morrow I will, if possible, send a packet to Dorchester.

" The King of France, accompanied by the Regent, set off for Dover this morning, intending to reach that place to-day, and to get into the yacht directly, where they were all to dine. It seems this his most Christian Majesty was able, with help, and platforms to avoid steps, to get through his several ceremonies, and they say he is only lame from gout.

" I wish it may be true, as I have been told, that the Prince has already sent two very handsome state carriages with horses for the King and the Duchess of Angoulême, and that it was intended they should be in waiting for them at Boulogne. It would be a very hand-

[1] Youngest daughter of second Earl Spencer, married Lord George Quin, second son of first Marquis of Headfort.

some and acceptable present, and done in excellent taste, but such a preparation would, I think, have got into the newspapers, and besides there seems hardly to have been time to get them ready, ship, and land them.

"I have a note from Lady Harriot, pressing me to go to Lansdowne House this evening, and as I dine with the Sturges Bournes,[2] which is in the neighbourhood, perhaps I may. I write in haste."

When Louis XVIII. was summoned from his retreat at Hartwell to assume the Crown of France, he was invited by the Prince Regent to make a public entry into London.

On April 20th the royal state carriage was sent forward to Stanmore, where his Majesty was to break-fast. He was drawn into the town by the populace, and was met at the door of the inn by the Prince Regent and his suite about two o'clock. The procession was then formed, headed by a hundred gentlemen on horseback. Two detachments of Horse Guards, royal carriages with outriders and servants with white cockades followed, and lastly the state carriage, drawn by eight cream-coloured horses, conveying the King of France and the Prince Regent.

The Duchess of Oldenburg had sent invitations to the Queen and Princesses, and Princess Charlotte to come to the Pulteney Hotel—where she had apartments during her stay in London—to see the royal procession, which were accepted by all but her Majesty, and they were joined by the Russian Ambassador, Countess Lieven, &c.

---

[2] Right Honourable William Sturges Bourne, M.P. for Hastings, joint Secretary of the Treasury under Mr. Pitt; in 1827 Secretary of State for the Home Department; First Commissioner of Woods and Forests; "Lord Warden of the New Forest," which latter appointment he retained till his death in 1845.

About half-past five o'clock the *cortége* reached Cumberland Gate, and on opening out into Piccadilly the view was most striking, as every window and balcony was full and waving with the Bourbon flag, or wreathed with white of some sort; and the streets lined with carriages.

His Majesty entered Grillion's Hotel, in Albemarle Street, leaning on the Prince's arm, who conducted him to the apartments which had been expressly prepared for him with crimson hangings, embroidered with gold *fleurs-de-lys*, where the Duchesse d'Angoulême, the Prince de Condé, and the Duke of York, as well as the foreign ambassadors, and some of the ancient French *noblesse* were waiting to receive him.

After an address from the Prince Regent, to which the King replied, his Majesty took the Ribbon of the Order of the St. Esprit from his own shoulder, and the Star from his breast, and, assisted by the Prince de Condé and the Duc de Bourbon, invested the Prince Regent with them.

Louis XVIII. left London on April 23rd, accompanied by the Duchesse d'Angoulême, &c., and on arriving at Dover was again met by the Prince Regent, who remained with him until the following day, when the King embarked on board the *Royal Sovereign* yacht, and, escorted by the Duke of Clarence in the *Jason* frigate, and attended by the English fleet, reached Calais the same afternoon.

THE SAME TO THE SAME.

"*Temple, April 26th,* 1814.

"Though you will most probably have Lord Wellington's Despatches in your paper, yet you will not grudge a letter which will ensure William Shirley's safety, and it is possible you may not have the full returns so as to satisfy yourselves. I see no name of any officer of his regiment, except Colonel Vivian's, who commanded another brigade.

" As to the Bayonne business[3] we are still in the dark. The accounts are very different from one another, but cannot be entirely discredited. It is highly probable that there were more prisoners than killed or wounded if it was a surprise. We may now congratulate ourselves that Lord Wellington's fighting is over; it is satisfactory that he should have been so well received in Toulouse *before* what had happened at Paris was known there.

" It is most confidently said, as from the authority of Lord Castlereagh, and by those who must know whether it comes from him, that upon Bonaparte's being asked where he would go to first, said, ' to England,' as it was the only country where he could be safe, and the people of which he respected.

" This is certainly a compliment to us, but an instance of his meanness which exceeds every other. I write in great haste.

" Yours affectionately,
" C. B. WOLLASTON."

FROM THE SAME TO THE SAME.

" *Temple, April* 29*th*, 1814.

" I have just been despatching to Lady Harriot at Lansdowne House, a parcel containing various articles for my mother and you, which I hope she will convey safely to their destinations; I do not know on what day she leaves London, as I have not seen her since the party

---

[3] Bayonne was invested by the British force, January 14th, 1814 during which the French made a successful sally, and General Sir John Hope was taken prisoner. The French were eventually driven back, but the British loss was considerable.

there on Saturday, when I met, amongst others, Lady Mary Talbot, whom I was very glad to see.

" My mother's mind will have been relieved yesterday from all further anxiety about the two Shirleys, and happy I am that they have escaped. I heard that Despatches had arrived, and set off to look after them with no small apprehensions after breakfast on Wednesday, and got a sight of the *Gazette* before it was regularly published. We may now be considered as substantially at peace with all the world—the Americans excepted (who I hope will soon be sick of the contest). This suspension of hostilities is to be considered as a preliminary Treaty, and there will be no further arrangement till the definitive Treaty, which will take some time in settling. The terms of these preliminaries are very satisfactory, and I daresay none of the distant French garrisons will make any difficulty in withdrawing themselves and returning home. But I cannot help feeling that there must yet be much internal disquiet in France.

The Royal Family have hitherto acted with great prudence and judgment, but there are many about them who are much dissatisfied, and the people at present are, with their accustomed versatility, all for the Bourbons.

On the other hand, there must be many who are interested in preserving the remnants of the Bonaparte Government, and who are powerful. There are therefore materials for discontentments and disturbances, but *we* shall be out of the scrape, I trust."

FROM GEORGIANA LADY VERNON TO THE SAME.

" *Saturday, May,* 1814.

" MY DEAR MARY,—I fear that I have not any fresh dependable news to send you. Every moment brings something, but truth hard to get at, and until to-night's *Gazette* we can say nothing with certainty about the drawing-room; but this *I know*, that the Queen is very anxious to have it as soon as possible, and was in town for a few hours on Thursday to see a little about the alterations making at her house for the reception of the company.   It is an experiment—how it will answer remains to be proved.

" Was ever such a mean, despicable, as well as wicked, wretch as this Bonaparte ! I trust they will keep a sharp guard upon him.   It is thought that his last wife will not be permitted (even if she were willing) to accompany him. He should have every species of humiliation, and think himself well off that life is spared for repentance of his crimes.

" There never was so active a personage as this Duchess of Oldenburg.   She not only goes to see everything worth seeing, but goes into the very minutiæ.   At the bank the directors were dressed very smart to receive and communicate what she might wish to be informed of, but she presently questioned them out of their knowledge, and they were obliged to call the clerks to satisfy her on points of which they were totally ignorant.   I daresay she has her forefather before her eyes, and is determined to return as well instructed as the Czar Peter. I fancy she is a clever woman, and was very well instructed quite from youth.

" Entirely without *her* knowledge Madame de Staël[4]

---

[4] Anne Louise, daughter of the celebrated M. Necker, wife of the Baron de Staël Holstein, Swedish Minister at Paris ; the well-known authoress.   On account of her violent antipathy to Napoleon she was exiled from France in 1802, when she wandered over various parts of the Continent, visited England, &c.   For some time Madame de Staël resided at Coppet, on the Lake of Geneva.   She returned to Paris on the restora-

was carried into her apartment, she alone, or at best with only her ladies. The Duchess got up the moment she heard Madame de Staël's name, received her with the greatest coolness, but civility, stood all the time, so that Madame de Staël could not sit, and very soon said she was hurried by business, and dismissed her just civilly. Madame de Staël in a great rage at her reception—she deserved it by her impertinence in going.

" I heard another story, as a fact, of Madame de Staël, but do not vouch for it. It was Lady Caroline Damer, I think, who told it me—that Lady Hertford[5] had refused her being introduced to her, saying she did not wish her acquaintance. Some time after Madame de Staël met Mrs. Bankes,[6] and, taking her for Lady Hertford, went up to her, saying, how happy she was at last in seeing *la belle marquise*, of whom she had heard so much, and went on with a great deal of flattery ; Mrs. Bankes being in amaze for a time, so that it was not immediately that she could understand whom she took her for ; one does not hear so much of this lady since those grand operations at Paris and elsewhere."

We were kindly allowed to copy the following letter, and the contents are too interesting not to be inserted in my journal of this year :—

tion of Louis XVIII., where she died in 1817 (but was buried at Coppet).

[5] Isabella, eldest daughter and co-heir of Charles Ingram, ninth Viscount Irvine, wife of second Marquis of Hertford, K.G., Lord Chamberlain, &c. Lady Hertford became celebrated from her *liaison* with George IV., which continued for some years, but she was afterwards superseded in the King's favour by Elizabeth, Marchioness Conyngham.

[6] Frances, wife of Henry Bankes, Esq., of Kingston Lacy, for many years M.P. for Dorsetshire.

[PRIVATE.]

EXTRACT FROM A LETTER FROM CAPTAIN USHER, R.N., OF
H.M.S. "UNDAUNTED."

"*Off Corsica, May* 1*st*, 1814.

"I need not tell you with what humble gratitude I
thank God that this long and sanguinary war has at
length terminated, and with so much honour to our
country : the sacrifices that have been made by us for
the good of mankind have been unexampled in history.

"It has fallen to my extraordinary lot to be the gaoler
of the instrument of the misery that Europe has so long
endured, and I am sure you will believe me when I say,
that so far from allowing him to think that I bear in
mind any animosity towards him by a recollection of
what my country has suffered, I endeavour by my attentions to quiet his uneasy mind.

"It appears to me a dream when I look back six
months and see all Europe, prostrate at his feet, and now
absolutely my prisoner—it is a glorious finish to my
services.

"As Count Klam, Aide-de-Camp to Prince Schwartzenburg, will set off immediately for Paris and take
charge of my letter, I have only time to tell you that on
the 16th of April the white flag was displayed at Marseilles by the inhabitants, and out came to shake hands
with me my former enemies, but now my friends.

"I pushed into the anchorage before the town, but not
without meeting with some opposition from the military,
a battery having opened their fire and struck us—this
appeared to me such an act of treachery that I opened
my broadside, and in ten minutes silenced them, for I
now saw the inhabitants assembling on the ramparts
waving white handkerchiefs.   This determined me at all

hazards to anchor, soon after which the Lord Mayor and the municipality came off (forced by the people) to apologize for the act of hostility, and until they were assured that I was satisfied with the apology the town was in quite a state of insurrection. I immediately went on shore with Captain Napier (of the *Euryalus*, under my orders), and we were received by 50,000 people, who literally carried us to the Town Hall, where a speech was made by the municipality, after which we were carried to the Governor's, and with him and all the authorities went to hear the *Te Deum* chaunted. We then went in procession round the town, amidst shouts of the loudest joy and enthusiasm—" Vive l'Angleterre!" "God save our saviours, the English!" Such a mixture of mad joy and melancholy as was never before witnessed. I assure you I saw thousands of women with their hands clasped extended to Heaven, bewailing the loss of husbands, brothers, sons, &c., but partaking of the general joy of deliverance from a tyranny that cannot be conceived, much less described.

" When we returned to the Governor's the mob assembled round his house. He requested that we would drive out in his carriage about the town to satisfy curiosity : when we drove up to a part of this magnificent city where none but royalty are allowed to enter in a carriage, the mob tore down the iron rails, and we drove in. Our carriage was then stopped, and ladies came forward begging to be permitted to shake hands. We were soon suffocated with kisses. We then made a speech which was cheered by the loudest huzzas from 50,000 people.

" At church, at concerts, the opera, all places were alike, you could hear nothing but ' Vive les Anglais!' ' Vive Louis!' &c.

"When I entered the opera in the evening, they hurrahed for half an hour. I harangued and called out 'Everlasting peace and friendship with our *brothers* the French.' They called my idea *sublime*, and cheered with loudest acclamations. What a people!

"Now for Napoleon. On the 25th, Colonel Campbell drove into Marseilles, nominated by Lord Castlereagh to attend Napoleon. He said that he came by the express wish of Napoleon to request I would go round to St. Tropez (where it was intended he should embark), as he did not consider himself safe on board a French frigate which was ordered to convey him to the island of Elba. Next day I arrived at St. Tropez, but found that Napoleon had altered his route and was at Fréjus (a singular circumstance, as it was at Fréjus he landed when he returned from Egypt). At one o'clock I arrived and was introduced to the Russian Commissioner, Count Schouvaloff; Austrian, General Kochler; Prussian, Count Truxas; English, Colonel Campbell; and Count Klam, Aide-de-Camp to Prince Schwartzenburg. Soon after my arrival, Count Bertrand (Grand Mareschal) informed me that it was the Emperor's wish to see me. (He is still acknowledged Emperor and Sovereign of the Island of Elba.)

"When I was presented, he said that he was once a great enemy to the English, but now he was as sincere a friend. He said we were a great and generous nation. He then asked me about the wind, weather, distance to Elba, and other nautical questions. He then bowed and retired. He was very dignified—still the Emperor. I received his commands to dine with him; there was at table the Russian, Austrian, Prussian, and English Commissioners and the Grand Mareschal. The conversation was most interesting. He laughed when I asked him if he did not issue his Milan decree for the purpose of forcing America to quarrel with us, which he did not deny. He said all his plans were on an immense scale and would have been finished in four or five years. I have not time to repeat this interesting conversation.

"That night we began and embarked all his carriages, six in number, and immense baggage. Next morning he sent for me, asked how the wind was, and made up his mind to embark at eight in the evening. At seven o'clock an immense mob formed round his hotel; he sent for me and I remained half an hour alone with him. His sword was on the table and he appeared very thoughtful. At one time there was a great noise in the street. I said to him, 'The French mob are the worst I have seen.' He answered, 'They are a fickle people.' He then appeared in deep thought, but recovering himself, rung the bell and ordered the Grand Mareschal to be sent for— asked if all was ready.

"Being answered in the affirmative, he turned to me and said in his usual quick way, 'Allons.' The stairs were lined on each side with ladies and gentlemen. He stopped a moment and said something to the ladies which I could not hear. He then walked to the carriage and called for me (not a safe berth). He then called the Austrian Commissioner and the Grand Mareschal. I sat opposite to him and we drove off. My boats were about two miles from the town. We were accompanied by a Hungarian regiment of cavalry: it was a delightful moonlight night, the country which we passed through a Paradise.

"When the carriage stopped, the bugles sounded and the regiment was drawn up. What an interesting scene now opened: the bugles sounding, drums beating, neighing of horses, people of every nation of Europe to witness the embarkation of this man who had caused such misery to them all. I told him that the boat was ready and we walked together to her. He was handed into the boat by a nephew of Sir Sidney Smith, who is my fourth lieutenant—rather an odd coincidence, Lieutenant Smith had been confined in prison seven or eight years. I introduced. The Emperor seemed to feel his conscience prick him. He only said, ' Nephew to Sir Sidney Smith! I met him in Egypt.'

" When we went on board he walked round the ship. My people crowded round him, and for the first time in his life he felt confidence in a mob. His spirits seemed to revive suddenly, and he told me the next morning that he had never slept better.

" Next day he walked about the ship, asked me a thousand questions, and seemed quite initiated in all nautical matters.

" At breakfast and dinner there was a great deal of conversation. He spoke of the Scheldt expedition. I asked him if he thought we would have been able to succeed. He said ' No,' and turning a little towards the Austrian Commissioner he said, ' I wrote from Vienna that the expedition was intended against Antwerp.'

" He told me that his principal motive in annexing Holland to France was for naval purposes, and that he thought the Zuyder Zee particularly well adapted for exercising his conscripts. At breakfast one morning the Emperor asked me to bring-to a neutral brig that was passing. I said, laughing, that I was astonished his Majesty should give me such an order, as it was contrary to his system to denationalize. He turned round and gave me a pretty hard rap, saying, ' Ah, capitaine.'

" When we were passing the Alps, he leaned on my

arm for half an hour, looking earnestly at them. I told him he once passed them with better fortune. He laughed and liked the compliment. He told me that he had been only once wounded, and in the knee by an English sergeant. He looks uncommonly well and young. He is changed much for the better, being now very stout.

"He showed me a portrait of the King of Rome, who is very like his father. He likewise showed me one of the Empress, who is rather pretty.

"We had a smart gale. When off Corsica the Emperor asked me to anchor off Ajaccio, the place of his birth, but the wind changing made it unnecessary. In the gale I told him I had more confidence than Cæsar's pilot —the compliment made him vain."

THE MARCHIONESS OF LANSDOWNE TO MISS VERNON.[7]

"*Paris, Rue Neuve des Petits Champs, No.* 89,
"*May,* 1814.

"MY DEAR AUNT,—It was quite impossible to have a more prosperous journey than we had. We landed at Boulogne Monday afternoon, and arrived here Wednesday evening, having never been delayed by the want of horses, and having found the country in a state of the greatest tranquillity, which is ensured by a Prussian garrison in every village. We have a very pretty apartment, very clean, and beautifully furnished with satin,

---

[7] Elizabeth, youngest daughter and co-heiress of Richard Vernon, Esq., and of Lady Evelyn Gower, daughter of first Earl Gower, and widow of John Fitz Patrick, first Earl of Upper Ossory. Miss Vernon always resided with the Honourable Miss Fox (sister of Henry Richard, third Lord Holland) at Little Holland House, Kensington, which adjoined the grounds of Holland House. Miss Vernon died 1830. Some pretty lines were addressed to the "Three Miss Vernons" by the Honourable Horace Walpole.

in a private house with a balcony, from which I can see all that is going forward when I remain at home. I saw the gardens of the Tuileries yesterday, and whilst we were walking the King and Royal Family went to mass, and then came forward and showed themselves to the people: the applause was not great.

"'Madame'[8] is evidently the person who excites most feelings of enthusiasm. We dined with Mr. Vernon[9] and Lord Gower[1] at a restaurateur's in the Palais Royal, and afterwards went to the Théâtre Français, where I was charmed. One hears and sees so well, and the audience are so attentive that it must be a pleasure to act to them. To-night Lady Castlereagh is to take me with her to the opera. These are all the events that have taken place in the day and half I have been here: none of much importance as yet, as, excepting Lord Wellington, I have not seen any of the great men.

"There is, by all I hear, a dreadful want of society, therefore we have judged well in coming for a short time.

"I shall hope for a letter to-morrow: the wind has been so fair that the Packet must be over in a minute.

"Lord L. is gone to see M. de Lévis,[2] but I am obliged to close this before he returns, so cannot tell you whether he has seen him."

[8] Marie Thérèse, daughter of Louis XVI., married, 1799, Louis, Duc d'Angoulême, nephew of Louis XVIII., and died at Frohsdorf, 1851. She was staying at Lulworth Castle with her husband and father-in-law, Charles X., after his escape from France in 1830.

[9] Son of the Archbishop of York and of Lady Anne Leveson, daughter of the first Marquis of Stafford.

[1] Eldest son of the first Duke of Sutherland; born 1786; succeeded as second Duke in 1833; died 1861.

[2] Pierre Marie Gaston, Duc de Lévis, a French author.

FROM MISS VERNON TO LADY H. FRAMPTON.

"*Little Holland House, May,* 1814.

"MY DEAR LADY HARRIOT,—If I had had any news to have sent you it should have gone before this; but we have been in expectation since Tuesday of seeing Lord and Lady Lansdowne, and I parted with the dear children, who were looking better every day while they remained here. It was only last night, about eight o'clock, that they arrived at Lansdowne House, having been delayed four days at Calais, and of four Packets that sailed they were the last to reach Dover. Lady Lansdowne looked well; in the greatest possible delight with Paris and everything she had seen. I saw her only for half an hour, and cannot tell you much of their conversation: one talks and hears, but sitting down to write it becomes more difficult. They say there is more conversation about the new dress for Court, and the fashion of the head, high bonnets, &c., than of the Constitution.

" The Emperor of Germany is the one most difficult to deal with, the King of Prussia the favourite, and the Emperor Alexander the showman and hero. At the opera the applause was great, and all allusions caught at.

" The King rose, bowed, and pointed towards Madame, who cried much, and was quite overcome: the whole had a great effect. The other crowned heads were not present —at least not to be seen—but left all properly for the Bourbons; but the Russian commander of the troops in Paris, Count Sacken, had the bad taste to appear in the King's box and to show himself forward, which shocked every one, and was in the barbarian style.

" Lord and Lady Lansdowne breakfasted with

Joséphine [3] at Malmaison, and liked her much. Lord
Lansdowne declares that Louisa shall not disguise herself
with the high French head-dresses, but they agreed that
they would dress up Lady Elizabeth Feilding if she would
consent; but though she was shocked at the proposal
last night, I am not sure if she will not meet the new
fashions half-way at least. I never saw her look better
than last night.

" They think the difficulties seem to be got over, and
that the Peace will soon be signed. The King *acts his
part well*, but Madame is depressed, has a violent cough,
and appears really overcome and ill.

" Considering that I am going to set out for St.
Anne's Hill,[4] and have a bad pen and ink, I think I have
done tolerably to send you this scrawl, and though stupid,
compared to what it might be in other hands, will meet
your indulgence from the good intention, and show my
desire to gain your favour by my obedience !

" At home the fêtes, the balls, the Prince's quarrels
occupy us. He really wrote to the Queen to request her

[3] Empress Joséphine, born in Martinique, 1763. Mademoiselle
Tascher de la Pagerie came to France, where she married the Comte de
Beauharnais, Maréchal-de-Camp to the King and Minister of War,
who perished on the scaffold, 1793. Madame de Beauharnais herself
was a long time in prison. In 1796 she became the wife of Napoleon
Buonaparte, who divorced her for "reasons of State" in 1810. The Empress Joséphine died at Malmaison, and was interred in a vault in the
parish church of Ruel, June 3rd, 1814. The funeral ceremony was performed by the Archbishop of Tours, &c. Her son, Eugène Beauharnais,
subsequently Duc de Leuchtenberg, was made Viceroy of Italy by
Napoleon in 1805.

[4] Near Chertsey; at that time and until her death in 1842 the residence of Mrs. Fox, the widow of the Right Honourable Charles James
Fox. It was a mere cottage when Mr. Fox first went to live there, and
he planted nearly every tree. St. Anne's Hill is now the favourite
country residence of Lady Holland. The house is much altered and
enlarged, and the whole place improved.

to forbid the Princess of Wales appearing at the Drawing-room. The Queen wrote a civil letter to her, and enclosed this pretty request. The Princess, of course, gives up going, but wishes to know why she is forbid, and talks, as usual, of appealing to the public.

" White's[5] have given their tickets for the Royal Family to the Regent, and he excludes the Princess, of course, but they say also the Duke of Gloucester and his sister, the Princess Sophia, which does appear most extraordinary.

" Boodle's Club invite the Royal Family themselves and the Princess; therefore it is expected that the Prince will not go.

" Most sincerely yours,

" E. VERNON."

SIR GEORGE PAUL[6] TO LADY H. FRAMPTON.

" *Hill House, Minchin Hampton,*
" *May 24th,* 1814.

"MY DEAR LADY HARRIOT,—I have received a letter, written in a female style, with the Dorchester post-mark. It begins with a scratch for a place of date, and ends with a mark for a name, but neither the one or the other, or both combined, would lead me to ascertain the place whence, or the person by whom I had been flattered by the honour of the address. Fortunately, however, a part of the general cypher was less illegible, and I discovered something about ' our family ;' hence I inferred that my correspondent must be a genealogist, and this, in my opinion, *fixes* the author to be the Lady H. F.

" Assuming, therefore, that you are the *very* lady who

---

[5] The ball at White's took place on June 22nd, 1814.

[6] Sir George Onesiphorus Paul, Bart., of Rodborough, Co. Gloucester, a great friend of the Strangways family.

has done me the honour to address her wishes to me,
and that I have been so fortunate as to decypher her
meaning, I reply. Having opened your letter *first* by
the post, I received the first intimation of a design *in
action* by the club at Boodle's to give a fête in compliment of the present fortunate and distinguishing
hugging of the Kings and Emperors of Europe.

" On opening my next letter it was from a Boodle's
friend, giving me an account, not only of the purpose to
give a fête, but of the many extraordinary warlike circumstances attending this intended compliment to peace.
It is true, as you have supposed, that a subscription was
opened, and instantly 400 names were subscribed to the
purpose. In the midst of this union of design, our most
excellent Prince Regent threw a firebrand into the Society,
and all is intestine war between courtiers and country
gentlemen.

" It appears that the most noble managers of White's
ball, in order to oblige the Prince by excluding his dear
wife, had agreed to refer to the Prince Regent himself
the power to invite the members of the Royal Family.

" This excluding principle was (it seems) by certain
courtiers proposed in the club at Boodle's ; it was objected
to, and a ballot demanded on a question, and that question
was negatived by three balls to one. It was then ballotted
—' That the *managers* do invite *all* the Royal Family, as
done at the fêtes before given by the club,' and this
question was carried by a considerable majority. The
discomfited then proposed that ' The ball be postponed.'
The advocates for this point were again beaten, and it was
carried by three to one that the ball should proceed as before intended. And the next day after my friend wrote,
namely, yesterday, the managers were to be chosen, I
believe, by ballot. The most important consequence of

this convulsion is that the only person in the club fit to manage a fête (Charles Herbert),[7] and who conducted the former ones given by the club (being one of the Prince's family), declines having a part in the management. It is said that the courtiers intend to withdraw their names, but there is a question whether they can do so.

"The Regent, it is supposed, will not accept of his invitation, and will do his utmost to injure the fête. If his design should extend to the obstructing the royal strangers it will destroy your purpose in attending the fête; but otherwise I should imagine the country gentlemen will be required to do something extraordinary to render the absence of his Royal Highness less regretted.[8]

"You have addressed your letter to London, whilst, since the middle of March, I have retired to witness the works of the budding spring amongst my trees at Hill House, and this without any present determined intention to change the scene for the sight of Kings and Emperors.

"You will be surprised that any strong measures should be taken in my favourite club at Boodle's (' *There, where* I have garnered up my heart ') without my wishes and my hand in the design. But I cannot part with a beloved object by halves. I cannot take a little and decline a little of what I like.

"As to your ticket, I can, as you perceive, at present

---

[7] In the list of the officers of the King's Household for the year 1791 the name of Charles Herbert appears as one of the Grooms of the Bedchamber to his Majesty. Mr. Herbert held the same post in 1804, but is not subsequently mentioned.

[8] The ball at Boodle's Club was, after much discussion, eventually given up.

say little; because I know in fact nothing of what is designed, and being hitherto resolved (*in toto*) to avoid the Imperial bustle.

"Whether the spirit of support to my brother squires may rouse my dormant gallantry must be determined by coming events, when known. But be assured that it will be an inducement to me to engage, if only to convince you, that I cannot easily refuse a request of yours.

"Being, my dear Lady Harriot,

"Ever sincerely yours,

"G. O. PAUL."

1814.

(Journal continued.)

June.

AFTER the expulsion of Napoleon from Paris, and the first possession of that city by the allied armies, all the great Princes and generals—the Emperor of Russia and King of Prussia setting the fashion—came to England, where the madness to see persons who had become so famous was carried to an extravagant height : people from the most distant parts of England flocking to London to get a peep from a garret window or an area grating at a hero or a Prince as they passed.[9]

[9] June 6th, 1814. The Emperor of Russia, the King of Prussia, Prince Royal of Prussia, and his brothers, Marshal Blucher, Count Hardenburg, Baron Humboldt (the King's Chamberlain), Count Nesselrode, General Czernischeff, Sir Charles Stewart, our Ambassador at Vienna (subsequently third Marquis of Londonderry), &c., landed at Dover with H.R.H. the Duke of Clarence from the *Impregnable*, which was escorted by the *Royal Sovereign* and *Royal Charlotte* yachts, and the next day proceeded to London. The Emperor went to the Pulteney Hotel, where he was met by his sister, the Grand Duchess of Oldenburg. He showed himself at the balcony, and shortly afterwards paid a visit to the Prince Regent in a private manner. The Prince had had apartments newly fitted

My mother not going from home, and being too old to be left alone, I remained at Dorchester with her, receiving those nephews and nieces from Moreton and Cliff who were too young to accompany their parents on such a sight-seeing expedition.

My brother, James Frampton, went to stay with our aunt, the Dowager Lady Vernon—a widow since June, 1813—and Lady Harriot, to Lansdowne House.   Later in the season the Framptons took a house in Clarges Street.

In default of personal narrative, I will give extracts from letters daily received by us.

From C. B. Wollaston to his Sister.

"*Temple, June 3rd,* 1814.

"MY DEAR MARY,—Your letter of last week reached me at Radwell, and I felt much obliged for it, but I am vexed at my mother's cold, as it will discourage her from getting out in any weather.   On Wednesday I returned home from Hatfield, where I left Dr. and Mrs. Arnold, who were intending to stay there a few days longer.   We had had a walk in the park on the preceding evening, and it was rather pleasant, but not summer-like, but on Wednesday morning I scarcely ever had a more disagreeable drive in a cold, blighting, *thick* east wind.

" I went into the park to see the Drawing-room company, and happened to be just in time to see the Prince pass, or rather I should say the Horse Guards which *concealed* his carriage.   He went at a brisk trot.   Where I was, all was silence, but in the street and near the palace I understand that he was *hooted* and shouted at,

up for him in the Duke of Cumberland's house at St. James's, but the Emperor preferred to remain at the hotel.   The King of Prussia went to Clarence House, St. James's.

notwithstanding that the park guns had just been firing for the conclusion of the Definitive Treaty. Nothing was ever more absurd and wrong-headed than his conduct on this occasion. If he had left the Princess without notice, she would have continued in the oblivion into which she has sunk since last year; but he has now brought her out again, and made himself so detested by the populace that he will probably be insulted whenever he shows himself, in the midst of all these potentates and the galas and rejoicings which are to take place.

As yet the Definitive Treaty is not made public. The new boundaries of France, and the conditions which the Continental Powers may finally conclude, are of more consequence than the Colonies we give up; but these important matters do not as yet appear to be arranged.

" It is now given out that the Sovereigns do not leave Paris until Saturday, probably they await the conclusion of *their* Treaties.

"If the bet you mention was on *my* having read " Thalaba " *through*, I can settle it decisively by stating that I never read one line of it.

" This, however, upon reflection may not be strictly true, for I remember Bowles once showing me a large quarto, and reading out of it, or with me, a passage which he considered as very fine. It is possible that there may be a mistake between Southey's "Thalaba " and his " The Curse of Kehama." The latter I never read through, and most probably never shall, but I was much struck by some extracts from it in the *Quarterly Review*, and *talked* of buying it and reading more, though I have never yet done so. I believe we must buy one of the horizontal thermometers.

" Yours affectionately,
" C. B. WOLLASTON."

THE DOWAGER LADY VERNON TO MARY FRAMPTON.

"*Saturday, June 4th,* 1814.

"MY DEAR MARY,—I write to-day, though I have nothing particular to say. Georgiana has received Selina Shirley's letter this morning, and I am glad they are to have a private lodging, as at this particular bustling time an hotel would have been most comfortless. By that I find that Lady Harriot is of the party. I wish I could accommodate both husband and wife, but that is not possible, as I have only one small room for James.

" The town is full of nothing but this very unpleasant business of the Prince and Princess of Wales. At this time, which should be all gaiety and happiness, to have such a cloud, and really brought about by the intemperance of the Prince, I do think is vexatious, and throws a damp on everything and everybody—filling some with extreme wrath (Charlton Wollaston, for instance), and others almost in despair. There is little doubt the Lady has been lying quietly by to take advantage of any false step of her amiable husband, and that it was imprudent in the extreme to give her this opportunity of complaint. She has roused the world again most strenuously in her favour, and every one must say, whatever their opinion may be of her, that *he* is greatly in the wrong. The manner in which he is talked of by all ranks of people is frightful, and should our excellent King be taken off shortly, the consequences are greatly to be dreaded.

" I heard lately that the only pleasure his Royal Highness now has is *expense* of all sorts, and the sums of money he throws away is beyond all belief.

" I fancy the rough treatment the Prince met with on his return from Buckingham House alarmed him not a little.   He did not attend Lady Bridgewater's[1] assembly last night, as proposed, and you see the business in the House of Commons.   Her Royal Highness's letter to the Speaker is violent, and shows the blackest intentions, and how it will end, Heaven only knows.

" Our weather is dreadful, damp and bad, and makes my poor arms ache without mercy. I hope Mrs. Frampton is not the worse. I cannot but wish your mind sufficiently at ease to have accompanied this party, but I know you would have had no enjoyment, so forbear saying more on the subject. I was very glad to get an invitation for the Shirleys to Lady Anson's ball, as it will be capital in its way. I saw Lady Ilchester on Wednesday. Lady Theresa is a nice, upright little child.

" To-night the Harbords[2] are going to see Mr. Kean in ' Iago ;' good judges of acting are highly pleased with Kean. We see a strong sort of connection in air and gentlemanlike appearance. He never is out of his part for a moment, entirely absorbed in the character he undertakes, and nothing for an instant draws him from it—that is excellent. He has kept low company, and it will be difficult to draw him out of such society, which produces in some instances bad taste. I, of course, speak others' language, but take my opinion from the best judges I converse with.

[1] Charlotte Catherine, only daughter and heiress of Samuel Haynes, Esq., married, 1783, John W. Egerton, seventh Earl of Bridgewater, a general in the army, who died (s.p.) 1823.   On the death of his brother, the *last* Lord Bridgewater, 1829, the title became extinct.

[2] The Honourable Edward Harbord, who succeeded as third Baron Suffield, 1821, married, 1809, the Honourable Georgiana Vernon, only child of George, second Lord Vernon. She died 1824, and Lord Suffield married secondly, 1826, Emily, daughter of Evelyn Shirley, Esq., of Ettington, and died 1835.

"All our plans and movements must be very late this year. In the meantime I have a very comfortable habitation, and am truly thankful for it. Georgiana has got the better of her Drawing-room fatigues, and joins me in love.

"Believe me, yours most affectionately,

"G. VERNON.

"How extraordinary poor Josephine's death just now! It was a sore throat."

FROM JAMES FRAMPTON TO MRS. FRAMPTON.

"*Park Place, June 9th,* 1814.

"MY DEAR MOTHER,—When I have a moment's time I always begin a letter, that I may tell you all we see and do, and send it off when the sheet is full. About an hour after I sent my letter yesterday I had a very perfect sight of the Emperor Alexander, who came out on the balcony at the Pulteney Hotel,[3] and bowed several times to the people; Piccadilly, St. James's Street, the Park full of double rows of carriages, and people on horseback and foot innumerable, to see them all go to the Queen's house.

"To-day I have seen the Emperor twice, going to and returning from Carlton House, where the Prince held a Chapter of the Garter, and invested the King of Prussia, and, I believe, Lords Liverpool and Castlereagh, with the Garter. It is very entertaining to see all the streets full of carriages, horse and foot people, to see these sights.

---

[3] The Pulteney Hotel, No. 105, Piccadilly, "Hertford House." Built by Novosialski about the year 1780, for the Earl of Barrymore, but left unfinished at the Earl's death. It was burnt, but subsequently repaired, was opened as the "Old Pulteney Hotel," and so continued for some years. In 1829, however, the house was in possession of the Marquis of Hertford.

The Emperor is very like his portraits. I should not know the King of Prussia's face again if I saw it. I also saw three little boys finely dressed in a royal carriage, with full-dress liveries, &c., who I take to be the Princes of Prussia, and a gentleman, who I believe is their tutor, with them.

" I dine at Lord Ilchester's to-day, to meet a Frenchman who was civil to him, and to help him talk French, in which Harriot will be of more use. I had rather dine at home. I may perhaps go to Lansdowne House, where there is an early party, but I shall prefer the Opera. The Drawing-room, it is said, is postponed, probably it will never take place.

" I have not yet seen Platow or Blucher. I waited some time in the crowd to-day before the door of the former, but he did not come out. Some Russian troops, I believe about 8000, are coming here on their way home, and are to be encamped near Southampton. The Crowned Heads go to-morrow to Ascot Heath Races, as it is said. Great preparations are making for the illuminations, which I think will be beautiful—they are to last three nights. I have heard that one of the reasons why White's *fête* is put off is that the Duke of Wellington may be present.

" I went through the King's Mews to-day to see these people's curious collection of carriages, and I saw more queer carriages arrive full of foreigners to-day. The Emperor gets up very early, and is out and about at seven o'clock in the morning. He went to St. James's to see the guard mounted *incog.*, and spoke to the officers and soldiers without their knowing who he was, he then went to Westminster Abbey and the British Museum. To-day, I believe, he has been to see the London Docks. They are to go to Oxford next.

"*4.30 o'clock.*

"Since I have been writing this, I have got up twice to look out of the window on hearing the huzzas of the people on some of these folks going by. The weather, luckily, is very fine. As for Blucher, he was drawn about various parts of the town yesterday by the people.

"*Friday, June 10th.*—I was at a party at Lansdowne House last night to see Blucher, but I stayed until near two o'clock—he did not come. However, I saw the Prince Royal of Wurtemberg, Prince Czartorisky, Baron Köller (who went with Bonaparte to Elba, and with whom Harriot got acquainted and heard all about it from him), Counts Metternich, Meervelt, and all the foreigners you ever heard of. Had I stayed a quarter of an hour longer I should have seen Blucher, as he came with Prince Radziwil, Sir Charles Stewart, &c. I am quite vexed with myself, but there were not ten people left in the room when I came away, and even Lord Lansdowne had given him up. He was at the Opera also, so I missed him both ways. I am glad your Dorchester illuminations went off so well; our children must have been in ecstasies at them, and the town must have been pretty by Mary's description. I am delighted that Lord Cochrane [4] and Co. are found guilty. I suppose they will be expelled the House. Nothing could be clearer, I am told, than the evidence.

"*Saturday, three o'clock.*—I had a very good view of Blucher this morning. On the multitude cheering him he came to the window and bowed. To-night they are all to be at the Opera. I dine with Dr. and Mrs.

---

[4] This refers to the famous trial of Lord Cochrane, Honourable Arthur Cochrane, and M. de Berenger, &c., respecting the fraud practised on the Stock Exchange, and conspiracy for raising the funds, which took place June 8th and 9th, 1814.

P

Arnold, and Moysey and I have agreed to set off from thence at seven o'clock to be able to get in. White's fête is to take place on the 20th. They are certainly to be present. There is to be a review on Tuesday in Hyde Park. On Wednesday they are to be at Oxford, as is believed, and on Saturday they all dine with the Lord Mayor. To-day the Emperor receives the City address. Harriot and I walked about last night, and saw some of the illuminations, they were very beautiful, but we could not get down to the public offices, nor could I by myself afterwards, though I tried twice.

" How very amusing is the account of all these great people at Ascot! they must be surprised at the English altogether, and the Emperor is said to be much struck with the population, and the quantity of carriages, and that all ranks of people are so well dressed. Nothing can be more entertaining than London, as everybody seems wild. The Ilchesters go to Oxford to see the sights there. I have been to the panorama of the Battle of Vittoria, which is very well worth seeing.

" Yours ever,

" JAMES FRAMPTON.

" I have seen Lady Caroline Damer this morning, who seems very well."

MRS. SHIRLEY TO HER SISTER, MARY FRAMPTON.

" Friday, 10th, and Saturday, June 11th.

" We dined in Park Place yesterday, and met Charlton. Selina went afterwards to the opera, and saw Blucher very well, who was in the Duchess of York's box with some of the Prussian Princes. The Harbords walked home from the opera. The illuminations were very beautiful indeed. We were in a great crowd yesterday morning, as we went to the King's Mews to see the foreign carriages. There were ten standing there, and more not far off. We met three more arrivals of foreigners in Prussian regimentals. They shook hands with the mob in passing, as the people held out their hands to them, and which, as the carriages are so low, could easily be done. I never saw anything like London now—so very gay and full. I have not yet seen the Emperor, but mean to sit in my carriage opposite his house, and by that means they say it may be done, as he comes to the window when the mob call for him to appear. He is very early, and goes about unattended with his sister.

" The dresses for White's ball are all silver ; Selina's, though not an expensive one, will cost 20*l.*, I daresay. The ball is put off till the 22nd. It is said the Regent deferred it in hopes of Lord Wellington's arrival.

" Only think of a report last night that he was murdered in Spain ! I have heard from Charles [5] that he is detained at Bordeaux by a sprain in some frolic during a leave of absence, after escaping in so many battles. He hopes to join his regiment at Passages, and to return soon with them.

" His brother William is coming all through France with his hussars.

" The Royals and grandees are all gone to-day to Ascot Races. I hope the Regent is becoming more popular again, with the mob at least. They say that Lord Liverpool has spoken to the Prince on the subject. He and Lord Castlereagh have each received the Order of the Garter.

" *Saturday*.—A magnificent ball at Lady Anson's,[6] or

[5] Charles, second son of Mrs. Shirley, then in the Coldstream Guards.

[6] Frances, sister of Sir Frederic Hamilton, Bart. ; wife of General Sir George Anson, G.C.B., &c., brother of first Viscount Anson, sub-

I should rather call it assembly, for there was a great crowd and very little dancing. I remained until near three o'clock, and then went away just before supper, leaving Selina with the Harbords; they came home at six. There were a great many of the Princes, &c., but not the Emperor, or King, or Blucher, or Platoff.

" The Prince of Orange slightly trod on my foot in the crowd, and very civilly turned round to beg pardon. He is unfortunately plain and mean-looking, but seems to have a very pleasing and quiet manner.

" The two Princes of Prussia were dancing in the same set with Selina; one of them with a pretty Miss Fitz-Clarence.[7] They are nice-looking youths. The odious Prince of Wurtemberg was there—a fright in all ways; and Mecklenburg, &c., also Count Schwartzenburg's aide-de-camp, a great man, I was told. I saw Sir Charles Stewart introduce him and several others to Lady Anson, and heard them making the Emperor's excuses, ' La cause un diner à Frogmore.' All this made it very entertaining."

FROM MRS. FISHER TO MARY FRAMPTON.

"Windsor, June 11th, 1814.

" You are so interested in all that concerns your friends, that I must tell you I had a good view of all these Royal personages at Ascot Races on Friday. The Emperor of Russia and Duchess of Oldenburg I saw better than any of the others, as they were in an open carriage, and made a half-minute stand close to us. The Emperor has certainly quite an English face.

" I do not in general like a crowd, but I ventured into

sequently Equerry to the Duchess of Kent, Groom of the Bedchamber to Prince Albert, and Governor of Chelsea Hospital; died 1839.

[7] Sophia, married, 1825, the first Lord de L'Isle.

a pretty great one in order to get a good sight of all the Royal strangers when they had taken their station in the stand prepared for them; and I saw the King of Prussia, the Regent, the Duchess of Oldenburg, the Queen, the Princess Augusta, the Emperor of Russia, all standing side by side as I have named them. I was retiring much gratified and well satisfied, when a cry was raised that Marshal Blucher was coming. The air resounded with the cheers the populace gave him, and in a few minutes after arrived General Platoff, the latter being the only person in regimentals.

"I really wish that the Emperor and King had worn some mark to distinguish them, as the common people could not know who they were, they were so plainly dressed. When I was trying to get a peep at Blucher, a farmer-like looking man told me I was too short to get into a crowd. I could not resist answering him, 'So I am, but yet I have as much curiosity to see Marshal Blucher as if I was taller.' He then said to a gentleman who was with me, 'Let us lift the lady up,' and in a moment I was seven feet high and saw all perfectly.

"I was glad to hear the Regent cordially cheered; the Queen and Princesses also; but Blucher and Platoff were the cry, and the populace appeared ready to eat them up. They will have but a poor idea of an English horse-race, as they stayed only for one heat, and that an indifferent one.

"They came to see the Castle here, but so *incog.* that very few people had an idea it was them. They were afterwards entertained at Frogmore, and the Queen very goodnaturedly asked all the Eton boys to a collation in Frogmore Gardens, where they had a fine sight of all the Royal Family.

"When Marshal Blucher came into the garden he

saluted Miss Eliza Cookson,[1] a very pretty-looking girl, and the Etonians gave him a cheer when he did so. He saluted Mrs. Keate,[2] whom he had known as a child. Miss Poole, the housekeeper, and the Queen's dressers, who all came forward to get a sight of the Marshal, were also saluted."

C. B. WOLLASTON TO MARY FRAMPTON.

"*Friday, June* 10*th.*

" Though you probably have letters from all quarters, yet you will not regret the numbers in such entertaining times. The streets are now a constant assembly in the neighbourhood of the residence of these great personages. Carriages, horsemen, and foot-passengers of all descriptions and qualities being constantly on the look-out.

" I have been Emperor-hunting two mornings. On Wednesday I was upon the watch near Buckingham House, but was obliged to go away in order to be ready for dinner, with Mr. and Mrs. Stanhope in Tylney Street, just before the Emperor passed. Yesterday morning I found all the world assembled in Pall Mall and St. James's Street in order to see him pass to Carlton House, where there was an Investiture of the Garter, and I got a sight of him as he returned. I could have no doubt of his person from the likeness to the prints of him, but particularly to one with a full face.

I dined in Park Place, and went to the opera with the Harbords and Selina Shirley, without any expectation of the presence of any of these grandees; but in the course

---

[1] Daughter of one of the Canons of Windsor. She was extremely pretty.

[2] Wife of John Keate, D.D., Head Master of Eton College at that time, 1809 to 1834.

of the performance, Blucher [3] came into the Duchess of York's box with her Royal Highness. The opera was quite forgotten, and everybody was up and upon the benches : there were besides, several other of the Princes and generals and many foreign officers in different parts of the house. I wish they would all go about *ticketed*—it would save a great deal of trouble in finding out their names. Blucher, however, could not be mistaken. After the opera " God save the King " was sung. The illuminations were very splendid, the finest are amongst the public offices: and most particularly at Somerset House. There were also fireworks let off from the top of the Horse Guards.

" A very unpleasant report was circulated in the evening, of the Duke of Wellington being assassinated, but it does not appear to have the slightest foundation, and the *Sun,* in which Paper alone it appeared, ought to be punished for inserting it.

" Everybody, King, Emperor, and all, are gone to-day to Ascot Races, so the town is comparatively quiet this morning.

" The Proclamation of Peace is to be on Thursday, and it is said that the Regent is to venture his person to

[3] Gebhard de Blucher, Prince de Wahlstadt, born 1742, at Rostock. During the Seven Years' War he entered the Swedish service, but subsequently that of Prussia. After the Peace of Tilsit, Blucher, although then aged seventy, commanded the Prussian Army, and eventually obliged Marshal Macdonald to evacuate the whole of Silesia. Blucher entered Paris on the 31st of March, and from that time all the Sovereigns gave their orders through him. Frederic William III. created him Prince of Wahlstadt, Field Marshal, and a Chevalier of *every order in Prussia.* He followed the Allied Sovereigns to England, where he was received with enthusiasm. On the 18th of June he arrived on the field of battle of Waterloo in time to decide the victory in favour of the Allies, refused the armistice proposed, and marched upon Paris. Blucher died 1819.

dine with the Lord Mayor on that day, with the other
sovereigns.

JAMES FRAMPTON TO HIS MOTHER.

"*June* 12*th*, 1814.

"Anything so entertaining as London at present, I
never saw; and I do not think any one at this moment
is quite sane !

"Instead of dining with the Arnolds, as we intended
yesterday, when I was just dressed and going to walk
to dinner, thinking the possibility of getting a coach out
of the question, a little dirty boy called, and told me that
he was sent to say, that if I would come to Mrs. Feilding's [4] *kitchen* at St. James's Palace, I should see a fine

---

[4] Sophia, daughter of the Honourable William Finch (second son of
the sixth Earl of Winchilsea), P.C., Envoy Extraordinary to the Court
of Sweden, 1724, Vice-Chamberlain to the Household, &c., and of
Lady Charlotte Fermor, daughter of the first Earl of Pomfret. She
married, 1772, Captain Charles Feilding, nephew of the fifth Earl of
Denbigh ; died 1815. Mrs. Feilding was Woman of the Bedchamber
to the Queen; she had apartments in St. James's Palace, and lived
with her mother, Lady Charlotte Finch, who was Governess to the
Princesses, daughters of George III. Mrs. Feilding's only son (subsequently Rear-Admiral Feilding), married, 1804, Lady Elizabeth, eldest
daughter of the second Earl of Ilchester ; died 1837.

LADY ELIZABETH FEILDING TO LADY MARY TALBOT.

[*Extract.*]   "*January* 23*rd*, 1809.

"Mr. Feilding luckily slept in the Palace the night it was burnt, and
could be of great use to his sisters, &c , saving *them* and their jewels,
&c.   Augusta, who had been confined to her bed with a bilious fever
for three weeks, was carried to the Duke of Cumberland's in a blanket.
Lady Charlotte Finch behaved heroically, and it was no joke to her at
eighty-five.   The Prince of Wales has written her a most *beautiful* letter
on the occasion, with an Agate Box of *sedative* pills, to quiet her nerves
after the fright.

"*January* 22*nd*, 1809.—About half-past two a.m. a fire broke out in
the apartments of the Duke of Cambridge at St. James's Palace.
H R.H. was in bed at the time, but happily escaped all danger.   The

sight; so off I set, and saw the Emperor, Duchess of
Oldenburg, Prince of Oldenburg, &c., and the Lord
Mayor go to present the Address—old Blucher being in
sight the greatest part of the time. In this kitchen
were Mrs. Arnold and Lady Harriot (Frampton). I
then ran back to Park Place, got some cold meat, and
set off for the opera, and never saw a more striking
sight. The Emperor of Russia, King of Prussia, and
the Prince Regent came after the first dance, and were
received with great applause, 'God save the King' was
sung, every one standing up, the house as full as possible.
The Princess of Wales came in soon after, and was
applauded, and the Prince made a bow across the house,
but whether he mistook the applause as belonging to
them, or a bow for her, or, as I suspect, a gesture
that might suit either purpose, nobody knows. After
the opera, when the rest were gone, she came forward
and curtseyed, and was again applauded. Another box,
next to the royal box, was filled by Prussian and other
Princes without end, and as you came out, at every turn
you were shown Princes of different descriptions.

"*Sunday.*—To-day I hurried my breakfast to go with
Lady Harriot and Lady Elizabeth Feilding to the Greek
Chapel. They would not admit us, but we saw the
Emperor, &c., arrive.

"Afterwards I saw Platoff[5] mount on horseback and

---

sentinels immediately gave the alarm, and, as soon as possible, engines
arrived, but at first there was great difficulty in procuring water. The
fire raged with great fury for some time, and the whole interior of the
south-east angle fronting Marlborough House, and including the first
southern turret, was entirely destroyed."

[5] Count Platoff, or Platow, born about 1765, on the banks of the
Don, subsequently Ataman of the Cossacks. After the Peace of
Bucharest (May, 1812) he joined the army destined to prevent the
French from penetrating into Russia. At the head of twenty regiments

go with his Cossacks to the park, where were the Royal Dukes, the Emperor, King of Prussia, and a long &c., —and such a multitude of people as were never before seen—some hundreds of thousands were there.

"The Emperor says he has seen nothing but *heads* since he landed at Dover. Another of his remarks was, what had become of all the poor people in England, for they appeared so well dressed, that he could not suppose there was any distress. It is quite ridiculous how wild London is : the bankers say that they had never so many mistakes in their books, bills forgot to be accepted, &c. No tradesman can get anything done. To-morrow —Monday—I hear they go to Woolwich—Tuesday, a review. Oxford, &c., follows ; and on Saturday they dine at the Mansion House. There is some idea that the Naval Review [6] will be put off on account of the expense. I hope not, as I want to give them a grand idea of our Fleet.

"*Monday, June* 13*th.*—They all dine to-day at Lord Stafford's, Lady H. F—— is to go somewhere into the house to see them. They went to Lady Salisbury,[7] last

of Cossacks, during the disastrous retreat from Moscow, he caused the French army as much harm as the cold and famine, and regained from the soldiers the booty they had taken, as well as making a great number of prisoners. When the Allied Armies were approaching France, Platoff was charged to occupy the country between the Rivers Seine and Marne, and the inhabitants long remembered the pillage and incendiaries caused by his undisciplined troops. Platoff entered Paris with the Allied Sovereigns, and accompanied them to London, where he was received with triumph, and presented by the City merchants with a Sword of Honour. He died in Russia, 1818.

[6] The Naval Review at Portsmouth took place on June 25th, 1814.

[7] Mary Amelia, daughter of the first Marquis of Downshire, married 1773, James, first Marquis of Salisbury, K.G. Lady Salisbury always kept up the habits of the last century, and went in a Sedan chair, instead of a carriage, even to the Drawing-rooms, as long as she was able to attend them. When I first went out in London, and even after my

night, and the streets at half-past one o'clock were crowded with open barouches full of ladies. I am to go to Lord James Murray's [8] one day, to be in the room with Platoff. He now lives at Lord M.'s, having procured but a poor lodging for himself. The populace do not know the names of Barclay de Tolly and of Chernitscheff [9] so well as the others, but these being famous

marriage, I used to see her occasionally at evening parties, when her Sedan chair, with porters and footmen, in the handsome blue and silver liveries of the Salisbury family, was always in attendance. She used also to have regular Sunday card parties, which custom happily ended with her life. Lady Salisbury was unfortunately burnt to death when the west wing of Hatfield House was destroyed in 1835, at the age of eighty-five.—H. G. M.

[8] Son of the fourth Duke of Athole, a Major-General in the army, subsequently (1821) Lord Glenlyon. He then resided in Cumberland Place; died 1837. His son succeeded, as the sixth Duke of Athole, in 1846.

[9] On the accession of the Emperor Nicholas, in 1825, the Minister of War, subsequently Prince Tschernitscheff, was as much esteemed as in the reign of his predecessor on the throne of Russia, and was equally renowned by his French campaigns and his previous stay in Paris. He was elegant and attractive, and although, as Minister of War, the most busy man in the kingdom, he always diffused a gay spirit into any society that he entered.

"*Paris*, 1810-11.—Parmi les Chevaliers de l'Ambassade dans la suite du Prince Kourakin était le brillant Comte de Czernicheff. On le croyait uniquement occupé du désir de plaire, tandis que son seul but était de servir son souverain en cherchant de découvrir les plans de Napoléon, afin de pouvoir les faire échouer. C'est, dit-on, à lui qu'est dû le fatal résultat de la campagne de Russie, pour laquelle l'Empereur avait conçu des plans admirables; il fut obligé de les changer promptement, lorsque M. de Czernicheff fut en possession de tous ses secrets. M. de Rovigo, dans ses Mémoires, dit que M. de Czernicheff était encore en France lorsque l'on sut qu'il était possesseur de papiers important; que le télégraphe aurait pu transmettre l'ordre de l'arrêter, mais qu'on ne le fit pas, pour lui éviter trop d'humiliation. Je crois me rappeler que sa tête fut mis à prix, et qu'il eut deux heures d'avance sur le télégraphe. Ce qui est positif, c'est que j'ai revu M. de Czernicheff en 1814, et il a dit qu'il n'avait échappé que par une activité miraculeuse au sort qui le menaçait."

people, should also be cheered. Chernitscheff has performed so many gallant actions [retook Winzengerode,[1] &c.] that it is supposed at Platoff's death he will be elected Hetman of the Cossacks. Prince Paul of Wurtemberg[2] is a sad blackguard. Lady Lansdowne was presented to the Emperor, and he kissed her hand; he likes England and London very much, and dislikes Paris."

MRS. SHIRLEY TO HER MOTHER, MRS. FRAMPTON.

"*Monday, June* 13*th.*

"While I have a few spare minutes, I begin a letter, but really the town is quite wild, we are all alike, and no one knows where they are likely to be two hours beforehand. These great people lead us entirely astray. Yesterday I waited in the crowd opposite the Pulteney Hotel, and saw the Emperor in the balcony and afterwards get on horseback and trot away. All these great people rode in the park. The crowd is so great everywhere where he is, that the Emperor says he would willingly stand one or even two whole days to be seen on London Bridge if they would let him alone afterwards. It is lucky we have not much business to do, for nothing can be done.

---

[1] Ferdinand, Baron de Winzingerode, Général Russe. After the Peace of Campo-Formio, 1797, he quitted the Austrian Army, and entered that of Russia. Aide-de-camp to Emperor Alexander I., subsequently Ambassador Extraordinary to Berlin. Winzingerode was taken prisoner in 1812, by the corps of Marshal Mortier, and, when conducted before Napoleon, he reproached him so unjustly and violently that his life was probably owing to the French marshals, who interposed in his favour. The convoy which escorted him to Metz was attacked by Général Tchernischeff, when he succeeded in escaping, and returned to Russia after the Battle of Leipzig. The Marshal died 1818.

[2] Younger son of Frederick, King of Wurtemberg, and stepson to his second wife, the Princess Royal of England, daughter of George III. He married a Princess of Saxe Hilbourghausen.

We sent for the shoemaker, Ayton, but he was gone to see the sight, so whether we shall get Fanny's shoes I know not. I went with Mr. Fremantle, the manager of White's fête, yesterday to see the decorations and the whole place which is built up, a monstrous space very well managed and very grand indeed it will be. Selina will be in luck to get to it, but I doubt if it will be finished by the 20th, they were at work on Sunday. We went to a quiet church and heard an excellent sermon before we went with the crowd. It is very amusing for a little time, being so new and odd. People are now so early too, we had a visit soon after eight o'clock this morning before we were dressed, so we could not receive the gentleman. I daresay it was to offer us a sight of them somewhere. At dinner in Tylney Street yesterday, we met one of the Stanhopes, who was a prisoner at Verdun five years, and lately returned, a wild youth. He says he lived very pleasantly there, they were civilly treated and with respect, and had much liberty, very different from our way of treating French prisoners.

" This is a quiet day, as they are all gone to Oxford, but it is now very hot here."

LADY HARRIET FRAMPTON TO MARY FRAMPTON.

" *Lansdowne House, June 14th,* 1814.

" I have been hoping every day to tell you that I have succeeded in seeing the Emperor, but until last night never arrived at anything more than a sight of the top of his head. Yesterday I got Lady Stafford's [3] leave to sit on her staircase while they all came up to dinner, and Mrs. Campbell and I had a very comfortable place on the

---

[3] Elizabeth, Countess of Sutherland in her own right, the wife of George Granville, second Marquis of Stafford, K.G., created Duke of Sutherland in 1833. The " Duchess Countess."

landing-place, and afterwards saw them all at dinner, being close behind the Emperor, King of Prussia, &c., so that except in a private party of one's own it was impossible to see them better. Mr. Frampton enjoys London more than I ever saw him do, everybody is so wild. Every street has a mob to see some famous person who lodges in it. I had a delicious treat of famous people one evening at Lansdowne House: amongst the rest I talked some time with General Köller, who accompanied Bonaparte in the carriage to the coast, and was with him at Elba nine days.

" There were twenty-two Princes of blood-royal at Lord Stafford's dinner. The King of Prussia and his two brothers are very good looking, one handsome. The Emperor is very like a fair Englishman, and very prepossessing. The fête at White's is on Monday certainly. The Grand Duchess of Oldenburg told Lady Lansdowne that the Emperor must go on the 21st, so what is to become of the Prince's fête nobody knows.

" On the populace cheering Blucher the other day very much, and almost forcing their way into his house, he brought out a bust of Lord Wellington to them, as much as to say that he desired the mob to reserve their applauses for *him*."

MR. FRAMPTON TO HIS MOTHER.

" *June* 15*th*, 1814.

" The town has been a little more quiet yesterday and to-day, as all these great folks are gone to Oxford. They return this evening.

" We went to the Opera last night: there were two new dancers who were thought good. The heat of yesterday was extreme, and we had a violent thunderstorm in the night: to-day is warm and pleasant. We go in the evening, or rather at midnight, to a ball and supper at Mrs. Walker's (Mrs. General Jones'[4] sister). I believe it is to be a waltzing ball, which I shall like to see. Barclay de Tolly[5] and others of these Generals are invited. The Emperor, King of Prussia, and all the foreigners were astonished at Woolwich, where they were shown 20,000 cannon ready for service, and everything in proportion. They say, 'Tout est beau en Angleterre,' and will not believe the scale on which everything is done until they see it.

"I have been this morning to see the Cossack horses, we could not get into the stable to them, but looked in at the window.

"We saw all Lord Cathcart's[6] Cossack horses, and his orderly man, an Englishman who had followed him

[4] Maria Antonia, daughter of Henry Swinburne, Esq., of Hamsterly Hall, Durham (author of "Travels in Spain and the two Sicilies"), and granddaughter of Sir John Swinburne, Bart. She married, 1811, Major-General Oliver Jones, son of Robert Jones, Esq., of Fonmon Castle, Co. Glamorgan. General and Mrs. Jones were in Dorsetshire during the years 1812-13, when they were frequently staying at Moreton, accompanied by Miss Swinburne.—H. G. M.

[5] Michel Prince, a Russian Field-Marshal, descended from a Scotch family settled in Livonia since 1689. In 1810 the Emperor Alexander named him Governor of his recent conquest of Finland, and Minister of War. Subsequently he was Commander-in-Chief of the Army, and under him Wittgenstein commanded the Russians, Blucher the Prussians, and the Grand Duke Constantine the Imperial Guard. Barclay beat Vandamme at Culm, and assisted at the Battle of Leipzig. He entered Paris with the Allies 31st of March, 1814, and accompanied the Emperor Alexander to London. Barclay de Tolly then rejoined the army at Warsaw, and eventually returned to St. Petersburg. He died at Insterburg, in Prussia, 1818.

[6] William Schaw, tenth Baron, K.T., K.A.M., &c., &c., born 1755. Lieut.-General, 1801. Appointed in 1807 Commander-in-Chief of the Expedition to Copenhagen; created in 1814 Earl Cathcart. He was for some time Ambassador at St. Petersburg.

everywhere, and had been at the battle of the Borodino and wore a medal for it. He spoke very highly of the Russians and Prussians, but not at all well of the Austrians. He had fortunately escaped being wounded in any action, but had had four horses killed under him, and one ball through his cloak. He seemed a very intelligent man. I believe Harriot wrote you an account of the dinner at Lord Stafford's, where twenty-two or twenty-four Princes of Royal blood sat down to dinner.

"It is doubtful whether there will be a Naval Review, from the ships being sent to different parts, but they are trying to collect them.

LADY HARRIOT FRAMPTON TO MARY FRAMPTON.

"The two boys are here, and we are contriving to get them a window for Saturday, to see the procession to Guildhall, which is no small difficulty, as windows are let at fifty guineas, so we have no chance but from Paul or Snow's[7] father and mother, as they have boys who are their schoolfellows. I saw all the great people (though no crowned heads) at dinner at Freemasons' Hall. The toast given with Platoff's health was ' The man who drew his sword on the banks of the Don and never sheathed it till within the gates of Paris.' It was a very fine sight.

"It is true, I assure you, that we can get no new bread of a morning, for, if sent, the journeymen now convey it (and lose it, I suppose) to the Pulteney Hotel, where they stay all day long. No milk sometimes, as the cows are all frightened out of the Green Park by the constant huzzas, and many people cannot get their clothes washed, as the washerwomen work for Princes and Kings.

[7] Messrs. Paul and Snow, the well-known Bankers in the Strand.

" Engagements are broken, and no one stands on any ceremony, the confusion beggars all description."

THE DOWAGER LADY VERNON TO MRS. FRAMPTON.

" I have seen all your children but Lady Harriot. James it is a delight to me to see and to be of use to, for my own gratification in the first place, and in the second to show how truly sensible I am of his attentions to me when I was particularly in need of them. He is in high health and glee, and delights in seeing London in its present wild state. It is a great pity that some public place should not be appointed that all these great people might appear in their proper situations, visible to the eye of every one. I doubt the Emperor prefers privacy to state ; one can only be sorry in that case, and say to oneself the man is in the right, but he should give up a little of his own pleasure to gratify others. I hear that he is highly gratified with the eagerness of the world to see him, and their strong expressions of regard, but wishes he could be allowed sometimes to go about in peace quietly. Our Prince Regent is never so happy as in show and state, and there he shines incomparably. The black side of his lanthorn is domestic life. It is said, but not advertised, that there is to be no Drawing-room next Thursday. The two days these great people were at Oxford seemed an extraordinary calm. Another observation of the Emperor I was pleased with—that he remarked one thing in the English he had never seen elsewhere—that they were all *heart*. The Emperor is fond of dancing, and at Lady Cholmondeley's ball picked out Mrs. Arbuthnot,[8] and danced two English country

---

[8] Harriet, daughter of the Honourable Henry Fane, son of the eighth Earl of Westmoreland, wife of the Right Honourable Charles Arbuthnot. She was a great beauty, and much admired by the Duke of Wellington.

dances with her. He afterwards waltzed with Lady Jersey, whom he admires, to the great discomposure of the Regent, who has quarrelled with her. The Emperor went to her ball at two o'clock in the morning after returning from Oxford.

"The King of Prussia [9] is of a more serious turn, and has never got over the loss of his wife, and I fancy keeps aloof with his boys when he can.

"As I cautioned you against Madame d'Arblay's novel, I now recommend you 'Mansfield Park' [1] if you meet with it. It is not much of a novel, more the history of a family party in the country, very natural, and the characters well drawn.

"Mr. Harbord and Georgiana were on Saturday at Lady Castlereagh's till near five o'clock, and saw the Emperor, King of Prussia, &c. The former dancing first with a pretty girl, a Miss Rawdon,[2] of the Moira

[9] Frederic William III., succeeded 1797; died 1840. He married, 1793, Louisa Augusta, daughter of Charles Louis, Duke of Mecklenburg Strelitz (niece of Queen Charlotte of England). She was loved and revered for her virtues. Every Prussian regarded her, and spoke of her, with a love approaching adoration. The unfeeling insolence with which Bonaparte treated her, after the Battle of Jena, is matter of history, and from that moment the health of the Queen visibly sank. She died in 1810.

In the grounds of Charlottenburg is a small Doric temple, which is the tomb and monument of Louisa, Queen of Prussia. The body lies in a vault, and above, on an elevation, is a full-length portrait statue of the Queen reclining on a sarcophagus, by the sculptor Rauch, and universally considered to be his masterpiece.

[1] One of the incomparable novels by Miss Austen. They are all true pictures of real life, and have deservedly preserved a lasting reputation.

[2] Elizabeth Anne, only child of the Honourable Theophilus Rawdon, son of the first Earl of Moira. She married, 1817, General Lord William Russell, second son of the sixth Duke of Bedford, G.C.B., Envoy Extraordinary and Minister Plenipotentiary at the Court of Berlin; Aide-de-camp to the Queen.

family, and afterwards waltzed with Lady Jersey, who is wild about waltzing, and is knocking herself up completely.

"The Prince Regent was very ill yesterday, was bled copiously, and could not dine with the Merchants.[3] It is doubtful whether he can attend the grand procession to-day.

"The Emperor is to stay till Thursday, and then I hope take his final departure. There has been quite enough of it; it makes all sorts of people so thoroughly idle from morning till night, and one cannot help feeling afraid that something unpleasant may arise, the Opposition are seemingly so much favoured by the Emperor."

JAMES FRAMPTON TO HIS MOTHER.

"*June 20th*, 1814.

"The boys came up to see what could be seen, and were in high luck. They got a place at a window in Mr. Paul's house near Temple Bar, from whence they saw the procession into the city as well as possible, and a magnificent sight it was. It is supposed that the review at Portsmouth is postponed, and that these Royal folks stay a few days longer.

"The regular London assembly ladies are heartily tired of their stay, as everybody is made uncertain by it, and they cannot have their usual dinners and parties. The entertainment at Guildhall,[4] as well as the procession thither, were very fine, I am told. We go to a full-dress party at the Duke of Cambridge's to-night, to meet the Queen, but not these foreign potentates.

[3] On June 17th a grand entertainment was given to the Emperor of Russia, and King of Prussia, &c., by the Merchants and Bankers of London at Merchant Taylors' Hall.

[4] This entertainment took place on June 18th.

"The marriage of the Princess Charlotte is certainly put off, but probably these Russian Princes have no hand in it, though I daresay they will have the blame. I sincerely wish that they were gone, for now the novelty is over, the fine world and the political world begin to pick holes and find all the fault they can. The King of Prussia is more popular at Court than the Emperor. I have an order to disband the Yeomanry, but it is as well not to announce this until it is done in form.

"There was a review in the park to-day, and a Proclamation of Peace—both worth seeing.

"The Prince Regent was very much pleased with his reception at Oxford. At the opera on Saturday his wife was applauded and hurra'd, and 'God save the King' called for. On Tuesday when she was there she was not noticed. The Duke of Wellington is not yet arrived."

FROM THE SAME TO THE SAME.

"Park Place, June 21st.

"We move into our own house in Clarges Street to-night. We are to give ten guineas a week for it.

"Instead of none of the great personages being at the Duke of Cambridge's last night, the following list will tell the names of those who attended it, and which I send for your amusement :—

"Emperor of Russia, King of Prussia, Grand Duchess of Oldenburg, Prince Royal of Bavaria, Prince Royal of Wurtemberg, three Princes of Prussia, Duke of Orleans,[5] Prince of Mecklenburg, the Hereditary Prince of Orange, looking in good spirits (and I hear he thinks himself so ill-used by the Princess Charlotte that he is not vexed

---

[5] Subsequently Louis Philippe, King of the French ; died at Claremont in 1850.

about it, but carries it with a high hand)—the Queen, Princesses Elizabeth and Mary, Princess Sophia of Gloucester, the Dukes of York, Kent, Sussex, Cambridge, and Gloucester, and perhaps some more whom I did not know. Lords Beresford, Hill, and Sir C. Stuart, Prince Gargarini, the Duchess of Oldenburg's attendant, so not much of a Prince.

" The feast at Guildhall, every one says, was the most splendid that could be seen. White's ball very magnificent and well conducted. I believe I told you that 80 and 100 guineas were offered for a ticket for this ball. Such is the temporary insanity."

THE DOWAGER LADY VERNON TO MARY FRAMPTON.

" Park Place, June 25th, 1814.

" I certainly have lost James, but I hope all may turn out for the best. Clarges Street is very near me, and we can have access frequently and at any time of need at either house.

" Mr. Harbord was at Carlton House last night. He had an invitation in a strange manner by *a list* sent from Carlton House on Sunday to meet 'the Queen.' No invitation for Mrs. Harbord. He sent an excuse, and yesterday came a similar invitation. We thought, after consultation, that Mr. Harbord must go, which he did. All the foreigners there—a stupid fine party with music. No notice taken about Georgiana. I do not believe that the Queen and Princesses knew him. What makes all this particularly remarkable is, that *he* has never been invited to anything at Carlton House since he married, and this was no card, merely a list carried about from the Prince with a verbal message. The Prince bowed, but took no further notice of him. The marriage of the Princess Charlotte and the Prince of Orange is quite at an end.   I suppose bad advisers and not a good disposition in the young Princess the real cause.   I have heard that he wrote a very proper letter, manly and affectionate, taking his leave, and hoping at the end of it she might not repent her determination.   Unless the Prince is an ambitious man, he is not to be pitied.   They are all gone to-day, except Blucher and Platoff.   They stay to amuse themselves some time longer."

THE SAME TO THE SAME.

"*June 29th.*

" The Duke of Wellington is arrived.   The members of White's Club are going to give him a dinner.   I trust he will have every honour shown him ; at present everything seems quiet.   The Duke went about six o'clock to his own house, stayed some little time with his wife, and then went to his mother, Lady Mornington, stepping out without being known, though there was a collection of people at the door.

" I believe the Prince of Orange is gone.   He is most popular, very much liked indeed, and I am sorry to say that the Princess Charlotte has not gained much ground by her behaviour to him.   You will see by the speech of Lord Castlereagh that the Princess of Wales is to be further provided for ; if got rid of, it will be a good thing. She has few supporters left, and would have had *none* but for those injudicious letters about the Drawing-room.

" There are great works going on in the two parks. In the lower part of our Green Park an immense building is erecting, supposed for fireworks, but for what *now* and when to be exhibited no one can tell.   The work is massive to a degree of strength one cannot see the necessity of.   In St. James's Park much the same work.   It will spoil our parks for a length of time.   London is in a state of quiet just now; nothing of amusement to look forward to more than common.

"I wish you had better weather for your haymaking! the mornings and evenings are more like winter or very early spring than near the end of June. I have been walking in the park with my grandson in my winter pelisse, and yet at times cold."

MR. WOLLASTON TO MARY FRAMPTON.

"*June 29th,* 1814.

"The town is in a state of quiet, and I believe many families have left it, but the arrival of the Duke of Wellington will again revive curiosity. I wish he had partaken of the festivals which have already been given, and that a stop could be put to the proposed magnificent fête at Carlton House and the display of fireworks; for with this unfortunate rupture of the Royal match and the continued difficulties respecting the Princess of Wales, there will be nothing but ill-blood and ill-humour. Her mother will exult in having been the cause or pretext of the rupture, and it is impossible not to feel provoked that so much inconvenience, if not more serious distresses, should have been brought on by the intemperate and selfish measure which again called the public attention to a person who had been deservedly forgotten and laid aside. The Thanksgiving Day and the Exhibition on the following one have rather embarrassed my plans."

JAMES FRAMPTON TO HIS MOTHER.

"43, *Clarges Street, June 29th,* 1814.

"MY DEAR MOTHER,—You seem to be so much amused by our letters that I write again to-day to tell you that there was a very splendid party at the Queen's house last night. The Regent, Duke of Cambridge, Princesses Elizabeth and Mary were there, and the Duke of Wellington, Blucher, Platoff, and foreign princes without end, and all the other fine people that could be thought of. Lady Mornington looking as happy as possible, and as for the Duchess of Wellington, it did one good to see any creature so delighted. I heard many peers say that the Duke's very modest manner of receiving the thanks of the House of Lords was quite striking, and that he gave the greatest praise to the Ministers for the manner in which he had been supplied with everything that was required. The Queen's house, which I had never seen before, struck me very much, and all these great people covered with Stars and Orders of every description added much to the brilliancy. There were a great many people there whom I knew, so it did very well, but I did not get away until twelve o'clock. I was then carried by the Grosvenors to Lady Ducie's, where I stayed only a few minutes. I have heard, but I think it doubtful, that the Duke of Wellington is to go to the bar of the House of Commons to-day to receive the thanks of that House, as there is a precedent for it. There is a fête for him at Wanstead[6] to-day. White's, as I believe I told you, is to give him a dinner; the East India Company another.

"I will write to Lady Susan O'Brien about the prints. I can get likenesses of most of them for five shillings, but the best of the Emperor is a guinea. I have bought it for myself and several of the others, thinking you would like to see them. Though we regret the cold weather for every one else, it is fortunate for Lady H., who is not accustomed to be in London in the summer."

[6] This place belonged to Catharine, daughter and heiress of Sir James Tylney Long, Bart. She married, in 1812, William Wellesley Pole, Lord Maryborough, who succeeded as fourth Earl of Mornington, 1845, and died 1857. He was nephew to the Duke of Wellington.

On the 1st of July, 1814, the thanks of the House of Commons were formally given to the Duke of Wellington for his distinguished military services.

The following extract is from a letter of Lady Harriot Frampton :—

"*July 1st*, 1814.

"Mr. Frampton is just come in highly delighted having seen everything without the least difficulty. He was particularly struck with knowing long before the Duke of Wellington came into the House that he was approaching it, from the cheers of the populace on the outside and from a great distance. A chair was placed for him, and he made a very good speech, and the Speaker [7] a very good answer. It was a curious sight to see a peer in that House, and especially one coming to return thanks for the thanks of the House."

THE DOWAGER LADY VERNON TO MARY FRAMPTON.

"*Park Place, July 2nd*, 1814.

" I write to thank you for your letter and good account of your mother. Nothing can be better than Lady Harriot, and James is enjoying everything that is going forward, particularly the seeing the Duke of Wellington in the House of Commons yesterday. It must have been a noble and affecting sight, and I would rather have been witness to that scene than all the fine shows, balls, &c., though I believe it was very overcoming. I hope I may see this great personage before he leaves England again.[8] I have invited the little Framptons, and I think Lady

---

[7] The Right Honourable Charles Abbot, Speaker of the House of Commons from 1802 to 1817, when he was created Baron Colchester.

[8] In July, 1814, the Duke of Wellington was appointed Ambassador Extraordinary and Minister Plenipotentiary to the Court of France.

H. F. will also be able to come, to see some of the fireworks and park shows, which it is now said will take
place next week.   I grieve for the park, which is sadly
cut to pieces.   We met yesterday *the* Mrs. Fitz Herbert
and her *protégée*.[9]   She was driving herself in one of the
fashionable carriages which resemble your old phaeton,
only lighter.   They have four wheels and one horse, and
go at a great rate.   One could not help moralizing, as
the road she was on was the very one where the Princess
of Wales is driven almost every day in her phaeton.   The
Princess Charlotte goes into the park daily—the only
place where she is permitted to go—and stares at everybody with perfect *sang-froid*.   At present the Prince will
not admit of the Duchess of Leeds'·resignation.   I cannot imagine how it will end."

JAMES FRAMPTON TO MRS. FRAMPTON.

" Clarges Street, July 3rd, 1814.

" MY DEAR MOTHER,—You will like to hear that I distri-

[9] Miss Mary Georgiana Seymour, second daughter of Admiral
Lord Hugh Seymour, son of the first Marquis of Hertford.   He
married Anne Horatia, daughter of James, second Earl Waldegrave (and
of Mary, daughter of Sir Edward Walpole, afterwards Duchess of
Gloucester), and died in 1801.   Miss Seymour married in 1825 Colonel
the Right Honourable George L. Dawson Damer, P.C., third son of the
first Earl of Portarlington, who died in 1856.   They resided at Came,
in Dorsetshire, after the death of Lady Caroline Damer; and Mrs.
Dawson Damer's death in 1848 was universally lamented.

In March, 1847, Georgiana, eldest daughter of Colonel and Mrs. G.
Dawson Damer, married Viscount Ebrington, now Earl Fortescue.   At
that time Prince Louis Napoleon, afterwards Emperor of the French,
was on a visit to them at Came.   He attended the wedding, and his
name appears as one of the witnesses.   That of my father is the next
on the marriage register : he was requested to sign it *immediately* after
Prince Louis Napoleon, as being the oldest friend of the family, as
well as the oldest *person* present. Mr. Frampton was then seventy-eight.
—H. G. M.

buted your pound note amongst your grandsons yesterday, which made them very happy. The Duke of Wellington was again received at the opera last night by the house all standing up and clapping and cheering, and the performers singing 'See the Conquering Hero comes.' I came in in good time for this. There are various vessels with three masts on the Serpentine river. As these were to have been jointly for the visit of the Sovereigns, the peace, and the marriage of the Princess Charlotte, and as two of these reasons have passed by, there is room for the whole to be quizzed, of which the Opposition do not fail to avail themselves. As I go to the launch to-morrow I write this to-day."

P.S. by Lady Harriot Frampton :—

" *July 4th.*

" Everybody is wild about this launch at Woolwich. It is of the *Nelson*, they say the largest ship ever built, but I fancy a *show* ship, as it is fitted up beautifully, particularly the cabin, with every sort of wood from every part of the world. Nobody knows when the fireworks are to be; some say on Friday. I am really afraid of the rockets setting the town on fire, so I heartily hope they will not take place until after we are gone, but I can get nobody to join in the wish.[1] I have not seen the ships in the Serpentine river, but they have three masts and apparently two rows of guns, though they say the lower row is only painted canvas. They were built, I believe, at Deptford, and towed up some creek to Chelsea, and thence brought *overland*, and of course Hyde Park gates

[1] The National Jubilee eventually took place on August 1st, which was also the centenary of the accession of the family of Brunswick to the throne of England, and the anniversary of the Battle of the Nile. In addition to the fireworks in the Green Park, a fair was held in Hyde Park, and a naval action took place on the Serpentine, &c.

were obliged to be pulled down to let them through. They were launched by a horse and rope on the opposite side dragging them in. This, to be sure, seems ridiculous and expensive, and appears to be universally laughed at. Mr. F. goes to-night to see Hogarth's pictures."

Thursday, July 7th, 1814, was the day appointed for the thanksgiving for the restoration of peace, when the Prince Regent went in state to St. Paul's Cathedral. The Dukes of York, Clarence, Sussex, Cambridge and Gloucester were in the procession, but neither the Queen nor Princesses took part in the ceremony. "I went to the house of Dr. Heberden, who then resided at No. 85, Pall Mall, and saw the whole procession perfectly—as well as the Prince Regent in his state carriage with the cream-coloured horses, &c. I was then eight years old."—H. G. M.

FROM LADY HARRIOT FRAMPTON.

" July 22nd, 1814.

" Last night Mr. Frampton and I were at the ball at Carlton House, given by the Prince Regent in honour of the Duke of Wellington. The rooms were all beautifully furnished and painted beautifully, but on the basement story, and were consequently so low that I think a tall man might have touched the ceilings with his hands, which took off extremely from their splendour.

"The supper laid out in one room for the Queen was very handsome, as the ornaments were quite beautiful. There were fifty covers, and the plateau down the middle of the table was covered with exquisite groups in silver gilt. The centre group was above three feet high, and each one of the figures was so beautifully executed that they might have been ornaments in a drawing-room, and everything else, even the salt-cellars, was in the most excellent taste. All was in gold or silver gilt, which made the silver plate, set out in the deep-recessed windows, look cold and poor, although in reality it was very massive and handsome.

"The plates only were of china, and I recognized them as a set of the finest Sèvres porcelain which Lady Auckland had once shown me at Beckenham, as having been a present from Louis XVI. to the late Lord Auckland,[2] when he was Ambassador at Paris, and I regretted that they should have been obliged to part with them. Each plate had a large bird painted in the centre of it.

"All the rooms were studded with W's in honour of the Duke of Wellington, who, however, seemed to do all he could to avoid notice.

"The Queen and Princesses Augusta and Mary came in their *chairs*, entering by the garden from the Park."

1815.

HON. CAROLINE FOX [3] TO LADY ELIZABETH FEILDING.

"*Milbrook, near Southampton,*
"*January 11th,* 1815.

"MY DEAR LADY ELIZABETH,—I have just heard from Bowood of your kind intentions towards me, and though I do indeed suspect they were rather suggested by the *beaux yeux* of my letter-case than my own *beaux yeux,* they shall not go unrewarded, and I will give you the gleanings of all the transalpine news I have heard (not, however, all my brother's) since we took leave of each

---

[2] William Eden, first Baron Auckland, Secretary of State for Ireland, P.C., and Ambassador to France, &c.; died May, 1814. He married Eleanor, daughter of the Right Honourable Sir Gilbert Eliott, Bart. They resided at Eden Farm, Beckenham.

[3] Sister of Henry Richard, third Lord Holland, born 1767; died unmarried, 1845.

other in the breakfast-room at Bowood on the last
morning of the old year. To begin with the latest,
therefore, first—I received this morning a beautiful ring
from Lady Holland,[4] which, had it not been for the few
melancholy words which accompanied it, I should have had
the greatest pleasure in wearing ; but really they make me
feel it like a mourning ring. She says it bears upon it
that which she thought a few days before would have
been her resting-place, viz.—a tomb—but, though better
then, she had been quite prevented from partaking in the
gaieties of the English colony, which have been brilliant
and good-humoured. Her chief amusement at home has
been listening to, or reading, the narratives of those who
have lately visited Elba, some of whom, like Mr. Vernon
and Fazakerley,[5] have been favoured with four hours' eager
and active conversation with certainly the most extraordinary man that has appeared in the world since the days
of Cæsar and Alexander. He speaks, they say, with an
indifference amounting to insensibility of past events, as
if they neither reflected credit nor discredit upon himself,
' On m'a dit que vous avez été en Égypte,' said Napoléon
to Fazakerley. ' Oui, sire, j'y ai passé quelques mois '—
' Eh bien ! Je vous montrerai une chambre Égyptienne,'
and he carried them into an apartment covered with pictures of Mamelukes, Arabs, and camels ! ' Est-ce que
l'on parle de moi dans ce pays-là ?' and hearing that one
of the Pacha's officers had assumed his name, he laughed
exceedingly, and said, ' Ainsi donc il s'appelle Bonaparte.

    [4] Elizabeth, daughter and heiress of Richard Vassall, Esq., married,
first, Sir Godfrey Webster, Bart., and was subsequently, in 1797, the
wife of Henry Richard, third Lord Holland, who died 1840. Lady
Holland survived until 1845.
    [5] John Nicholas Fazakerley, Esq., M.P., married, 1822, the Honourable
Eleanor Montagu, daughter of the fourth Baron Rokeby. They were
habitués of Holland House and Lansdowne House.

Mais que dit-on des Français ? ' 'On les admire beau-
coup *comme guerriers*.' 'Mais comme administrateurs ? '
This was a puzzling question, but he took the answer
good-naturedly—that they certainly were much preferred
to the Turks.

"From thence, by some rapid transition, Napoléon
went to Europe, and talked of the last campaign, and of
all the events of his life to which the conversation led
him. 'Things,' he said, ' were not yet settled. Mais
pour moi, je me regarde comme mort.' He spoke of
Marmont's [6] conduct with feeling and expressions of
astonishment, but without violence. Of the Bourbons he
said but little, and did not seem to consider their footing
in France as very secure. In short, for almost four hours
he talked incessantly of emperors, kings, ministers,
battles, intrigues, of his own conversion to Mahometan-
ism,[7]—of which he gave a most amusing account,—and
only seemed anxious for his guests to suggest any topics
upon which th ey wished for information.

" It is something in any one's life to have passed several
hours with such a man—to have laughed and disputed
with him (for he then bore contradiction very well), and
to have conversed quite as familiarly and with as much

---

[6] Auguste Frederic Viesse Marmont, born 1774 ; created Duc de
Ragusa, 1807 ; Maréchal de France, 1809. Marmont was the one
of all his generals the most trusted by Bonaparte, but basely deserted
him when the Allies entered Paris (1814). The Emperor Napoléon
would not believe this when the announcement was first made to him ;
he thought it so *impossible*. After the abdication and flight of Charles X.,
1830, Marmont wandered about in exile, and died at Venice, 1852.
Louis Philippe steadily refused to countenance him in any way.

[7] Immediately subsequent to the capture of Alexandria, July, 1798,
Bonaparte circulated a proclamation, in which he stated that there was
no god but God ; who had no Son nor associate in His Kingdom ; that
the French, true Mussulmen, had overthrown the Pope, who excited
Christians against the professors of Islamism, &c., &c.

ease as with any private gentleman. He took a profusion
of snuff, and once or twice, in the heat of conversation,
put his hand upon their sleeves, calling them *Mon cher*.
He spoke well of Josephine, and his mode of contempt
for any one who had more reputation for sense than he
deserved, was saying, ' C'est un homme d'esprit,' so he
called Metternich.

" Yours sincerely,

" CAROLINE FOX.

" To be quite *English*, Napoléon talked of *Tom* Bull.
Lucien[8] has accepted the title of Roman Prince—rather
as a security for his person and property than from any
value he attached to so empty an honour."

FROM THE SAME TO THE SAME.

" *Milbrook, Southampton, Jan. 20th*, 1815.

" MY DEAR LADY ELIZABETH,—Pray observe my prompt-
itude to obey your wishes. Here I am sitting down to

---

[8] Lucien Bonaparte, younger brother of Napoléon Bonaparte, born
at Ajaccio, 1775 ; Prince de Canino, 1814 ; Prince de Musignano, 1824 ;
Prince Bonaparte, 1837. Died at Viterbo, 1840. His first wife
(married 1793) was Mademoiselle Christine Boyer, who died 1801. She
was the mother of Charlotte, the wife of Prince Gabrielli, and of Christine,
who married, 1824, Lord Dudley Stuart, and died 1847. We frequently
met Lord and Lady Dudley Stuart at the old Duchess of St. Albans at
Holly Lodge, and subsequently in Stratton Street. Lady Dudley was
plain, and odd-looking, ill-dressed, and with nothing *distinguée* about
her.

In June, 1835, Mr. Mundy and I dined with Sir Francis and Lady
Burdett, where amongst other guests—Lord and Lady Dundonald, Mr.
Rogers (the poet), the Duke and Duchess of St. Albans, &c.—we met
the Prince de Canino, and I sat next him at dinner. The Prince was
very quiet and pleasant, and I much enjoyed having the opportunity of
conversing with him.—H. G. M.

The Prince married secondly, 1803, Alexandrine de Bleschamp, who
died 1855. From this union is descended the present Lucien, Prince
de Canino ; created a Cardinal, 1868. He is their grandson.

answer you by return of post; and first of all I must tell
you that I can now look at my beautiful ring without a pang, since I have had the pleasure of receiving
several very cheerful letters from Lady Holland since I
wrote to you last.   She is evidently capable of enjoying
herself, and had been to Mrs. Macdonald's, who has her
nights among the English round of routs, which Lady
Holland says, though approaching too much the size of
London assemblies, are yet brilliant and agreeable, the
parties giving being in perfect harmony and good-humour,
and living very sociably among one another.   So I have
no scandal or *tracasserie* to relate, and, *faute de mieux*,
must return to Elba, after telling you that both my
brother and Lady Holland are quite in love with Lucien
Bonaparte and his wife—the wife for whose sake he
refused sceptres, power, and even liberty, and was wise
in the preference they say, since it is impossible to see
them without being convinced of their mutual attachment.
Their manner towards each other and towards their
children is affectionate and kind, and in their *ménage*
they seem perfectly happy.   The manners of Lucien are
pleasing and gentle, his voice sweet, like that of his
brother's, his conversation sensible, judicious, and feeling,
but of rather too grave a character.   He professes himself a great friend to rational liberty, and ascribes the
evils of despotism rather to the nature of despotism
itself, than to the character of the individual despot.
Lucien's tone is to praise England, not only for the happiness of the people but that of the Ruler too, who,
being limited, cannot fall into the misfortunes of a despot.
He is ambitious of the character of a man of letters, very
anxious for the success of his poem in England,[1] and my

---

[1] "Charlemagne; or, The Church Delivered," an epic poem, in twenty-
four books, by Lucien Bonaparte, of the Institute of France, &c., &c.;

brother says, that after seeing him and liking him so much, he shall be quite unhappy if it fails. Pray, then, tell me if you hear anything or nothing in its praise, but I much fear it will escape severity of criticism more from the paucity of its readers than any other cause.

" Lucien lives upon good terms with his brother Louis,[2] and with Cardinal Fesch[3]—a ruddy personage, concerned to have parted with the goods and grandeur of this life,

translated into English verse by the Rev. Samuel Butler, D.D., and the Rev. F. Hodgson, A.M.   2 vols quarto.

[2] Louis Bonaparte, born at Ajaccio, 1778 ; created King of Holland by his brother Napoléon, May, 1806 ; but abdicated 1810, when he took the title of Comte de St. Leu. He married, 1802, Hortense Eugénie, daughter of the Vicomte de Beauharnais (who perished on the guillotine, 1796), and of Joséphine, subsequently the first wife of the Emperor Napoléon, and died at Leghorn, 1846.

Queen Hortense separated from her husband in 1807, and indeed it was from the beginning the most ill-assorted union possible. The Countess de St. Leu died in Switzerland, 1837.

[3] Joseph Fesch, born at Ajaccio, 1763, son of a Swiss officer in the French service, and brother (on the mother's side) of Maria Letizia Ramolino, mother of Napoléon Bonaparte. Educated at the Seminary of Aix, he had just taken orders when the troubles began in that country, and Fesch was necessitated to throw off his clerical dress, and to enter the army. In 1796 he became Commissary-General in the Army of Italy, then commanded by his nephew, Napoléon Bonaparte. After some time, however, he resumed the ecclesiastical habit and profession, and, on the signing of the Concordat with the Pope, was in 1803 appointed Archbishop of Lyons, and in the same year received a cardinal's hat, and was sent as Ambassador from France to Rome. In 1804, Cardinal Fesch accompanied Pope Pius VII. to Paris, to assist at the coronation of his nephew, and the following year he was appointed Grand Almoner of France, &c. In consequence, however, of his spirited and firm conduct in opposing some of the Emperor's schemes, and particularly his violent treatment of the Pope, Fesch fell into disgrace at Court, and retired to his See of Lyons, where he remained till the approach of the Austrians in 1814. Nevertheless, after Bonaparte's escape from Elba, the Cardinal followed him to Paris, but eventually retired to Rome, accompanied by his sister, Madame Mère, where he died in 1839.

but treated with respect by the Pope,[4] for his conduct while the latter was a prisoner at Fontainebleau.

"Now for Elba. Your friend Charles writes me word that Lord Ebrington spent six days there, dined with the Emperor, had a long *tête-à-tête* with him, and saw him once or twice besides. In all these conversations he was perfectly frank and unreserved, and very entertaining.

" Of Murat,[5] the Emperor said that his timidity of

---

[4] Pius VII., Bernabo Chiaramonti, elected Pope 1800. In 1804, by command of the Emperor Napoléon, he was summoned to Paris to perform the ceremony of his coronation, which took place on December 2nd, and the Pope returned to Rome in May, 1805. Bonaparte confiscated the provinces of Benevento, and subsequently took possession of all the States of the Church; but when, in 1809, he proceeded to declare Rome itself an Imperial city, Pius excommunicated him; in consequence of which act he (the Pope) was forcibly compelled to quit the Quirinal, and carried off first to Grenoble, and afterwards to Savona, from whence he was removed to Fontainebleau, where he remained till January, 1814, but was sent back to Rome in May. During the "Cent Jours," fearing Murat (who was still King of Naples), Pius VII. took refuge for three months at Genoa. All his estates had been restored to him. Pope Pius VII. died at Rome, August, 1823.

[5] Joachim Murat, born 1771; son of a small innkeeper at La Bastide (Lot). Being destined for the Church, he received a liberal education, but he entered the army shortly after having become an Abbé. Aide-de-camp to Bonaparte 1795, he covered himself with glory in Egypt, Syria, St. Jean d'Acre, Aboukir, &c. After their return to France, 1800, Napoléon gave him the hand of his youngest sister, Caroline Annonciade, to whom Murat always remained devotedly attached. Commandant of Paris, 1804, Murat created the Military Commission which condemned to death the Duc d'Enghien, and in 1806 he was created Grand Duke of Berg and Cleves, during which sovereignty his good administration was much appreciated.

In 1808, at the earnest solicitation of his sister, Napoléon bestowed on Murat the crown of Naples, when he was proclaimed by the title of "Joachim Napoléon." He quitted Naples, 1815, and took refuge in Corsica; but, endeavouring to return again to Naples, was betrayed by the captain, landed at Pizzo, where he was captured, and shot on Oct. 13, 1815. His widow took the title of Comtesse de Lipona, but was more usually called Princess Caroline. She died at Florence, 1839.

character was such, that in planning he was *presque poltron*, but in executing and in the field he was noble and brave, and always found where his activity and bravery could be of most advantage. 'Enfin,' he concluded, 'c'est un lazzarone magnifique.' Those who have seen Murat say this is excellent.

"At Tilsit (Bonaparte said) he had had a great deal of conversation with the Emperor Alexander, who, he observed, had been educated by a *philosophe*, and that they disputed about elective and hereditary monarchies ; *he* (Napoléon) taking the side of the hereditary, Alexander of the elective. 'Pour prouver,' he thinks he hesitatingly added, 'qu'un Empereur de Barbares pouvait avoir des idées libérales.'

"And here my anecdotes end ; ' Je n'en ai plus.' "

CHARLES LEMON, ESQ., TO HIS SISTER-IN-LAW, LADY
HARRIOT FRAMPTON.

"*London, April* 18*th*, 1815.

"MY DEAR HARRIOT,—We dined at Lansdowne House yesterday, and I think the account of our dinner will amuse you.   There were no wits or poets, but many very extraordinary people whom I was very glad to see.   Gallatin, the American Plenipotentiary, with his most penetrating Italian countenance, was there.   Sir James Macintosh, General Ramsay, Mr. Dumont,[6] Mr. Murray (just from Paris), and a little Frenchman fresh from the Tuileries,

[6] Pierre Etienne Dumont, born 1759 ; Protestant minister at Geneva, 1781 ; but, having adopted democratical ideas, he quitted Switzerland, and went to St. Petersburg.   From thence he was invited by Lord Shelburne, subsequently Marquis of Lansdowne, to go to England, in order to superintend the education of his sons.   Dumont was at Paris during the early part of the revolution in 1788 and 1789. He returned to Geneva in 1814, when he renounced the ecclesiastical character, and became one of the representative Council.   He died at Milan, 1829.

who knew everybody and everything. His account of Bonaparte's advance was more like what we heard than I thought the event made it possible to believe. He says that Bonaparte had certainly not more than 6000 men at Lyons, and that at Fontainebleau he had been joined only by Ney's division of 6000 more, so that even at the gates of Paris 12,000 faithful soldiers would have been in a condition to have disputed with him the possession of the place. But it was long certain to the people in Paris that not one of the National Guard would fight against him; and this little M. Pichon, who commanded one battalion of them, said that when the Comte d'Artois reviewed them on the Thursday before Bonaparte entered Paris, the conduct of General Dessolles (who was the General-in-Chief) left the impression very strongly on their minds that he had already made his terms with Bonaparte, and looked upon the whole ceremony as a piece of useless parade.

"Ney, just before he left Paris, made a demand of 150,000 francs for his corps, and the King gave him 300,000. He was met by somebody when coming out with this order, and said, ' Auparavant j'étais traître ; à présent je suis traître et demi.'

" It seems certain that Bonaparte's plot was laid long ago, though not at the time of his abdication, which some people think. This was disputed yesterday, when I suggested that if this had been the case, he would never have thought of coming to England, which by Lord Castlereagh's letter he really proposed doing. Mr. Dumont said that at a dinner given at Geneva by Lord Huntley to some officers of the regiments which were sent back, one of the party proposed the health of Bonaparte, to which Lord H—— objected, and they then gave " Le violet qui paraît au printemps." This was in

December, and at a dinner at Paris in January, at which a friend of M. Dumont's was present, the same toast was given, which, though *he* did not understand it, seemed to be perfectly understood by three-fourths of the company.

"In the French papers extracted this morning, I see that Bonaparte is very angry with Talleyrand, and if he has refused to re-rat, it will be the best symptom which has appeared for some time. I am afraid that ministers will be mistaken in the expectation that by their declarations they can make the French understand that by fighting against Bonaparte we are not fighting *for* the Bourbons, but mean to leave them entirely at liberty in the choice of their Government. Talleyrand, in pleading the cause of the King of Saxony, said that his case was the case of all the Sovereigns of Europe. "Seulement, c'est une horloge qui retarde."

Lady Caledon told my sister, Lady De Dunstanville, that the change of signs over the shops at Paris was quite like a piece of harlequinade; on the first change they had turned the faces of their boards to the wall and painted the back with Bourbon emblems, and on the second they had only to turn them back again, and the whole place was revolutionized in a moment. This was all done in one night, and the Bourbons sent to the wall for another opportunity.

"Your affectionate,
"C. LEMON."

FROM THE SAME TO THE SAME.

"*London*, 1815.

"MY DEAR HARRIOT,—*dat feci factum!* Three and a half long hours have we spent in the most useless and miserable squeeze, without being able to speak scarcely to a soul excepting the few to whom chance joined us at starting, and every one of which one wishes at Jericho for getting in the way. There were some beautiful arrangements meant to throw the press further from the Queen's throne-room, but they had the effect of making a throng at the bottom of the stairs that really was dangerous even to men. The Drawing-room always leaves me in a troubled state of mind, made up of fatigue and indignation! Charlotte was invited to the Queen's house the day before yesterday, but she was so ill that she could not go, and consequently was obliged to volunteer a morning visit yesterday to apologize—in which visit little Charley behaved very ill, and did everything most shocking to Majesty. I did not pick up many entertaining things, but you shall hear all I can recollect. The Prince passes his time in playing Patience with Lady Hertford. The new knights were presented at the Levée yesterday, and received each a small star and a large card containing a list of fees— which cards all the Navy Knights deposited in the outer room, and swear they will not pay 108*l.* each for their honour, which is not worth 6*d.*

"Lord Kinnaird has brought back a good squib from Paris. It is a conversation between two Voltigeurs, one of whom was asking of the other, the account of what had happened: to which he replied, 'L'histoire en est très courte: le tigre s'échappa d'Elbe; le monstre resta trois jours sur la mer; le traître débarqua à Fréjus; le chef de Brigands avança à Grenoble; Napoléon entra à Lyons; l'Empereur arriva à Versailles; Sa Majesté se couche ce soir aux Tuileries.'

"Good-bye, the (post) bell is ringing."

EXTRACTS FROM LETTERS OF MRS. CAMPBELL,[7] IN ATTEND-
ANCE ON H.R.H. THE PRINCESS CHARLOTTE, TO LADY
HARRIOT FRAMPTON.

" *Warwick House, June*, 1815.

" I write a line, as you desire, but to amuse you is
quite out of my power while in this fearful suspense
as to the news from the army. The reports of yesterday and to-day are very bad, but nothing is confirmed.
Lord Bathurst[8] wrote Princess Charlotte, that there
was some skirmishing on the 17th, but that the Duke
had taken up the position he *had planned* in case of the
French advancing towards Brussels, and had joined his
forces with the army under Blucher. Still I fear the
account of the death of the Duke of Brunswick[9] is true,

---

[7] Vide Note 9, page 125. After the flight of the Princess Charlotte
from Warwick House to Connaught Place (July 12th, 1814), which was
followed by the immediate dismissal of Miss Knight, a most improper
person to have been placed near H.R.H., though only in fact as " reader,"
the Prince Regent earnestly solicited Mrs. Campbell again to accept a
post about the Princess, his daughter. This she positively declined,
and, amongst other reasons, alleged her delicate health. The Regent,
however, was *peremptory*, and in fact *would take no denial*, the strongest
proof of the entire confidence he felt in Mrs. Campbell's principles, and
the greatest compliment he could pay her. The Prince Regent sent his
own carriage to No. 31, Old Burlington Street, where Mrs. Campbell was
staying, with first a *request*, and then a *command*, that she should
attend him at Carlton House; so that, although extremely unwell, she
was obliged to submit. He detained her there all night, *giving up his
own apartment to her*, and the Prince would not allow Mrs. Campbell to
leave Carlton House until she had given her consent to his wishes.

From that time she was installed as Woman of the Bedchamber in the
Princess's establishment, and, on her marriage in 1816, became her
Privy Purse, &c., which appointment Mrs. Campbell held until the
lamented death of the Princess in 1817.

[8] Henry, third Earl Bathurst, K.G., Secretary of State for the War
Department; died 1834.

[9] William Frederic, Duke of Brunswick Wolfenbuttel, born 1770;
married Marie Elizabeth, daughter of Charles Louis, Hereditary Prince of

it is stated so very particularly in the Papers. Princess C—— was much attached to him, and is much affected.

" *June 22nd.*—I send you the horrid detail. I have had a line from my brother,[1] and cannot be thankful enough that he escaped on the 18th, but still I live in terror—the intelligence we get hourly is dreadful. My brother says he never witnessed so horrible a scene, and hopes never to see the like again; only four officers of his regiment escaped. The 7th Hussars suffered dreadfully, but that is to come.

" Major Hodge is killed, and Colonel F. Ponsonby is dead. Lord Uxbridge is dead of his wound ; the leg was taken off above the knee. Lady Ilchester has been out, trying to obtain any information respecting Tom Strangways, but cannot get any particulars; it is, however, some comfort to know that he is alive, which it is said few of the artillery are, and he is not said to be dangerously wounded.

" Of course we will write to all if we get any intelligence. I am ill, and bewildered with it all. Only three of the Duke's staff escaped; my brother, Lord March,[2] and this Major Percy who is come with the news ; and the list published is what he had collected himself, not the regular return, which will be frightful. I cannot write more.   Ever yours,

"A. C——.

Baden. He was killed at the Battle of Quatre Bras, June 16th, 1815. (Nephew of the Princess of Wales, and first cousin of the Princess Charlotte.)

[1] " Colonel Dawson Kelly, who was on the Duke of Wellington's staff, but took the command of his regiment (the 73rd) at Waterloo, when the officer previously in command, Colonel Harris, was wounded. Colonel Kelly had two horses killed under him in the battle, and brought a third with a bullet in it to England, where it died at a great age at Lord Ilchester's, at Melbury.

[2] Born 1791, afterwards fifth Duke of Richmond.

" Miss Mercer [3] is just come, and says Lord Uxbridge is still alive.   Her two cousins in the 7th are wounded."

" *Warwick House,*
" *Saturday, June 24th*, 1815.

" I have not anything new to tell you.   No despatches had arrived an hour ago, as Lord Castlereagh [4] sent Princess Charlotte a message to say so ; but you have the comfort of knowing that William Shirley is safe. Lady Ilchester sent over to Captain Fraser,[5] of the 7th, who arrived from Lord Uxbridge yesterday.   His answer was that Shirley was safe, and he believed he was almost the only man who was so.

" Mrs. Gwatkin left me yesterday to go to inquire after her nephew, young Blackman of the Coldstreams.   She soon got her answer that a ball through the head had ended his troubles on the 18th.

" You really cannot conceive the state of agitation we live in, and though I am thankful for my brother's safety on that day of horrors, yet I do not dare feel that my day is not coming.

" Ever your affectionate
" A. C."

" Lord Uxbridge set out for Brussels a few hours after."

<hr>

[3] The Honourable Margaret Mercer Elphinstone, born 1798, daughter of Viscount Keith, who died 1823.   She married, 1817, Auguste Charles, Comte de Flahault, and died 1867.   Their eldest daughter became, in 1843, the wife of Henry, Earl of Shelburne, subsequently fourth Marquis of Lansdowne.

[4] Lord Castlereagh was at that time Secretary of State for Foreign Affairs.

[5] Subsequently Colonel Sir James Fraser, Bart.

FROM THE PRINCESS CHARLOTTE TO H.R.H. THE DUKE
OF YORK.

"*Warwick House, May 23rd,* 1815.

"DEAREST FREDERICK,—I quite forgot, when you were
with me on Sunday, to present Giles Strangways (which
I had promised him to do) to you, as he is very sensible
of your kindness in so immediately giving him his Commission, and he is very desirous in consequence of paying
his respects to you.

"He is to be the bearer of this letter with General
Garth, who is to present him to you. I feel quite convinced he will not disgrace the Profession, or any notice
you may be so kind as to take of him.

"Believe me,

"Dearest Frederick,

"Ever your very affectionate Niece,

"CHARLOTTE."

THE DOWAGER COUNTESS OF ILCHESTER, IN ATTENDANCE
ON THE PRINCESS CHARLOTTE, TO THE SAME.

"*Warwick House,*[6] *June 23rd,* 1815.

"Colonel Percy,[7] who brought home the despatches,
and whose list (alone) the *Gazette* gives, says that it is
impossible to do justice to the kindness and attention of
the inhabitants of Brussels to all the wounded men, as
well as to the officers. They think that they cannot do
enough for them, they feel so much gratitude for their

[6] Warwick House stood at the end of Warwick Street, which
stretched from Cockspur Street towards Carlton House Terrace, but
terminates in a *cul-de-sac*. The site of the house itself, between which
and the gardens of Carlton House there was a private communication by
a gate, of which the Princess Charlotte had a key, is now occupied by
livery stables.

[7] The Honourable Henry Percy, fifth son of the first Earl of Beverley ;
Aide-de-camp to the Duke of Wellington.

exertions, and Colonel Percy says no invalid could be better nursed at home than they are at Brussels. This is a very great comfort to all, and all the comfort we can receive about Tom Strangways till some immediate intelligence arrives from him. I cannot describe to you what I feel for poor Mrs. Shirley till the returns come.

" Tom's wound is an assurance of existence, and we are led to expect a dismal addition to the killed. The 7th Hussars have suffered very severely; Major Hodge is certainly dead, and most of the 7th wounded. Thank God, Giles [8] was not there. He regrets his absence, in which feeling I cannot sympathize.

" Dear Mrs. Campbell hears that her brother took a command in the course of the last day, and Colonel Percy, who came to answer Princess Charlotte's inquiries, says he heard that he had been highly approved. I hope the Duke will name him in the next despatch, for which we are out of breath with impatience.

" Princess Charlotte feels deeply the Duke of Brunswick's death.

" Your affectionate
" M. ILCHESTER.

" Giles tells me that he has just heard that Shirley is safe. Nearly every other officer of the 7th wounded or dead.

" The Duke of Cumberland has been here. It is rumoured that the Queen will not receive his Duchess, and I believe it. What money he will get I do not know."

---

[8] The Honourable Giles Fox Strangways, second son of the Countess of Ilchester. He had not long been gazetted into the 7th Hussars, and consequently had not yet joined the regiment. He died unmarried, universally regretted, 1827.

C. B. WOLLASTON TO MARY FRAMPTON.

" Downing Street, July 7th, 1815.

" MY DEAR MARY,—My letter will again travel amidst the shades of the laurels of the second capitulation of Paris, and Mr. —— will again have an opportunity of proclaiming this extraordinary news from the top of the coach.[9] What will happen next who can say? Louis XVIII. will, I suppose, walk (or rather be carried) quietly into Paris, but Bonaparte will sneak off, and I strongly suspect he will be found to have been in the American vessel which is said to have been edging out of the harbour of Havre, and which was followed by some of our cruisers till she was lost in a fog. As you say, the changes are so frequent and so unexpected that one has less confidence in the continuance of circumstances which at the instant are so flattering and so favourable. At all events the proud city of Paris cannot escape the historical stigma of having twice capitulated to a foreign force in two successive years. I am very sorry for, and shocked at, Whitbread's death, though I strongly disliked his line of politics.

" I am glad the question was carried against the Duke of Cumberland.[1] It is right that the Regent should

---

[9] I well remember, when a girl of eight or nine, frequently seeing the Mail coach come into Weymouth, covered with branches of laurel, in token of some great victory. My father and mother were at that time staying at Weymouth, and our house commanded the whole Esplanade, in the centre of which was, at that time, the Post Office : and on the arrival of the Mail thus decorated, which was then not until the afternoon, my father used eagerly to set off to obtain the latest news !— H. G. M.

[1] Ernest Augustus, Duke of Cumberland, fifth son of King George III., born 1771, married at Strelitz, May 29th, and in London, August 29th, 1815, the Princess Frederica Sophia, daughter of Charles Louis, Duke of Mecklenburg Strelitz, born 1778. She had previously married first, in 1793, Prince Frederic Louis Charles, son of Frederic William II.,

know that he cannot carry everything as he likes. It is scandalous in him to have given the Royal consent to a marriage with a woman unfit to be received here. It shows the badness of his principles.

"As to the Military Convention,[2] I feel by no means disposed to quarrel with it, as many are. What could be done better than removing the French troops and giving free access to Louis XVIII. if he chooses to come there? Let the French say what they may hereafter, it is a more complete conquest of their capital than that of last year, and upon what principle could the Allies stipulate for any alteration in the Government, the restoration of the King, or the delivery of any traitors, except Bonaparte, not so much as a traitor as the person against whom the war was undertaken? But there can be little doubt that he had withdrawn himself before. I fear he is not and will not be caught. Paris could not have been attacked without much bloodshed on both sides, and moreover a doubtful issue. I trust that now there will be no more fighting; and if Louis is well received at Paris, the example will be followed in every other part of the kingdom.

"Yours affectionately,

"C. B. WOLLASTON."

CHARLES LEMON, ESQ., TO LADY H. FRAMPTON.

"*Henbury, Macclesfield, August 13th,* 1815.

"MY DEAR HARRIOT,—Your threat terrified me into a

King of Prussia, who died 1796; and secondly, 1797, Prince Frederic William of Solms Braunfels, who died only in 1814. The Duke succeeded to Hanover, June 20th, 1837. The Queen of Hanover died June 21st, 1841. Queen Charlotte would never receive the Duchess of Cumberland.

[2] Convention of Paris, July 3rd, 1815.

determination of writing immediately, but it afterwards occurred to me that by waiting a day or two I should have something better worth sending you, and the picking of a man's brains who has just returned from the Princess of Wales, and has lived with all the strange people who form her society at Naples. My friend is Dr. Holland,[3] who published his travels in Albania, &c. He was physician to the Princess of Wales, and has been with her during all her tour. He gives a very different opinion of Murat from what I understand Lord Holland thought of him, and represents him as a stupid, grinning, ungainly ruffian. His Court, however, is by far the most magnificent Dr. Holland has seen, and it was supported by a tax something like our income tax, only amounting to 38 per cent. This tax, together with the total decay of their trade, has so impoverished the country that large tracts have been let pass out of cultivation for want of capital; and of the whole coast of Naples nearly two-thirds produces nothing but rushes and agues.

" It will take a considerable time before this can be restored, for these parts are now so unhealthy that the labourers employed usually die before they can drain sufficient to support them. The Neapolitans therefore were very glad to get rid of Murat, and did not much care who came after him, provided they were at peace with England.

" By what Dr. Holland says, as well as from what he does *not* say, I suspect he has seen some strange frolics in the society to which he belonged.

" If you have a soft place in your heart I think you must feel for Bonaparte. Necessary or not, it is a sad future for him, and they do not seem to have shown any

[3] Subsequently (1853) created Sir Henry Holland, Bart.

inclination to make it less so. What puts me in a passion is that the only exception which has been made to the order to admit nobody to see him has been made to accommodate Lord Lowther. Why put him before 16,000,000 of his fellow-countrymen who have never been hissed off the course at Newmarket? I rather believe we shall leave this place about the 28th.

" Yours affectionately,

" C. LEMON.

P.S.—" Dr. Holland says it was curious to see the different reception which the news of the Battle of Waterloo met with in the Prussian and Saxon States. In one they were all joy, in the latter all sorrow, and it was difficult to conceive how the same event could be a source of happiness and misery to people living within a few yards of each other."

1815.

(Journal continued.)

DURING the time of the Princess Charlotte's residence at Weymouth this year, she was accompanied, as before, by Lady Ilchester and Mrs. Campbell. Everything that was said or done was most scrupulously and jealously watched, consequently the anxiety and responsibility of these ladies in charge of H.R.H. were very great. My brother and Lady H. Frampton had a house at Weymouth during this autumn and winter (1815-16) on account of the health of their eldest son.

The Princess Charlotte arrived at Weymouth from Cranborne Lodge at the end of July, and from that time my father and mother went to the King's Lodge, with very few exceptions, every evening.[4]

---

[4] In my father's pocket-book diary are the following entries :—

"Monday, September 21st, 1815.—H.R.H. Princess Charlotte, Lady

My father used constantly to sail with the Princess, and generally also accompanied her on any expeditions— to Portland, Lulworth Cove, Corfe Castle, &c., occasionally, as at the little *hostelries* of the latter places, where the Princess had luncheon, acting as her privy purse.[5]

My mother (who disliked sailing as much as my father enjoyed it) was, however, once or twice prevailed upon to accept the repeated invitations of H.R.H., when I was included in the party on board the Queen's yacht, *The Royal Charlotte*. I well remember the Princess saying to me " Are you sick, Harriot ? " and in my confusion I answered, whilst making my curtsey, " No, *thank you*, ma'am," to her great amusement. She wore yellow Hessian boots and the high bonnets then in fashion. We had a capital luncheon in the state cabin—cold meat, &c., of course—as hot luncheons were unknown until at least twenty years after, but the Princess took

Rosslyn, Miss Cotes, and Lord Rivers dined at Moreton. The party in the house to meet H.R.H. were Lord and Lady Ilchester and William Strangways, Miss Frampton and Charles Strangways."

" October 5th, 1815.—Went to Portland with the Princess Charlotte."

" Tuesday, November 21st, 1815.—H.R.H. Princess Charlotte, Lady Augusta and Lady Charlotte Greville and Mrs. Campbell dined at Moreton. The remainder of the party were the Honourable Mr. and the Honourable Mrs. Harbord, Sir William and Lady Maria Oglander, Mr. and Mrs. Seymour, Mrs. Selwyn, and Miss E. Murray (sisters of Lady Ilchester), Lord Ilchester, Mr. Grosvenor, Mr. Lemon, Captain Stephen Digby, and Mr. Frankland, afterwards Sir Robert Frankland Russell, Bart."—H. G. M.

[5] The Princess Charlotte had also visited Moreton when staying at Weymouth the previous year.

My father's pocket-book diary says :—

" September 22nd, 1814 ⎫
" October 26th,   „ ⎬ The Princess Charlotte came in the morning.
And—   ⎭

" October 31st, 1814.—Went to Corfe Castle to meet the Princess Charlotte."—H. G. M.

her repast seated on a sofa on deck with the plate on her lap. When asked what H.R.H. would like to have, she said " cold beef," and then called out rather loudly, " with plenty of mustard."

Later in the autumn and during the winter Princess Charlotte was accustomed to read aloud of an evening, whilst the ladies at the Royal Lodge worked. She had been well instructed, and read beautifully, and my mother especially used to enjoy this, which, indeed, every one of the party found a great improvement on the sameness of the usual conversation. Amongst other works, H.R.H. read Southey's " Roderick " from a copy which my father happened to have, and, of course, the book at once became an historical possession.

MR. STAPLETON COTTON [6] TO WILLIAM MUNDY.

" *Rue de Bourbon, Paris, December* 12*th*, 1815.

" MY DEAR MUNDY,—In case you have not received my letter, I write to you again. Am I not lucky? I have been to balls, operas, and concerts every night, but have not had a day's shooting. I have got a new watch, and am quite a dashing fellow. I believe my father will give a ball on New Year's Day. Lavalette[7] has escaped;

[6] The Honourable Robert Henry Stapleton Cotton, son of the first Lord Combermere, by his first wife, Lady Anna Maria Pelham Clinton; born 1802, died 1821. He was a very favourite Eton friend of Mr. Mundy, who greatly lamented his premature death.—H. G. M.

[7] Antoine Marie Chamans, Comte de Lavalette, born 1769, son of a shopkeeper. After the seizure of the Bastille he entered the National Guard, and, always an enthusiastic admirer of Marie Antoinette, remained faithful to the King and Queen as long as any royalty existed, and being consequently compromised, his only mode of avoiding proscription was to enrol himself in the army, where he served with distinction. After the Battle of Arcole Bonaparte made Lavalette his aide-de-camp, and also conferred on him in marriage the hand of Emilie Beauharnais,

they searched our house, as it belongs to Beauharnais, a relation to Madame Lavalette.

"I have got a new horse, for which my father gave sixty guineas. They have nothing but wood fires here, I shall be very glad of an English one, they cook with charcoal. The Duke of Wellington dines here to day. How goes the new gun, and the ferrets? send me one in a letter.

"I am, dear Mundy, your truly affectionate,
"Most devoted and obedient servant,
"ROBERT HENRY STAPLETON COTTON."

1816.

MARIA, COUNTESS DOWAGER OF ILCHESTER, TO LADY
HARRIOT FRAMPTON.

"Cranborne Lodge,[8] January 3rd, 1816.

"MY DEAR HARRIOT,—I know you will be glad to hear that we have accomplished successfully our journeys.[9] We

daughter of the Marquis de Beauharnais, brother of the first husband of Joséphine, and in 1808 created him a Count of the Empire, &c.

On the return of Louis XVIII. in 1814, Lavalette was *destitué* and excepted from the general amnesty, subsequently tried and found guilty. The only hope was in his possible evasion. The execution was fixed for the 21st of December, 1815. On the previous evening, when Madame de Lavalette was admitted to a final leave-taking at the Conciergerie, she managed to change clothes with her husband, and in this manner he escaped, having friends who concealed him in Paris for a week or two. On the 10th of January, assisted by the English General, Sir Robert Wilson, and his compatriots, Captain Hutchinson and Mr. Bruce, he left Paris and reached Mons in safety; from thence he retired to Bavaria, but in 1822 was allowed by Louis XVIII. to return to France, where he died 1830. The Countess de Lavalette lost her senses, but survived until 1855. Their daughter had become the Baronne de Forgat.

[8] Cranborne Lodge was in Windsor Park. The Princess Charlotte first took up her residence there after the rupture of her engagement to the Prince of Orange.

[9] On leaving Weymouth, where the Princess Charlotte had resided

got to Salisbury at a quarter past four, and here a
quarter before five, and I do not think Princess Charlotte
over-fatigued by any of it. She tired me by sitting up
too late at Salisbury, where the Pembrokes [1] and Talbots [2]
came in the evening with Mr. and Mrs. Alfred Harris.[3]
The Queen and three Princesses came this morning;
she is indeed altered. All seemed happy to see Princess
Charlotte. The Queen was certainly very nervous, and we
talked on various uninteresting subjects, and steered
clear of all inquiries or allusion to past correspondence,
&c.

"I am sorry to say I perceive the Queen to be much
shrunk and to have lost much of her presence of mind.
We sleep at the castle on Friday night, but do not go
there before, so we shall have some rest. Mrs. Campbell
goes to London for the time we are absent. The
Princess speaks of the charms of Dorset in very gratifying terms, but does admire her Home, so she calls
this, very satisfactorily, and is delighted by the execution
of her orders in the furniture, &c. In short, there is an
air of happiness and content about her which I have not
seen before.

since July 1815. H.R.H. was very partial to that place, where she felt
more at ease and happier than elsewhere, and which also suited her
health. On the morning of her departure from Weymouth I accompanied my mother, who went to the Royal Lodge to pay her respects,
&c. When the Princess embraced Lady Harriot Frampton, on taking
leave, she could not control her tears or her voice, she was so sorry to
quit Dorsetshire.—H. G. M.

[1] George, eleventh Earl of Pembroke, and his second wife, Catharine,
daughter of Count Woronzow.

[2] Charles, grandson of first Lord Talbot, Dean of Salisbury. He
married, 1796, Lady Elizabeth Somerset, daughter of fifth Duke of
Beaufort.

[3] The Honourable and Rev. Alfred Harris, Prebendary of York,
second son of second Earl of Malmesbury; died 1823. He married,
1812, Maria, daughter of the Rev. Dr. Markham, Dean of York.

"Lord Ashbrook[4] is here to-night, and I trust poor
Dr. Short happy in his home; he went off this morning.
I will not say that we either of us met with any out-of-
the-way civilities, and towards Mrs. Campbell I could
have suggested some which were omitted—prudence
and caution seemed to be the order of the day, but the
poor Queen was certainly unusually agitated.

"Lady Elizabeth Talbot told me she had heard that
Lady Feilding[5] had resigned, but the Queen said, 'We
must hear something of Lady Feilding at Brighton;'
beyond this I know nothing.   They all seem to have
unfeigned pleasure in the idea of Princess Charlotte being
there, so I hope all will be *smooth*.   Pray let me hear
how you go on in our absence, and tell Mr. Frampton
that I am to have a bust as well as himself, but it is to
be a corrected one with the hair raised, not as a crop.

"I feel as if I was living in a cloud at present, and
that it is uncertain whether the sunshine will dispel it or
what else may environ us and keep us in the *mist*.

"*Thursday morning.*—I have just got a letter from
dear Giles, dated the 23rd, not more than five leagues
from Calais, where they landed on the 19th at four
o'clock in the morning, after a boisterous passage of
fourteen hours.   He says he has a bad cough, but hopes
it is getting better.   He makes himself well understood,
and is the best Frenchman of the *four*, and has not had a
moment to himself.   They have orders to remain in their
quarters, he believes until the English troops on their
return have cleared the roads, but he is impatient to
join the regiment, thinking it fated that he never shall.

[4] Henry, fourth Viscount Ashbrook.   It does not appear that he was
in any way attached to either of the Royal Households.

[5] Mary, daughter of T. J. Powys, Esq., widow of William, Viscount
Feilding, eldest son of sixth Earl of Denbigh, who died (s.p.) 1799.   Lady
Feilding's name does not appear in any list of the Royal Household.

" Giles says it seems very odd to spend Christmas in
an obscure French village, but has bought a fine turkey
for his feast, and has good claret at 1*s*. 3*d*. a bottle.   He
complains of its being very cold, and the ground covered
with snow.

" Your affectionate,
" M. ILCHESTER."

MRS. CAMPBELL TO LADY HARRIOT FRAMPTON.

" *Cranborne Lodge, Windsor, January* 26*th,* 1816.

" MY DEAR LADY HARRIOT,—I have just received your
letter, which is not very cheering, but the weather here
is equally bad.   I have not been out, nor one of us
since the day we arrived here, but within this hour daylight seems inclined to peep out a little.   I cannot give
you any account as to which brother [6] it is, but believe he
is third ; all is silence as to us.   Not from any wish of
hers, the Princess, that it should be so ; but so it is, and
we do not even remark upon the paragraphs in the papers.
But the Princess asked if you had said anything about
her, and to my reply, ' A great deal,' she smiled, and
desired me to tell you she has not forgotten her promise
to you. [7]

" I may tell you all I know, but that all is nothing.
No confidence has been placed in me, so I am as free
to discuss the subject as the rest of the world, but it is
a very great satisfaction to me to tell you that I have
heard nothing but good of the Prince.   I inquired of
military men in London, who I could depend upon being
open and candid with me, and the account was that he
is a sensible and rather reserved man, and not dissipated

----

[6] This refers to Prince Leopold of Saxe Coburg.

[7] The Princess Charlotte had promised to write to Lady Harriot
Frampton whenever her marriage was positively settled.

as the generality of foreign princes are. I believe his name is Leopold, but I expect the first certain information that we here shall have will be through Parliament, the week after this. Not a word has been said to Lady Ilchester, and we are in complete ignorance as to everything intended, which, considering how nearly it concerns ourselves, is not very agreeable. Princess Charlotte expects to go to town early. She is always kind and affectionate to me, and, indeed, to the others also.

"We are quite quiet here; no visiting, which is a great comfort. Dr. Short is here, and stays in the house, as it was not worth moving his family and settling at Windsor for so short a time. The Princess is better, but not well yet. She was very happy at Brighton, and the accounts of the Prince Regent are better. When I have anything to tell you, you may depend upon my writing.

"Ever your very affectionate,

"A. CAMPBELL."

DOWAGER COUNTESS OF ILCHESTER TO LADY H. FRAMPTON.

"*Cranborne Lodge, February 2nd*, 1816.

"MY DEAR HARRIOT,—I have thought of writing to you ever since I left Brighton, but really the obscurity in which we, who should see (Mrs. Campbell and myself), live, is so singularly ill-judged that the effect of it is to keep one's faculties suspended, and so, for fear of stumbling on the subject we are to know nothing of but from the newspaper, I am fearful of speech and pen. However, I may say that the fortnight at Brighton has had a happy effect on Princess Charlotte's spirits, and she has an air of cheerful content that would please you. You have no idea how much her manners daily softened by witnessing the address of the Queen and Princesses, with whom she regularly went round the circle, and paid individual attention to all the company, and she really looked very handsome, being always elegantly dressed, and every one seemed delighted to have her under her father's roof.

"It certainly was a great gratification to the Prince to find it really gave so much pleasure to the Princess, for certainly he had been led to suspect that she did not like to come, which was a complete mistake, of which he is now convinced. The gout came very provokingly to mar the pleasures of the fortnight, but he could see his family daily, and all ended most harmoniously. The Chinese scene is gay beyond description, and I am sure you would admire it, as well as the manner of living at the Pavilion, though the extreme warmth of it might, perhaps, be too much for you. Every one was free in the morning of all Court restraint, and only met at six o'clock punctually for dinner to the number of between thirty and forty daily, and in the evening about as many more were generally invited; a delightful band of music played till half-past eleven, when the Royal Family took their leave, and the rest of the company also, after partaking of sandwiches. The evenings were not in the least formal. As soon as the Queen sat down to cards everybody moved about as they pleased, and made their own backgammon, chess, or card party, but the walking up and down the gallery was the favourite lounge. All the rooms open into this beautiful gallery, which is terminated at each end by the lightest and prettiest Chinese staircases you can imagine, made of cast-iron and bamboo, with glass doors beneath, which reflect the gay lanterns, &c., at each end. There are mandarins and pagodas in abundance, plenty of sofas, Japan and China. The centre of the gallery has a skylight, but each staircase communicates to a large room, into which, at one end, the Queen's apartments opened; at the other the Princess's and mine. The effect of this centrical common room is very good. There was in it an excellent fire and books and newspapers, and from one set of rooms to the other there is a private communication round the skylight, so that you need not go down at one end to get up by the other to the Queen's apartments from ours. I was glad to come back, though I was pleased there. Our going to London may be sudden. For my part, I shall be sorry to be too soon fixed there; but we must do as we are bid a little longer.

"Now pray tell me all about yourself. This stupid letter is not worth postage, but I have no frank. Remember me most kindly to Mr. Frampton, and to James, Harriot, Louisa, and Charlton. I hope their education prospers.

"Ever affectionately yours,

"M. I."

MRS. CAMPBELL TO THE SAME.

"February 22nd, 1816.

" MY DEAR LADY HARRIOT,—Your last letter was a great comfort to us, for we felt your silence a proof that poor James [8] was not so well; but the weather is now much more in his favour. The Royal Family make constant kind inquiries about him, and so did Mrs. Arthur Stanhope, who was here two days ago with the Queen.

"To-day we put on mourning for a week [9]—which week I hoped to have got over quietly here; but, alas! the Lover is arrived. I only know it from the agitation and pleasure the Princess showed on the receipt of a note

---

[8] James, eldest son of Mr. and Lady H. Frampton, who died 1818.

[9] Caroline Louisa, Grand Duchess of Mecklenburg Schewerin, died January 20th, 1816. She was daughter of Charles Augustus, Grand Duke of Saxe Weimar. This death is also alluded to in the letter of February 27th.

this morning. I did not ask any questions, as I never surprise her into any confidence or communication. Now we *must* be told, but I shall always regret the ill-judged silence imposed upon her towards the only persons who could have been of any use to her from a knowledge of what was going on, or rather from being allowed to speak, for we knew what the rest of the country knew. I suppose Princess Charlotte will soon write to you, and till then I shall not give any message for you. She is going over to Windsor with Lady Ilchester, so it is probable the embargo will be taken off our tongues when it can be of no use, as the bustle, &c., which will now commence will prevent all reflection. I am in a little of an agitation myself, which has put all out of my head I had to say. I am really sorry to go to town, and hear it never was more unhealthy than at present. What an extraordinary death is that of the Duchess of St. Albans [1] and her child! It is, however, considered a fortunate thing from the rumours prevalent on the subject. The Papers are come and the arrivals stated, so they will come back from Windsor with some plan. Probably we shall be off directly, though it is not unlikely the Princess may go to Brighton if the Prince Regent cannot come to town. Lady D. Herbert is to marry Lord Normanton. I have kept this open, hoping they would come back and that I might add more, but they are not come, and it is near six o'clock, so with kind regards to Mr. Frampton, I must end.

" Your affectionate,

" A. C."

[1] Louisa Grace, daughter of John Manners, Esq., and of Louisa, Countess of Dysart; married, 1802, Aubrey, sixth Duke of St. Albans, who died 1815. The child Aubrey, seventh Duke, died February 19th, 1816, a few hours after his mother. The dukedom then reverted to his uncle William.

THE COUNTESS DOWAGER OF ILCHESTER TO THE SAME.

" *The Pavilion, Brighton,*
" *Monday night, February 26th.*

" DEAR HARRIOT,—Your letter reached me as I was leaving Windsor this morning, and I lose no time in telling you that Prince Leopold is enchanting as far as appearance and manner, and imagination cannot picture a countenance more justifiable of love at first sight.   There is a particularly soft and gentle expression blended with positive manliness of cast.   Everybody seemed pleased, and indeed Princess Charlotte's taste is not bad.   You may imagine how very anxious I feel, and how pleased I am at the prospect of resigning my charge into such hands ; how soon I cannot tell.   I have some reason to think that Weymouth may come into the plan of a projected diversion of time for *him*.   Of course, if it is so, I will write to you directly : but *mum*, or I will never give you a whisper again.

" Princess Charlotte seems so happy and looks so pretty that she must please and flatter the object of her choice, and if his countenance and the character given of him are honest, he is really something superior.   The Prince speaks English, I am happy to say, and is like an Englishman in all but the ease, elegance, and deference of his manners.   I understand he is well informed, fond of reading, accustomed to business, has a taste for music, interests himself in agricultural pursuits, and likes botany, and is of a reserved character, very gentle, but very firm. I hope I have said enough to please and interest you, but I must add that his figure is tall and good; his face, if not strictly handsome, is positively interesting, but I think it handsome.

" On Friday we go back to Cranborne.   Pray let me

hear from you there, if you have any gratitude for this undelayed detail of my first impressions."

MRS. CAMPBELL TO THE SAME.

"*Cranborne Lodge, February* 27*th*, 1816.

"MY DEAR LADY HARRIOT,—I am here by myself, and very solitary it is at night, but as the Queen said so decidedly that she should return on Friday, I thought it best to remain in good air as long as I could, for no doubt we shall go to town very soon now. Princess Charlotte did not enter upon the subject[2] with me before she went, as the Prince Regent had not taken off the restriction, but she told Lady Harcourt how much it hurt her not to say anything to me before her departure. I only regret it for *her* sake, as I feel I might have done some good, the opportunity for which is now lost, as her head will be full of jewels, houses, dress, appointments, &c., so that nothing I could say would make any impression. There does seem to be a fatality about royalty, that those who would serve them cannot do so.

"*Wednesday.*—I have just had a long letter from Princess Charlotte, full of happiness. Alas! I can make out but little of it. She says her tongue is at last untied, and it is a weight of thousands taken off her; it is extremely kind as far as I can make out. The Princess says she cannot write to you from Brighton, but will on her return here. They come back on Friday, as settled. Lady Ilchester is quite in love with Prince Leopold, and says he is quite to *my taste.* The Prince Regent in good spirits, and wheels himself about in his chair, but cannot walk yet. No plans of any kind mentioned; indeed, they had been but one night there. I do not expect to hear anything until they return. I dread a Drawing-room

---

[2] Of H.R.H.'s approaching marriage.

directly, though I trust not this day week, as the papers
state. Here is a north-east wind fit to destroy me if I
was obliged to go to a Drawing-room. Well, ' sufficient
unto the day is the evil thereof.' I have been reading one
of Gisborne's sermons [3] on the subject of fears and *plans*
for the future. His are the best sermons, to my mind,
that I ever read. This is a dull letter, but you will insist
on hearing that I have nothing to tell. Remember me to
Mr. Frampton, James, and all, and believe me,

" Most affectionately yours,

" A. CAMPBELL.

" We are in mourning for some Princess till Friday.
Bailie says that the Duchess of St. Albans had been in a
consumption for some time."

THE DOWAGER COUNTESS OF ILCHESTER TO THE SAME.

" *March 4th*, 1816.

" MY DEAR HARRIOT,—I hope you and Mr. Frampton
will enjoy the sight of my present *hero* very soon, for he
is going to Weymouth, when of course you will—that is
Mr. Frampton—call upon General Cartwright [4] who I
believe attends him there. The Queen's kindness and
proper feeling in the conduct of all this is beyond all
praise, and gives a most desirable dignity to this interesting event, and the necessary attention to etiquette has
already had a good effect in softening both the mind and
manner of the Princess, and when I confess to you the
impression I have of Prince Leopold's character from my
own observations as well as from what I hear, you will
believe in the anxiety I must feel that *she* should be every
way deserving of the happiness I think in her power, if
she is capable of the attachment he seems formed to

[3] Sermons by the Rev. Thomas Gisborne, of Yoxall, Co. Stafford.
[4] General W. Cartright, Equerry to the King, 1808-20.

excite.   Of course I depend on you not to quote *me*
for anything but *general* approbation and praise.

"I do feel a very great satisfaction in giving up my
charge into such hands.   Of establishment, &c., I can
say nothing beyond the value set on Mrs. Campbell's
continuance, and this puts *her* in a very flattering point
of view.

" God bless you all.

" M. I."

MRS. CAMPBELL TO LADY H. FRAMPTON.

" *Cranborne Lodge, March 6th,* 1816.

"My DEAR LADY HARRIOT,—I find that Princess Charlotte has written to you this day.   She sent her letter to
the Duke of York to frank before she told me.   I do
not know what she may have said respecting the Prince,
but she told me he did not wish to enter into any society,
and that Mr. Frampton, Harry,[5] &c., were only to write
their names as having inquired for him.   I should not,
however, be surprised if he did not go to Weymouth after
all; but if he should, I beg as a particular favour that
you will not name me to Prince Leopold, though I am
fully sensible of the kindness of your intentions.   Princess Charlotte has so far marked her special favour for
me, that I am the only person she has made a point of
retaining, if I will stay, and the Prince Regent, as I hear,
has been most gracious on the subject of my remaining,
so I wish it to rest there for the present.

"As I do not know one atom as to what is intended,
or who are to form her establishment, I remain silent.   I
have every wish to do what she wishes, and should be very
sorry to leave her to strangers at first; but it is very
possible that I may feel myself unequal to the situation,

[5] Lord Ilchester.

therefore I beg of my friends to say nothing about my staying or going at present.

" The reason of my writing to-day is to say that I have sent off a print of the Princess Charlotte, by *her desire*, directed to you.[6] The bust is not forgotten for Mr. Frampton, but the Princess intends to sit again before any more are made, that the hair may be altered, so this print is to fill up the gap in your recollection till the bust is done. I hope it will arrive in time to be included in your letter, as it will save another of thanks.

" It is framed and packed in a box, and goes by the coach from Windsor to-morrow; so if you wait one day, you may receive it.

" ' Highness,' is what Prince Leopold is entitled to as a younger brother—Serene Highness now and then is thought civil—as people say Royal Highness to the Duke of Gloucester occasionally.

" The Queen is in town ordering the wedding garments.

" Remember me to Mr. Frampton.

" Ever yours affectionately,

" A. C.

" Prince Leopold knows that I am the person Princess Charlotte wishes to keep."

FROM H.R.H. PRINCESS CHARLOTTE TO LADY H.
FRAMPTON.

" Cranborne Lodge, March 6th, 1816.

" DEAR LADY HARRIOT,—In compliance with the promise I gave you some time ago and which (consistent with one of silence I gave the Regent at Brighton) I could not sooner fulfil, I take up my pen to confirm the reports as well as the accounts (which I have no doubt Mrs. Camp-

---

[6] This portrait is now at Markeaton Hall (1880). My mother said that the side of the face next the crown was as like the Princess Charlotte as possible, the other is represented too fat.—H. G. M.

bell and Lady Ilchester have already written you) of my approaching marriage with the Prince of Coburg—an event that makes me exceedingly happy as it fulfils wishes that I had long formed. No royal marriage I believe, ever promised to the individuals what this one does in point of domestic comfort, as without exaggeration I think I may say that he is a very charming and very superior person.

"It is possible that the Prince may go to Weymouth for a little while, but if he does, his object will be that of retirement, and therefore that object will be entirely defeated if any particular notice is taken of him. I do not mean to say that the names should not be left at the house, but that is all, I know, that would at present be agreeable to him.

"I cannot close this letter without assuring you of my constant inquiries after James, and that I take a very sincere interest in his recovery. I trust you are in pretty good spirits about him, and that you and Mr. Frampton, as well as all the rest of your children, have been well.

"May I beg you will remember me particularly to Mr. Frampton, whose attentions to me I shall not easily forget! Poor little James too comes in for a share of my remembrances, as well as my friend Henry,' who I pre-

---

7 Second son of Mr. and Lady Harriot Frampton, subsequently of Moreton, Co. Dorset. He married, 1833, Charlotte Louisa, seventh daughter of Robert Willis Blencowe, Esq., of The Hayes, Middlesex, and died 1879. He was then a boy of about twelve years of age. The Princess Charlotte was very partial to him, and on more than one occasion amused herself by learning how to make *ducks* and *drakes* in the sea from the beach on her occasional visits for the day to Abbotsbury! H.R.H. was peremptorily forbidden by the Prince Regent to remain even for a night from Weymouth. She used therefore to stay as long as she possibly could do so at Melbury, Abbotsbury Castle, Moreton, &c., and return to the King's Lodge between twelve and one o'clock a.m.—H. G. M.

sume is much grown. I have not forgot to make en-
quiries about your German friends, the Knesebecks, but
as yet have had no answer from the Duke of Cambridge.

"Believe me to be, dear Lady Harriot,

"Yours very sincerely,

"CHARLOTTE."

MRS. CAMPBELL TO LADY HARRIOT FRAMPTON.

"*Cranborne Lodge, March 25th.*

"MY DEAR LADY HARRIOT,—The Queen and two Princesses are gone to have a Drawing-room; fortunately for
me, Princess Charlotte could not with propriety appear
there till Prince Leopold is with her. I feel it fortunate
because no time has been given for preparation. I have a
bad cold, and my maid has been ill and confined to her
room for nearly a week. Miss Goldsworthy is dead, and
poor Lady Catherine Poulett at Clifton. Lord Poulett
and Mary [8] set out for town as soon as all was over.

" The Income Tax having failed is a gain to me, but I
regret it, for I really think it was the best tax we could
have for another year or two, and I cannot think how we
are to get on without it.

"Princess Charlotte's business was got through very
handsomely, and she was much pleased, but I must own
I was sorry that no one called upon Lord Castlereagh to
name the ladies who were paid out of the £30,000 a year.
I, for one, can declare that I have never received a
shilling in nearly two years that I have been in the family.

"We have not heard of any one being appointed for
the Establishment, but I understand some have refused,
The Princess still thinks the marriage may take place
before Easter, but I trust it will not, and indeed I do not

---

[8] Daughter of John, fourth Earl Poulett.

T

think a public marriage of that kind ought to take place during Lent, and just upon Passion Week.[9]   There was a report of its being at Brighton, but that would cause such discontent that I hope it will not be attempted. Camelford House[1] is bought for the Princess Charlotte, and will do *as it is* for this season, and when she leaves town it is to be added to and newly furnished.   Alas ! it is beyond a walk for me to any one I care for ; in truth I begin more and more to dread that I shall not be able to hold the situation, though I shall be silent till I know what it is to be.   I hope better weather may enable me to bear the first of the bustle ; to-day is a bitter east wind.

" I am plagued to death with letters of congratulation, applications for *places at Court* and petitions.   They have all their share as well as me, and if it was not for the trouble of answering, it would be amusing.   We all compare notes when the post comes in, and some of the letters are very funny.

" *Wednesday.*—Nothing new to-day, only that Mrs. Louis[2] is ordered up to town by the Queen on some business respecting the wedding clothes.

" What a horrible business Sir R. Wilson's[3] is likely to

<hr />

[9] Easter Day fell on April 14th in the year 1816.

[1] In Park Lane at the end next Oxford Street, subsequently the residence of Sir Charles Mills, Bart.

[2] Mrs. Louis was the principal dresser and personal attendant on H.R.H. the Princess Charlotte.   After the death of the Princess she remained at Claremont as confidential housekeeper in Prince Leopold's establishment until her own death.

[3] Sir Robert Wilson, Knight, son of Benjamin Wilson, F.R.S., born 1777.   In 1793 he enrolled in the Flemish army, when he greatly distinguished himself.   Subsequently he entered the English army, and in 1808 took the command of the Portuguese Levies.   In 1812 Sir Robert Wilson was sent to Russia as British Military Correspondent of the Allied Armies.   After the peace Sir Robert Wilson visited Paris, where in January, 1816, he engaged with Captain H. Hutchinson (afterwards

turn out! General Long saw Lady Wilson on her return from Brighton.   She said the Prince Regent received her as a King should do a subject, that is, as a father would a child.

" It is thought that he and the others will fall a sacrifice to a weak government and a faction which will rejoice to see English blood flow on a French scaffold. I wished them punished, but certainly never thought of death for them. I have nothing more to say. Remember me to Mr. Frampton.

" Ever yours affectionately,
" A. C."

THE DOWAGER COUNTESS OF ILCHESTER TO THE SAME.

" *Cranborne Lodge, March* 24*th.*

"MY DEAR HARRIOT,—I received your stray letter this morning, directed to Brighton, where we have not been since I wrote to you from thence, so do not heed the newspapers, which only tell the truth *par hasard* and do not come forth *upon oath.*

Earl of Donoughmore) and Mr. Bruce in effecting the escape of Comte Lavalette, who, having been condemned to death as an accomplice of Bonaparte, had escaped from prison by changing his dress with his wife. The three Englishmen were tried at Paris, March 22nd, pronounced guilty, and sentenced to three months' imprisonment. In consequence of this and the conduct of Sir Robert Wilson at the funeral of Queen Caroline he was dismissed from the army, September, 1821, and all his foreign orders returned to their respective sovereigns. After a few years, however, he was restored to his rank, was made Colonel of the 15th Hussars, and a General, 1841. In 1842 Sir Robert Wilson was appointed Governor and Commander-in-Chief and Vice-Admiral of Gibraltar. He died in London, 1849. In May, 1830, my father, mother, and myself, dined with Sir Francis and Lady Burdett in St. James's Place. Amongst the party were the Duke and Duchess of St. Albans, Sir Robert Wilson, and Lavalette Bruce (as he was called). I sat between the two latter !— H. G. M.

" I can yet only speak from surmise, but I apprehend that Weymouth may not be blessed with the presence of Prince Leopold before he is blessed with a wife. Camelford House is fixed on as the town residence, and will be very comfortable from what I hear of it. A Drawing-Room on Thursday next, but I am thankful to say we escape it. The wedding cannot be till after Easter, but I suppose *then* immediately. No one appointed (to my knowledge) but Mrs. Campbell and Colonel Addenbrook. Princess Charlotte very happy by anticipation, and flattered by the handsome manner in which her establishment is provided for by the two Houses ; in short, all is 'couleur de rose' *now*, and that makes me serious, who *know* we must expect in this life so many variations.

MRS. CAMPBELL TO THE SAME.

" *Cranborne Lodge, April* 18*th*, 1816.

" MY DEAR LADY HARRIOT,—Prince Leopold is to come to Windsor on Monday, so Princess Charlotte will dine there every day till they go to town, and she has just offered me leave to go to town, which I shall accept, as I have everything to prepare, though I feel anxious to be as long in good air as I can.

" No favours are to be given, and the Queen's household is not to attend, only those in waiting. This is the intelligence of to-day, for every day brings some change.

" The Bust came,[4] and is so ugly and unlike, that I told Princess Charlotte I was sure it would only mortify Mr. Frampton, who, I would answer for it, would rather wait till she could give him one that had some resem-

---

[4] Alluded to in a previous letter. Most unfortunately H.R.H. was prevented from again sitting for her bust, and consequently Mr. Frampton never received her promised gift, to his very great disappointment and regret.

blance, and as I have no doubt the Princess will sit to one of the first-rate sculptors this year, I hope you will approve.

" Colonel Addenbrook [5] has been given this, which will do very well for an empty house.

" Remember me to Mr. Frampton and all,

" Ever your affectionate,

" A. C.

" Prince Leopold is not to be a Duke, so you may set the people's minds at rest; he is wise enough to decline it at present."

FROM CAROLINE, COUNTESS OF MOUNT-EDGCUMBE, TO MRS. MUNDY.

" *Cotehele, March* 18*th*, 1879.

". . . Do you remember, on the occasion of Princess Charlotte's marriage, that old Queen Charlotte wanted Mrs. Campbell to go bodkin with her and Prince Leopold to Claremont ? considering that it was so improper that they should drive there without a chaperon ! Mrs. Campbell, however, strenuously resisted this command, greatly to the Queen's disgust ! "

THE DOWAGER COUNTESS OF ILCHESTER TO J. FRAMPTON, ESQ.

" *Cranborne Lodge, April,* 1816.

" DEAR MR. FRAMPTON,—Thank you for becoming Harriot's secretary and giving me so far a good report of dear James.

" General Gordon is Governor of Jersey, and is the favourite friend and governs the favourite island of

---

[5] Equerry to the Princess Charlotte. He was still attached to the household of Prince Leopold in 1825.

Colonel Addens; but General Baillie, the late Lord Uxbridge's nephew, is Governor of Guernsey, and will be equally ready to attend to any recommendations or introductions of Colonel A., but the latter says the Jersey Governor he recommends as the *pleasantest*, and that he is hospitality itself.

"The 25th seems now to be the appointed day, and I wish it was over. All I know is that Lady Rosslyn,[6] Miss Cotes,[7] and myself attend in the train to deliver over our charge, and that when the marriage is over, the new ladies are to be introduced to Princess Charlotte, and by her then presented to the Queen.

"Lady Rosslyn's attire, I hear, is to be *magnifique*, so I must do my best not to be outdone and send my bill to Lord Castlereagh, who informs the world of causes for excess of expense in the Princess Charlotte's establishment.

"I cannot report well of Mrs. Campbell, and I am far from being at my best; two days' absence would do me a world of good, but that I have asked and am denied, with many a kind word written by the Princess Elizabeth."

THE COUNTESS DOWAGER OF ILCHESTER TO LADY H. FRAMPTON.

"*April* 28th, 1816.

"MY DEAR HARRIOT,—I tried to write to you yesterday, but it was impossible. This whole week has been a continued Duty, but it is the last week and my mind feels so

---

[6] Charlotte, daughter of first Viscount Courtenay, second wife of first Earl Rosslyn, by whom she was left a widow in 1805.

[7] Charlotte, daughter of John Cotes, Esq., of Woodcotes, Co. Salop, by his first wife, Lucy, daughter of Viscount Courtenay, Woman of the Bedchamber to the Princess Charlotte. Her sister Lucy was also attached to the Princess's household. They had been with H.R.H. at Weymouth during the preceding winter. The Miss Cotes both died unmarried.

light. I am much pleased with my *Hero* still,—indeed all I hear and see is most estimable, and Princess Charlotte is very fortunate to have such a lord and master, but that he will be.

"I have received a magnificent present from the Regent—his own picture superbly set in diamonds. He gave it me on Princess Mary's birthday,[8] saying, 'I feel myself much obliged to you.'

"Dear Mrs. Campbell has been in town since Monday. Alas! her spirits are hardly equal to looking forward at all, but I trust the next week well over and she will be happier. I know she is *not* forgotten, and it would have done you good to hear what Princess Charlotte said *à son sujet* to Colonel Addenbrook. When he lamented her delicacy of health, she said, 'I am not blind to it, but I am ambitious Mrs. Campbell should start with me, but give up without scruple when she finds the duty too much for her. I wish her to feel my house her home when it suits her to be with me, as I shall always be glad to see her.' She added more than it would be fair to repeat. Nearly this, Princess Charlotte has also repeated to me, saying, 'Mind, it is Mrs. Campbell's own fault if she lets me interfere with her comfort.' This is a cordial to me, and highly creditable to Princess Charlotte, and I must add that the pleasure she expressed at my having received so handsome a present from the Regent has greatly enhanced its value, for she said, 'If my approbation was of value to him I would tell him I approve.

"Lady Rosslyn has a cypher in diamonds which I have on the reverse of my picture. Mrs. Campbell, the Cotes, and gentlemen are none of them forgotten, but how remembered I do not know yet. Lady Rosslyn, Miss Cotes,

---

[8] April 25th.

and I attend at the marriage, and are all to be cast off together when the new ladies are presented after the ceremony. I do not know that I am clear, but you cannot think how hurried I am, and how much you should be obliged for this.

"I stay in Burlington Street till after the Queen's birthday,[9] then fly down to Abbotsbury. Love to all your dears.

"Your affectionate,

"M. Ilchester."

Mrs. Campbell to the Same.

"*Warwick House, May 6th*, 1816.

"My dear Lady Harriot,—I suppose I am in utter disgrace, but it has been quite out of my power to help that. I have hardly had time to live, much less to write.

"The marriage was very impressive, and Princess Charlotte's manner just what you could wish. The account in the papers was more exactly what it was than I could have given, for we only saw a part.

"We were taken from one room to another, every one finding out that we were in the wrong place, till at last we were brought back to the room we set out from, and then taken from that to the apartment where Princess Charlotte and Prince Leopold were. She presented us all to him; that is, Lady Rosslyn, *me*, and the Miss Cotes. The Prince bowed civilly, but said nothing, except when I was named, when he said, 'Ah! Mrs. Campbell,' and smiled. A moment after he was called out by Lord Cholmondeley and taken to the altar, and soon after the Duke of Clarence came for Princess Charlotte, and we followed her.

[9] May 19th.

"After all was over, we returned to that same room, and were presented to the Queen; that is, Lady E. Murray, Lady John Thynne, *me*, and Miss C. Cotes. Next morning I had a letter from Princess Charlotte to forbid my going down to Oatlands, which I sent in to the Prince Regent, and asked leave to remain here till Camelford House was ready; so here I am.

"My mornings are taken up with writing to Princess Charlotte, paying her bills, &c. It rains without end, so I get little or nothing done for myself.

"Not a morsel of cake have I got, and Lady Ilchester only a scrap from Princess Mary. The Regent sent me a very pretty diamond cross by Princess Elizabeth, who wrote a very gracious note with it. No brevet has taken place, nor any other compliment. Lady Ilchester's picture is magnificent. Lady Rosslyn was given a cypher, set round with very fine diamonds, and the Miss Cotes a set of amethysts and one of chrysolites, very handsome.

"Miss Madelene Carnegie is going to marry Sir Andrew Agnew. She is the youngest of the ten, and Miss Julia Somerville is to marry a Mr. Head,[1] of the Engineers. I am going with Harry and Caroline to Mrs. Banke's assembly; Lady Ilchester goes with Mrs. Mills,[2] who looks pretty well again.

"I beg you will tell us of James; and do not fancy, because we have not time to write, that we do not care. By us I mean Lady I. and myself, for she has stayed with me till now, but goes up to Burlington Street, to

[1] Subsequently Sir Francis Bond Head, K.C.H. &c., late Lieutenant-Governor of Canada, &c.; created Baronet 1837; died 1875. He married the Honourable Julia Somerville, fourth daughter of thirteenth Lord Somerville

[2] Elizabeth, daughter of the Honourable Wriothesley Digby (son of William, fifth Baron Digby); married, 1786, William Mills, Esq. Their third son, Charles, was created a Baronet 1868.

remain, to-morrow. Mr. Lemon returns home on Wednesday; I have seen little or nothing of him. I had a most affectionate and kind letter from Princess Charlotte to-day. The only command she has to give me is to make myself happy in her house, and look cheerful.

" Remember me to Mr. Frampton.

" Ever, my dear Lady Harriot,

" Your very affectionate,

" A. CAMPBELL."

THE DOWAGER COUNTESS OF ILCHESTER TO THE SAME.

" *May*, 1816.

" I have just seen the ceremony of the City Address, presented by the Lord Mayor, and 250*l*., &c. The hurry and bustle in which all were to kiss the Queen's hand was truly ridiculous, and I am glad I have seen it. The Queen received it on a throne.

" One of the Aldermen or Common Council-men said to me, ' We have four addresses to-day. We have been to the Regent, and now to the Queen, and we are going to the Princess, and to address afterwards Prince Leopold; and after all this, we shall be in very good time for dinner.' You cannot imagine how proud he seemed of such great performances. I cannot say how Mrs. Campbell is, for since she took possession of Camelford House, on Saturday, I have not seen her.

" *Wednesday.*—I have literally not been able to finish this, I have been so fully engaged in writing letters of consequence.

" I feel quite uncertain about getting out of town, which is no small mortification to John,[3] who naturally

---

[3] The Honourable John Fox Strangways, her youngest son, father of the present Earl of Ilchester.

wishes to be at Abbotsbury.   Since I began this, I have
seen Mrs. Campbell.   The inconvenience of her abode is
unparalleled and indescribable."

THE MARCHIONESS OF LANSDOWNE TO LADY H. FRAMPTON.

" *May 20th*, 1816.

" MY DEAR HARRIOT,—I have been a long time in
writing, but I have had no time.   I went to the Drawing-
room, and have been dead tired ever since.   Princess
Charlotte looked beautiful.   Mrs. Campbell is looking
well for her, and if she *would*, might be very happy;
but she will think of every disadvantage and discomfort
more than of the opposite side of the picture.

" I leave town next Saturday, and go with the children
to Bowood for a fortnight, after which Lord Lansdowne
will join me there, and we shall set off as soon as
we can.

" Mr.[4] and Mrs. Smith are still expected; Caroline, I
fear, no better.   There is a clever physician at Florence
and at Parma.   What shall I bring you from Italy?

" Mr. Brummell[5] has absconded, and left all his friends
to pay the money they were security for.

" There is a very curious novel come out, ' Glenarvon,'
written by Lady Caroline Lamb,[6] in which she tells her
own history.   A great deal of it is literally true.

---

[4] Robert Percy Smith, Esq., of Cheam, Surrey, Judge Advocate-
General in India, always known as "Bobus Smith;" died 1845; married,
1798, Caroline Maria, second daughter of Richard Vernon, Esq., and of
Lady Evelyn Gower, widow of John Fitz Patrick, first Earl of Upper
Ossory.

[5] George Brummell, Esq., the celebrated "Beau Brummell," once the
associate of George IV. when Prince of Wales.   He resided on the
Continent for many years, and died at Caen in April, 1840, aged sixty-
two.   Mr. Brummell had latterly been confined in a lunatic asylum.

[6] Lady Caroline Ponsonby, daughter of third Earl of Bessborough

" Good-bye. This is a sad scrawl; but I have more to do than I can do, besides having a headache.

" Yours affectionately,

" L. L."

[7] CHARLES LEMON, ESQ., TO LADY H. FRAMPTON.

" London, February 26th, 1816.

" Auckland gives a dim account of the society at Paris, excepting for a few individuals who have credit to get introduced to the best of the disaffected sets. He was almost every day at Talleyrand's, where people talked openly of the Government, and said that a revolution might be lighted up any moment; but they are afraid they shall not be able to stop it. If any person in whom they could not confide was present, the hint given was by the lady of the house asking if he had a headache, and then politics were not spoken. He says all the people laugh at the Government as a thing they consent to tolerate for a time. Auckland passed Louis driving through the streets without any of those acclamations which used to follow the Emperor, and his cabriolet driver said, ' Comme on crie, " Vive le Roi;" on peut à peine s'entendre parler!' There was a report yesterday that the ultra-Royalists had joined in an association to support the Bourbons in the following order of succession : Louis XVIII., Monsieur, the Dukes de Berri and Angoulême, Ferdinand of Spain, to the exclusion of the Duke of Orleans. They are in love with the Inquisition and Ferdinand's vigorous Councils. Hobhouse has published

married 1805, William, afterwards second Viscount Melbourne (born 1779, died (s.p.) 1848). Mr. Lamb succeeded to the title in July, 1828, but Lady Caroline Lamb died the preceding January.

[7] This letter has been transposed to avoid the interruption of the series relating to the marriage of the Princess Charlotte.

some very entertaining letters from Paris. He is a strong anti-Bourbonist, and there seems to be some ground for being so.

"I went to the French play on Thursday, and was very much entertained. I saw Benjamin Constant [8] there,

[8] Benjamin Constant de Rebèque, one of the most distinguished political writers and orators of France, born at Lausanne, 1767. During a temporary banishment by Napoleon, he travelled and resided for some time with his compatriot, Madame de Staël, and after the Battle of Waterloo passed some time in England. Constant again returned to Paris, and after the Revolution of 1830 was invested with the "Présidence du Conseil." He died in December of the same year. Amongst his most ambitious works are "Mémoires sur les Cent Jours," "De la Religion," &c., and in 1816 B. Constant published his only novel, "Adolphe," alluded to in the letter of Sir C. Lemon.

In the month of October, 1845, we were at Lausanne on our way to Italy, when the following anecdotes were related to us by Madame de Polier Vernand, who had resided at Vernand, near Lausanne, during part of the French Revolution, when so many illustrious *émigrés* took refuge in Switzerland. Her husband, who died in 1821, was Lieutenant-General of the armies of the Swiss Confederation. Madame de Polier was well acquainted with Madame de Staël, who was then living at Coppet, near Geneva, where, in 1807, Madame de Polier saw her act Racine's "Andromaque." The other characters were sustained by Madame Récamier, M. Benjamin Constant, M. de Sabran—a Frenchman who lived much with them—and M. d'Hermanches, a clever man, who afterwards married a daughter of M. de Polier. She described Madame de Staël's figure as being extremely large, nothing good but her hand and arm, as her face with projecting teeth was very plain, and the costume required for the character being white muslin with full draperies, she did not appear to advantage *until* everything was forgotten in the extreme charm of her voice and enunciation, both of which were *perfection*. Madame Récamier was very handsome, with dark hair and eyebrows, but without much expression, and Madame de Polier described her acting as resembling a girl saying her lesson. M. Constant had a tongue too large for his mouth, so speaking did not suit him. At that time he was Madame de Staël's favoured lover. Another anecdote struck me so much that I cannot refrain from inserting it here, particularly as it was told by Madame de Staël *herself* to Madame de Polier. It appears that although Lord Byron was a first-rate Italian scholar, he

who has a novel in preparation, which was rehearsed last night at Lady Charlotte Campbell's,[1] in a private reading, and Dr. Holland says it was much approved.

"After the French play there was some pretty waltzing, the smooth, tasteless oil of Castlereagh swimming round with Madame de Lieven.   People say that she has abated much of her hauteur since it has been known that Princess Esterhazy[2] is coming, who is said to be everything that is most captivating.   There is a sight for you to see when you come to London, some beautiful sculptures from a Grecian temple, which are at the British Museum.

"Good-bye, dear Harriot.

"I am, yours affectionately,

"C. LEMON."

FROM THE SAME TO THE SAME.

"*Melbury, June 28th,* 1816.

"I do not know all the characters in 'Glenarvon,'[3]

was not equally so as regarded French, and being, as every one knows, most absurdly susceptible, nothing would induce him to speak that language in public.   Madame de Staël said that Lord Byron was constantly in the habit of rowing over from the Villa Deodati on the opposite shore of the lake to spend the afternoon at Coppet.   He used actually to interrupt the most agreeable conversation at dinner by requesting Madame de Staël herself to tell the servant to change his plate, or to ask for what he wanted.—H. G. M.

[1] Lady Charlotte Campbell, daughter of fifth Duke of Argyll, married first, in 1796, Colonel John Campbell, of Shawfield and Islay; secondly, 1819, the Rev. Edward Bury, and was again left a widow in 1832.   In 1819 Lady Charlotte Campbell was one of the Ladies of the Bedchamber to the Princess of Wales.   An authoress of note.   Lady Charlotte Bury died 1861.

[2] Marie Thérèse, daughter of Charles Alexander, Prince de Tour et Taxis; born 1794; married, 1812, Prince Paul Anthony Esterhazy, Ambassador from Austria to the Court of St. James's from 1816 until 1844.   The Prince died 1866.

[3] "Glenarvon," a novel, by Lady Caroline Lamb.

but I will tell you all I do know. I am not surprised at your being struck with a few detached passages; but before you have read one volume, I think you will doubt at which end of the book you began. There is no connection between any two ideas in the book, and it seems to me to have been written as the sages of Laputa[4] composed their works. Glenarvon is Lord Byron; Lady Augusta, the late Duchess of Devonshire; Lady Mandeville—I think it is Lady Mandeville, but the lady who dictated Glenarvon's farewell letter to Calantha is Lady Oxford.[5] This letter she really dictated to Lord Byron, to send to Lady Caroline Lamb, and is now very much offended that she has treated the matter so lightly as to introduce it into her book. The best character in it is the Princess of Madagascar (Lady Holland), with all her Reviewers about her. The young Duke of Devonshire is in the book, but I forget under what name. I need not say that the heroine is Lady Caroline's own self.

" There is one personage who goes off the stage in a fine way, with some degree of poetical effect. She wraps her cloak round her horse's eyes, and rides over the cliff. Take away this and a few other short passages, and there remains only a deliberate vindication of the love of a married woman for another man, and upon the old plea of necessity. It is a mischievous book, but interesting as giving a true picture of the sentiment and moral sophistry of that set. I have given you much more than you asked for on this subject.

" Your affectionate
" C. LEMON."

[4] Vide "Gulliver's Travels," Voyage to Laputa.

[5] Jane, daughter of the Rev. James Scott, wife of Edward, fifth Earl of Oxford, died 1824. Their second daughter, Lady Charlotte Harley, born 1801 (subsequently the wife of General Bacon), was the "Ianthe" of the Proem to Lord Byron's "Childe Harold."

1816.

(Journal continued.)

" DURING Mr. Wollaston's abode at Cheltenham, in the month of July, the Duke and Duchess of Wellington came there, the former to drink the waters. He was followed constantly by crowds, and the little Duchess nearly trampled on in their eagerness to get a sight of him.

" The first night of his arrival they surrounded the Duke's house, got into the garden, and knocked at the door, desiring him to show himself, which he refused to do."

1817.

C. B. WOLLASTON TO MARY FRAMPTON.

" *Temple, February* 3, 1817.

" You will before this have had the account of the disturbances on Tuesday.[6] It is rather amusing to observe that the Ministry and Ministerials all affirm strenuously that the holes in the glass of the state carriage were made by bullets, and the Opposition and their adherents as positively that the effect was produced by a stone.

" Now it seems to me to be perfectly immaterial whether it was one or the other, except as far as the person is concerned who fired the shot or threw the stone, whom they have not the smallest chance of catching, for most undoubtedly there was a very serious and alarm-

---

[6] January 28th, 1817. As the Prince Regent was returning from the House and passing at the back of the garden of Carlton House, the glass of the carriage was broken by a stone, or by two balls from an air-gun, which appeared to have been aimed at H.R.H.

ing disposition to violence, and if the mob could have got at the Regent I have no doubt that they would have pulled him out of the carriage. I saw the procession pass and re-pass from the window in Downing Street, towards the Park. I never saw before such a throng of people, and when the carriage had passed the parade on its return and got into the road under the wall, I heard the shouting and screaming and roaring so loud, and saw the crowd pressing so much that way with the Life Guards hustling amongst them, that I thought there was something more than common curiosity or common signs of disapprobation in the tumult. I did not know what had happened until afterwards. To say the truth I am not sorry that it has happened, as I can perceive clearly that the hands of Government will be strengthened by the alarm, and that something will be done to put down the haranguing at tumultuous meetings, as was the case in the year 1795, which produces the mischief by irritating and inflaming discontent to its height. I propose taking the two Shirleys to Drury Lane to-morrow. Kean acts a tragedy, " Oronooko," and there is a pantomime afterwards."

From the Same to the Same.

" *Downing Street, February 19th,* 1817.

" I got a pound's worth of the new silver this morning at the Bank. The shillings and sixpences are a pretty coin, but the head on the half-crown is so uncommonly large, and the neck so like a shoulder of mutton, that I think it disgracefully ugly, though the die is said to have been made by a famous Italian artist.

" The inconvenience in small payments, such as hackney-coach fares, &c., has for some days been very great. I saw one of the offices for exchanging money crowded round by a multitude of poor-looking people this morning, so I hope they are not very nice in making the exchange. I have not heard of any complaints or disturbances on that account.

"Yesterday's Westminster meeting passed off without much observation. Mr. Hunt,[7] I understand, was driven off in triumph by his friends."

[7] Mr. Henry Hunt, the notorious political agitator, born 1773, the son of a rich Wiltshire farmer. For many years he regularly attended Devizes Market, and married the daughter of Mr. Halcomb, the landlord of the Bear Inn at that place. No man attended more strictly to farming, and no farms in the kingdom were in better condition than his. In the year 1801, when the apprehension of a French invasion was so great that the Lord-Lieutenant of the county caused letters to be written to the churchwardens, requiring from every parish a return of movable property, live and dead stock, &c., that of Mr. Hunt was valued at upwards of 20,000*l.*, the whole of which he voluntarily tendered to the Government, to be at their disposal in case of an invasion. He also engaged to enter himself and three servants, completely equipped, and mounted upon valuable hunters, as volunteers. This liberal and patriotic offer was much appreciated, and he was appointed to one of the highest ranks in the Wiltshire Yeomanry; but, carried away by his uncontrolled disposition, he unfortunately got into a serious misunderstanding with the commanding officer, Lord Bruce, in consequence of which he received an intimation that his services were no longer required. Hunt was so indignant at this, that on the next field-day he rode up to Lord Bruce, and demanded satisfaction. For this offence Hunt was sentenced to pay a fine of 100*l.*, and to be imprisoned for six weeks. In prison he met with some Radicals, to which may be attributed his subsequent political sentiments. When Hunt entered he was only a discontented person, adverse to all control; he left the prison one of the most headstrong apostles of universal reform. He took to going about from town to town in a fanciful equipage like a mountebank, collecting and haranguing the people as he passed, a sort of political propaganda.

Amongst the largest assemblies which he provoked were those of Westminster and Spa Fields in 1816—1819, and after the last tumultuous one at Manchester, which was only dispersed by force, and which

The Same to the Same.

" *Temple (April or May)*, 1817.

" I add to the parcel the manuscript from St. Helena [8] Harris [9] having desired me to send him one to Cambray, stating that the book was prohibited, but had made a great sensation in France, induced me to read it, and I liked it so well that I bought a copy for myself, which may amuse you and my mother.

" It cannot be written by Bonaparte himself, nor by any one immediately connected with him, for it contains a strange historical inaccuracy. It supposes the attack upon Poland, and the battles of Eylau and Friedland, and the Peace of Tilsit, to have immediately followed the victory of Austerlitz and the Peace of Presburg, and to

caused the death of many persons, Hunt was arrested, and condemned (15th May, 1820) to two and a half years' imprisonment, and a fine of 2000*l.*, &c.

After many failures, Hunt at last succeeded, during the excitement of the Reform Bill in 1830, in defeating Lord Stanley as a candidate for Preston ; he was again re-elected 1831, but the end of that session was likewise the termination of his Parliamentary career. During a journey on business, Hunt was seized with paralysis, which ended his singular life in February, 1835.

" At the time of Hunt's political visit to Bristol in 1817, a detach-ment of the 23rd Lancers, then stationed at Weymouth, were ordered to that place, to assist in keeping the peace, &c. They escorted Hunt into the town, playing ' The Rogue's March.' "—" Reminiscences of W. M."

[8] " Manuscrit venu de Ste. Hélène d'une manière inconnue."

Battle of Austerlitz. . . .	December 2nd, 1805.
Peace of Presburg	December 26th, 1805.
Battle of Jena and Auerstadt . .	October 14th, 1806.
Battle of Eylau	February 8th, 1807.
Battle of Friedland. . . .	June 14th, 1807.
Peace of Tilsit	July 7th—19th, 1807.

[9] John Greathed Harris, Esq., of the Middle Temple (of the family of Greathed Harris, of Uddens, Co. Dorset), Deputy-Judge Advocate on the Continent of Europe 1815 till 1819, when he retired.

have preceded the battle of Jena and the destruction of the Prussian monarchy, which is a complete change in the order of events, and never can be supposed to have escaped from anybody who had been a party to them.

"But it is a very well written abstract of Bonaparte's history and *motives*, calculated to keep up the recollection of him, and a regret that his system was defeated. There is an epigrammatic terseness in the observations which are like his style in his bulletins and speeches."

CHARLES LEMON, ESQ., TO LADY HARRIOT FRAMPTON.
"*Carclew, September* 13*th*, 1817.

"MY DEAR HARRIOT,—The story of the Russian officer, I thought you must have heard from Colonel Cutcliffe.[1] He found him walking on the esplanade at Weymouth with his young boy, who was very much crippled by a grape-shot at the battle of Smolensko. He had been in the whole of the Moscow campaign and in that which followed, up to the taking of Paris, from which place he was sent to *Cherson*. He had hardly arrived there before he was ordered back again, and arrived at Paris a second time, and after all the business was done, he was offered half-pay in Russia if he chose to go there, but he thought he could provide for this poor boy better by seeking his fortune in South America, and was on his way to Lisbon when Colonel Cutcliffe saw him. He had lost his portmanteau at Salisbury, containing all his wealth, amounting to 6*l*., when Colonel Cutcliffe met with him and very humanely gave him money and a recommendation to a gentleman at Falmouth, asking his assistance in procuring a passage to Lisbon.

[1] Colonel Cutcliffe was in command of the 23rd Lancers, at that time quartered at Weymouth.

" We had rather an interesting personage yesterday at dinner, Colonel Gossett, who commanded the engineer part of the expedition to Algiers.[2] He had been sent some years before to all the Barbary States as Secretary of Legation to Sir William A'Court, but, in fact, quietly to survey the defences. He knew Sedi Useph and all the story of his murdering his brother in his mother's arms; but if you have not read the ' Ten Years' Residence in Tripoli '[3] this will be gibberish to you. Colonel Gossett gave me some very interesting anecdotes of the battle—one very characteristic of a sailor's coolness which passed under his own eye.

" The *Queen Charlotte*, Lord Exmouth's flag-ship, had expended all her wads, and had for some time been loading with dead men's jackets, &c., which failing also, he saw a sailor coolly take off his jacket and ram it into the gun, and just afterwards swearing at himself for being such a fool that he had ' gi'en 'em his tobacco-box in the pocket o' it.' Another fellow he heard, as he was ramming down a ball, say, ' This will raise the price of masonry in Algiers.' Lord Exmouth *must* be a great man, though he does love to flatter the powers that are. His coolness and determination were prodigiously fine: of this I could tell you some anecdotes that are good in every respect except in being too long for a letter. I hope Ilchester may have some good sport. I asked a farmer who rents a tolerably large farm here, whether he had any birds on it, and his answer was that he believed

---

[2] The bombardment of Algiers by Lord Exmouth took place August 27th, 1816. I well remember, when a girl of ten years old, seeing the fleet pass down the Channel from the beach at Weymouth, when walking with my father, who told me that the ships were Lord Exmouth's fleet going to Algiers. It was a grand sight.—H. G. M.

[3] " Narrative of a Ten Years' Residence in Tripoli," by Richard Tully, Esq., late British Consul, 1816.

there were three old ones! You may guess that my shooting journal will not give me much trouble.

"Yours affectionately,

"C. LEMON."

MRS. CAMPBELL TO LADY H. FRAMPTON.

"*Claremont, October* 24*th*, 1817.

"MY DEAR LADY HARRIOT,—I write a line to beg that as you are coming to town that you will bring up with you ' Santo Sebastiano,' the novel I left for your reading last spring. It belongs to Princess Charlotte, and I have often been afraid of its being asked for since. Do not send it here, but leave it in Burlington Street for me to convey when I go up—which, however, I greatly fear will not be whilst you are in London. I told Princess Charlotte this morning that you were to be in town on Monday. She said, ' Oh, dear! you must see Harriot somehow,' but there it ended.

" I have so much to say to you that does not do for writing, that it will be a great mortification not to see you. Sir Richard Croft will have been a fortnight here to-morrow, and he is quite at home ; but that he was from the first.

"Lady John Thynne [4] is very pretty, pleasant, and unaffected, and a great comfort to me.

" I find nature intended that I should not dwell alone, for it does not agree with me.

" Dr. Short is here, and is to stay until the event is

---

[4] Lady John Thynne, Mary Anne, daughter of Thomas Master, Esq. ; wife of Lord John Thynne, third son of first Marquis of Bath. In 1838 he succeeded his brother as Baron Carteret, and died 1849, when the title became extinct. She was one of the Ladies of the Bedchamber to the Princess Charlotte.

over, so we meet at dinner nine[5] in number. I long to hear how the Royal visit went off at Melbury,[6] I hope you went over to help it out. How long do they remain at Weymouth? I fully expect the Bath water to be the death of the Queen.

"Remember me to Mr. F. and all.

"Ever your affectionate,

"A. C."

THE DOWAGER COUNTESS OF ILCHESTER TO LADY H. FRAMPTON.

"*Sydney Place, Bath, November 7th,* 1817.

"MY DEAR HARRIOT,—We return to Windsor to-morrow. I think you will be glad to hear that the Queen is better than we could expect after the severe shock this sad event has given her.

"The calamity is strikingly awful, and appears to be unusually unexpected. The first express we had yesterday to announce a dead son, assured us of poor Princess Charlotte's safety, but a few hours after brought the last dismal news. Poor dear Mrs. Campbell and Lady John gave good reports as late as six o'clock Wednesday evening, and at two o'clock the following morning all was over, so they were kept completely in the dark, and did not witness her sufferings. Poor soul! we hear she

---

[5] The Prince Leopold, the Princess Charlotte, Lady John Thynne, Mrs. Campbell, Baron de Hardenbrock, Colonel Addenbrooke, the Rev. Dr. Short, Dr. Stockmar, Sir Richard Croft.

[6] The Duke and Duchess of Gloucester visited Lord and Lady Ilchester at Melbury from October 20th until the 23rd, when Lady Harriot Frampton was one of the party. On November 4th their Royal Highnesses drove over from Weymouth, where they were staying at the King's Lodge, and spent the day at Moreton; and on the 6th the Duke of Gloucester shot at Moreton.

bore them with great fortitude and resolution. I feel very anxious about dear Mrs. C., she has so much to go through now, under the melancholy circumstances of the house. Lord John Thynne has just gone to them, and thank God they have Dr. Short at Claremont. I know you would wish to hear something, but you cannot doubt the general dismay and grief of all around. Indeed, in a public and private point of view, here is an important chasm made to our future hopes and expectations. Love to all around you.

" From your affectionate,
" M. ILCHESTER."

LADY CHARLOTTE LEMON TO THE SAME.
" <i>Deans Leaze, November 8th</i>, 1817.</div>

" MY DEAR HARRIOT,—I had a letter from Lady Isabella[7] to-day to say that the Duchess of Gloucester was pretty well. They set off this morning to Bath, and go to London on Monday, not to return to Weymouth.

" She says the Duke of York broke the intelligence to the Prince Regent, who was quite stunned on hearing it. We can think of nothing else.

" Yours very affectionately,
" C. A. LEMON."

THE DOWAGER COUNTESS OF ILCHESTER TO LADY HARRIOT
FRAMPTON.
" <i>Windsor, November 10th</i>, 1817.</div>

" MY DEAR HARRIOT,—I have just seen the Queen, who has shown me a paper of Dr. Baillie's, stating every circumstance respecting the confinement. . . .

---

[7] Lady Isabella Thynne, daughter of first Marquis of Bath, Lady of the Bedchamber to the Duchess of Gloucester.

"The only reflection which *calms* my mind upon the subject is, 'that not a Sparrow falls to the ground without permission.'

"Nevertheless, Sir R. Croft [8] ceases to be an object of jealousy with his brother accoucheurs, and Mrs. Griffiths with her sister nurses. All the absent must be thankful.

"I have at last heard from dear Mrs. Campbell; she assures me that she is well, and evidently is wound up to the duty she is engaged in. She says scenes of affliction do not disagree with her, and that 'this is one of real woe. The sight of poor Prince Leopold is grief enough. Dr. Short he does not like to lose sight of, and the Queen tells me she understands that on Saturday the Prince received the Sacrament from him. It is a heartrending business.

"Mrs. Campbell says that she and Lady John Thynne had seen Mother and Babe put into the last sad receptacle; they sit up alternately, and never are absent from the room at the same time. The grief here hourly increases as the whole sense and extent of the calamity is enforced upon the mind.

"*I* have just been told that I shall be called upon as Chief Mourner. God knows I sincerely grieve for her, and recall many amiable traits and gratifying circumstances which at the time claimed a real affection for her, which, till now, has been chilled somewhat by neglect; but, my dear Harriot, I have before this time had occasion to observe that great happiness does not agree with the human mind, and I suppose no two persons have ever been so entirely left to the indulgence of their own feelings as the Prince and Princess have been, it appearing a point of duty in all that they should

[8] Sir Richard Croft, Bart., M.D. He shot himself in February, 1818.

not be interfered with. The last duty I was called upon
to fulfil was to attend at her wedding, and now so soon
to follow her to the grave! C. Cotes is also sent for, I
believe, and Lady Harrowby and Lady Rosslyn, but on
no account name these circumstances till they are made
public, for all may be changed before the next week is
over.

"The Duke and Duchess of Gloucester come to-
morrow. They are now at Carlton House. I have
many letters to write, but could not help complying
with your request as far as I could.

"Of the dear Queen I fear we cannot yet say what
the effect of all this may be to her; however, she
sleeps well, but I cannot say looks so. I go on writing
to you when I have more to do than I and my pen can
well manage to-day. God bless you all.

" Ever, dear Harriot,

" Your affectionate,

"M. I."

THE DOWAGER COUNTESS OF ILCHESTER TO THE MARCHIONESS
OF LANSDOWNE.

" Windsor, November 11th, 1817.

"MY DEAREST LOUISA,—As you are now at Moreton
you will hear from Harriot the particulars I gave her
yesterday of all I then could learn of the very sad termination to all our hopes in dear Princess Charlotte.
Every hour increases our sense of this affliction, as preparations are making for the last melancholy duties,
and all who so recently attended her the " happy
bride," are to follow her and the much-wished-for son
to their graves. Mrs. Campbell assures me she is not
ill. I long, yet dread to see her, but we shall meet on

Tuesday at the end of all our dear Princess's earthly pomp. I do not wonder that you should doubt the first intelligence, we could not believe it.

"I have just seen the Duchess of Gloucester. She is very much overcome indeed, and tells me many little circumstances which are very interesting. She says that ten days ago, when dear Princess Charlotte had taken the Sacrament, she, soon after the Service, gave her hand to Dr. Short,[1] and said, 'I have not now a wish ungratified, any change must be for the worse.' When informed that her child was dead she said she was sorry for the Prince, and added, 'I hope we may be more fortunate another time,' and certainly showed no sign of fear the whole time.

"I have just got a letter from Mrs. Campbell. The Prince has had a bad night. He often comes into *the* room, which she says she thinks does him good, and the Regent is gone to him to-day, meaning to stay no more than ten minutes; but the sooner their meeting is over the better. The Regent has so implored to have the Duchess of Gloucester with him for a few days at Brighton till all is over, that the Duke has consented, being much affected by the manner in which it was asked.

"All this is for Harriot as well as for you, and the Duke of Gloucester sends grateful messages to her and to Mr. Frampton, but I have not time to give all now.

"Ever your affectionate,

"M. ILCHESTER."

FROM MRS. CAMPBELL TO LADY H. FRAMPTON.

"*Claremont, November 11th,* 1817.

"MY DEAR LADY HARRIOT,—I have received your kind

---

[1] Chaplain to the Princess Charlotte and to Prince Leopold.

letter, but had intended to write even if I had not, as I felt sure you would wish to hear of me. I am not ill, and I hope may keep up till after the Funeral, though at times I feel the want of sleep, but to-night is my turn to go to bed.

"Like you, I was not aware till the blow came, how deeply it would wound. Never was human being so deplored. As yet it appears a horrible dream, and when in the midst of some of the very feeling letters I receive, it comes across me, 'Shall I show her this?'

Prince Leopold is calm, and exerts himself all in his power. He sees us all, and even tries to employ himself; but it is grief to look at him. He seems so heartbroken. Dr. Short is a great comfort to him, and walks out with him. To-day the Prince came, and sat an hour and a half with me, but it only served to augment my regret that the tie is broken which bound such a man to us. Oh! had it been the will of God to have spared either mother or child! Either would have been a consolation to lessen the affliction for the loss of the other.

"*Wednesday.*—I was in bed last night, but it only seems to give me a clearer view of the calamity which has befallen us. There is much I could say if with you, but I cannot write, indeed I have not time, for I am bewildered by the letters I receive, and have to answer. After the Funeral I think of going to Burlington Street to collect my confused thoughts, and consider how I can begin life again, now, at the end of it.

"The Prince has all the hair; he spared me a little bit, of which you shall have half.[2] He also gave a bit to

---

[2] The Hair is placed in a Brooch which formed one half of a Clasp for a Belt given by the Princess Charlotte to Lady Harriot Frampton at the Royal Lodge at Weymouth on Christmas Day, 1815. It is now in my possession.—H. G. M.

the Regent, at his request. Many have asked for it, but I do not think he will part with any to them. My kind remembrances to Mr. Frampton. No one possessed a higher place in Princess Charlotte's opinion than he did, and she had impressed the Prince with the same. God bless you, my dear Lady Harriot.

"Ever your affectionate,

"A. C."

THE DOWAGER COUNTESS OF ILCHESTER TO THE SAME.

"*Windsor, November* 16*th*, 1817.

"The poor Queen feels deeply. She was very fond of Princess Charlotte, and now every affecting circumstance and retrospect of this sad event is harrassing to a degree. It has been the will of God that we should lose Her, but to think how ill-managed she *appears* to have been is heart-breaking."

MRS. CAMPBELL TO THE SAME.

"*Cattemont, November* 18*th*.

"MY DEAR LADY HARRIOT,—You are so kindly anxious about me that I write a line to say that I am really not ill. The Prince had a good night, and has remained most of this day in the room with Her. I shall miss my visits there as well as Him. In the mornings I said my prayers by Her and her Child. She and the Prince had appointed me Governess to it, and it was to have been given entirely into my care. This, although a great addition to my loss and sorrow, has done me much good, as convincing me that the Princess's *heart* was not changed, nor her *opinion*, though her manner *was*. Had they but told me so, or had Dr. Short so far trusted me—for he knew this—how much pain and wear of spirits would it not have saved me!

"I was fully persuaded that both the Prince and Princess wished me to resign, at the very time they had settled on my remaining for life. They were to have gone abroad in the summer, and left the Child with me. How I should have loved it, and how happy I should have been! and I had not even the small comfort of enjoying it in hope.

"We leave this at six, this evening; whether we shall have to sit up all night, we do not know, but I hope not, as I should be sorry not to be able to go through the next day.

"I can say nothing as to Sir R. Croft. His interest was that the Princess Charlotte should do well, and she had the utmost confidence in him.

"I am convinced that he acted to the best of his judgment and with great anxiety about her.

"I do not see that anything can be said at present about the Bust. There is but one in the house, and it is as like *you* as *her*, and was turned out and sent to Mrs. Louis' room long ago. Dr. Short can mention it some time or other; but everything that the poor Princess touched, wore, or even looked at, is endeared to the Prince so much that I do not think he will part with anything.

"I have had many applications for even a bit of ribbon that had belonged to her, and so has Lady John, but we cannot get it.

"Lady Ilchester will write to you from Windsor after to-morrow. I have more letters than I can read, not to say answer.

"When I leave this I shall go to Burlington Street, if convenient to Harry.

"Your affectionate,

"A. CAMPBELL.

" What a change has this sad event made to me ! but I do not think about it just now ; if I live, I shall have time enough to reflect upon it."

MRS. CAMPBELL TO THE SAME.

" 31, *Old Burlington Street, November 29th,* 1817.

" MY DEAR LADY HARRIOT,—I am very grateful for your kind letter, but so oppressed with business that it is out of my power to write to my friends.

" I came here on Tuesday, and, without being selfish, I may be allowed to feel a pang at quitting such a Home —for I do not know what. Life to begin again, at its close !

" I am not ill, but really overcome by the kindness of friends. To be alone and to get my business settled would give rest to my mind ; but the former I am not permitted to be, so many have claims to come in, and of course cannot get on with the latter. Prince Leopold will set out for Weymouth early next month, therefore it is a great object that I should give up my papers ; but I see little hope of it. Lady Caroline Damer has lent him *Came*,[3] and he will, I believe, go there first.

" The Prince is calm, but it is the calmness of settled grief. He goes to Weymouth because the poor Princess liked it.

" God bless you all.

" Ever your affectionate,

" A. C."

[3] Came House, near Dorchester, in Dorsetshire, one of the seats of Lady Caroline Damer, who herself resided at Milton Abbey. On the death of Lady Caroline in 1828 Came devolved, by her bequest, on her kinsman, the Right Honourable Colonel George Lionel Dawson Damer, and is now the property of his son.

THE DOWAGER COUNTESS OF ILCHESTER TO THE SAME.
                          " *Bath, November* 27*th.*

" MY DEAR HARRIOT,—I am sure that I have written to
you, but where my letter has gone I cannot tell.   I was
inwardly grumbling at not hearing from you when I
received yours this morning.

" I am very anxious about dear Mrs. Campbell, in
every way.   She looked a shadow at the Funeral, but
would not admit that she was otherwise than well.   I
am, however, sure that perfect quiet is quite essential at
the present moment to mind and body.   I only wish that
this Bath duty [4] had not occurred, for I am sure otherwise
I could have been spared to her, and my mind would
have been less harassed than it is, for I cannot quite
rally after all the last week's melancholy circumstances;
however, I have great comfort in my colleague, Lady
Melville,[5] who is kindness and feeling itself.   I never
knew her before.

" The Queen is pretty well, and still is sanguine as to
the effect of the Waters.   Princess Elizabeth's looks I do
not like.   The sight of Prince Leopold at the Funeral I
shall never forget; indeed, it was heart-breaking.

                          " Yours affectionately,
                                        " M. I."

FROM MRS. CAMPBELL TO THE SAME.
          " *Old Burlington Street, December* 6*th*, 1817.

" MY DEAR LADY HARRIOT,—It was not in my power
even to read your letter of to-day till after the post was

----

[4] Lady Ilchester was in attendance on Queen Charlotte at Bath.

[5] Anne, daughter and heiress of Richard Saunders, Esq., M.D., married second Viscount Melville, Lord Privy Seal in Scotland, &c.   Vis-
countess Melville was Lady of the Bedchamber to the Queen (1816), and
in that capacity attended the funeral of the Princess Charlotte.

gone. I am getting on as to business—have not above a dozen bills now to pay—have gone over all accounts, and have only to copy the one book into the other, and fifteen letters remaining to answer, this not one of them. But every trades-person takes up so long a time, and so many artists come to beg me to look at the pictures they are at work upon, and so many particular friends *must* come in, that even now I cannot say when I shall have done.

"Prince Leopold does not go until near Christmas. The Baron [6] was here yesterday, and gave but a bad account of him, and he has a pain in his face. I take it the Prince means to make acquaintance with Mr. Frampton from the way he inquired the distance to Moreton, &c., and I know he is highly impressed as to his character, and the poor Princess always did Mr. F. justice, so he has him on his mind. I hope to give up my papers next week, but have no idea of leaving this until after Christmas. I have promised to visit Mrs. Scott and also Lady Liverpool, who offered me their houses as my home at the first, and I must look a little into my own affairs when the other is finished. Louisa has pressed me most warmly to go to Bowood and to make that my road to Dorset. I have left it open, not liking to refuse so much kindness, but Lord Lansdowne will be returned, and then I shall not be wanted. If I can do so I shall certainly pay you a visit, and I am very grateful for all your kind arrangements. The medical report does not satisfy people here. For my own part, all I have witnessed has lowered the profession extremely in my opinion, but of that when we meet. Mrs. Louis knows my opinion for long previous to the confinement, but I could prevent nothing nor remedy what I disapproved, so the less I say the better. To-morrow

[6] Baron de Hardenbrock, Aide-de-Camp and Equerry to Prince Leopold.

will be poor Prince Leopold's birthday. Much was planned for that. Oh! it is a sad change, and to me most of all. Remember me to Mr. Frampton. I will write if I hear of anything being settled as to the Prince's going to Dorsetshire. My love to all,

" Ever, my dear Lady Harriot,

" Yours affectionately,

" A. C.

" *Monday* (8*th*).—I have a very indifferent account of the Prince Leopold this morning."

1818.

" *Old Burlington Street, January* 1*st*, 1818.

"MY DEAR LADY HARRIOT,—I write a few lines to tell you that Prince Leopold is to set out for Came on the 5th, and will not stop by the way. I asked what he would wish as to the gentlemen in the neighbourhood, as I knew my friends there would wish to pay all attention and respect, but not to annoy him by calling if not agreeable. He said, ' After some time, there were some that he should wish to know—Lord Ilchester and Mr. Frampton, Charlotte was partial to, and they were good.' Now I should recommend Mr. Frampton to ride over some morning soon, and to leave his name, and then to wait to hear from him.[7] The Prince's intention is to go to Weymouth if he finds he can be retired there, and to stay for six weeks or two months.

[7] During the residence of Prince Leopold in Dorsetshire, he paid a visit to Moreton. The following extract is taken from my father's pocket-book journal :—

" *March* 24*th*, 1818.—H.R.H. Prince Leopold of Saxe Coburg, Sir Robert Gardiner, and Dr. Short came in the morning."

The Prince drove over from Weymouth, had a collation, and afterwards walked about the grounds.

"I finished my business yesterday, and closed the account at the banker's, and sent the book and balance of the money to the Prince, so my occupation and the year have ended together; it was a fatal year to me, and I have no great hopes from the future.

" Colonel Addenbrook does not go with Prince Leopold, which is unfortunate, as he knows Weymouth, which Sir Robert Gardiner does not. The Baron and Dr. Stockmar [8] go with Prince Leopold. If Mr. F. makes acquaintance with any of these gentlemen, he will find the Doctor the smallest body, but the largest mind of the party; but this is quite private information for yourselves. The little man is shy and very retired, or I should say *retiring.* They all talk English well now, the Baron the least, although he was the only one who could speak it at first.

"I am to go next week to Coombe Wood for two days to Lady Liverpool. I have been to see a bust that a man is moulding of the Princess Charlotte, and think it the most like thing that there is of her; should it succeed I do not yet despair of Mr. Frampton getting his, as I should have no scruple in mentioning the promise should an opportunity offer hereafter.

" My love to Mr. F. and all.
                    " Ever, my dear Lady Harriot,
                              " Yours affectionately,
                                        " A. C."

[8] Christian Frederick von Stockmar, appointed by Prince Leopold of Saxe Coburg, on his marriage with the Princess Charlotte, as his physician, but after the death of H.R.H. he resigned that office and became his Private Secretary and Comptroller of the Household. Stockmar accompanied the Prince on his accession to the throne of Belgium, and always remained attached to him, but would never accept any official appointment. He died at Coburg, 1863.

FROM LADY SUSAN O'BRIEN TO HER NIECE, LADY HARRIOT
FRAMPTON.

"*London, March 5th,* 1818.

"MY DEAR HARRIOT.—I have received your work safely,
and am very much obliged to you for it.   I exhibited it
yesterday at Lord Malmesbury's,[9] where I dined.   There
was a large company, some geniuses, no doubt, and if you
had been seated as I was between Lord Lansdowne and
Sir W. Scott, I daresay you would have extracted more
from their brains than I did, though I found them agreeable neighbours.   Lord Amherst[1] was one of the party,
and *he* really was one whom you might have questioned to
great advantage and amusement, but I was a mile from
him, and only looked at him with a sort of respect from
all the perils he has gone through.

"I think my friends have all been kind and glad to see
me again, Mrs. Damer looking very well and very friendly.

"I have made my Gloucester visit, and had a gracious
reception from the Duchess, and a visit from the Duke—
so all is right as to my Royalty's.

"I have two nieces in London, the Lady Herberts,[2]
who are very fond of being with me; they come very
often, and carry me about visiting whenever I wish to
go.   Indeed I have met with no difficulties of any sort,
and have passed my time not unpleasantly hitherto.

"We were almost demolished last night by the storm.
When I came home I found everything in dismay, the

[9] James Harris, C.B., a diplomatist of the first rank.   Created Earl
of Malmesbury, 1800.   Died 1820.

[1] William, first Earl Amherst, some time Ambassador to China, and
afterwards Governor-General of India.

[2] Lady Harriot and Lady Emily Herbert, daughters of Henry, second
Earl of Carnarvon.   Lady Emily married, 1822, Philip Pusey, Esq., of
Pusey.   They were great-nieces of Lady Susan O'Brien.

skylight broke in, and smoke and soot an inch deep,
owing to the pots on a neighbouring house having been
blown down. Happily nobody was on the stairs when
they fell, or they would have been killed. I hear to-day
of roofs blown off and various mischief: I hope I shall
not hear of trees lost at Stinsford or Melbury. I dined
on Monday at Lady Vernon's; she said her accounts from
Moreton were better.

"Pray, when you see Mr. H. Browne, ask him if he
did not sleep remarkably well the night after we met in
Old Palace Yard. We were patient listeners to the whole
life and adventures of the Duchess of Gordon, and I was
so composed by the narration, that I went home and
slept nine hours without waking.

"God bless you.

"Ever your affectionate aunt,

"L. S. O'BRIEN.

"I had written so far, when I received yours. You
will like to hear that Lady Sarah,[3] fearing I might leave
London before Mrs. G. Napier could spare her after her
confinement, has come to town, to spend a week with me

---

[3] Lady Sarah Napier, the youngest daughter of Charles Lennox,
second Duke of Richmond, born February, 1744-5. She was the first of
the ten unmarried daughters of Dukes and Earls who supported the train
of Queen Charlotte at her nuptials on September 8th, 1761. Lady Sarah
Lennox married, 1762, Sir Charles Bunbury, Bart. (who died 1821),
from whom she was divorced in 1776, and in 1781 she remarried the
Honourable George Napier, son of fifth Lord Napier, who died 1804, by
whom she had with other children, General Sir Charles Napier, G.C.B.,
General Sir George Napier, K.C.B., and General Sir William Napier,
K.C.B., author of "History of the Peninsular War." He married, 1812,
Caroline, daughter of the Honourable Henry Edward Fox, third son of
Henry, Lord Holland, youngest brother of the Right Honourable C. J.
Fox. Lady Sarah died 1826.

An interesting account of the life of Lady Sarah Napier is given in
"Holland House," by the Princess Marie Lichtenstein.

before it. This is a great pleasure to me, as I should
have been sadly vexed to have missed seeing her. We
hope Mrs. Campbell did not hear of her brother's death
till she was settled at Melbury. It will be a great
affliction to her, though, as she knew of his being very ill,
perhaps no surprise."

LADY SUSAN O'BRIEN TO HER NIECE, LADY MARY COLE, AT
PENRICE CASTLE.

" *Stinsford, February 7th,* 1818.

" The elections everywhere have been most disgraceful
to the country (Weymouth as bad as anywhere), and the
language and conduct are so revolutionary and atrocious,
that one cannot help fearing what it may come to.

"I had a letter from Lily[4] yesterday; the Whigs
triumphant; of course she is, and preparing to be one of
the ladies attendant on Sir Samuel Romilly's procession
from Covent Garden to Brooke's, where there is to be a
grand breakfast.

" This, their great favourite at present, I think very
much resembles Necker. A worthy, good sort of man in
private life, much beloved and esteemed by his family and
friends—so was Necker; longing for alterations, improvements, and economy—so was Necker; both from Geneva,
and with republican ideas of perfection and strong balance
that way, both meaning well, but the former doing more
mischief in France than probably the most profligate
Minister could have done. Here, I hope, the parallel
will cease, but certainly both the language and behaviour
of revolutionary mobs have been very scandalously
encouraged."

[4] Lady Elizabeth Feilding, her niece.

1819.

From H.R.H. Prince Leopold of Saxe Coburg to Mrs. Campbell.

"*Coburg, March 12th*, 1819.

"Dear Madam,—It is so long a while I had not the pleasure of conversing with you, that I think it high time recommending myself to your remembrance. Stocki, though, as it seems, somewhat in a dilatory way, has given you from time to time accounts of our life and proceedings, which renders needless my relating to you our adventure on the road. At first I did not derive the comfort from my stay here which I had every reason to expect, but the young and happy *ménage* of my brother,[5] as well as the sight of his fine child, gave me almost more pain than I had strength to endure.

"Time, which softens by degrees the most acute feelings, has kindly exercised its power on me; more accustomed to the sight of these objects I enjoy now somewhat more tranquillity, but still I avoid as much as possible the sight of the poor little child.

"I live here in the quiet and very snug house of my respectable and amiable mother,[6] who feels extremely happy by my being about her. I breakfast in her room, then I remain the longer part of the forenoon reading or talking to her. The latter part of the day I pay my visits to the other branches of the family, finishing it at the Castle, where my mother generally is present. Last week

[5] Ernest, Duke of Saxe Coburg, succeeded 1806, died 1844. He married, 1817, Dorothy Louisa, only daughter of Emile Leopold, Duke of Saxe Gotha, who died 1831. Their eldest son, Ernest Augustus, is the reigning Duke of Saxe Coburg and Gotha.

[6] Augusta Caroline, daughter of Henry, twenty-fourth Count Reuss d'Ebersdorf, married, 1777, Francis, Duke of Saxe Coburg, who died 1806. The Duchess survived until 1832.

I have been frightened by an attack she had, which might have proved dangerous without a speedy adoption of the proper remedies. She was affected all on a sudden by a sort of an inflammatory bowel complaint, to which several persons of very robust constitutions had fallen victims in the course of this extraordinary winter. It gave me the greatest uneasiness, but thank Heaven, after applying leeches the pain abated, and though still extremely weak she is slowly recovering. I hope that the spring will amend her health. She is always very much affected when I speak of my fast approaching departure. She says that at her time of life adieus may easily prove the last, but I trust to Heaven that if she takes good care of herself such an event may be far removed. Unfortunately, my eldest sister [7] suffers from

[7] Sophie, Comtesse de Mensdorf-Pouilly. The Governor of the fortress of Mayence for Austria was, in 1830, the Duke Ferdinand of Wurtemberg. His Duchess was a sister of Prince Metternich. The Vice-Governor was Field Marshal Count Mensdorf-Pouilly. He was still a very handsome man, who looked especially splendid in his uniform of a Hungarian General. He was very much liked in Mayence, where the pleasantest balls were those given by him. In addition to a well-provided buffet, there was always a hot supper for six or eight hundred persons—generally only the ladies were seated, and the gentlemen attended on them. The Count had distinguished himself at Regensberg, where Bonaparte was wounded; but when the Princess Sophia of Saxe Coburg fell in love with him he was only a major. In her youth it was said that the Princess was a pretty and merry girl; but at this time she was between fifty and sixty, and the mother of five sons. The Princess used to relate how she had once shocked the Grand Stewardess by jumping out of a window to escape from a Prince, a visitor at the Court of Coburg. She was now, however, somewhat lame, so that she could only walk with difficulty. Her complexion was dark, and the shape and form of her head not in the least like that of her brothers, the father of Prince Albert, or the King of the Belgians; but there was great intelligence in her brown eyes. Mademoiselle von Wiesenthau was the Princess's Dame de Compagnie—a very lovely young lady, with whom all the officers were in love. The

violent spasms since her last confinement, which have till now resisted every attempt of cure, though I have consulted the most eminent physicians on the Continent; her state is truly alarming, and gives me great pain. So, my dearest Mrs. Campbell, we are always assailed by some new misfortune when one hoped to have overcome the last.

"Poor Lady Ilchester's death has very much shocked me; so unexpected an event must have been particularly painful to you, who were such a warm friend to the whole family; if you have an opportunity, pray express to Lord Ilchester the very sincere interest I take in his calamity, of the bitterness of which, alas! few can be better judges than myself. Strange it is that most of the ladies who were Charlotte's friends are no more. Poor Lady Althorp, Lady Grant, &c.! Do you think the bustle of this life has already effaced Charlotte's memory in the minds of the people? I hope not, but new events exercise a strong influence on the human mind, and for that very reason it is my pride that I am a living monument of those happy days that offered to the country such bright prospects; and so I trust it will be made difficult to them to forget Charlotte as long as they see me.

"I should already sooner have thought of returning to dear old England, but I greatly wanted quiet and retire-

Princess was much afflicted with ennui, and liked to be amused and to see everything, and was especially fond of observing the life of the people, and went therefore everywhere, and without any other escort than Mademoiselle von Wiesenthau. She could easily do so, as the German people, even of the lower class, generally behave extremely well. Especially she never failed to attend military reviews, when she was usually seated on some eminence on the very battle-field, enveloped in the smoke of gunpowder, and surrounded by soldiers. In fine, she was very kind to the poor, though by no means rich.

ment, fallen from a height of happiness and grandeur seldom equalled, to accustom myself to the painful task of leading so very different a life. I will not dwell on this subject, when I know you understand me so well. My health is rather improved, but still not what it was in 1817, and probably never will become so again.

" I hope you will at the approaching more propitious weather visit Claremont sometimes, and look a little on your protections in the flower garden, and even the poultry yard.

" I think of leaving Coburg in April, if the state of health of my mother or sister give me no immediate cause of alarm, and in the meantime recommend myself to the continuation of your friendship, assuring you that I shall ever entertain the most sincere sentiments of regard and esteem for you.

" Dear madam,

" Your very sincere friend,

" LEOPOLD."

MRS. CAMPBELL TO DOWAGER COUNTESS OF ILCHESTER.

" Old Burlington Street, June 27th, 1819.

MY DEAREST LADY I.,—We have had a sad, wet day, but John and I went to St. George's Church at four o'clock, and we also went in the rain to see and take leave of Louisa Lansdowne, who is to be off by seven o'clock in the morning. She had so bad a headache that she was obliged to put off her ladies yesterday, and let it be a gentlemen's dinner for the Royal Dukes, but is well again to-day. I gave her a packet for you.

" My day at Marlborough House [8] was very satisfactory.

---

[8] Marlborough House, the residence of H.R.H. Prince Leopold. On the death of the third Duke of Marlborough in 1817, it was bought by the Crown for the Princess Charlotte and Prince Leopold. H.R.H. died

There were no ladies, so that I was there as one of the family; the Bishop of Salisbury[9] and a Sir Lewis —— somebody, whom I had met before, but forget his name; the Baron Stockmar, and Sir Robert.[1] The Prince was so kind, it was very gratifying. I sat by him, and after dinner he showed me the house, and sat on the sofa by me all the evening, and, except to the Bishop, spoke to no one but me. He said he had many things for me to assist him in, and that he should send Stocky to me very often as his little spy upon me, what I was doing with myself; and his manner was such that I found it impossible to bring in my plan of going to Ireland, and, indeed, regret more than ever the necessity for that visit.

" The Prince told me his plans, and that he was going to Scotland for six weeks in August, which I was glad to hear, as then he will be absent part of the time. He also told me of his parties for the next month, and who he was going to ask, and all in a way that was very gratifying. He inquired with much interest for Harry, you, Framptons, &c., entering quite with interest into the alterations at Moreton, and asked me over and over if I thought that ' Charlotte' was still thought of and remembered in Dorsetshire. The Prince has laid out a great deal of money on Marlborough House, in painting before the completion of the purchase, but the Prince lived in the house for some years.

[9] The Right Rev. John Fisher, Bishop of Salisbury from 1807 until 1825. He had been Preceptor to the Princess Charlotte.

[1] Sir Robert Gardiner, younger brother of Lieut.-General Sir John Gardiner, R. A., was in the Peninsular War and at Waterloo. On the marriage of the Princess Charlotte he was appointed principal equerry; was military aide-de-camp to George IV., William IV., and Her Majesty; General 1841, Governor of Gibraltar from 1848 till 1855. He married the daughter of Lieut.-General Sir John and Lady Emily Macleod. Sir Robert Gardiner died 1864.

and cleaning it, very handsome carpets to the whole range of apartments, and silk furniture, and on my asking if the silk on one sofa was foreign, he seemed quite to reproach me, and said I should never see anything that was not English in his house, that he could avoid. I could not help wishing that Mrs. Williams had been with us to judge of the sum that Prince Leopold must have expended in the last three months on English manufactures—magnificent glass lustres in all the rooms, &c. He has also purchased a large collection of fine paintings, which are coming over, and though that is giving money out of the country, it brings a value back.

" The Prince told me that it was a painful task to attend the christening[2] at Kensington, but he thought it right.

" *Monday*.—Your letter of Friday has just come, and

[2] The infant daughter of their Royal Highnesses the Duke and Duchess of Kent, born May 24th, 1819, was baptized at Kensington Palace June 24th following.

The following extract is from "Recollections of the Early Years of the Present Century," by the Honourable Amelia Murray :—

"It was believed that the Duke of Kent wished to name his child 'Elizabeth,' that being a popular name with the English people; but the Prince Regent, who was not kind to his brothers, gave notice that he should stand in person as one Godfather, and that the Emperor of Russia was to be another. At the ceremony of baptism, when asked by the Archbishop of Canterbury to name the infant, the Prince Regent gave only the name of 'Alexandrina;' the Duke requested that one other name might be added. 'Give her the mother's name also, then,' 'but,' he added, 'it cannot precede that of the Emperor. The Queen, on her accession, commanded that she should be proclaimed as 'Victoria' only."

Extract from a letter from Miss Murray to Mrs. Mundy, September 19th, 1868 :—

"I am happy to find that the Queen has not been annoyed by anything I have inserted in my little book. She sent me one correction, which was a very new bit of information, viz. that it was not 'Elizabeth,' but '*Georgiana*' that the Duke of Kent wished to name her."

I am always thankful for a good account of the dear ones at Melbury.

" We have had a tremendous thunderstorm, with such a torrent of rain as will injure the hay very much, and another is coming on, so no business to-day. I have no time to write to Harriot, so think, perhaps you would send this on for her to read and burn. Poor Dr. Short has been dangerously ill at Exeter when on a visit on business to Mrs. Popham. Mrs. Short and his daughters were sent for, but he is now recovering. Poor Addenbrooke has gained a lawsuit by Lady Pitt's death, and is so worried, I fear it will hurt him very much. She made several foolish wills, and the amiable Lord Howe wants to set them aside, and disputes 4000*l.* left to Colonel Addenbrooke, the only friend the poor old soul had on earth.

" Ever your very affectionate,

" A. C."

1820.

THE DOWAGER LADY VERNON TO MARY FRAMPTON.

" *Muddiford, October 2nd*, 1820.

" I have to-day a letter from a sort of neighbour of the delightful Queen, who says she is in the habit of seeing a person whose business often obliges her to call upon this fair lady. She says that the Queen is low, very averse to quitting her domain, lies in bed the greatest part of the day complaining of the cold and general climate. Says that ' Dear William ' (meaning Austin) has never been well since he came to England ; and, in short, is not well in health, and completely out of sorts. Very *disagreeably dirty* in her person, and her establishment and mode of life very extraordinary and comfortless, and unbecoming her situation.

"I hope she will be disgusted sufficiently to set off to dear Bergami, but the Radical party will not suffer her to depart till a little more mischief is completed. This will be cooked up before the Parliament meet for business, and I have no doubt is now cooking; the *Times* are giving a strong helping hand, no doubt.

"I have a letter from Mrs. Kerby, speaking of her affairs, the prospect of which is melancholy enough. Her daughter is engaged to marry a younger son of Lord Le Despencer's, who is to be a clergyman, a younger brother of Mr. Stapleton, who married Miss Bankes.

"God bless you.   Kind love to all.

"Ever yours most affectionately,

"G. V.

"A beautiful day, the sea quite enchanting.   I have made a new sort of walk, and long for my nephew back again to *see it*."

C. B. WOLLASTON TO MARY FRAMPTON.

"*December 1st*, 1820.

"On dating my letter, I am not sorry to find that on this day three weeks I may hope to be with you.   I wrote to James on the day of the procession[3] to St. Paul's, and you will like to hear that it passed off without riot. Indeed, I am glad that it took place, for if anything can make the Queen feel her degradation, such a *blackguard*

[3] November 29th was the day appointed by the Queen to return public thanks for the result of the late proceedings against her.   She was escorted from Brandenburg House, Kensington, by about 150 horsemen, and great numbers of people joined the cavalcade as it passed onwards, and at Temple Bar the procession was met by the Lord Mayor and Sheriffs, &c.   The Queen was attended by her Vice-Chamberlain and Lady Anne Hamilton, and was accompanied by Sir Robert Wilson, Mr. Hume, Mr. Hobhouse, &c.

set as attended her on this occasion must do so. The multitudes were immense that poured in from every quarter, but curiosity as well as affection would contribute to this, though I believe the language amongst them and the disposition to support her cause were strong enough. Scarcely a person of respectability was, however, seen in her train. You saw the names of her attendants, and of the five Members of Parliament. But where were all those peers and clamourers of the House of Commons who declare their satisfaction of her innocence, and their indignation at the ill usage she has met with? With such opinions it is base in them not to show themselves on such an occasion. To continue *my* politics. I have a strong idea that there will be a change in the Ministry after Parliament meets. I believe that Lord Liverpool wishes very much to retire, and it is true that the King sent for and saw Lord Granville. They were together at the Cottage in Windsor Park upwards of two hours, but during that time the King *is said* to have talked all and left no room for Lord G. to say scarcely a word, and I apprehend that the conversation ended without any great satisfaction on either side, Lord Granville having declined taking any place, or interfering in any arrangement. But if the Ministry *are* changed, *most certainly* I will not engage under a new master, whoever he may be.

" Yours affectionately,
" C. B. W."

1821.
C. B. WOLLASTON TO MARY FRAMPTON.
" <i>Curzon Street, January</i> 25<i>th</i>, 1821.</div>

"I have been better pleased with your account of my mother than with that which she gave of herself in her preliminary postscript, and I trust that you, too, will soon recover your usual strength.

"I dined on Wednesday at Lord Harrowby's with the Ryders only, Lady Harrowby is with Lady Ebrington at Dawlish. This party led to the proposal of another which I shall like much ; either Lord Harrowby [4] or Ryder will take me to-morrow to the latter's, Hertfordshire Place, and bring me back on Tuesday, and I am promised a lesson in whist, though I do not really intend to play with them, notwithstanding my study of Bob Short and Matthews.

"I think, by the conversation of these sage politicians and ministers, that the prospect of things is more favourable, and the Queen going down; but still the Liturgy question [5] hangs over their heads, and they are determined not to flinch on that point, though it is not denied that it would have been better if the name had been inserted at first. It is expected, and with confidence, that the majority will be in favour of ministers; but I fear that it will not be a predominant majority, and therefore that the question will still be kept up so as to create irritation and dissatisfaction."

THE SAME TO THE SAME.

"*March 1st*, 1821.

"The King did not go to the Concert,[6] as had been talked of; but he told the Archbishop of York at the Levée that he should come on some future night. The

---

[4] Lord Harrowby was at that time Lord President of the Council.

[5] This refers to the omission of the Queen's name in the Prayer for the Royal Family.

[6] Concert of Ancient Music, of which the Archbishop of York was one of the Directors. Lord Darnley was also a Director.

Queen is going to try her luck at a concert at the Mansion House this evening, but I really flatter myself that she has sunk considerably lately, and that there is much less interest about her. She has changed her mind about the Parliamentary allowance, and, notwithstanding her message, takes the arrears and the annuity. With the former she has agreed to purchase the Duke of Cambridge's House in Audley Street. This looks too much like staying here, but she may think it right to have a place of residence in England, and yet take her departure to the Continent.

"I wish I could get a sight of the Comet, as you have done, and perhaps I may do so next week at Bernard's; but it seems likely to disappear in this latitude before long, unless it should, as is the more common practice with those of its kindred, change its position, and keep in the visible part of the heavens.

"I have just been reading 'Anastasius.' It is not by any means a book for our Book Society."

FROM THE SAME TO THE SAME.

"Curzon Street, March 23rd, 1821.

" In the first place, as a supplement to my last letter to James, I must say, in justice to the Directors, that at the Ancient Music Concert every arrangement was made for the convenience of His Majesty and the public, and the Directors changed their doors and staircases for that night. The concert bill was sent to the King, and he was requested to make alterations in it, and Lord Darnley was as well pleased with the civility of the answer, as all persons, with very few exceptions, are, when Kings or Princes are the parties who proffer the civilities. So the concert began and ended with " God save the King," and besides, it was by much the best we have had this year, and indeed contained almost all the best things which the Directors ever give us, so we must be contented with the refuse for the rest of the season.

" The King makes himself a strange figure by drawing in his great body with a broad belt, and by the close buttoning of a kind of uniform jacket more than dress-coat, and hiding the lower part of his face with a large black neckcloth, and then swelling out his shoulders and the upper part of his person with tags and embroidery, and covering it with orders, instead of the simple Star and Garter worn by his father, and yet for a man of near sixty he contrives to look young by the help of a wig without powder; and his air and manner were as graceful as they used to be. So all this went off well, as did the opera the night before, and I believe the Drawing-room yesterday, without the Queen, though she certainly wrote to Lord Liverpool to declare her intention of going, and preparations were made to receive her. She was not to be stopped in her way to Buckingham House, but, on the contrary, to be treated with due honours, but when there was to be received by the Ministers, who were to show her into an apartment below stairs, and tell her that she could not see the King in the Drawing-room above.

" She has taken possession of Cambridge House, and one of her carriages was seen at the door at about the hour of the Drawing-room, but she certainly did not go her-self as late as three or four o'clock, when I was in the Park, where great crowds were collected. Her Majesty's popularity has, however, certainly evaporated, and is no longer dangerous.

" I shall not make my appearance till later than I had intended, and shall probably be delayed to within a short time of Easter."

THE SAME TO THE SAME.

"*Downing Street, May,* 1821.

"The Queen is going to the opera to-night. I wish she had chosen any other. I do not wish to see or hear of her, but her visits to the play have not answered. On the last occasion she went *incog.* into the stage box. 'God save the King' was called for, and the word 'King' pronounced emphatically. There was some groaning and hissing at her. This is the account on *one* side. The Coronation will certainly take place if the King's *wen*, or the remains of it, will suffer the crown to set easy on his head, and if he has not a fit of the gout. As the Queen has announced her intention of being in England, it is to no purpose to wait for her departure.

"Yours ever affectionately,
"C. B. WOLLASTON."

THE SAME TO THE SAME.

"*Curzon Street, June 7th,* 1821.

"Princess Augusta and the Duchess of Clarence were last night at the 'Messiah' in the Ancient Music Room. The former sat where her Mother used, and looked very like her. I have not seen her before for many a year."

"*Curzon Street, June 22nd.*

"The Queen has commenced a tour round the minor theatres, by way of bringing herself to the recollection of the mob, and preparing a stir at the Coronation. She began at Astley's, and was well received. The preparations are going on rapidly. I wish it was well over.

"Yours affectionately,
"C. B. W."

FROM MRS. CAMPBELL TO LADY H. FRAMPTON.

"31, *Old Burlington Street, July*, 1821.

" MY DEAR LADY HARRIOT,—The newspapers will give you the details of the Coronation[7] far better than I can, and moreover I am going to take leave of Prince Leopold, who sets out to-morrow for Coburg, and at five o'clock Emily Murray and I are to be with the Duchess of Gloucester, so you may judge how much time I have. Nothing could be finer than the sight, and Prince Leopold the most beautiful part of it. The King looked fagged out, and the canopy, with all those carrying it, and the train, took from the dignity of his appearance. When he had done with that he looked very dignified and graceful and pleased.

" We are well now, but were dead tired with the heat, length of time, and no food. No accommodation was made for ladies, or for those going in with tickets.

" Mr. Horner[8] looked very well, and so did Harry, but the coronets are most unbecoming things, and take from the height. Lord Londonderry looked very handsome."

1823.

FROM HENRY KER SEYMER, ESQ.,[9] TO MARY FRAMPTON.

"*Pisa*, 1823.

" The coins used here called 'Pisis' are crown pieces

[7] The Coronation of George IV. took place on July 19th, 1821.

[8] Thomas Strangways Horner, Esq., of Mells Park, Co. Somerset; in 1820 Gentleman of the Privy Chamber to King George III. He was in attendance on his relative, the Earl of Ilchester, at the Coronation ; died 1844.

[9] Henry Ker Seymer, Esq., of Hanford, Co. Dorset, married Harriet, sister of Horace, third Baron Rivers ; died 1834. Their second daughter became the wife of Edward Denison, Bishop of Salisbury.

of different dates, but not made at Pisa, as might be supposed from their name, there being no mint in Pisa.

" The money is coined at Florence, *that* mint has long been proud of the purity of the gold and silver, and therefore when prudence or necessity requires a greater degree of alloy to be used than is consistent with the dignity of the Florence mint, they stamp ' Pisis ' on the coin produced."

1824.

FROM THE SAME TO THE SAME.

" *Florence*, 1824.

" Mrs. Seymer and my daughter, Harriet, were presented at a private audience to the Grand Duke and Duchess.[1] I also was present. The Grand Duke was very affable. He told me that he had once accompanied Bonaparte in an excursion to Cherbourg, on which occasion he had seen the shores of England, and that the noise of the *feux de joie* for the Emperor had brought an English frigate very close into Cherbourg to see what was going on; the idea occurred to the Duke of the possibility of their all being taken prisoners and carried off to England, which amused him very much, and I daresay at that time he desired no better."

1825.

FROM LADY HARRIOT FRAMPTON TO MARY FRAMPTON.

" *London, May* 11*th*, 1825.

" On Monday Harriot and I dined at Lansdowne

---

[1] Leopold II., Grand Duke of Tuscany, succeeded his father, the Grand Duke Ferdinand, June, 1824 ; died 1870. He married Marie Anne Caroline, daughter of Prince Maximilian of Saxony, who died 1832.

House—a small party to meet Lady Cochrane.[2]   It consisted of Miss Fox, Lord Auckland, and Miss Eden, Lord Porchester,[3] Mr. McDonald, Mr. E. Stanley, and Mr. Portman. Lady Cochrane is a most attractive and interesting person. She is scarcely twenty-six, and very handsome, and has been married ten years. She has been twice round Cape Horn, once over the Cordilleras, has been twice stilottoed, and one of her children died in consequence of the hardships it underwent in some flight. Besides which she has had the variety of being like a queen in South America, with public days, guards, &c., for months, and in one earthquake lost 400 horses, some thousand *beeves*, and 20,000 sheep, as well as all her fine furniture. Lady Cochrane told it all with such nature and spirit that with the addition of a most changeable and intelligent countenance, it quite entranced both ladies and gentlemen.

" She has much of a Spanish countenance, and has lived so much abroad as to speak with a foreign accent, and can hardly help speaking Spanish when she is eager, but she is an Englishwoman.

" When asked whether the Patagonians were really such giants as is commonly reported, she replied that many of them were certainly extremely tall, and gave as an instance that their own servants and attendants used to put out the candles or lamps suspended from the ceilings by merely reaching up their arms when standing on the floor."

[2] Katharine, daughter of Thomas Barnes, Esq., married Thomas, Lord Cochrane, afterwards tenth Earl of Dundonald.

[3] Succeeded, 1833, as third Earl of Carnarvon; author of " The Moor," " Portugal and Gallicia." Married, 1830, Henrietta, eldest daughter of Lord Henry Molyneux Howard. Lord Porchester's mother, the daughter and heiress of Colonel Dyke Acland, was first cousin to Lady Lansdowne and Lady Harriot Frampton, &c.

FROM COLONEL ADDENBROOKE TO J. FRAMPTON, ESQ.

"*Marlborough House, May,* 1825.

"DEAR SIR,—Lady Harriot said what was very true. I offered her Ladyship the box at the play-house, but since that time I have the higher authority of the Prince[4] himself to accommodate her Ladyship thus. I enclose an order from *authority* for Covent Garden on Monday night, and hope to be acquainted with her Ladyship's convenience for Drury Lane some other evening during the ensuing week. The box there is only engaged for the first night of *King Lear* by Lady Torrens. If Lady Harriot can use Covent Garden either this night or to-morrow, it is quite at her Ladyship's service.

"Pray say to Lady Harriot that I warned the Prince of the possibility of his seeing Lady Harriot walking in the garden here. 'In that case,' said the Prince, 'she shall not be alone, for I will certainly join her and ask her Ladyship concerning her health.' Lady Harriot will understand this.

"Always, my dear sir,
"Your faithful and obedient servant,
"F. A. ADDENBROOKE."

1827.

FROM JAMES FRAMPTON TO HIS SISTER, MARY FRAMPTON.

"*London, June,* 1827.

"Charlton and I went last night to the opera, and heard the first act of the 'Mosé' and the first act of 'Tancredi.' Pasta sang very beautifully in the latter. The Queen of Wurtemberg[5] arrived last night. We

---

[4] H.R.H. the Prince Leopold of Saxe Coburg.

[5] Charlotte Augusta, Princess Royal of England, daughter of

heard the guns saluting her while at the opera, which is unusual, as in general no salute takes place after sunset. Prince Borghese is in London; he married Pauline, Napoleon's sister, as you may remember, but she is happily now dead.

"I think my little scheme of a week's visit to Dorsetshire is much less likely to take place than when I wrote yesterday. The weather is not so hot, as there is a high N.E. wind; and we are asked to dine at Lord Ducie's on Friday, to meet the Duke and Duchess of Gloucester.

"Moreover, Pasta performs 'Medea' on Thursday next. It is the last time that opera is to be performed this season, and I should like to see it again. I went last night to see 'Maria Stuarta,' which was very heavy, though a duet was pretty, and Pasta's acting before she was beheaded was good. The two Harriots are at Almacks. I have been to see the statue of Milo, by the young man of whom I told you, and the group of Sampson slaying the Philistines, and I think them most wonderful performances for any one, particularly for a young blacksmith in the country.

"Ever yours,
"JAS. FRAMPTON."

FROM THE SAME TO THE SAME.

"June 16th, 1827.

"Yesterday we had our dinner at Lord Ducie's, which

George III., second wife of Frederick Charles, King of Wurtemberg. He died 1816.

June 18*th*.—My aunt had a select party, with music, at Lansdowne House, to meet the Queen of Wurtemberg, at which we were of course present. Her Majesty was very gracious to my mother, and I was also presented to her. The Queen wore a turban headdress, and I thought her like those of the Royal Family whom I had seen, most like the Princess Augusta.—H. G. M.

was much as royal dinners usually are. The Lords had just thrown out the Game Bill, which pleased them. We were about twenty, and I liked the Duke of Northumberland,[6] who was one of the party. The new Attorney-General, Scarlett,[7] was also there, whom I have never seen since I was at Cambridge, and should not have remembered at all. I never was acquainted with him. Charlton and I were accidentally walking through St. James's Park yesterday, and saw the Queen of Wurtemberg coming out of the Palace. She did not appear to me at all larger than any other fat woman, and did not occupy a larger space on her side of the open carriage. Her face is oldened and more sallow, and I suppose I should not have known her elsewhere; but I recollected, I thought, the sort of features; but the Duchess of Gloucester told Harriot last night that she should not have known her.

"William Bond, whom I met yesterday, told me that many new King's Counsel had just taken their places, and amongst them the Mr. Williams who had been one of the Queen's Counsel; but that the King had desired that the name of Mr. Denman should never be mentioned to him. He was the most abusive of all, and compared the King to Nero.

"The Duke of St. Albans is to marry Mrs. Coutts to-day.

"I find there is to be a select party, and Pasta, at Lansdowne House, on Monday; but I like her much better at the opera than in a room.

"As nobody took up the Corn Bill in the House of Lords last night, it falls to the ground for this year.

[6] Hugh, third Duke, K.G., Ambassador Extraordinary at the Coronation of Charles X., 1825, subsequently Lord-Lieutenant of Ireland.

[7] Sir James Scarlett, Knight; created, 1835, Baron Abinger.

The present Ministers are very angry with the Duke of Wellington, and as much so with their old ally, Lord Grey, for the part he took."

FROM MRS. SHIRLEY TO MARY FRAMPTON.

" Cliff, June, 1827.

" MY DEAR MARY,—I write on my return from my drive to Milton Abbey. The day was lovely, and the country in great beauty. Lady Caroline Damer was quite glad to see me, and means to visit you some Thursday. She had heard from Lady C. Waldegrave a pleasing and good account of the King, who had kindly asked her to attend his sister while in England. She was with the Royal Family when the Queen of Wurtemberg arrived: the King had been waiting patiently several hours for her. The meeting was very kind on all sides, the Princess Sophia the most affected by it (added to waiting so late for dinner). They all dined together about nine; then the King went back to Windsor. Although well, he is on crutches, and very lame; no wonder he cannot have Drawing-rooms, &c. Lady Caroline bade me tell you all this.

" Yours ever,
" P. B. S."

FROM JAMES FRAMPTON TO MARY FRAMPTON.

" June 26th, 1827.

" MY DEAR MARY,—We have heard of John Strangways. The letters from him are gone to Melbury, but Mr. Stratford Canning's [8] account to Lord Anson is that they were disguised as pilgrims going to Mecca, and were discovered two days' journey from Aleppo, and seized and

---

[8] Created Viscount Stratford de Redcliffe, 1852.

conveyed as prisoners to that place. They communicated their situation to the French Consul, who immediately procured their release; but previous to it Mr. Anson [9] showed symptoms of the plague, and was placed in some house belonging to the Consul, out of quarantine, where he had all the medical attendance that was to be had, and John attended him to the last. John was after that, as you know, safe in quarantine, and is coming home as soon as he can."

FROM C. B. WOLLASTON TO MARY FRAMPTON.

"Westbrook, Thursday, June 7th.

"MY DEAR MARY,—I propose being at home on this day week, and in some respects I should not be sorry to advance my day of departure, for there are many people coming here or expected, for it is a sort of open house to the family and its connections at all times. I found Lord Harrowby here on Monday, and he went away yesterday morning. I was very glad to meet him, and had a great deal of amusing political conversation with him in a long ride we took together to see the thorns in Lord, or I should rather say, in Lady Bridgwater's park, which, though going off, were still in high beauty; and also at other houses here. He looks old and harassed. Is always kind and friendly to me, and expresses himself so to all of us. I also found here Lord Sandon and Lady Frances.[1] I like Lord Sandon very much. He is easy and quite unaffected, very open and conversible. A

[9] The Honourable Henry Anson, fifth son of Thomas, first Viscount Anson; died 1827.

[1] Daughter of the first Marquis of Bute, wife of Lord Sandon, married 1823; died 1859.

staunch supporter of the present Government, and much inclined to Whiggism. Not so his uncle, who is very lukewarm in his support, and does not seem to like the present arrangement. As to Lady Frances, she is a most singular person in appearance, and altogether unlike anything I ever saw, except in a picture. The upper part of her face is very beautiful, but when she speaks, and particularly when she smiles, her features curl up, and she is almost plain. She is very fanciful in her dress; sometimes like a Madonna, which agrees best with the character of her countenance; the hair quite flat on the head, and tied in a large knot behind, which is concealed by a long white veil fastened on the top of the head and flowing backwards. This was the first attire I saw her in, and I was very much struck by its singularity and effect. Sometimes she has nothing on her head, and the hair, of which there is a great deal, tucked up as close as possible—never any curls. Lady Frances plays on the guitar, and sings to it trifling things, but in too low a pitch of voice, which does not suit her. Perhaps my general musical *fastidiousness* prevents my being properly sensible of its merit, but others are delighted, and she certainly *looks* to great advantage during the performance. She seems to be really very amiable and unaffected in her manner. The family are very fond of her. The Bishop's [2] eldest daughter is going to be married to Sir George Grey's eldest son,[3] who it seems is a lawyer. This seems to please them all much, and is a very satisfactory *spiritual* as well as temporal connection, more so in the former than the latter view at

[2] The Honourable Henry Ryder, D.D., Bishop of Lichfield and Coventry, third son of the first Lord Harrowby.

[3] Subsequently the Right Honourable Sir George Grey, Bart., P.C., &c., &c., second Baronet.

present, as the means are but small at setting out. In
this house there is never any lack of fires, and it is well
that this is the case, for more cold and sour weather at
this season I never remember.

"There has been abundance of rain, and everything
looks beautiful, but I fear the cold high wind of last night
must have blighted and injured whatever it met with.
This is certainly one of the prettiest places I ever saw for
variety of ground, and the walks and pleasure-grounds
are disposed in excellent taste."

1828.

REMINISCENCES.

LADY CAROLINE DAMER.

"AT the time of the Duke of Cumberland's marriage he
called upon the Princess Charlotte, who received him as
usual without alluding to his change of state. After
some time the Duke said, "But, Charlotte, you do not
wish me joy." "Of what?" was her answer. "Of my
marriage, to be sure." "As the Queen has not informed
me of it, I did not think it proper to mention it," was
the Princess's discreet reply. The Duke took leave of
her immediately. Queen Charlotte just before this visit
had announced to the Duke of Cumberland that his wife
could not be received at court on account of her
character.

The Princess of Wales, afterwards Queen Caroline,
was at a party with the old King and Queen, when some
allusion was made to the King's (George III.) privy purse.
She said, "It should be called a ridicule." "Why so?"
"Oh, because it is always empty."

In 1827 and the following year a son of Sir Michael
Seymour was Chaplain to George IV., and preached at his

private chapel every Sunday. The pew fitted up for the King was hidden by a large screen, so that neither the clergyman nor any of the congregation knew whether his Majesty was present or not. The uncle of Mr. Seymour, Sir William Knighton, told him never to preach sermons on mere moral duties and virtues, the safe course was to keep entirely to doctrinal explanations, &c.

Mr. Okeden [4] was in Switzerland at the same time with Lord and Lady Conyngham and their sons when boys; he was very intimate with the family, and at that time Sumner, afterwards Bishop of Winchester, was tutor to the boys. In a confidential conversation with Mr. Okeden Sumner lamented having attached himself to that family, and said that he had mistaken his interest by so doing, as they were never likely to be of any use to him in advancing him in the world. Lord Mount Charles, then very young, had formed an attachment to a Mdlle. Monnaie, the daughter of a banker, I believe, at Geneva, and Lady Conyngham lamented the connection—much fearing her son would be drawn in to marry her. Mr. Okeden recommended to Lady C. sending Lord Mount Charles home to England, and that she should employ Mr. Sumner to represent to the family that notwithstanding the beauty, &c., of the young lady, such a connection could not be sanctioned by his father and mother.

This advice was followed, and the future Bishop executed the commission so perfectly that he himself became the husband of Mdlle. Monnaie, to whose character or connections for him there was no objection.

---

[4] D. Parry Okeden, Esq., of Turnworth, Co. Dorset, married first, Mary, daughter of the Rev. J. Harris, and secondly, 1817, Lady Harriet Capel, sister of the sixth Earl of Essex; died 1833. He was an intimate friend of Mr. Wollaston, and his agreeable society was much appreciated at Bowood.

When Lady Conyngham became the Favourite of George IV., all this was remembered to his advantage, and he became thoroughly aware that he had been by good fortune much truer to his own interest than he had supposed.

REV. J. L. JACKSON.

George the IVth, soon after Dr. Sumner was made Bishop of Winchester, sent to him to say that he intended to receive the Holy Communion. By some mistake the Bishop arrived half-an-hour later than the King expected, which irritated His Majesty extremely, and on the arrival of the Bishop he found him in a state of mind which he judged quite unfit for such an ordinance. After hearing with the greatest respect and humility the King's expressions of anger at the delay, which were in one instance accompanied by an oath—the Bishop expressed the greatest sorrow for the unfortunate mistake, but firmly, though couched in the most respectful language, refused to administer the Sacrament to him whilst his mind was in its present agitated state. At first this only enraged His Majesty still more, but the Bishop remained steady to his resolve, and left the palace. In a week the King sent for Sumner again, shook hands with him, and thanked him for his previous refusal, and requested, if he then thought it proper, that he might receive the Sacrament from his hands.

EXTRACT FROM A LETTER FROM ENNIS.

"*July*, 1828.

"During the contest between Mr. Vesey Fitzgerald and Mr. O'Connell in County Clare which excited so much interest from being the first attempt made to elect a Roman Catholic to serve in Parliament, such was the order maintained through the influence of the Roman Catholic priests, that although 40,000 people were assembled, there was no riot or confusion whatever, not a drunken man seen amongst the mob, and a greater degree of quietness prevailed than is commonly seen at the chairing of an uncontested candidate in England. A trait of Irish feeling, truly National, took place during the heat of the election.

" Mr. Butler, a very respectable Irish landlord, a friend to Mr. Vesey Fitzgerald, addressed his tenants, and appealed to them to know if he had not uniformly behaved to them as a kind landlord, &c. ; to this they all assented, but declared they could not vote as he wished them to do, it being contrary to their duty to their God and their Country.

" Soon afterwards these men were harangued by a person of the opposite party, who in the course of his speech, ventured to abuse their landlord, Mr. Butler, upon which they immediately seized upon him, drew him from the crowd, and gave him a severe thrashing, for speaking disrespectfully of the very man whose wishes and requests they were at that moment opposing."

FROM C. B. WOLLASTON TO MARY FRAMPTON.

" Westbrook, St. Albans, September 12th, 1828.

" The latter part of my Journey was more fortunate than the setting out, and indeed I may consider that I met with an unusual piece of good luck. I had been looking at the Outer Court at Windsor, the only part of the Castle to which strangers are admitted, without very special favour, and was going back to the inn, when I met Hobhouse, the late Under-Secretary of State, and after our greeting, I found he had an order from Sir H. Taylor, to see the interior, and he made no difficulty of carrying me in his suite, so we were shown the whole, by Mr. Wyattville in person. It is still, however, seen imperfectly, for the few rooms which are finished are papered up, and the furniture covered, corners of which were of course only shown; but nothing can conceal the dazzling splendour of the gilding, which seems to be much overdone, and Mr. W—*ville* said it was "His Majesty's taste." The ceilings are a mass of gilding and pannelling, pilasters, &c., the same. The great Dining and Drawing-rooms, are more unfinished, but as what was done *was* uncovered, they were better seen than the finished rooms.

"St. George's Hall is pulled to pieces—unnecessarily, and lengthened, so that it will, I should think, have more the appearance of a *gallery*, but it is choked with scaffolding, and only a specimen of the Gothic ornaments put up here and there. The whole is no longer ' Old Windsor Castle, ' it is completely altered, raised, machicolated, and with new Towers added—and so raised, that they are now obliged to raise the Round Tower also, to give it a proper height above the walls of the Castle.

"Mr. Wyattville was himself worth seeing—a busy-bustling, vain little man, but not at all pompous, though such a person as one might expect to be gratified by the addition of *Ville* to his name.

"There is a gallery over a colonnade, added within the Great Court, which is already nearly filled with pictures, but it is narrow and low, and although it affords a communication, and a good place to walk in bad weather, it must not be supposed to be *intended for pictures*, as a National Museum. I do not know what has become of the rooms which used to be shown, and whether they are absorbed in these apartments—for our guide was so rapid in his movements, and his elocution, and seemed so much to presume that we were masters of the plan of the Castle, that I was quite lost.

" The terrace will, I suppose, be always shut up from the public. On the side towards the little park, where the old King used to walk, a kind of large bastion for a flower garden, fountains, &c., is thrown out. More of this hereafter.

" Yours affectionately,

" C. B. W."

FROM SIR CHARLES LEMON, BART., TO HIS NIECE, LOUISA C. FRAMPTON.

" *Carclew, September 28th,* 1828.

" I wish you had been with us yesterday, for I think the show would have amused you. Lord Clinton and Sir William Freemantle arrived at Falmouth the day before, and the landing of the little Queen of Portugal[5] was fixed for twelve o'clock yesterday, but it did not occur to the good folks that the tide would not suit to land in the harbour, where preparations had been made for her, much after eleven o'clock, and she arrived before Lord Clinton was dressed, or the mayor had got his speech by

---

[5] Maria da Gloria, born 1819. On the abdication of her father, Pedro d'Alcantara, 1826, she succeeded to the throne of Portugal. The Queen married, 1826, her uncle, Don Miguel; secondly, in 1835, Auguste, eldest son of Eugène Beauharnais, Duc de Leuchtenberg, who died the same year (s.p.) ; and thirdly, 1836, Ferdinand de Saxe Coburg Gotha. The latter is father to Louis Philippe [born 1838], the reigning King of Portugal. The Queen died November 16th, 1853.

heart. The speech was afterwards presented to her printed in gold letters on satin.

"A group of young girls dressed in white with flowers received her at the quay and strewed flowers under her feet as she walked to the carriage which took her to the house of old Mrs. Fox, a Quaker. Strange to say that as the object of it was a child, this frenchification was not ridiculous. At Mrs. Fox's were assembled a great many naval officers in full dress, many Portuguese, and Lord Clinton and Sir W. Freemantle in gold and feathers, and a dozen or two of Quakers: there was no medium between all this gold lace and mob caps. The little Queen held a circle here, and people were admitted to kiss her hand. After about an hour she withdrew to her dinner and then walked round the garden, and was quite in the humour for a romp with the flower girls.

"At half-past two the carriages were ready and they went to Truro, where the Mayor read an address, I hope as well worded as that at Falmouth, 'Praying that under her august rule in Portugal, the ancient alliance between the two countries may be maintained and strengthened for the mutual benefit of both.'

"Lord Clinton told me that he was ordered to receive her as Queen; still this may mean queen in virtue of her husband, Don Miguel's rights, and not a simple declaration of the sentiments of Government on her right."

FROM MRS. SHIRLEY, OF LOUGH FEA AND ETTINGTON, TO MARY FRAMPTON.

"*Coolderry, September 29th,* 1828.

"MY DEAR MISS FRAMPTON,—I think we shall not be in Dublin on our way back till towards the end of October, at least if this country remains pretty quiet. There is evidently very great excitement on both sides, and I cannot imagine how both of them can be allayed and pacified. Evelyn (Mr. Shirley) I am sorry to say, is a very violent *Brunswicker*, for I do not fancy these new clubs will do any *real* good, but everything here is *Party*, and no one allowed to stand neuter. I abhor the Catholic Association as much as any Orangeman could, particularly as I am sure they have done the *simple* Catholic question more harm than any other thing. We have very nearly had some serious work in this country with that vagabond ' Jack Lawless,'[6] as they call him.

I believe Mr. Shirley wrote his mother word of his not having been allowed to enter *Ballibay*. He has abandoned his intention of entering the town of Monaghan, nor do we believe he will *dare* go further north. Certainly had he got into Monaghan, his life would not have been worth five minutes' purchase, and so the magistrates told him, and I know of one who told him that ' he had sufficient evidence to justify his putting him into Monaghan Jail, which he would undoubtedly do if he came to the town.' He therefore only went to some chapel a few miles short of it, where he abused Lord Rossmore and Westenra (though the former has just sent 25*l.* to the Association, and desired to be a member of it), but Lawless *fully* expected Lord R. would invite him to his house and protect him, which his Lordship (*why*, we cannot conceive) positively refused to do. It puts me strongly in mind of the true saying, ' When rogues fall out,' &c. To our dismay Lawless returned to Carrick on Saturday evening; however, he left it again

---

[6] A person put forward by the Catholic Association, for the purpose of agitating and haranguing the people in the North of Ireland.

yesterday, and I trust for good, as I hear he is to be in Dundalk to-day.

"I have never met with the Mémoires you mention, but I have somewhere met with a review of 'Les Deux Cousines.' I subscribe here to a Dublin Library, but as country folks can never get the newest works, I have been contenting myself with some *not very* old ones which I had not read. I am now going to read 'The Last of the Mohicans,' which the clever Dr. Robinson told me was one of the cleverest works of the sort he ever read.

"Believe me, yours truly and affectionately,

"E. SHIRLEY."

FROM MAJOR WILLIAM SHIRLEY, 7TH HUSSARS, TO HIS MOTHER.

"*Clonmel, October 8th*, 1828.

"Here I arrived on Sunday, by *forced* marches, from Dublin, which I left on Thursday, with a squadron of the 7th and two guns, under the command of Major Walcott, of the Horse Artillery, to enforce, should it be necessary, the Lord Lieutenant's Proclamation (which you, I suppose, have seen in the newspapers, forbidding all Meetings). I believe the people of this town did not like the looks of the guns, and our entrance into the town on a Sunday had a good effect; but I am sorry to say the Catholic Association had sent their orders to have no more meetings previous to the Lord Lieutenant's Proclamation, so all is at present quite quiet. The priests, with a few more rascals of attorneys, are the cause of all the disturbance. I found Lord Clonmell here, who introduced me to Mr. Bradshaw, his agent, with whom I dined yesterday and the day before, and returned home at night unmolested by any one. It is the opinion of the magistrates and gentry of this country that nothing will be attempted until the meeting of Parliament, when, if Mr. O'Connell is not allowed to take his seat in the House, there will be some lives lost. On Sunday week there was an assemblage here of about 2000 people, with about 100 on horseback dressed in green uniforms, with white sashes and epaulettes, and a band of music; they marched in good order through the town, and towards evening dispersed. They had no arms with them; but it is supposed those are hidden on the mountains or in the bogs. I do not know how long we shall remain here; but Sir John Byng told me he should withdraw *us* as soon as possible, but leave the artillery. We had very bad weather for our march, and had two days' very long marches, about thirty English miles a day.

"I have got my men and horses into barracks, which, however, are very much crowded; but in these times it is better than having them quartered in the town.

"Sir J. Fraser is at Kilkenny with another squadron, and I hear there are seven infantry regiments at the Lord Lieutenant's command on the other side of the water.

"I do not suppose I shall be able to get leave for some time, if at all this winter. I am under the command of Lieutenant-Colonel Moberley, of the 76th Regiment, who was my cornet at Bourgoiny, in France."

1830.

(Journal continued.)

The months of January and February were very

severe—much suffering attended the state of the poor
from the preceding summer having been too wet to
enable them to get in their turf for fuel; the villages in
these districts, where turf constitutes the common fuel,
were particularly ill off. The cold continued until the
23rd of March; from that day till the 1st of April the
weather was most extraordinarily warm and bright—a
very hot sun, with the thermometer at noon from 63° to
67°. In the night, or early morn of the 1st of April, a
considerable fall of snow began, which continued for
many hours, lying some inches deep on the ground.
The illness of George IV. commenced at the latter end
of March or beginning of April. However, the expectations that the King would be able to have a Drawing-
room on St. George's Day were kept up until within a
few days of the 23rd, when the first bulletin was issued.

Much murmuring was occasioned by the absence of
bulletins till they appeared, and afterwards at so little
being told in them; but the secrecy as to everything
that was going on at Windsor Castle was quite impene-
trable, and left a wide field for numerous conjectures of
all kinds. Sir William Knighton[7] was the person said
to manage all the private concerns, and to act in perfect
conformity to the King's wishes by keeping everything
secret, the King himself dictating the bulletins.

April 30th.—The final consecration of two Bishops
was delayed as the King was too unwell to sign the
necessary papers before it could take place; soon after
this time a Bill was brought in to enable the King to
affix a stamp, or to empower another person to sign for
him, such person having duly been nominated, and, in
the presence of the King, performing this act for him.

---

[7] Sir William Knighton, M.D., G.C.H., Keeper of the Privy Purse
to George IV.; created baronet 1813; died 1836.

This new power created very little objection or debate,
all parties feeling the necessity of the measure. The
arrear of signatures is said to amount to some thousands. The other business of the Session was, however,
much delayed by the uncertainty of many not knowing
what side to take, and the regular Opposition availing
themselves of this shabby disposition in the members.
The Duke of Wellington very unpopular, yet all looking
up to him.

The bulletins at the Palace were regularly delivered
in form, as in the time of George III., the Lord-in-
Waiting, in full dress, standing in one room at St.
James's to answer the inquiries, and the Yeomen of the
Guard in the anteroom drawn up as on a Levée Day.
Great numbers of ladies, as well as gentlemen, crowding
to read or hear the bulletin ; everybody in London afraid
of naming distant days for their balls and parties, lest
the expected death of the King should put a stop to all
gaiety. In the meantime the murmurs of tradespeople
began to grow loud and with some reason, for it became
almost a fashion in London to go to fine places in old
dresses on the pretence of the expected mourning, instead
of its being held a heinous offence against the laws of
dress to wear the same habiliments two evenings following.

In the country the dressmakers and milliners put off
their journeys for spring fashions, fearing to embark in
large purchases of any sort.

Madame Lalande was the new woman at the opera
this season, a finished singer, but with a thin, reedy voice.
Lablache, the man, with a most magnificent and powerful one ; but the great attraction at the opera was the
dancing, Mdlle. Taglioni uniting the grace of Hilligsberg
of the last century with the strength and activity required

in this period. She came late in the season, and all the world went wild to see her—fashion *only* was certainly not her charm, for as far as dancing can be called a science she excelled. On the English stage, much debased and little thought of as it is in modern customs, Miss Fanny Kemble, a niece of Mrs. Siddons, and brought forward by her, possessed some attraction, and although a young and unfinished actress, had natural genius, besides the advantage of a pretty person.

The middle of May and the King's doubtful state continued.

Prince Leopold, after accepting of the Sovereignty of Greece, declined it, on the pretence, or rather ostensible reason, that the boundaries of the kingdom and some other arrangements were not settled according to his demands. The general idea was, however, that the King's life being near its close, brought his niece, Princess Victoria, so much nearer the throne, that he might have pretensions to a Regency *here*, if on the spot, which he would entirely lose if elevated to the unquiet Government of Greece. This change of mind was supposed to cause embarrassment to Government, but more pressing and nearer cares made others soon forget and cease to talk of Greece and its doubtful Sovereign.

A Bill for putting the Jews on the same footing with dissenting Christians was brought forward and defeated in the House of Commons. Many were violent out of the House against this concession to them, and many did not object to the measure who it might have been supposed would most have done so. My own feelings, I confess, revolt at the idea of a Jew and a Christian being equal, and in this *liberal* age, should the Bill in future pass, I could only reconcile it to myself by the thought that this as well as every other event relative to those most extraordinary people is permitted, and will tend to their ultimate conversion and the completion of prophecy, though in a way far different from that which appears probable to human eyes.

FROM JAMES FRAMPTON TO MARY FRAMPTON.

" May 25th—26th, 1830.

" We had a large dinner on Saturday at Mr. Bankes'— eighteen in number—Lord and Lady Sidmouth, Miss Addington, and Sir William and Lady Heathcote amongst the party. Lord Sidmouth inquired after Charlton Wollaston, and was very gracious, but so very ponderous in his observations that I could not help saying to myself, 'Is it possible that man could ever have been Prime Minister?'

" We have been over Buckingham Palace, which is certainly a very fine house, and would look most magnificent when full of company at a Drawing-room. The entrance and basement storeys, however, are much too low, but this the King (George IV.) particularly insisted on, liking to inhabit low rooms himself; and this has injured the effect of the whole building. The staircase also appears to me much too small and narrow, and I cannot approve of the immense pillars in Scagliola, some imitating Lapis Lazuli, of which, if you can get a bit as large as your hand, it is worth a large sum; and others, if one may say so, of marble not in existence. The walls of the entrance and staircase are of strawberry and cream-coloured Scagliola, and no such marble is known! But the reception-rooms are very splendid, both as to size and in the beautiful ornaments of the ceilings, doors, and inlaid floors, as far as are finished, which, however, even if they had the money, which they have not, could not be completed for nearly two years. The private apartments are likewise very comfortable, excepting the present King's own bed-room, which is long and narrow, with the bed in an alcove, and there *is* room for a Queen, as there are larger and better apartments upstairs. The garden is laid out in most excellent taste, and on the whole it is much better than *I* at least expected. The Marble Arch [8] at the entrance to the palace will be very handsome, and the view from the portico through that to the Birdcage Walk very pretty."

FROM THE SAME TO THE SAME.

"*June 3rd*, 1830.

"The King's danger increasing momentarily; the report of the Duke of Clarence being unwell is not true. It is positively asserted that a regular Opposition to Government has been arranged within these few days.

"*June 5th*.—The accounts of the King from all hands, which we heard last night at Lansdowne House, were so bad, that I suppose now all must very soon be over. No dependence can be placed on the bulletins, but it is supposed that the last bulletin before the event will give pretty plain indication of what is to follow. On Thursday there was the old opera of *Don Giovanni*. The house was immensely and early crowded, yet they say that the new man, Lablache, does not make a good Leporello, as he is so enormous. Taglioni, the new dancer, is superior to anything ever yet seen, so that the other dancers cannot conceal their delight.

"*June 7th*.—The King still alive. The ladies have

---

[8] The Marble Arch was removed to its present situation in Hyde Park, 1851.

three balls to-morrow night.   We dine with the Duke
of Norfolk to-night; Almack's, Wednesday; Lansdowne
House, Friday."

(Journal continued.)

GEORGE IV. lingered on until the 26th of June. The
Duke and Duchess of Clarence were in bed when the
Duke of Wellington came to announce his accession to the
throne, and the Duke, finding it was yet early, returned
to bed, saying that he wished particularly to do so,
having never yet been in bed with a Queen!

William IV.'s very easy, familiar manners, and the
amiable and sensible qualities of Queen Adelaide, rendered
them, luckily for England, most popular, and although
the King, walking alone about the streets as he did at
first, was blamed as *infra dig.*, yet it assorted much more
with the temper of the times than the secluded Court of
George IV., who was forgotten almost before the ceremony of his funeral took place, and soon afterwards the
famous Cottage in Windsor Park, with all its expensive
and luxurious appendages, was razed to the ground. The
King and Queen lived in great union with every branch
of the Royal Family, but less so with the Duke of Cumberland than any other. In the autumn the King and
Queen went to Brighton, where they were received with
the greatest enthusiasm. A triumphal arch was erected
near the entrance of the town, under which they were to
pass, composed of the usual materials of such erections, but
with the addition of sailors and children at intervals in
the arch, holding colours, &c., and the effect was said by
good judges to be very beautiful. The populace met the
King and Queen on the road, and wished to draw the
carriage; but the King would not allow the horses to be
taken off, and called out to the people, "You want to

see me, and I want to see you, so you may depend on my going at a foot's pace, but I only request you to let the horses draw us."

In this manner they proceeded, and their Majesties remained at Brighton until the meeting of Parliament brought them to London, having large family parties, and other company daily at dinner.

The sad death of Mr. Huskisson at the opening of the Liverpool and Manchester Railway happened in September. His disobeying the order, and getting out of the carriage when particularly requested not to do so, at a peculiarly narrow part of the railroad, was the cause of the accident. Lord Sandon and one or two others were out at the same moment, but, being more active, were re-seated in time. Lord Sandon described the crash of Mr. Huskisson's thigh, on the engine with its immense rapidity passing over him, as the most appalling sound he ever heard. Lord Wilton took up the arteries and stopped the bleeding before the arrival of a surgeon, but all idea of saving his life was vain. His poor wife was in one of the carriages not far behind, and after the first shock behaved heroically.

The month of August, 1830, was distinguished by the fatal folly of the King of France, Charles X., reprobated by all parties, and which probably will entail disturbances and discontents by again exciting a revolutionary spirit, not only throughout his own kingdom, but also through Europe.

In a letter from Lord Auckland to Lord Lansdowne, he details a long conversation the former had with Marmont, Duc de Raguse, soon after his arrival in London, in which Marmont declared that the day preceding the sending forth the fatal Ordonnances, he had a conference of some hours with the Ministers then in power, who were perfectly silent as to any changes or any strong measures projected by them, and that he (Marmont) in consequence was equally surprised at their appearance as the most ignorant of the Parisians.

The whole Royal Family were obstinate in their belief that there was no danger to them in these measures, and when at St. Cloud within hearing of the cannon and tumults of Paris, they were occupying themselves as usual without a thought of their danger, and the King was obliged to be told that he *must* go, before he would at all credit the necessity of it. Their journey to Cherbourg was performed with extreme slowness, probably with the idea that they would still be recalled. At Cherbourg the Dauphiness and the Duchesse de Berri [9] were robbed of their clothes, and on their arrival at Cowes were obliged to be supplied by Lady Anglesey and Lady Grantham for immediate use. Charles did not land at Cowes, and refused to be addressed as King by those who waited upon him there. The Duchesse de Berri was soon seen in a shop in the town. She and the Dauphiness lodged at the Fountain Inn.

Mr. Weld offered Lulworth Castle as a temporary asylum, and thither they removed in steam-vessels. Charles wished much to land at Lulworth Cove, but the wind did not permit this, which, however, he would not believe until Mr. Humphrey Weld was called to him to testify to the impossibility of it. Whilst at Cowes, Lady Grantham [1] invited the French Royal party to a luncheon,

[9] The Princess Caroline, daughter of Francis I., King of the Two Sicilies, married Ferdinand, Duke de Berri, 1816, who was assassinated at Paris, February, 1820.

[1] Henrietta, daughter of the first Earl of Enniskillen, wife of Thomas Philip, Lord Grantham, K.G., who succeeded as Earl De Grey, 1833.

and Lady Listowel to tea the day of the regatta; this the
ladies declined, but the Duc de Bordeaux and his sister
went to the luncheon. The French captain was invited
to the great Yacht Club dinner, and made a very neat
speech on his health being drunk.

The French Royal Family remained at Lulworth until
October. Soon after they were settled there Mr.
Frampton went to leave his name at the castle, thinking
that attention due to ex-royalty, however he might join
in deprecating the folly which led to their residence in
England.

EXTRACT FROM MR. FRAMPTON'S NOTE TO ME.

" My visit at Lulworth Castle to-day was happily performed. When the groom took my card to desire that
it might be delivered to the Duc de Luxembourg, the Duc
himself happened to be at the door, and came down the
steps to receive me. He was very civil, and said that
he would immediately present me to the King.

" I explained that I merely came to pay my respects
and to say that I should be happy to be of any service
in my power during his Majesty's stay at Lulworth; this
he understood, and on opening the door from the
entrance and saloon, he found the King there, so asked
permission to shut the door for a moment against me, to
prepare the King for my reception.

" The Duc de Luxembourg then showed the King and
the Duc d'Angoulême into the saloon and came back for
me, and brought me just within the saloon where they
were all standing close to the door. He then presented
me, and the King spoke to me in very bad English. I
answered him and explained why I came, &c., and then
said in my bad French that if he would speak to me in

French I should understand him, although, not being accustomed to do so, I spoke French ill. After some little talk about the country round Lulworth, George III. at Weymouth, &c., the King asked how far off I lived, and on hearing that it was only six miles, he desired the Duc de Luxembourg to write down the name of the place. The Duc said he knew that already, as I had called before, and then added something about M. Moutardier,[2] who, I suppose, had explained who we were, and that I was a magistrate, as the King asked me if I was much troubled by business.

"I then thought it was high time to go, as he seemed not to know what else to say; so I again repeated my reasons for having come, and made a bow, when the King wished me 'Good day,' and put out his hand and shook hands with me, which surprised me very much. The Duc de Luxembourg and another gentleman then accompanied me to the steps, where I got on my horse and rode away.

"The Duc d'Angoulême was present, and I was also presented to him, but he said nothing. The King, a tall, thin, gentlemanly man, the Duc d'Angoulême the reverse, a very mean-looking person.

"There was a woman dressed exactly like an English monthly nurse, only not so neat and clean, in a large white cap, with a round and sallow old face standing just behind them in the saloon; she retired soon after I entered, though, I think, not out of the room, but we were all so close to the door that I could not even see the organ, as the door opened against it. I cannot think who she could be.

"After I was on my horse I was so astonished at the

---

[2] The Chaplain, who resided at Lulworth Castle for a number of years.

King having shaken hands with me that 1 thought he
might have put out his hand for me to kiss, until I
recollected that he did not put out the back of his hand,
as our King and Queen do, but on his saying, 'I wish
you a good morning,' he put his hand out with the palm
uppermost, and on my putting out my hand, he took
hold of it and shook it.   Six weeks ago the odds would
have been high that I did not shake hands with Charles X.
at Lulworth Castle.   I tried three times, as well to the
King as to the Duc d'Angoulême, to find out whether
they would like Lady Harriot and the girls to call on
the Duchesse d'Angoulême, but they always avoided
giving an answer.   The King always spoke to me in
English, but very unintelligibly, and I wish that he had
spoken French.   They were all evidently pleased at my
having called, and were very civil.   The house seemed
all in a bustle, with various people and servants in the
entrance hall, moving things, and giving directions, &c."

Friday, September 10th, 1830.—I drove over to Moreton with Fanny Shirley to see the Framptons, and to
make arrangements with them respecting the intended
marriage of Harriot F. with Mr. William Mundy, and
we were all sitting in Lady Harriot's dressing-room, surrounded with trinkets, patterns, &c., when Churchill,
the Butler, came up and said that some French people,
he believed ladies' maids from Lulworth Castle, were
come in a gig, which they had left at the gate, and had
walked towards the house.   As far as he could make
out, they wished to see the flower garden, so, he added,
he had just pointed out the way to it, and would, if Lady
Harriot approved, send the gardener to them.   She
desired he would be civil to them, and in a short time we
saw two housekeeper-looking persons coming again to-

wards the house. Lady H. Frampton, who was very busy writing letters, asked me to go and speak to them, for, she said, the dress of Frenchwomen in a morning is so unlike ours, that they may be something above servants, and Mr. Frampton is so particularly engaged that I doubt his being able to go to them. Accordingly Fanny and I went down to the library where was Louisa F., and in a few minutes Mr. Frampton, who had gone out to the visitors, notwithstanding his business engagement, came into the room accompanied by the two persons, whose dress was undoubtedly inferior to that of most house-keepers. We began talking a little, partly in French and broken English, when we clearly perceived from their manners that they were gentlewomen. Presently Lady H. Frampton and her daughter Harriot came in, when the former inquired of one of them, "Si Madame la Duchesse d'Angoulême était encore à Lulworth," upon which she was answered, "Moi, je la suis," the other lady saying at the same moment, "C'est elle-même." Our surprise, of course, was extreme, but we immediately made proper curtseys, &c., and expressed how much we were shocked and distressed at the mistake, &c.

The Duchesse then requested that Mr. F. would send to the place where she had left their carriage, to ask the gentleman who drove her to come in, and a very gentle-manly person, who spoke English fluently, soon joined us, who was, I believe, the Comte de S. Aubin, but we could not then ascertain his name. They were accom-panied by an old handsome dog, who walked about per-fectly at its ease, as if accustomed to such visits. The ladies went all over the house, and said how much they admired the gardens, the outside of the church, and very particularly the obelisk. The Duchesse congratulated my niece on her approaching marriage, and asked whether she had ever seen her fiancé, expressing some surprise at hearing that they were well known to each other. She took away a little pencil drawing of Moreton, which she caught sight of when in Lady Harriot's dressing-room upstairs, saying, "Ah! que c'est fidèle! je le garde, made-moiselle," which of course Harriot was obliged to consider a great honour, but as Her Royal Highness immediately folded the drawing in half, she rather regretted the loss of her little sketch.

They would not take any refreshment, and after remaining about half an hour, went away in a heavy shower, their equipage being a miserable low four-wheeled open carriage with two seats, drawn by a rough pony, no servant with them. The name of the attendant lady was Madame de St. Maur. She was dressed in a black douilette with a worked pélérine, the Duchesse in a shabby light brown, or rather yellowish shawl, cotton stockings, ' very short petticoats, and both wore coarse, weather-beaten straw bonnets. The Duchesse was much altered since I caught a glimpse of her, fifteen years ago, when passing through this town of Dorchester. She is grown old and plain, but not so cross-looking as it is said that her unparalleled misfortunes have made her. Lady Harriot said afterwards that she ought to have recognized the Duchesse from the peculiar redness of the whites of her eyes, having heard that this was occasioned entirely from the constant weeping during the years of their troubles.

The gentleman called Charles X. "the King," although he takes the name of Comte de Ponthieu. When they had driven off, the butler said that he so completely took them for servants, that dinner in the servants' hall being just sent in, he was on the point of asking if they would go in with him, and eat something! On my expressing to the attendant gentleman how much I was astonished on discovering to whom I had the honour of talking, he answered that it was just what the Duchesse liked, to surprise people. She must possess rather a singular character, and well deserves the praise of having the most manly mind of her family. Her spirit and personal courage was great. In the year 1818, Mr. Okeden happened to be at Paris, and he related to me a strong instance of those qualities, displayed at a moment when she had no time to prepare her mind for their exhibition.

At the annual fair held at Vincennes, the crowd was extreme, and the pressure very great and dangerous to the people, on the arrival of her carriage with herself and attendants in it, preceded and followed by a detachment of guards on horseback. The mob murmured, and cries were heard; the "La Dauphine," then only Duchesse d'Angoulême, dared not venture to the fair unaccompanied by guards. Upon which she stood up in her carriage, ordered the coachman to stop, and then, in the most cool and dignified manner, commanded the troops to retreat, and leave her. The order was immediately obeyed, and the Duchesse then drove several times backwards and forwards through the fair, accompanied by the applause instead of the hisses of the crowd.

EXTRACT OF A NOTE FROM MY NIECE, HARRIOT FRAMPTON.

"*Moreton, September* 29*th.*

"You will like to hear about our expedition to Lulworth, which was most successfully accomplished. My mother, Louisa, Mr. Mundy, and myself drove over there yesterday. On arriving at the castle we were immediately shown into the great saloon, which was empty. After a time the door at the upper end was thrown open and some one announced ' Le Roi.' The king came down the steps accompanied and followed by Madame la Dauphine and her husband, the Duc d'Angoulême; subsequently the Duc de Bordeaux and his young sister, ' Mademoiselle' entered the room. The latter appeared very glad to have some one to talk to, and told me how much she liked riding over the hills, &c., on her donkey. On Mr. Mundy being presented as my fiancé, this naturally led to some conversation about our approaching marriage, and the Dauphine seemed amused and interested when my mother mentioned the English fashion of sending wedding cake on such occasions, but I am sure one has always heard of a Gâteau de Noce, so I am surprised that this should have appeared a novelty to them. Perhaps, however, as *Royalty* they were above such knowledge. The Duchesse de Berri [3] was absent, so we did not see her, which was unfortunate."

In the middle of the month of October, Dorsetshire witnessed the departure of the ex-royal family of France from Lulworth Castle. The ex-King and Duc de Bordeaux went by sea to Holyrood House : the rest abhorring "la triste mer," proceeded thither by land, the Duchesse de Berri and Mademoiselle stopping in London. Their departure from the County was regretted, they had afforded much historical gossip to the neighbouring families, all but the King having shown themselves everywhere, and, being great walkers, moved about in all directions, unlike English people, and much to the amusement of all ranks. The consumption of food during their stay was immense, and one of the reasons whispered for

---

[3] Mr. Mundy met the Duchesse de Berri a few weeks afterwards at Kedleston, where she was on a visit to Lord and Lady Scarsdale.— H. G. M.

Charles Xth's departure was, that so many dependents lived upon him owing to his residence being remote from any town. The freedom from arrest might be another motive for preferring a palace, as certainly in one instance, unfair advantage, as I must call it, was taken of his unfortunate situation, and he was in danger of being seized for money said to be due during his last residence in England. Charles himself denied the debt, and a trial in our English Court of Justice is to take place. The good done amongst the poor during their stay was great. Nothing is permitted to appear a second time at the Royal table, and therefore it was given to the poor, who, like true Englishmen, complained that the meat, &c., was boiled to a *poultice*, and they could not therefore enjoy it. The King lived in great anxiety from an idea that a party in France wished to make themselves masters of the person of the Duc de Bordeaux, and he applied to my brother, as a magistrate, to guard against this danger. Mr. Frampton recommended a communication with the Home Office; in consequence of which Sir Robert Peel sent a person from the police office to hover about the castle and watch over any strangers, &c., with orders to report and communicate with my brother in the first instance. I never heard, however, that any suspicious character was seen near Lulworth.

The boy, the Duc de Bordeaux, was a fine interesting child with very dignified manners when told to do his honours. Mademoiselle lively, and talking English or French equally well.

The 28th of October, 1830, was an eventful day in the annals of the Frampton family. Harriot Frampton, my brother's eldest daughter, being married on that day to

Mr. William Mundy, only son of Mr. Mundy, of Markeaton, M.P. for Derbyshire. The day was uncommonly fine, the wedding a grand one, the house being quite filled with relations and friends. Lord Ilchester, his brothers, the Dowager Lady Ilchester, Lady Elizabeth Feilding, Sir C. Lemon, &c., being amongst the guests. My niece had six beautiful bridesmaids, her cousins, Lady Theresa Strangways, and two Miss Feildings, (daughters of Admiral and Lady E. Feilding) her own younger sister, Louisa F., and two Miss Seymers, daughters, of Mr. Ker Seymer, of Hanford, very old friends of our family. She was the first Miss Frampton who had been married at Moreton since the reign of Queen Elizabeth. The bride was dressed in the finest embroidered white India muslin over white satin, a wreath of orange flowers in her hair, and a deep Brussels' lace veil over all. The bridesmaids all in white, with white hats. Carpeting was laid from the house to the church for the little procession, and school-girls strewed flowers on the paths as it proceeded. The church and churchyard were crowded with the villagers, and altogether it was a very pretty sight. Everything went off well; the parting from one so amiable and much beloved, and who had been so happy at home, the only drawback. Indeed, her departure from the county was regretted by all, as my niece was universally popular. They went to her uncle's at Melbury for the honeymoon. There was dancing upstairs as well as downstairs, in the evening, a bonfire, and beer given away to the villagers, yet everything passed off quietly.

The month of November began auspiciously, the weather fine, a popular King and Queen, and great expectations from the opening of Parliament, &c. On the 2nd of

November, the King's going to the House and his return was hailed as it ought to be; but the unpopularity of the Duke of Wellington was extreme, so as to render his life in danger from the pressure of the crowd, stones being thrown at him, &c. The new police, established the preceding year to replace the old and useless watchmen, were set upon by the mob, aided by all the thieves and pickpockets in London, and many were much hurt. All these circumstances occasioned serious alarms, lest there should be danger, not to the King's person, but of bloodshed amongst the crowd, if he and the Queen went, as was intended, to dine at the city feast on the 9th of November. The dinner was consequently given up, which caused intense disappointment to the city, where the outcry was immense, and the Ministry much blamed, others, however, saying that the precaution was necessary. A large body of troops was moved to the capital, and the good conduct and forbearance of the new police was such that, although much of the popular cry was directed against them, the order they maintained was so universally acknowledged that these very attacks established them as the most useful defence of the metropolis. As the month advanced it became very gloomy, more than its proverbial horrors ever displayed before. An universal spirit of dissatisfaction pervaded every class. The plentiful harvest, good potato crop, remarkably fine autumn weather without frost to impede the labours of husbandry, appeared to have no effect in lessening the murmurs of discontent; whilst incendiaries, whose steps could not be traced, spread rapidly from Kent—where the setting fire to corn-stacks, barns, &c., first began in the month of October—to the adjacent counties. These incendiarisms were in general unconnected with the riotous mobs which nearly at the same time assembled, breaking and destroying machinery used in husbandry, paper-mills, &c., and also surrounding gentlemen's houses, extorting money and demanding an increase of wages.   These mobs rose very unexpectedly, and spread with alarming rapidity.

On the 22nd of November the first risings took place in this county.   Mr. Portman[4] immediately promised to raise the wages of his labourers, and by doing this without concert with other gentlemen, greatly increased their difficulties.   My brother, Frampton, harangued the people at Bere Regis, and argued with them on the impropriety of their conduct, refusing to concede to their demands whilst asked with menaces.   This spirited conduct caused him to be very unpopular, and threats were issued against him and his house.

November 28*th*.—Notice was received of an intended rising of the people at the adjacent villages of Winfrith, Wool, and Lulworth—the latter six miles off—which took place on the 30th.   My brother, Mr. Frampton, was joined very early on that morning by a large body of farmers, &c., from his immediate neighbourhood, as well as some from a distance, all special constables, amounting to upwards of 150, armed only with a short staff, the pattern for which had been sent by order of Government to equip what was called the Constabulary force.   The numbers increased as they rode on towards Winfrith, where the clergyman was unpopular, and his premises supposed to be in danger.   The mob, urged on from behind hedges, &c., by a number of women and children, advanced rather respectfully, and with their hats in their hands, to demand increase of wages, but would not listen to the request that they would disperse.   The Riot Act was read.   They still urged forwards, and came close up

---

[4] Of Bryanston, Co. Dorset, subsequently created Viscount Portman.

to Mr. Frampton's horse; he then collared one man, but in giving him in charge he slipped from his captors by leaving his smock-frock in their hands. Another mob from Lulworth were said to be advancing, and as the first mob seemed to have dispersed, Mr. F. was going, almost alone, to speak to them, when he was cautioned to beware, as the others had retreated only to advance again with more effect in the rear. The whole body of the constabulary then advanced with Mr. Frampton, and, after an ineffectual parley, charged them, when three men were taken, and were conveyed by my brother and his son Henry, and a part of the constabulary force, to Dorchester, and committed to gaol. I was at Moreton that day with Lady Harriot F. Our gentlemen returned about six o'clock; they described the mob they had encountered as being in general very fine-looking young men, and particularly well-dressed, as if they had put on their best clothes for the occasion. That night James Shirley[5] and I sat up at Moreton. Many threats had been reported to us as having been made in the course of the day, and, during the dispersion of the mob, against Mr. Frampton's person and property, but no fire took place on his estate. There was one announced to us watchers, but not being very near Moreton, we had nothing to do but to lament over the wickedness which occasioned that and so many other incendiary fires. It subsequently proved to have been a hayrick, at the village of Preston, between Moreton and Weymouth, which had been set on fire; but though one man was strongly suspected, no legal proof against him could be procured.

There were no soldiers in the county, all having been

---

[5] The Rev. James Shirley, nephew of Mr. Frampton, at that time Rector of Moreton.

sent towards London, Wiltshire, and Hampshire, where
the riots raged first; and in the beginning of December
hourly accounts of the assembling of mobs, for the purpose of breaking thrashing-machines, increase of wages,
and extorting money, &c., arrived. Under these circumstances, it was judged necessary to block up all the lower
windows of Moreton House, as well as all the doors, with
the exception of that to the offices. The Mayor of Dorchester ordered the staff of Dorset Militia to go to Moreton
to defend the house, nightly patrols were established, and
Mr. Frampton or his son sat up alternately for many
nights. My sister-in-law also took her turn in sitting up
with another woman, Lady Harriot saying that they were
more watchful than men. Spies were certainly sent from
the rioters to see the state of the house, &c.[6]

London being comparatively, indeed really, tranquil,
and large bodies of troops in the adjacent counties, my
niece, Louisa F., was sent by her father and mother to
accompany her cousins, the Lady Strangways, to London,
to be out of the way of alarm.

FROM THE MARCHIONESS OF LANSDOWNE TO LADY HARRIOT
FRAMPTON.

"*Lansdowne House, November 29th*, 1830.

"MY DEAR HARRIOT,—Your letter to-day has made me
very anxious indeed. It is so sadly like what I have
heard of in Ireland, and which has left such deep and sore
impressions on the minds of the people there. I quite
shake, when I open the letters, for fear of what I may
come to. I have not seen any of the Burlington Street

---

[6] Moreton House escaped attack, doubtless from the mobs being aware
that preparations had been made for defence.

party yet; it is such a fog, but they all dine with my Louisa to-day (we dine with the King), and spend the evening, and as Henry [7] is coming home I hope they will be very merry. We are quite quiet at Bowood; they did not even make a riot at Calne upon the loss of their petition, which I fully expected, and the rest of the county is getting quiet and organized; the reason it is quiet, I believe; but it gives breathing time. We have a frightful number of prisoners at Devizes. Our yeomen have behaved well. In Hertfordshire Lord Verulam sounded the yeomen when they all refused to be enrolled, and told him if he had a meeting, it would only be for reduction of rents. It is considered that it is a very difficult point to decide whether it is a good thing or not to form new corps of Yeomanry, as it takes the farmers away from home when they are most wanted, and picks out the best men who would be specially useful in their own neighbourhood, and the very different recommendations— quite opposite, indeed—which come from equally well-informed, sensible men, render it very perplexing, and poor Lord Melbourne is not to be blamed for not having made up his mind. He sat up all the first night he was in office, and has been up at six o'clock every morning since to try to get through the business. Lord Lansdowne, who only has a part of Wiltshire to do as Lord Lieutenant, has been occupied by nothing else, and yesterday I never spoke to him for five minutes the whole. day. I shall be very anxious till I hear again from you.

" Your very affectionate,

" L, LANSDOWNE."

---

[7] Her second son, Lord Henry Fitzmaurice, afterwards fourth Marquis of Lansdowne.

(Journal continued.)

The town of Dorchester was well patroled.   No rising took place there or at Fordington; on the contrary, the latter were most active in extinguishing a fire at a place a mile distant where, however, two ricks of corn were burnt.   A troop of lancers arrived at Dorchester about this time, December 12th, and were joyfully received.   Most of the thrashing machines in this neighbourhood were, however, either laid aside or destroyed by the farmers themselves, and no rising occurred very near Dorchester.   The troop of lancers looked worn down by the fatigues of the riots in Wiltshire, but were immediately called upon to guard old Mrs. William's house at Castle Hill, upon which an attack had been threatened. This troop was soon relieved by three troops of 3rd Dragoon Guards, who were placed permanently in the barracks at Dorchester.   About seventy prisoners were at different times committed to gaol, and mobs and tumults became again rare occurrences.   But, alas ! the fires still continued at intervals, and no clue in this county any more than in others could be found by which to detect the perpetrators.   During the month of December the weather was favourable, and although there were a few days when the thermometer was as low as $14\frac{1}{2}°$ Fahrenheit, the frost was of short continuance, and labour was not stopped.   The natural phenomenon of the Aurora Borealis was seen to great perfection in this month.

Our Christmas was passed with a large family party at Moreton.   The house was unbarred and unblockaded with the exception of the one large window on the staircase. The carol singers from Mr. Frampton's own parishes ushered in Christmas Eve and Christmas Morn as usual, but no mummers were allowed to perform their ancient drama of the wonderful recovery of a man killed in battle by a little bottle of elixir drawn from the pocket of the doctor of the piece, or to personify the " Senses " from the ancient mysteries with their Latin names, " Tactus," " Visus," &c. The yule log, however, burnt on the large hearth of the entrance hall. The peacock in full plummage with its fiery mouth was placed on the dinner table, with of course the boar's head; the immense candles were well covered with laurel. The hare appeared with the red herring astride on its back, and the wassail bowl and lamb's wool were not inferior to former years.

FROM LADY ELIZABETH FEILDING TO LADY H. FRAMPTON.

(Extract.)

" *London, November* 17*th*, 1830.

" MY DEAR HARRIOT,—At the Queen's party seven brides were presented—Lady Ashley,[8] Lady Lilford,[9] Lady Fitzharris,[1] Lady Clanwilliam,[2] Lady Cholmondeley,[3] Lady Chesterfield,[4] and Lady Seymour.[5] What a constellation of beauty! The presentations were conducted in a very *unceremonious* manner, as you may imagine with our *citizen king*, who keeps up the historical parallel with France which has always prevailed, though not exactly at the same moment. The King forgot to kiss my sister,

[8] Lady Emily Cowper, daughter of Earl Cowper.
[9] The Honourable Mary Fox, only daughter of Lord Holland.
[1] Lady Emma Bennet, only daughter of the Earl of Tankerville.
[2] Lady Elizabeth Herbert, daughter of the Earl of Pembroke.
[3] Lady Susan Somerset, daughter of the Duke of Beaufort.
[4] The Honourable Anne Forester, the daughter of Lord Forester.
[5] Jane, the daughter of Thomas Sheridan, Esq.

Louisa, and shook hands with her instead. Some he kissed on both cheeks, some not at all, just as the fancy took him. Of course people talk of nothing now but Ministers coming in and going out, but all that you will hear from the newspapers."

1831.

(*Journal continued.*)

January 10*th.*—The Special Commission, in consequence of the late riots, fires, &c., came to Dorchester. In addition to the usual cavalcade which with the Sheriff and his train, javelin-men, &c., meets the Judges at Yellowham Hill, three miles from Dorchester, and from whence they are conveyed in the Sheriff's carriage, nearly 200 special constables with my brother, Mr. Frampton, at their head, and some carriages, went out to accompany and do honour to the Judges on this particular occasion. The procession, I think, extended a full mile, and the crowd was very great to witness their arrival, but the Judges had been delayed on the road, and it was dark before we entered the town. The Judges, Baron Vaughan and Alderson, dined with us afterwards, and we[6] had a large party besides, amounting to sixteen. Amongst others, Lord Shaftesbury, Mr.[7] and Mrs. Damer, of Milton Abbey, Mr. Bankes, Mr. Sturt, &c. The business at

---

[6] After the death of my grandmother Frampton, in 1829, my aunt continued to reside at Dorchester with her half-brother, Mr. C. B. Wollaston.—H. G. M.

[7] The Honourable Henry Dawson Damer, second son of the first Earl of Portarlington. He married Eliza, daughter of E. C. Moriarty, Esq., and of Lady Lucy, daughter of Simon Luttrell, first Earl of Carhampton (extinct); died 1841. His only son, Henry, succeeded his uncle as third Earl of Portarlington, 1845.

Milton Abbey was sold, and thus passed out of the family, in 1852.

Dorchester was finished in two days, and there were no capital convictions, only death recorded in about six or seven instances, which ensured transportation for life. After the heavy offences at the preceding towns, Winchester and Salisbury, this calendar was deemed very light. In the very week of the Special Commission four or five fires took place in the county, and several threatening letters were sent to the farmers in this neighbourhood. Mr. Murray,[8] the excellent clergyman of Stinsford, found one addressed to him, written on a dirty and rumpled piece of paper, threatening to burn barns and ricks close to him, at the foot of his bed. He supposed that it had been slipped into his pocket, and fallen from his clothes when he undressed at night.

January 26*th.*—It is hoped that Mr. O'Connel's run upon the Irish Banks, which brings ruin equally on his friends and foes, may, under Providence, be the means of checking the career of this very mischievous and clever man.

The whole of Europe is disturbed, no Government feels secure, and who will be King of Belgium, how long Louis Philippe will reign in France, or whether the Poles will be able to maintain themselves against the Emperor Nicholas, is equally uncertain. It is reported that Cardinal[9]

---

[8] The Rev. Edward Murray, third son of Lord George Murray, some time Bishop of St. David's, brother of Caroline, Countess of Ilchester.

[9] Mr. Weld was created a Cardinal in 1830. He died at Rome, 1837. Mr. Mundy and I passed some months at Rome in the winter of 1841-2, and found that the memory of Cardinal Weld was still cherished there. It was gratifying to hear how sincerely he was regretted by all, more especially by the poor, as his charities were very great. Several anecdotes were told me of him by his relations and our intimate friends, Mr. and Mrs. Bodenham (née Weld), Mr. and Mrs. Blundell of Crosby Hall, &c. The Cardinal was passionately fond of his grandchildren, some of whom used frequently to accompany him in his walks on Monte Pincio. One day a violent shower came on, when, of course, the two footmen, always,

Weld is to be Pope. No Englishman has been so since the reign of Henry II., when, A.D. 1155, Nicholas Breakspeare was made Pope by the name of Adrian IV. Mr. Weld is the head of a great Roman Catholic family in Dorsetshire, the owner of Lulworth Castle, a contemporary and playmate of mine in childhood, and a friend of later years. He married early in life a very agreeable and excellent person, a Miss Clifford[1] of Tixall in Staffordshire, by whom he had one daughter, who married the eldest son of Lord Clifford. His wife died young, and soon after her death Mr. Weld renounced his worldly possessions, and took Holy Orders. For some time he had the care of the Roman Catholic Congregations at Chelsea and its vicinity, in which he laboured so indefatigably as to injure his health. He was afterwards made Bishop of Canada, but never went to reside there, removed to Rome, where he was made a Cardinal about a year and a half ago, and is now talked of as likely to be Pope. In the war of the French revolution Mr. Weld had a commission in the Dorset Yeomanry. He was a man of mild, pleasing manners, very amiable, with a good deal of minor information, but not much reading, and I should not have supposed of a very powerful understanding.

and necessarily in attendance on a cardinal, instantly spread the red umbrella over His Eminence, whereupon he immediately included the children under the welcome shelter, to the great scandal of the beholders ! They considered it as little short of sacrilege that a cardinal's red umbrella should be used for any other than a member of the sacred college ! We were also well acquainted with Lady Acton and her son, the Cardinal ; another of those who, from his high moral character, did great honour to the English Roman Catholics, then holding responsible positions near the Papal throne.

[1] Mary Lucy, only daughter of Thomas Weld, Esq ., of Lulworth Castle, married, 1818, Hugh, eldest son of Lord Clifford. He succeeded as seventh Baron Clifford, of Chudleigh, 1831, in which year his wife died.

January 26th.—Since writing the above, his brother, Joseph Weld, the present owner of Lulworth Castle, in a letter to my brother, says that there is no chance of the Cardinal succeeding to the Papal Chair at present, and that the English newspapers have invented the report of it.

The last part of this month was passed tranquilly in Dorsetshire. If there were any discontents, they were only whispered, and no fires which could be traced as the act of incendiaries took place, and in general throughout the kingdom the state of the counties was less disturbed. Trade also began to revive, probably from the unsettled state of Belgium and the Netherlands.

Parliament opened on the 3rd of February with intense anxiety of all ranks and parties as to the reform in Parliament promised by the Government, and with all Europe in a state of ferment.

One of the motions made by Mr. Hunt on the first day of his appearance in the House of Commons, was for a petition to the King, to pardon all the unhappy men who had been convicted at the Special Assizes. Fortunately however, as they were already on board the Transports, and the wind fair, the petition would be too late. Care was taken at the deportation of these men to keep them separate from convicts of a different description, and to send them to those parts of New Zealand and New Holland where their agricultural knowledge and labour might be useful—thus very probably at a future time rendering our disturbances here a blessing to our Antipodes.

A curious movement in France gives hope there also, that even in our day we may see benefit arising from the overthrow of the Government.

In the heart of France, a considerable number of the

people have thrown off the authority of the Pope, declared against having the Service in Latin, and in many respects have assimilated themselves to the English Protestant Church. There being no established national religion, these opinions cannot be interfered with. May we not therefore reasonably hope that *real* religion may take root and spread, in the place of the infidelity or super-stition which has for years disgraced that fine, but, at least within the atmosphere of Paris, profligate country.

February 8th.—The Duc de Nemours, second son of Louis Philippe, King of France, is chosen by the Belgians for their King, but the rumours from London and from the Ministers there, repeat that his father will not permit him to accept the offer. He is only seventeen; it would therefore be annexing Belgium again to France. The French Government declare that they will not allow of the election of the Duc de Leuchtenberg,[2] son of Beauharnais and a Princess of Bavaria.

The magnificence of the parties given by the King and Queen at the Pavilion at Brighton are spoken of as realizing the ideas of the entertainments described in the "Arabian Nights," the dinners consisting daily of about forty persons. The King very temperate. The Queen, too, drawing some degree of line as to character in those she invites, has not even sent a card to the Duchess of St. Albans, the famous Mrs. Coutts, formerly an actress, Miss Mellon. The King consults Mrs. Fitz Herbert much as an old friend in matters relating to the fêtes, &c., and the Ministers speak of him as attentive to business, and ready and willing to do what is deemed right. I may

---

[2] Auguste, eldest son of Eugène Beauharnais, Duc de Leuchtenberg, and of Augusta, daughter of Maximilian Joseph, King of Bavaria. He married, 1835, Maria da Gloria, Queen of Portugal, and died the same year.

here mention that in conversation with my friend Mr. Humphrey Weld [3] he told me that *he had seen* the certificate of Mrs. Fitz Herbert's marriage to the late King when Prince of Wales, and that since his death she talked openly of it.

February 25th.—All Europe perturbed; France, it is feared, giving way too much to the Republican spirit, fomented, probably, by the Carlist (or old Bourbon) party, in order to create disturbances to the limited monarchy of Louis Philippe. His decisive answer, and refusal of the Government of Belgium for his son, is generally supposed to be very creditable to him.

The Republican Party have made him give up the fleurs-de-lys, and institute other arms for France.

A letter from Captain Markland to his wife now residing at Dorchester, from the *Briton* frigate stationed at the mouth of the Tagus, speaks of the state of Portugal as dreadful. Seventeen thousand persons are supposed to be in prison by Don Miguel's orders, and people are seized in their beds and carried off to prison without knowing their crimes. If there were revolutions only where so much must be to blame in the Government, no one would or ought to object to them.

Another letter, dated February 21st (1831), thus speaks :—" The country is in a most unsettled state, and with no prospect of amendment until a change of rulers has taken place.

" Athough the present Government *say* they respect everything British, no faith can be placed in a Portuguese. One English merchant was taken up, imprisoned, and ill-treated, but the English Consul (Mr. Hopner) had

[3] Humphrey Weld, Esq., of Chidcock, Co. Dorset, brother of Joseph Weld, Esq., of Lulworth Castle. His connection with Mrs. Fitz Herbert was through her first early marriage with his uncle.

him released in spite of the whole Portuguese Government.

"The English, by an old charter, have the privilege to protect six servants, though they may be natives. This the Government of Portugal wish to set aside, but we will not submit."

FROM HARRIOT G. MUNDY TO LADY H. FRAMPTON.

"We went to the Drawing-room on the 28th of May. Mr. Mundy was presented by Lord Ilchester, and my aunt, Lady Lansdowne, presented me. The King stood very near the entrance to the Throne-room, so that before I had time to collect my ideas my train was spread, and the King seized hold of me and kissed me on both cheeks very heartily! Then we passed on to make our bow and curtsey to the Queen, who stood at some little distance.

"My train was taken up again by John Strangways, who was one of the Gentlemen-in-Waiting to Queen Adelaide."

"June 15th, 1831.

"I am glad to tell you that I was able to go to the Queen's ball on Monday last, about which I had really felt very doubtful, and I enjoyed the first part very much.

"We arrived at the Palace early enough to see the King, Queen, and Princesses enter the ball-room and take their seats, the band of course playing 'God save the King' as they walked and *bowed* along. It was a splendid sight altogether. The supper was magnificent, and the immense height of the banqueting-room at St. James's Palace made the people look so small that it was quite different from anything I could have imagined, and the plate, as my Uncle Ilchester says, is more like the 'Arabian Nights' than anything else.

"We went to a small party at Mrs. Beauclerk's last night. The Duchess of St. Albans was there, and also Lady Dudley Stuart, who, by the way, is not at all interesting looking, and I cannot say at all handsome, but as she is a Bonapartist, I am glad to have seen her.

"We are provoked at having so many invitations for to-morrow.

"A *déjeûner* at Holly Lodge,[4] which I should have liked, having never been at one, a party at the Dowager Lady Dartmouth's, and the ball at Lansdowne House.

"Charlton goes with us to Lansdowne House, and I also propose to take him to old Lady Cork's,[5] unless he prefers the opera on Saturday, but she is so strange that she will amuse him highly."

FROM LADY THERESA STRANGWAYS[6] TO HER COUSIN MRS. MUNDY.

"*London, September 12th*, 1831.

"MY DEAR HARRIOT,—I suppose that Louisa has given

[4] Holly Lodge, Highgate. The villa residence of the Duchess of St. Albans, now that of the Baroness Burdett-Coutts.

[5] Mary, daughter of the first Viscount Galway, the second wife of the seventh Earl of Cork. Her eccentricities were notorious.

[6] Eldest daughter of the third Earl of Ilchester. At the Coronation of William IV., September 8th, 1831, she was one of the Train-bearers to Queen Adelaide.

In 1836 Lady Theresa Strangways was appointed Lady-in-Waiting to the Duchess of Kent, and, after her marriage to Mr. Digby the following year, Woman of the Bedchamber to the Queen, which post she held until 1856, when her husband succeeded to the title, on the death of the Earl of Digby.

you an account of the Coronation. I wish you had seen it, for it was a very fine sight, though a very fatiguing one for us Train-bearers, who had to stand the whole time (about five hours) and as we had (very absurdly, I think) trains ourselves as well, one to carry on each arm was no light weight, for there was not room for ours to sweep.

"I am just returned from the Drawing-room, where the Queen told Aunt Louisa that she was very much obliged to us for holding up her train so well, as it prevented her from feeling the weight of it.

"I am rather tired from the heat of the Drawing-room, so good-bye.

"Yours affectionately,

"THERESA M. FOX STRANGWAYS."

FROM LADY LOUISA FITZMAURICE [7] TO THE SAME.

"*Lansdowne House, September 12th.*

"MY DEAR HARRIOT,—I think you will like to hear of the Coronation, as you had so many friends acting in it. I went there as a spectator, with Miss Fox, Caroline and Horatia Feilding,[8] and Tom Strangways, who undertook to take care of us. Uncle John Strangways and Stephen[9] joined us at the Abbey. Papa walked in the procession as President of the Council, and his coronet was carried by Stavordale. We were so sorry that my brother Henry was not here, as he would have enjoyed it so much.

---

[7] Only daughter of Lord and Lady Lansdowne.

[8] Daughters of Admiral and Lady Elizabeth Feilding.

[9] The Honourable Stephen Fox Strangways, second son of Lord Ilchester, succeeded as Lord Stavordale on the death of his elder brother in 1837 ; died 1848.

Uncle Harry[1] was, of course, in his place as a peer, and we saw him do homage very well. Mamma was in her place as a peeress, but had also (which you may suppose she did not much like) to carry the pall over the Queen during the crowning and anointing, with the Duchesses of Richmond and Northumberland, and another, whose name I forget. Theresa's co-partners you have probably heard, as they were named in all the newspapers. She and mamma ended their day by dining at St. James's Palace.[2] Kerry[3] held the King's train, instead of Lord Lincoln, who was ill. So I had plenty of friends to watch for. We did not go very early, so we had not a very good place; we were in the south transept, behind the peers, and therefore saw the peeresses very well, but we saw nothing that went on near the altar.

" Some of the music was beautiful. I am glad to have seen it, but I do not wish to see another. It is a strange mixture of mummery and of what ought to be more serious. Mamma and Theresa are now at the Drawing-room.

" We go to Bowood to-morrow, and take Theresa with us; papa is to follow us when he can. Mamma is quite well again, as you may suppose from her being at the Coronation.

" Yours affectionately,
" LOUISA FITZMAURICE."

---

[1] The Earl of Ilchester.

[2] King William IV. and Queen Adelaide then resided at St. James's Palace. They afterwards moved to Buckingham Palace.

[3] Earl of Kerry, eldest son of Lord Lansdowne.

FROM THE "SUN" NEWSPAPER—IN MS., NO DATE.[4]

1. LD. EL—B—GH	Am-a-Tory.
2. SIR H. H—RD—GE	In-flamm-a-Tory.
3. SIR C. W—TH—L	De-clam-a-Tory.
4. SIR R. IN—GL—S	Con-serv-a-Tory.
5. MR. A. B—R—NG	Mi-gr-a-Tory.
6. MR. G—LB—N	Nug-a-Tory.
7. MR. PR—D	Pred-a-Tory.
8. MR. J. C. H—RR—S	Consol-a-Tory.
9. MR D—WS—N	Or-a-Tory.
10. LD. L—NDH—RST	Rot-a-Tory.
11. EARL OF H—RR—WBY	Emend-a-Tory.
12. DUKE OF W—LL—NGTON	Peremp-Tory.
13. SIR R. P—L	Fac-Tory.
14. MR. P—RC—VAL	Incant-a-Tory.
15. LORD AB—RD—N	Prevaric-a-Tory.
16. LD. WH—RNC—FE	Medi-a-Tory.
17. DUKE OF C—MB—L—D	Damn-a-Tory.
18. MR. CR—K—R	His-Tory.
19. LORD ELD—N	Dil-a-Tory.
20. MARQUIS OF L—ND—ND—RRY	Ful-min-a-Tory.
21. SIR H. H—LF—RD	Condolo-Congratul-a-Tory, *alias* Purg-a-Tory.

1831.

(*Journal continued.*)

THE death of Mr. Calcraft, early in September, threw

[4] 1 Lord Ellenborough.
2. Sir Henry Hardinge.
3. Sir Charles Wetheral.
4. Sir Robert Inglis.
5. Mr. Alexander Baring.
6. Mr. Goulburn.
7. Mr. Praed.
8. Mr. J. C. Herries.
9. Mr. Dawson.
10. Lord Lyndhurst.
11. Earl of Harrowby.
12. Duke of Wellington.
13. Sir Robert Peel.
14. Mr. Percival.
15. Lord Aberdeen.
16. Lord Wharncliffe.
17. Duke of Cumberland.
18. Mr. Croker.
19. Lord Eldon.
20. Marquis of Londonderry.
21. Sir Henry Halford.

N.B.—Found in a packet dated 1830-31-32.

all Dorsetshire into combustion. He had never been happy since his reception in London, after he had been returned for Dorsetshire. A gloomy melancholy never left him, and he put a period to his existence by cutting his throat, and was found by his daughter, on her return from church, quite dead in this horrid manner. His eldest son, married to the Duke of Manchester's daughter, was residing at Rempstone, the family place, and the first notice of the event was the express which was sent to acquaint him with the catastrophe; and instantly the first inquiry made was, who would offer themselves to represent the county?

Mr. Bankes positively declined again to stand, alleging that his age (seventy-two) entitled him to withdraw from public life. Eventually the candidates were Mr. Ponsonby and Lord Ashley. The latter had married Lady Emily Cowper, who doated on her husband, and was a warm Tory, although a niece of Lord Melbourne, who was Secretary-of-State at this time, and her father, Lord Cowper, being also a Whig; Mr. Ponsonby's wife, Lady Barbara, a Roman Catholic, and a niece of Lord Shaftesbury. As Lord Ashley wished his wife to join him during the violent contest which ensued, we received her at our house, at Dorchester, on October 5th; and Lady Ashley remained with us until the 18th of October, the day after her husband was elected. She was pretty, very young in ideas, and unknowing of common things; but very good-tempered, amiable and interesting, and perfectly unassuming, most desirous not to give any trouble, and civil to every one. Lady Ashley was most anxious for her husband's success, and nervous to a great degree on that subject.

On Monday morning, October 18th, numbers came early into Dorchester, some with banners, and altogether in somewhat regular order. This was the day of the declaration of the poll. It was to open at 8.30 a.m., in order to be open the seven hours prescribed by law, and soon after breakfast we walked to a bank, from whence we overlooked the scene of action at Poundbury.[5] Much ill-will showed itself. A party of Lord Ashley's friends had established themselves on the top of the first entrenchment, from whence the other party determined to dislodge them, and made a regular attack. They chased one unfortunate man who was on horseback, hunting him round and round until he was obliged to dismount and seek for shelter through some paling belonging to the barracks. The special constables were either unable or unwilling to do their duty, and great confusion and danger of bloodshed was likely to ensue. Mr. Wollaston rode in amongst the combatants, and there was still some respect shown to a magistrate, as excuses were made as he rode through them, to him individually, for pressing upon him; but a determined spirit of violence still continued, and broken heads were beginning to be numerous. Mr. Wollaston then rode down the town, and fortunately at that moment a large body of mounted yeomen, who had assembled to escort Lord Ashley when elected, rode into Dorchester, and were requested to appear in the field, which they did, and all became temporarily quiet. At about half-past 3 p.m., a majority of thirty-six was declared in favour of Lord Ashley. Every window in the street through which he passed was crowded, but the shops underneath were shut, fearing the crowd. Lord Ashley rode as usual, bare-headed; his brother John on foot, leading his horse, and preceded

---

[5] An ancient Earthen Fortification, half a mile west of Dorchester, much resembling that at Amesbury, in Wiltshire. Here the Knights of the Shire were elected.

and followed by from 300 to 400 mounted horsemen, chiefly gentlemen and farmers—a very handsome and respectable *cortége*—large numbers following on foot; and there was much cheering. The procession had not quite reached the King's Arms Hotel, about half-way down the street, when a cry was raised that the Sheriff was in danger; and the alarm was too true. The yeomen having gone off the ground with Lord Ashley, left the poor Sheriff (Mr. Damer, of Milton Abbey) and his assessor (Mr. Philip Williams, who had made himself personally unpopular) at the mercy of the Ponsonby mob, who commenced pulling down the booth in which they were, attacking their carriage, &c. Mr. Ponsonby stood before them to protect them; but his interference would have been in vain, had not the yeomen at once galloped back and rescued the Sheriff and Mr. Williams from their dangerous situation, and escorted them safely to their lodgings. The Yeomanry were all in plain clothes, others belonged to none of the troops, but were merely farmers.

The evening passed quietly, and as few drunken riots occurred as could be expected at the conclusion of so severe a contest. Blandford and its neighbourhood still continued its lawless proceedings, and the High Sheriff remained the following day at Dorchester, from apprehension of being attacked in passing through Milbourne. He returned home the next day without any unpleasant occurrence; but a house was destroyed at Blandford, and the windows of several others broken. Lord and Lady Ashley went to Moreton on the 19th of October, and from thence proceeded by Wimborne, &c., as a route which it would not be thought likely they would take; the whole country was, however, in so disturbed a state that it was deemed advisable for them to travel with a pair of loaded pistols in the carriage. This, however, was kept secret from Lady Ashley.

October 19th and 20th.—At Sherborne a considerable mob assembled. They proceeded to Sherborne Castle— Lord Digby's—where they broke every pane of glass which they could get at, and tried to force the great gates leading into the court of the castle. A large party were staying in the house; they were playing at some round game, when a yell was heard, and a volley of stones shivered the glass about the room, and put them to flight. A troop of yeomanry were called out immediately, and two more arrived before morning at Sherborne Castle; but in the town, where the mob still continued disorderly and to break windows, they could effect little as to quelling them, and the yeomen were much annoyed, and several of them seriously injured and knocked off their horses by the stones thrown at them. My brother, Mr. Frampton, Colonel of the Yeomanry, was at the time attending the Quarter Sessions at Dorchester, but started in full costume for Sherborne the moment he heard of the disturbance. He had an escort with him; but although some murmurs and cries of " Ponsonby for ever !" pursued him in two or three of the villages through which he passed, no efforts were made to detain him. On arriving at Sherborne my brother found that arrangements were made, and of which he approved, for the withdrawal of the troop of Yeomanry from the town upon an understanding that a troop of regulars should remain there, and tranquillity was pretty well restored, but many windows were broken, and the house of the clergyman, the Rev. Mr. Parsons, much injured.

November 5th.—Various rumours spread of intended mischief on this night, but all passed quietly, and whether

Lord Ashley's effigy, or that of Guy Fawkes was burnt, made happily no difference as to riot or confusion. The only difference was that no stuffed Guy Fawkes were brought to our door, as was the common custom of the day, and that the fireworks were more prolonged, lasting from dark until near midnight. Apprehensions had been entertained of riots, and the guard at the gaol was increased, and a day or two previously special constables had been sworn in and organized for the town, ready to be called upon if required. All the regular troops had quitted the barracks to go to Bristol, and at this time the safety of the county, as far as military were concerned, rested with the Yeomanry. As soon, however, as the riots at Bristol were quieted and a sufficient force fixed there, two troops of the 3rd Dragoons returned to their head-quarters at Dorchester.

On the morning of the 5th intelligence had been received that a mob from Poole were intending to attack Lord Eldon's place at Encombe, and also Corfe Castle. Mr. Bond's troop of Yeomanry were in consequence called out, and stationed on and about the bridge at Wareham, thus effectually guarding the only approach from Poole to those places, excepting by sea, across Poole Harbour. All, however, passed off quietly, but the minds of the common people are wickedly excited by persons of a somewhat higher class going amongst them raising penny subscriptions to form a fund to pay Mr. Ponsonby's expenses towards petitioning Parliament against Lord Ashley's return to Parliament, and talking the same language to induce them to give to it as was without scruple used to influence the votes and opinions of the mob in the two late contests, viz. that " Reform " would give them meat as well as bread in abundance by paying only a quarter, if so much, of the present price for those articles. How can the poor resist such tempting language?

November 6th.—A good, well-printed paper has been sent out this day to contradict the falsehoods which have been printed and stuck about the town with a deep black border. This last was denominated the "Black Lists;" it denounced the Lords and Bishops who voted against the Reform Bill as almost all pensioners of Government, and living on the taxes raised from the poor. Amongst the principal lies in this list was the assertion that all Lords-Lieutenants of Counties received large salaries, the amounts of which were I think stated, for their services instead of the honour being purely gratuitous, and indeed attended with expense to those holding it; but here again, how can the lower classes know whom to believe when such positive assertions are made? A letter from near Bagshot mentions the alarm of the Bishop of Winchester, from threats having been made that his palace would be consumed, and in consequence troops were ordered there to guard the palace and himself and family.

The proclamation issued by Government, and the effect produced by the King himself coming suddenly to town without previous consultation with his Ministers, is likely to be useful, as there was a general idea spread amongst the lower orders that the King being in *favour* of Reform, they were supporting his wishes by their lawless endeavours to procure it, and that he would not allow the soldiers to act against them as they would cry out for "The King and Reform." The riots at Sherborne, as well as at Wareham and Yeovil, partook in some degree of electioneering excitement. Those at Bristol were of a still more frightful character, as the following letter will show :—

FROM THE REV. J. L. JACKSON [6] TO C. B. WOLLASTON, ESQ.

"*Clifton, October 31st and November 1st*, 1831.

"As reports may have reached Dorsetshire from Bristol, I now write to assure you and our other friends that at present we are unharmed by fire and the mob. I do not think that report could have gone beyond the horror of our actual condition last night. During the whole of Saturday Bristol was in a state of considerable ferment from the arrival of Sir C. Wetherell, the Recorder. In the evening the multitude assembled before the Mansion House in Queen Square, and smashed the windows by a volley of stones in the front of the building. The Recorder was then at dinner with the Mayor and Corporation; the people then went away. But yesterday morning when I was going down to Bristol to serve the church of a friend, I learnt that the populace had actually broken into the Mansion House, had forced the cellars, and were destroying and gutting the house.

"I proceeded to the church, which was at no great distance from the Mansion House, and went through the prayers, but whilst reading the Commandments I heard two distinct charges of pistol firings. In fact the military, two troops of horse, who had been summoned, then fired. The congregation became alarmed, and dispersed without my giving them a sermon, but only a few words of exhortation to repair quietly to their own homes, and look after their servants and dependents. I also quitted the church and walked home without receiving the slightest insult or interruption, but the knots of men standing about the streets were of the most awful

[6] A connection of Mr. Wollaston; his wife being sister of the celebrated man of science, Dr. William Wollaston.

character. Three individuals were killed by the soldiers and more wounded. In the afternoon we heard that the multitude was assembled in much greater masses, and about four o'clock we saw the new City and County Gaol in flames; afterwards the Bridewell and another prison in the Gloucester Road, about a mile from Bristol. In the course of the evening Queen's Square was fired and the Bishop's palace. Of Queen's Square two whole sides have been burnt down, including the Mansion House and what must be of irreparable loss to such a place as Bristol, the Custom House. The cathedral was preserved, and is still standing, but was attempted. Other property to an immense amount is also destroyed. This morning an actual slaughter has taken place; it is supposed, though of course nothing precise can be known at present, that above seventy persons have been killed, besides a large number who have been wounded. The military charged through some of the principal streets, cutting right and left. What will be the event of this evening and night I know not, but I believe that the events of yesterday will never be effaced from the recollection of my family while memory holds her place.

"*November* 1.—Thus far had I written yesterday when I was called to attend a meeting of the respectable inhabitants of Clifton for the defence of the place. About two hundred householders were enrolled and divided into four parties, each party under the command of half-pay officers. By this precaution we have slept last night securely in our beds, and Clifton, thank God, has been uninjured. Five houses had been particularly threatened by the incendiaries, and might now with many others have been smoking in flames. This mode of attack is tremendous, it is by applying phosphorus to the doors. Much praise and many obligations are due

C C

to the military for their forbearance at first, and for their decision latterly. The magistrates, police, and constables were wholly inefficient. Indeed one of the worst features of many which are bad is the rotten state of the public mind, not only amongst the very low, but in the different gradations of society, even to the highest and most influential. It is a fact that the Bishop's palace was plundered and fired by not more than ten men and a rabble of mere boys. It is also a fact that the fires of Sunday night appeared to cause a degree of exultation amongst many not of the lowest class. Just as I am closing my letter I hear that two more fires occurred last night, and that they would certainly have been multiplied but for the presence of the military; also that Bath is in a considerable ferment. Of course reports will be exaggerated, but may God preserve us and our guilty Land! Our wretched Ministers have raised a storm which, I fear, it will not be in their power to direct or control.

"Yours, &c.,

" J. L. JACKSON."

FROM HARRIOT G. MUNDY TO LADY H. FRAMPTON.

" *Markeaton, October 8th*, 1831.

" MY DEAR MOTHER,—*Sunday, October 9th,* 8 *a.m.*—Since writing the enclosed we have had direful events, but I am thankful to say that nothing serious has happened excepting breaking all the windows. Last night, just as we were nearly all in bed, and Mr. W. M. and I quite so, a large mob came from Derby (having just heard of the failure of the Reform Bill), and surrounded the house, shouting and halloaing, and smashed all our windows, and broke in many doors and frames of windows. Luckily we

were very strong in point of men-servants, and Godfrey
Mundy[7] is here, but I must say they did not show much
inclination to enter.   We are going to send off for troops
to Nottingham—sixteen miles—which is our nearest
point, so expect to be quite strong and secure before
night.

"You need not be the least alarmed, as we are all quite
well, and I only write because you may have worse
accounts by the newspapers."

THE SAME TO THE SAME.

"*Markeaton, October* 12*th*, 1831.

"MY DEAREST MOTHER,—We have not been visited
again, for which we cannot be too thankful, as I have no
dependence on the strength of our fortifications or on our
forty men, if they really chose to attack us with all their
force, for we have no military guard, and a super-
abundant quantity of windows, principally without
frames, which by no means increase their power of
resisting a mob.   I have now been *four* nights without
undressing, but I get so tired that I sleep quite as comfortably lying on my bed as I ever did, and by that means
am all ready for any alarm.   We have had one or two,
but fortunately they proved false ones.   Mr. W. Mundy
comes to bed for a couple of hours at six o'clock, when it
is broad daylight.   I hope he will not suffer, but it is a

---

[7] Subsequently Major-General Godfrey Charles Mundy, Lieutenant-
Governor of Jersey. He married, 1848, Louisa, daughter of the
Honourable and Rev. William Herbert, Dean of Manchester; died 1860.
Author of "Our Antipodes," &c. He was eldest son of General Godfrey
Basil Mundy, of the Shipley "*Miller Mundy*" branch of the family
and of the Honourable Sarah Brydges, youngest daughter of Admiral,
first Lord Rodney, who died 1871, aged ninety-one.   Godfrey was elder
brother of Sir Rodney Mundy, G.C.B., who died December, 1884.

terrible strain on his mind, having everything to do and his father to manage completely; he asks his son 50,000 questions where one would be quite sufficient, and about nothing at all just in the midst of all his bustle. However, his temper is proof against everything, and he is as cool and quiet as possible. We hear that Derby was very quiet last night, and that some of the people are *going* to work again as usual, but we cannot feel at all secure yet, as if the refractory people are dispersed and driven out of the town, they are very likely to form into parties and annoy the country. I am happy to say that Godfrey will not leave us till to-morrow, but what we shall do when he is gone I cannot think. The worst of being so near the town is that one hears the shouting and halloaing of the people and any guns that are fired, which is very disagreeable, as one never knows whether they may not be at the door the next minute. If my brother Henry was not captain in the yeomanry, I should invite him here to help defend us."

"*Markeaton, Thursday, October* 13*th*, 1831.

"MY DEAR MOTHER,—We are more comfortable as far as the present is concerned, but have not a very agreeable prospect for the winter. Some fresh troops have arrived from Sheffield, and we are lent some yeomanry from Staffordshire, so that the town is kept very quiet, as they relieve one another, and take it by turns to patrol the streets. We have not been attacked again, and are tolerably defended, as I must say the tenants and labourers came to our aid instantly—many even on Saturday night—and have stood very firm ever since. With *them* Mr. Mundy is very much liked, as he is so very kind and liberal about their rent and money matters, and they understand him. Mr. W. Mundy is extremely

popular, and always has been so. Only think of poor
Mrs. Wilmot at Chaddesden (*née* Mundy of Shipley)
hearing the mob halloo out when they threw a stone up
to the nursery where her three poor little children—the
eldest not three years old—were all crying from fright,
'I wonder how many of those little brats we've squashed
now?' I undressed *nearly* for the first time last night,
but I cannot help being in a great fuss about Mr. W. M.,
which prevents me from going to bed as the rest have
done all the time. All the neighbouring counties are
inclined to be uproarious, but I hope we may get some
troops stationed at Derby. The Duke of Devonshire is
come down to stay in case we want our Lord Lieutenant.
Godfrey Mundy goes to-day."

THE EARL OF ILCHESTER TO HIS NIECE, MRS. MUNDY.

"*House of Lords, October* 12*th*, 1831.

"MY DEAR HARRIOT,—We have been, I assure you,
looking out for accounts from Derby ever since the com-
motion first began, and great anxiety we have felt. I
trust ere this reaches you that it has again subsided in
consequence of what took place in the Commons, and
from the other symptoms of the certainty of a Reform
Bill being now carried. I saw Lord Lansdowne soon
after I got your letter, and he was to see Lord Melbourne[8]
at the Levée, and would state what he could for you; he
said he knew that they were quite aware of what was
taking place, and would do their utmost. He was, however afraid that troops were very scarce in that part of
the country. We have heard also of the occurrences at
Nottingham and its neighbourhood, from which place
they will not be able to spare many, I should fear.

[8] Secretary of State for the Home Department.

"There has been an immense assemblage of people to-day in the neighbourhood of St. James's, but it seems to be going off peaceably. I shall leave town Friday, or in the beginning of next week. The Parliament will be prorogued for about six months, either on Friday or Monday.

"Affectionately yours,

"ILCHESTER.

"*Wednesday*."

THE EARL OF ILCHESTER TO THE SAME.

"*October* 13*th*.

"MY DEAR HARRIOT,—I wrote you a few lines yesterday to tell you how much we all thought about you, and that I was assured that all practicable assistance was about being rendered.

"I afterwards saw Lord Melbourne, and he said his accounts were more favourable, and that you would have Troops before the time he was speaking, so I trust your anxiety and alarm has ceased. I shall like, however, to hear again from you to certify the fact.

"Yesterday was a great day with us here, but upon the whole there was less outrage. than, with such an immense concourse of people collected, might have been expected.

"The Dorset election goes on still. Lord Ashley is six ahead—1746 for Lord A., 1740 for Mr. Ponsonby. I daresay you hear more than I do about it from the Moreton anti-reformers. Remember me kindly to Mr. Mundy, and believe me,

"Affectionately yours,

"ILCHESTER."

From Mrs. Mundy to Lady H. Frampton.

"*Markeaton, Saturday night,*
"*October* 15*th,* 1831.

"My dear Mother,—After my letter was gone to the post I received yours. We perceive that, you do not think much of our mob, which considering your own troubles last year is not surprising, but I assure you that our situation was rather terrific, and, indeed, we do not think ourselves as extraordinarily out of the reach of a second edition yet. Conceive how horrid it was on Sunday morning, just as we had finished our doleful breakfast, having been up all night, and having the yells of the multitude and the crash of windows and doors still ringing in our ears, to have a gentleman (Mr. Meynell) ride up, saying that he was just come from Derby (where he expected to have been annihilated by the mob, as they threatened him, and told him that they should visit him), that they had forced the town gaol and liberated twenty-three prisoners, were proceeding to the county gaol, which he feared could not resist long, and were then coming on to us to Kedleston (Lord Scarsdale's), and to his place. We distinctly heard the shouts of the mob, not having a window or shutter whole, and if they had come at that moment we could not have offered the slightest defence or resistance, as the whole of the lower rooms were open, and anybody could have walked into them as easily as possible. Fortunately the gaoler made a gallant defence, which delayed the rioters until the dragoons arrived from Nottingham, which was only just in time, as they were preparing to scale the walls, and if so, or they had attacked it with powder, it must have given way.

"To-day a detachment of the 18th Foot arrived from

Manchester, so we feel tolerably secure, and privately we attribute these to my uncle Ilchester's great kindness in speaking to Lord Melbourne, as I am sure that his and Lord Lansdowne's mention of us makes them think less lightly of our situation, and we feel very grateful in consequence. We are very thankful for our preservation, as you may believe, for the Nottingham rioters plundered much more; and at Colwick, near Nottingham— Mr. Musters' place—they entered, seized the furniture and pictures, which they made into a bonfire before the door, and utterly ruined it. Only Mrs. Musters and her daughter were at home. Mrs. Musters was ill in bed, and she was obliged to be carried out of the house and laid under a bush for safety. This is dreadfully brutal for an English mob, and makes one's prospects sadly gloomy. They say that Mr. Muster was *excessively* unpopular, and that if he had been found at the moment, he would certainly have been murdered. With regard to your plans, I am sorry to say that it will be quite out of the question for us to receive you at present—we have but one room left entire, excepting Mr. W. Mundy's dressing-room, where *he* dresses and *we* dine, and everything is so demolished—both doors and windows—that they say it will require at least a month to make us again decent, even supposing they were to set to work to-morrow; but as we by no means feel sufficiently secure for that, we are only going to have the library, &c., made habitable for the present. It is wonderful how admirably Mr. W. M. manages everything. He is obliged to rely entirely on himself, but orders all so coolly and quietly, never seeming impatient, that it is quite delightful to see, and he always finds time for me !

" Your affectionate daughter,

" H. G. M."

From William Mundy to Lady H. Frampton.

"*Markeaton, October 20th,* 1831.

"My dear Lady Harriot,—I want to tell you how much interested I have been about the progress of your election, more particularly from having been present at the last, and now I must congratulate you upon its successful termination. We are beginning to breathe again after the late turmoil, which has now quite subsided; and as I hope and believe that we shall have some troops at Derby through the winter, I have no doubt we shall remain quiet. As Harriot has already described the whole to you, I will not recur to it again further than to express my admiration of her coolness and composure throughout the bustle. She was of essential use by giving me some hints which were of great value at the time, and altogether behaved just as I expected she would do in any emergency. I am happy to say that she does not seem to have suffered from the alarm. It is surprising that Derby should have been almost the only place in the kingdom to riot on this occasion, which I can only attribute to the constant excitement in which the inhabitants have been kept by the Radical party, by holding no end of public meetings, getting up petitions upon all occasions, &c., so that they were ready charged for an explosion. I hope Mr. Frampton thinks we did right in not firing upon the mob the other night, taken by surprise and unprepared as we were for such an attack; as my idea is, that it is not well to begin a fire unless one is prepared to keep up a brisk one, and with the few guns and pistols we could muster at the moment it would have been impossible to defend all the doors and windows if they had been determined to force an entrance, though the first man who *entered* I should certainly have shot.

"I am now told that many of these rascals themselves repent having visited us, and regret that they did not go to Lord Scarsdale's instead, before the Hussars arrived to impede their further operations. We have never had any answer from Captain Corry [9] about the place to procure Hand Grenades. I hope he received Harriot's letter. I do not think that my father and mother are likely to leave home this winter, indeed I think *now* this neighbourhood, having had its explosion, is perhaps less likely to be disturbed than any other part of the kingdom, as the people will remember, for some time at least, that bullets can kill.

> "Believe me, dear Lady Harriot,
> > "Affectionately yours,
> > > "W. MUNDY."

"We are much obliged for the polling-paper, which is indeed a curious document."

The country, however, continued in so unsettled a state that it was deemed advisable for Mr. and Mrs. Mundy, with their daughters, to remove to London in the middle of December, and when Mr. W. Mundy and I went to dine at Kedleston, about that time, he took a pistol in the carriage for safety. We remained at Markeaton all the winter alone. A *ci-devant* artilleryman, recommended by old General Mundy, was stationed in the house as a precaution, and he remained there until the spring.

[9] Captain Armar Lowry Corry, R.N. (subsequently Admiral Corry), went to the Baltic during the Crimean War, 1854, in the *Queen* line-of-battle ship; and whilst there a spar accidentally fell on his head, which incapacitated him for further service; he died 1855. The Hand Grenades were not allowed by Government to be purchased.

1832.

(*Journal continued.*)

ONE of the most absurd of all possible lies of the day is the rumour, that Mrs. Fitz Herbert is endeavouring to convert the King to Roman Catholicism. Another report is that the Queen is unhappy, and wishes herself back in Germany. Poor woman! she has had little happiness of the domestic kind since she became Queen. Her opinions are supposed to be anti-reform.

February 23rd.—The King's Levée was numerously attended.

The fogs in London unusually thick this month. On February 24th, the day on which the Queen's birthday was kept, the Duke of Devonshire gave a full-dress ball. A letter from my niece, Harriot Mundy, says that she and Mr. Mundy had great difficulty in reaching Devonshire House, even from the short distance from the hotel they were staying at in Albemarle Street. Link-boys with flambeaux walking one on each side of the horses' heads. Many were prevented from getting to the Ball at all, and many accidents happened. The fog also penetrated into the interior of the house, so much so as to spoil the effect of the lighting up of the rooms.

Owing to the illness of the Princess Louise, the Queen's niece, the Drawing rooms announced are postponed until May, when notwithstanding her illness, and of the Queen's maternal attention to her, they must for the good of trade and other state purposes be held.

This is an age when every woman talks on every subject, and the prettier and younger they are, so much the more foolishly do they talk, or at least, so much the more are they listened to, on subjects far beyond their comprehension, and although all may not openly declare, as a very young friend did to her aunt, Mrs. McTaggart, not long ago, that she had just plunged into the depths of metaphysics, yet all think it necessary to talk on matters they do not understand; but every age has its peculiar foibles, and there is much of good as well as evil in the present times.

Active charity was never more practised, all impurity in conversation checked, and the toasts and coarse allusions of the last century abolished even in gentlemen's society. I trust there is much of real religious principle and useful practice following it, both in the society of the worldly and the so-called saints. I heartily wish the latter were not so exclusive, much good would ensue from the parties mixing.

The Duke of Wellington is said to be regaining popularity amongst the lower classes in London, and that instead of being hissed and hooted, people begin to take off their hats to him. The King has fixed to dine with the Duke of Wellington on his birthday at Apsley House.

I went to London towards the end of June. It was above two years since I had been in Town, and one of the new things which instantly caught my attention was the omnibuses, which resembled the old Millepede coaches of my youth revived, but going quicker and much more numerous. Another was the police walking about by day and night instead of the old watchmen, and the cabs driving incessantly and furiously about the streets.

From London we went to Salt Hall for a few days, intending to see Windsor Castle, but owing to the death of the Princess of Saxe-Meiningen, the Queen's niece, we could neither see the interior of the Palace, nor was there any service with music in St. George's Chapel.

On our road home we drove up the magnificent Long

Walk to view the equestrian statue of George III., very lately placed at the end of it.

The horse is magnificent, and the figure upon it may be well carved, and probably is so, but did not convey to me the proper likeness of King George III.

1833.

ANECDOTES OF THE DUKE OF WELLINGTON, from Colonel Gurwood, told me by the Hon. Colonel Dawson Damer, of Came.

Colonel Gurwood was looking over a collection of the Duke of Wellington's letters, and, being much interested by some of them written at the time he was on service with the Indian Army, told the Duke how very much he was pleased with one letter in particular, which he wished him to read. The Duke answered gruffly, and refused, saying, he did not wish to see his own old letters, and was quite cross on the subject. Colonel Gurwood still, however, persisted, and at length prevailed. The Duke sat down, took his own letter, and was soon quite absorbed in its contents, and lying back in his chair, exclaimed, as he went on, "Admirable," "Very good indeed," "Nothing could be better," &c., and, when he had completed the perusal, returned it to Colonel Gurwood, saying, "You may be satisfied that I am not a bit better general now than I was then; there was nothing in my succeeding Commands which exceeded what I did at that time; I have not improved at all."

The Duke of Wellington has been accused by the French of not having saved the life of Marshal Ney.

¹ Michel Ney, Duc d'Etchingen, created Prince de la Moskova, 1813, Maréchal de France, born 1769; the son of a cooper at Saar-

Some one named this to the Duke, to whom he answered
that he had nothing to do with it in any way, and could
not have saved him, or applied for him, as he was not at
that time on speaking terms with Louis XVIII., nor had
seen him for three weeks. On being asked how this
could be, the Duke replied, "When I went to the
Tuileries to pay my court to the King the first time after
his Restoration, Louis XVIII. would not speak to me.
I thought at first that the King did not see me; I tried
again, and still thought the same. I then went up to
him, and he immediately turned his back to me as quickly
as he could with his lame legs, and in the most determined manner. I consequently went away directly, and
resolved to go no more to the Tuileries. About three
weeks afterwards, Monsieur—afterwards Charles X.—

Louis. He was a non-commissioned officer when the Revolution began,
but rose so rapidly that in 1799 he became a General of Division.
After the Peace of Lunéville, 1801, Bonaparte, anxious to win all Re-
publicans to his party, brought about his marriage with Mademoiselle de
Lescans, a young friend of Hortense Beauharnais, and it was on this
occasion that Bonaparte presented to the General a superb sabre, which
had belonged to a pasha killed in battle, which, thirteen years later,
was to prove the fatal indication which delivered Ney into the hands of
his enemies. After the restoration of Louis XVIII., Ney submitted to
the King, who loaded him with favours. On Napoleon's return from
Elba, Ney assured Louis of his fidelity, and was sent against the
Emperor, at the head of 4000 men; but, finding his soldiers favourable
to the latter, Ney went over to the Imperial side. After the capitulation
of Paris, Ney decided on retiring to Switzerland, and had reached Lyons,
when finding that the routes were guarded by Austrians, and hearing of
the proscription of July 15th, in which he was personally named
as Traitor to the King, he stopped at the Chateau of Madame de
Bessonis, near Aurillac, which was indicated to him as a secure retreat.
Ney had not been there many days when, from the imprudence of
leaving on a canapé the precious sabre from which he had sworn never
to part, led to his being suspected, and ultimately arrested. Ney was
conducted to Paris, was tried, and condemned to death for high treason,
and was shot in the garden of the Luxembourg, December 7th, 1815.

came to see me, and inquired why I absented myself from
court, upon which I told him that I had for the second
time set the Bourbons on the throne; that I was in
possession of Paris, at the head of an army of 150,000
men at its gates, and when I went to the King to pay my
court he would not speak to me, and had turned his back
on me, an insult that no English gentleman would bear;
in which capacity I felt it much more than in either of
the former capacities, and should not go near the court
again unless excuses were made to me such as my honour
as an English gentleman could demand.

Monsieur left the Duke, and such messages passed
afterwards as enabled the Duke of Wellington to go to
the Tuileries in future.

It was during those three weeks that Marshal Ney was
shot.

ANECDOTE OF MARIA LOUISE, WIDOW OF NAPOLEON, GRAND
DUCHESS OF PARMA, &c., told of herself in confidential correspondence with Lady Burghersh,[2] wife of
our Minister at Florence, at that time, with whom
she was in habits of great intimacy, and related by
Lady Burghersh, to Mr. W. Bankes,[3] who related it
to me.

When sitting one evening, alone with Lady Burghersh, the conversation turned upon Napoleon, to whom
she (Marie Louise) said she had certainly believed herself
much attached, and was so, having been dazzled by his

---

[2] Priscilla Anne, daughter of the fourth Earl of Mornington ; married,
1811, Lord Burghersh, who succeeded as eleventh Earl of Westmoreland,
1841. He was a General in the army, G.C.H., &c., and a distinguished
officer and diplomatist ; died 1859.

[3] Of Kingston Lacy, Co. Dorset.

Military glory, and the greatness of his situation on the Imperial Throne, &c. Lady B. then asked if she had not kept up a correspondence with him, during the time of his residence in Elba? She answered, " Yes, she had certainly carried on such a correspondence to a much greater extent than was ever suspected." " Then why," said Lady Burghersh, " did you not join him during the Hundred Days?" The answer, " I could not," was made.

On being further pressed, as to the obstacles which prevented this, Marie Louise for some time, answered only, " that it was impossible," but at last ended by stating that being with child by another man, was the invincible reason which prevented it. That man[4] the Empress married immediately on the death of Napoleon, having had two children by him previously, and two subsequently to their marriage. Marie Louise was living with him as her husband when this conversation took place. She was much attached to him, declaring that she did not know what love meant until she became acquainted with him, and attended him most assiduously night and day, in his last illness.

He, on his part, never lost his respectful manners to

---

[4] Albert Adam, Comte de Neipperg, Général Allemand ; né 1774 ; mort 1829. Il entra dans l'armée autrichienne, mais il fut fait prisonnier sur les bords du Rhin par les Français. C'est à cette occasion qu'il eut un œil crevé. Remis en liberté, il se distingua dans la campagne d'Italie. Il épousa à Mantone la femme divorcée d'un Sieur Remondini de Bassano. Il prit une grande part à la Bataille de Leipzig en 1813. En 1814 il fut choisi pour Cavalier d'honneur de l'Impératrice Marie Louise, que les événements de France avaient rendue à l'Autriche, et il suivit à Parme cette Princesse, à qui, dit-on, il avait bien vite su plaire, et plus tard il l'épousa, dit-on, secrètement. Son fils ainé, le Comte Alfred de Neipperg, a épousé en 1840 la Princesse Marie de Wurtemberg. La Duchesse de Parme est morte 1848.

her, never sitting down in her presence when a third
person was present. He was said to be a very captivating person in mind and manners, although blind in
one eye.

The first acquaintance was made by Napoleon himself,
who after the fire at Prince Schwartzenburg's [5] which
caused so much alarm and mischief, invited all the
Austrians who had assisted their escape, to a breakfast

[5] On July 1st, 1810, was the fête given by Prince Schwartzenburg
at Paris, when many persons were burnt to death in the building erected
for the ball. The Emperor and Empress had scarcely retired when the
fire broke out, and shortly the lustres, ceiling, and beams, &c., fell,
crushing and wounding many. Ladies were crushed or trampled upon,
overtaken by the flames, suffocated and consumed, or injured; others
escaped to the garden almost naked, and hid themselves in the shrubs.
It is supposed that from sixty to seventy persons perished. Diamonds
and jewels, to the amount of many millions, were lost in the tumult.
Prince Kourakin, the Russian Ambassador, was thrown down by a
lustre, which broke his arm, and trampled upon, and the injuries he sustained by the fire lasted many months. He had in his hat a superb
solitaire, valued at 400,000 francs, which he lost, as well as his epaulettes,
worth 800,000 francs. Besides which, at the moment he was thrown
down, he was nearly losing a finger, on which he wore a superb ring in
brilliants. It is suspected that many were at this fête who were not
invited.

FROM CAROLINE, COUNTESS OF MOUNT EDGCUMBE, TO MRS. MUNDY.
        (*Extract.*)   " *May* 21*st*, 1871.
"In answer to your questions, Lady Brownlow * tells me that the fire
at Prince Schwartzenburg's happened *before her time*. She thinks the
ball was given in honour of the marriage of Napoleon and Marie Louise,
and the poor Princess Schwartzenburg was burnt to death. Lady
Brownlow knew the Prince well, when he was still Austrian Ambassador
at Paris, and she recollects that he never would go to a ball—always had
a sort of horror of one."

* Lady Brownlow, Emma Sophia, daughter of the second Earl of
Mount Edgcumbe, born 1791. In 1838 she became the third wife of
the first Earl Brownlow; died 1872.

"Slight Reminiscences of a Septuagenarian," from 1802 to 1815, published by the Countess Brownlow in 1867, is an amusing little volume.

at the Tuileries, where she first saw him, and asked the Emperor why he had brought a one-eyed person.

Marie Louise's first introduction to the man who became her husband when Duchess of Parma, was through the importunity of the Emperor Napoleon, who had an opinion of his courage and abilities.

She several times refused to have " ce vilain borgne " presented to her, and at last consented with great reluctance.

The consequence of the introduction—as given before —as well as this anecdote, are both from the same authority.

1838.

FROM LADY THERESA DIGBY TO HER COUSIN, MISS FRAMPTON.

"Buckingham Palace, February, 1838.

" MY DEAR LOUISA,—Many thanks for your *cadeau,* which arrived the day before yesterday. I intended to have written to thank you for it yesterday, but put it off till I came in from driving, when I found that I was so tired I was obliged to lie down and rest for dinner. I hope that we may be able to accomplish spending two or three days at Moreton on our way back, when you shall hear all the details of my life here; it is rather a dull one, though much happier of course since Edward has been in town, as he comes and sits half the day with me. We do not see the Queen till dinner time, and have the whole morning to do just as we like, with a carriage for each of us to go out when and where we like, so we have as much liberty as possible. After dinner we sit round the Queen's table, and work, or talk, or play chess, or do what we like, excepting the nights when there are grand people to dinner.

" My Aunt and Miss Lister went away last Thursday, and were succeeded by Miss Cavendish and Miss Pitt, whom I did not know before, but she inquired after Aunt Harriot and you.

" This is most miserable weather, is it not ?   The river is frozen, and 1 hear that water is very scarce.   Love to Aunt Harriot.

" Yours affectionately,
" THERESA DIGBY."

FROM MRS. MUNDY TO HER AUNT, MARY FRAMPTON.

"41, Queen Anne Street, May 31st, 1838.

" MY DEAR AUNT,—I am really sorry not to have been able to answer your last kind letter until to-day.

" I suppose you have already heard of our prowess in having gone to the Birthday Drawing-room on the 17th, then to a Full-dress Assembly at Lansdowne House afterwards—on the same evening—and to the Ball at the Palace last Friday (25th) which latter was very brilliant indeed.   Although the rooms at Buckingham Palace are not nearly so high, or large (with the exception of the one long Picture-Gallery) as at St. James's, yet it is a remarkably good House for a Ball, if one may so express it.   I have amused myself by drawing you a Plan of the Reception-Rooms, and shown where the Queen stood to eat her supper.   This shocked me dreadfully, and horrifies Grandmamma Ilchester, as there is not sufficient state in it.   Even William IV., who was quite Citizen King enough, always supped with the Queen in his private apartments with a select Party.   I told my Aunt Lansdowne of my disapproval, but she said that the

Queen liked to be able to move about, and that her object was to see, and, if she wished it, to speak to as many people as she could—in fact it arises from her extreme youth, but nevertheless I think it is a great pity. At all events the multitude ought not to be admitted to the Supper-Room until the Queen has herself finished.

"*Au reste* the Ball struck me as being more select than in the last reign."

FROM THE SAME TO LADY H. FRAMPTON.

"*Queen Anne Street, June* 27*th,* 1838.

"MY DEAR MOTHER,—I will do your commissions next week. At present [6] we are all mad. Stoppages in every street, and hundreds of people waiting on the line of road from Birmingham, to get lifts on the railway in vain. If my brother Charlton had not come by the Mail on Sunday, he could not have got here at all, as the coachman told him that people were waiting at Exeter for places. How very unwise not to put on more coaches! My uncle William Strangways has given Mr. Mundy a ticket for the Abbey in the best place he had to bestow, though not a very good one. The Queen herself was stuck for three quarters of an hour in Piccadilly the day before yesterday. She had been warned not to attempt Hyde Park, because from the carts carrying the fair goods, and the barriers admitting only one at a time, nobody could move there. The lower end of Regent Street, where is the barrier between that and Waterloo Place, was impassable, and so was Charing Cross, where we unwittingly went. I am thankful not to live in Belgrave Square, as no one can get upwards from thence at all. In the midst of all this,

---

[6] Queen Victoria's Coronation took place on June 28th, 1838.

the Duke of Wellington gives a grand party to-morrow
night, to which it is said that nobody will be able to get
on account of the illuminations and fireworks, &c. Conceive the Lady Elliots not being able to get out of their
own house without a Ticket! I suppose on account of
the barriers and scaffolding. Not a fly or cab to be had
for love or money. Hackney coaches £8 or £12 each,
double to foreigners!

"The Coronation will be a tremendous fag, especially
as John Strangways tells me that the scramble to the carriages to form the procession on returning will be beyond
description, because everybody must get into them somehow in the few minutes during which the Queen is dis-
robing. He says that even at the last coronation (of
William IV.), when there was no set procession, he saw
the Duke of Devonshire running halfway up Parliament
Street with his coronet on his head, and his robes
tucked under his arms, looking for his carriage which
could not get near the Abbey, although he was Lord
Chamberlain.

We doubt whether it will be worth while to remain in
town for the chance of any foreign fêtes, which after all
it is said that no one but Strogonoff will have space
enough in their houses to give ; at present there is only
a great ball at Stafford House on the 9th, and Sion
on the 11th of July.

"P.S.—I am in great perplexity, being pressed by my
Aunt Lansdowne to have a ticket for the Abbey, there
being one to spare, but as it is necessary to be there at
5 a.m., which is as soon as the doors are opened, I dread
the fatigue excessively. I may not see much, as that
depends on getting a good place, but certainly shall only
see the Peers do homage, though that, and the Queen
shown to her subjects and proclaimed, they say is very

fine, but I should like to see her anointed also ; very few, however, can do that."

FROM THE SAME TO THE SAME.

"*Queen Anne Street, June 29th*, 1838.

"MY DEAR MOTHER,—Although I did not go to the Abbey I could not find time to write to you yesterday, as I was persuaded to remain at Miss Burdett Coutts in Stratton Street to see the procession return from the Abbey, which I did in the hope of liking it better than I had done in going there ; but I confess that taken altogether I was extremely disappointed, though I can scarcely say why. John Strangways says it is because the squadrons of Life Guards were so small, and that what makes the processions on the Continent so splendid are the thousands of troops who always take part in them.   Then the line, at least in Piccadilly, being kept by Policemen and Rifles (whose dark uniform made them scarcely distinguishable from the crowd), took off from the gaiety extremely. The carriages too followed each other so excessively closely that they were in great danger of poling their neighbour's chasseurs, and one could scarcely tell which was which, or rather *which* was *who*, or have time to look at them before they were gone, for though their order was set down in a book (which I have kept), yet it did not specify how many carriages each would have, and the liveries were so fanciful and such a mass of gold, that one's wits did not help one at all.

"Strogonoff's carriage was magnificent, with crowns all over the top, not however of a proper *czarrish* shape, a large one in the middle, crimson and gold, with smaller ones of the same all round it.   All the horses with their manes dressed in the old-fashioned way with ribbons and nobs like shells, and silver and gold all over the harness, which was as thick and old fashioned as one could wish. Another was dressed with knots of nobs of leather, which I think was the carriage of the Mexican Ambassador, and which I liked very much. There was not nearly music enough, as from the great length of the procession a band was required much oftener, and there were only three, and also some sort of *Javelin* men to have walked in threes or fours between each carriage to have made a division. The Duchess of Kent and Duke of Sussex were excessively cheered in going, so was the Duchess of Gloucester a good deal, but the Queen herself not nearly so much as I expected. She was rather more so on returning from the Abbey, but by no means universally or heartily. The Duke and Duchess of Cambridge were cheered coming back, but not so much so as " Old Sussex, " as the mob called him.

" There was great excitement looking out for *Sowlt*,[7] as they called him, and when the Marshal was discovered on coming back, they gave him a hearty cheer, at which he looked as pleased as possible, peeping out of his glass carriage, which had little silver crowns all amongst the

[7] Nicolas Jean Soult, Duc de Dalmatie, Maréchal de France ; né 1769 ; mort 1851. Il entra dans l'armée à l'age de 16 ans. . . . Soult partagea avec Masséna la gloire du siège de Gênes, 1799. Il fut un des premiers généraux qui reçurent la dignité de *Maréchal d'Empire*, 1804. . . . A l'Époque du Couronnement de la Reine Victoria, Louis Philippe eut l'heureuse pensée de choisir pour Ambassadeur Extraordinaire, l'homme qui dans plus d'une circonstance avait balancé la fortune du héros de l'Angleterre. Soult fut accueilli par Wellington avec cordialité, par le peuple Anglais avec enthousiasme. Plus qu'octogénaire, il mourut peu de temps avant le Coup d'État Napoléonien, Novembre 1851. Il fut inhumé dans sa résidence quasi-royal de Soultberg à St. Amans.

rails round the top of it. Prince Esterhazy's carriage was very fine, and he wriggled about therein like an imprisoned worm. Schwartzenberg was covered with swan's-down (himself, not his carriage), and looked very well.

"Altogether, however, I regret the Abbey; but I should have been dead to-day had I attempted it, as I must have started at 5 a.m.; and Mr. Mundy walked home, which I could not have done, and so got here at a quarter before seven, but the carriage never arrived until half-past eight o'clock. Charlton got a very good place, and was delighted; Mr. Mundy also much pleased. They both walked about from ten o'clock last night until one o'clock this morning, looking at the fireworks and illuminations. In the Abbey, just as poor old Lord Rolle went up to do homage, somehow he slipped and rolled down the five or six steps from the throne, on his head, which was a frightful sight. The Queen rose up quickly, as if to help him, and then, recollecting herself, sat down again; but when Lord Rolle was lifted up, and would go again to do homage, the Queen advanced down several steps to meet him, which struck everybody with such admiration that there was a loud cheer through the whole Abbey. It was very stupid of the two peers who supported him to let him fall, and they thought he would be half killed, being eighty; but Charlton says that many of the peers were extraordinarily awkward in doing homage, and he concludes that the throne was very slippery. He also thinks that the Queen does not look so well as when she was at Melbury, and we think she has grown more like the Princess Charlotte.

"Noel[8] enjoyed his share of the gaiety exceedingly,

[8] Our son, Francis Noel Mundy, aged four and a half years. Now, 1880, of Markeaton, Co. Derby; married, 1864, Emily, third

and remarked, 'What a dear, young face the Queen has!'
Of course, he went with me to Stratton Street, and Smith
carried him nearly all the way home in his arms, after
the first procession had passed. As for myself, I do not
know what I should have done without John Strangways,
as he took me home in his cabriolet, the only means, as
my uncle William and Mr. Mundy had the carriage.

"To-night is the Full-dress Ball at Lansdowne House,
to which we look forward with much pleasure on account
of the many celebrities, as well as the different foreign
ambassadors, Soult, Esterhazy, &c., in their various
magnificent costumes, whom we shall meet there."

THE SAME TO THE SAME.

"*July 2nd*, 1838.

"They say that Soult is delighted at his reception, and
was quite overcome by the cheering, saying, 'Vraiment
c'est un peuple noble!' Everybody says that there never
was anything so orderly as the mob, fair, &c.; so I hope
all the world are become suddenly loyal."

1840.

FROM THE DOWAGER COUNTESS OF ILCHESTER TO LADY HARRIOT FRAMPTON.

"*Melbury, February 13th*, 1840.

"DEAR HARRIOT,—I rejoice to say that Harry is well,
and seems to have approved of all arrangements, and
seen the interesting little Queen, as usual with the accustomed partiality. He continues to see in her a most

daughter of the Honourable Richard Cavendish, of Thornton Hall,
Bucks.—H. G. M.

extraordinary character, as indeed, by every report which has ever reached me, I consider her to be. Every description of the happy pair is pretty, and I own that my anticipations are now glowing. How fortunate that the weather should so seasonably recover itself in sunshine and abatement of rain for the whole journey to Windsor! I do like the Dowager Queen being at the altar, and also that upon the close of the service the Queen should have darted up to her to give her a kiss. All seems to have been nice and kind on the part of Royals here. It would have been contrary to etiquette for the Dowager Queen to have been in the procession, and most happily, King Ernest was not at hand to spoil all; for as Heir apparent he must have acted the Father's part. His retaining a claim upon St. James's is too bad. The Duchess of Kent is going to Belgrave Square, at an expense of 1500*l*. a year to the Queen. I enclose Charlotte Neave's account, as I think it will interest you.

" Ever yours most affectionately,

" M. ILCHESTER."

FROM MISS CHARLOTTE NEAVE[9] TO THE COUNTESS DOWAGER
OF ILCHESTER (enclosed in the preceding).

" February 11th, 1840.

" MY DEAR AUNT ILCHESTER,—I must just tell you how well I saw the two interesting parties yesterday, thanks to kind Emily Murray, who looked well and happy in the procession. When the trumpets sounded, though really in discord, we were all eagerness, and felt both for Prince Albert and the Queen, for I know not which looked the most uncomfortable when going to the Chapel; but on

[9] Youngest daughter of Sir Thomas Neave, Bart., and niece to Lady Ilchester.

their return together they each had a colour, and with countenances much brightened. And just before the guns fired to announce that the ring was on the finger, a nice gleam of sunshine appeared, which my dear naval uncle [1] will, I know, join with me in being sure is a happy omen. The Duchess Mother was the only one, on returning, who looked sad, though not unhappy, which was truly natural. I was very fortunate, for Edward Digby saw me coming, and with his usual good-humour helped me to a seat, and shortly after he was pushed on till he was just before me, so I had an interpreter concerning the topic of the day. I heard a gentleman say that the Queen's orange flowers were shaking during the ceremony, but they both said all fairly out loud, 'obey,' and all. I liked the countenance of the father of H.R.H. (the Duke of Saxe Coburg), and he looked very well satisfied. William and John Strangways were near our seats, and many other friends, so time passed pleasantly; and after viewing the Chapel and waiting not an unreasonable time for the carriage, I was at home by half-past two. I am glad to say that when my sister took my Aunt Long into the Park and joined the rank of carriages near Kensington— for there was not an inch of space before—they saw Prince Albert and the Queen drive by, and had a good view of them, all smiles.

"Believe me, your affectionate niece,

"C. NEAVE.

"P.S.—The Duke of Norfolk, who was to sign first, kept the 'Parties' all waiting, thrusting his hand into one pocket and then into another, diving, without success, for his spectacles; but at last he fished them out of a third, and the 'Treaty' was signed in the Throne-room.

"I hear the illuminations were beautiful."

[1] Admiral Sir Henry Digby, K.C.B.

THE MARCHIONESS OF LANSDOWNE TO LADY HARRIOT
FRAMPTON.

"*Lansdowne House, February.*

"MY DEAR HARRIOT,—I send you a *Sun* newspaper,
which is reported to be the best account, but they are
all full of mistakes. The Queen did not wear her veil
over her face, but hanging quite behind like a drapery.
She looked very pale and pretty, and her hands trembled
very much when she took off her gloves, but her voice
was audible, and she looked at Prince Albert when she
said 'I will,' and once or twice besides in a very touch-
ing manner.

"The Archbishop of Canterbury did not spare us one
word of the Ceremony, which is very disagreeable, and
when one looked at all the young things who were listening, most distressing, however he mumbles a good deal.

"The Archbishop was very confused, and was going to
make Prince Albert put the ring on the Queen's right
hand. The Queen Dowager was dressed in such perfect
taste, no tinsel and diamonds, but velvet and ermine.

"The only thing I did not approve was that the
Duchess of Kent only squeezed the Queen's hand instead
of kissing her, which the Princess Augusta did most
affectionately.

"Little Princess Mary was a pretty incident, she
looked so happy, and when she came with her mother to
shake hands with the Queen, she drew her close and
kissed her.

"The Queen gave all her train-bearers a Coburg eagle
in turquoises, with large pearls in its claws. I saw the
Queen's dress at the palace, the lace was beautiful, as
fine as a cobweb, and the pattern like old Brussels.
Her train was trimmed with orange flowers growing in-

wards, all white, and was rich and light, and she had no
jewels on, which was very good taste, only a bracelet
with Prince Albert's picture. The park was as full of
people as if it had been a fine day, there was scarcely
room to get along at a foot's pace. Nobody, however,
was run over in their way to Windsor. Lady Sandwich
—the Lady in Waiting—and Baroness Lehzen [2] went to
Windsor, and Lord Byron and Major Keppel, the Lord
and Groom in Waiting, the rest were sent back to amuse
themselves in town.

"It was settled that they were to dine all together, and
then, *being all tired*, were to retire after dinner to their
respective apartments.

"This is all I can think of to interest and amuse you.

"Your affectionate,

"L. LANSDOWNE."

FROM THE SAME TO THE SAME.

(After the Queen was shot at the first time.)

"*June 24th*, 1840.

"MY DEAR HARRIOT,—I ought to have answered your
question before; I shall certainly be at Bowood the 1st
of August.

"It is fortunate that the Queen has her Grandfather's
nerves. Lord Albemarle told me that the wheel pos-

---

[2] Louisa Lehzen, daughter of a Hanoverian Clergyman. She first
came to England in 1818, as governess to the Princess Feodora of
Leiningen, a daughter, by her first marriage, of the Duchess of Kent,
and in 1824 she entered on the same functions as regarded the Princess
Victoria. In 1827 she was raised by George IV. to the rank of
Hanoverian Baroness, and in 1831 was placed about the Princess pro-
visionally, as sub-governess and Lady in Attendance which position she
held until the Queen's accession. The Baroness remained at Court until
1842, when she retired to Germany, where she died 1870.

tilion told him that he was sure Her Majesty must have looked down the barrel of the second pistol, for upon hearing the first, he looked round to see what idle person had fired, and he saw the Queen's head turned to look also in a line with it, and in a moment she *crouched* into Prince Albert's bosom and the shot went over her head. The postilion said he was so frightened that he pulled up, and then a voice said, ' Go on,' and he went on, not knowing whether he was alive or dead.

" She walked a quadrille, which I should think much less fatigue than sitting by the Duchess of Cambridge all the evening, but it is of course thought very wrong.

" I shall have beautiful music this evening, and wish you were within reach to hear it.

" Yours affectionately,
" L. L."

1842.

THE MARCHIONESS OF LANSDOWNE TO LADY H. FRAMPTON.

" *January*, 1842.

" MY DEAR HARRIOT,—I send you the *Gazette* about the Royal christening,[3] &c. I am afraid that there is no plan of Windsor excepting in Wyatville's great book, though there may be in some Windsor Guide.

"The State Rooms are divided as they always were. The Great Reception-Room and Waterloo Hall are the only new ones, I believe.

"The dinner in St. George's Hall, all on gold plate, with the beautiful sideboard of ornamental plate at each

---

[3] The christening of H.R.H. the Prince of Wales took place in St. George's Chapel, Windsor, January 25th, 1842. The King of Prussia was his godfather.

end and in the middle, made it look like a feast in a
fairy tale. Had there been more ladies the effect would
have been still better, there were not more than a dozen
to 150 men. The King of Prussia[4] has pleased every·
body; he has very gracious manners, and is full of
intelligence. His own society at home is composed of
remarkable people, and is very much *sans gêne*, and he
was much struck with the strict etiquette observed
here.

"Yours affectionately,

"L. L."

FROM LADY CAROLINE FOX STRANGWAYS[5] TO LADY HARRIOT FRAMPTON.

"31, *Old Burlington Street*,

"*May*, 1842.

"DEAR AUNT HARRIOT,—I will execute your commission
as soon as possible. I am puzzled how to send you an
account of the Ball,[6] which is happily over, but I will tell
you all I can about it. The Queen—who represented
Queen Philippa of Hainault—and her Court sat upon a
raised throne, upon which a great light was thrown by a
Bude light, and behind them were hangings of silk,
embroidered with coats-of-arms, &c.; above, quite high
up, was one of the bands, also dressed up. Everybody
came into this room and passed by her to make their
bows, beginning with the quadrilles. It was rather

---

[4] Frederick William IV.

[5] Youngest daughter of the Earl of Ilchester, subsequently married
Sir Edward Kerrison, Bart.

[6] This was a Bal Costumé given at Buckingham Palace in the spring
of 1842. Lady Caroline Strangways was one of those in the "Waverley"
Quadrille.

formidable going two and two to make our curtsey and bow, with everybody standing by to look and criticize.

" We then walked in procession through a lane kept for us through all the rooms, and after some time we danced our quadrille, which was a very pretty one, I think. Then others danced a mazurka in a Russian dress, and afterwards the Scotch people had their reel. It was a beautiful sight, but I was very glad when it was over to get rid of my dress, which was hot and stiff.

" The Queen's dress was not becoming, and she looked hot and oppressed. It was a heavy crown with gold things coming down on each side of her face. Prince Albert's dress was magnificent, and very becoming. He was, I think the best dressed person there. He had a sort of embroidered tissue, or cloth of gold, which cost fifteen guineas a yard, and which was so brilliant that all his other jewels and diamonds were quite eclipsed by it. He personated Edward III.

" My dress was approved, so I hope you will do the same. A red velvet bodice, cut square and laced down the front, with long hanging sleeves trimmed with gold, and gold fringes round the bottom of the skirt, red velvet embroidered shoes, a wreath of ivy-leaves and veil spangled with gold. I was sorry not to have been able to introduce the Croye arms anywhere after all, as you suggested.

" Theresa was a lady of the time of Louis XIII. It was a very pretty dress. She had her hair curled all round, which hung down to her waist, and was very becoming to her. Stephen was of Charles the Second's reign, with long curls, and a coat of watered blue silk, shot with silver, and loose yellow boots.

" I send you a programme[7] of our Waverley Quadrille, and if I see any tolerable account of this said ball I will certainly send it, but all I have as yet come across are very bad, and not written, I should think, by spectators. Theresa stays here till after the Birthday Drawing-room next Thursday, and then returns to her family at Minterne.

" Your affectionate niece,
" CAROLINE F. STRANGWAYS."

1843.

EXTRACT FROM A LETTER FROM THE HON. COLONEL DAWSON DAMER, OF CAME.

" June 10th, 1843.

" The King of Hanover took his seat yesterday, but, having done so, does not intend taking any part in politics. There never was a man so altered. He is

---

[7] PROGRAMME OF THE " WAVERLEY " QUADRILLE.

Rowena	LADY FRANCES VANE.
Ivanhoe	LORD BLANDFORD.
Queen Berengaria . . .	LADY ALEXANDRA VANE.
Richard Cœur de Lion . .	LORD CANTILUPE.
Isabel de Croye . . .	LADY CAROLINE STRANGWAYS.
Quentin Durward . . .	LORD DESART.
Anne of Geierstein . . .	LADY E. WEST.
Arthur Philpson . . .	LORD SEAHAM.
Catherine Seton . . .	LADY M. WEST.
Richard Græme . . .	LORD CURZON.
Isabel Vere	LADY JANE GRIMSTON.
Ernscliffe	MR. KERRISON.
Edith Plantagenet . . .	LADY E. CAMPBELL.
Kenneth the Scot . . .	LORD JOHN MANNERS.
Evelin Berenger . . .	THE HON. LAVINIA LYTTELTON.
Damian de Lacy . . .	THE HON. HUGH CHOLMONDELEY.

Led by Lady Delamere, in the costume of a former Lady Delamere, from a picture by Vandyke.

subdued in manner, *prévenant* to every one, and this proceeds from a religious feeling. He used to be as rude as a bear to the Duchess of Kent; now he is kind, amiable, and polite.

" The King cannot contain his delight at again visiting England. He declares that he has never been able to eat his dinner out of it, and he passes his time in visiting and recognizing his old friends.

" The Duchess of Gloucester takes him about to keep his mouth shut. He is very deaf, and grown very thin."

FROM MY NIECE, MRS. MUNDY.

" *Markeaton, December 6th*, 1843.

" MY DEAR AUNT,—As you wished to hear about our visit to Chatsworth, I will not delay telling you how well it passed off. You already know that the Queen and Prince Albert were there on the 1st, and as we drove through Belper *en route* we were amused by seeing, amongst the various decorations, one flag suspended from the top of a very high factory chimney! We were to stay at the parsonage at Edensor (with Mr. and Mrs. R. Wilmot), which is in the park, and the crowds of people and vehicles of every description with which it was filled, the waterworks and fountains playing, and the Royal Standard floating over the arched entrance, made the scene most animated. All were trying to catch a glimpse of the Royal party, who were walking on the terrace as we passed, and those who succeeded in their object cheered most heartily. The Duke of Devonshire had invited us for the evening, and on our arrival soon after nine o'clock we were ushered through the orangerie and statue gallery to the so-called banqueting or ballroom, which is a comparatively new apartment under

the tower, only finished since we were last staying at
Chatsworth, and quite distinct from all the other fine
reception-rooms. It is certainly a handsome room,
though the access is not good, being up a by no means
wide or handsome staircase. The only thing I admired
was the chandelier suspended from the centre. Between
each lustre was a real stag's head (the Cavendish arms),
which had a baronial effect. The Queen's sofa was
placed in a recess at the upper end, and as soon as she
entered the ball began. The Queen danced the first
quadrille with the Duke of Devonshire, and the Prince
with Lady Louisa Cavendish, who acted as lady of the
house. In the course of the evening she took one or
two *tours de valse* with Prince Albert, and finished by a
country dance with Lord Leveson,[8] evidently *con spirito*.
The Prince seemed much more animated than when I
last saw him before we went abroad two years ago. It
is unfortunate that the Ribbon of the Garter should be
so unbecoming to the Queen's small figure, particularly
in dancing. In one of the intervals the duke came up
and said we must be presented, though we had repeatedly
been at the Drawing-rooms and to balls at Buckingham
Palace, and as Mr. Mundy was high sheriff we were
obliged to go first, which was odious enough, but could
not be avoided. Only a few others were presented; in
fact there were scarcely any guests of note, which was a
mistake; excepting, of course, the house party. It
pleased me to see Prince Albert in conversation for a
long time with the Duke of Wellington, and his manner
struck me as particularly good, an indescribable mixture
of dignity and deference to an old man.

"The next morning (Saturday) we were on the *qui-vive*,
half expecting the Queen to come and see the village of

---

[8] Succeeded, 1846, as second Earl Granville, K.G., &c.

Edensor, of which the Duke is very proud; but I do not think you would admire these ornamental cottages more than we do, they are not in good taste or sufficiently rustic. The great conservatory was lighted up soon after dark, when Her Majesty drove through it. I wish we could have seen this sight, but it was impossible, as we were to dine at Chatsworth, and the addresses were to be presented before dinner. Mr. Mundy and the four county members were in a deputy-lieutenant's uniform, and the Duke wore his handsome lord lieutenant's dress. The Queen stood near one of the windows, with the Prince on her left hand. The Duke presented the addresses, which she handed on to Lord Jersey, who acted as Lord in Waiting, and after the Prince had received those addressed to him, the ceremony concluded with the presentation by the Duke of the five gentlemen themselves. The private band of the Duke played "God save the Queen" as we went in to dinner and also at intervals afterwards, as the Duke can hear conversation much better when music is going on. The Queen and Prince sat next each other opposite the windows, the Duke of Devonshire on the Queen's left hand, and then the Duchess of Buccleuch as Mistress of the Robes, the Duke of Bedford, Lady Portman, &c. On the right of the Prince was Lady Louisa Cavendish, and opposite to Her Majesty sat the Duke of Wellington, the Duchess of Bedford, &c. My locality chanced to be at the top of the table, which holds four in width, and was placed between our two M.P.'s. I think we were about forty-six altogether. You will like to hear who were the party: the Duke and Duchess of Buccleuch, Duke and Duchess of Bedford, Duke of Wellington, Lady Portman (Lady in Waiting), Miss Paget (Maid of Honour), Lord and Lady Normanby, Lord and Lady Beauvale, Lord

Melbourne, Lord and Lady Leveson, Lord and Lady
Waterpark, Mr. and Lady Catharine Cavendish, Lord
and Lady Emlyn, Mr. F. and Lady Emily Cavendish,
Colonel Cavendish, Mr. and Mrs. Brand, Lord Alvanley,
Lord Jersey, Lord Morpeth and Lady Mary Howard,
General Wemyss, Colonel Bouverie, Mr. and Lady Louisa
Cavendish, Mr. G. E. Anson, and some young Cavendishes
both male and female. Mr. Wilmot, as Chaplain, said
grace, and soon after Mr. G. Cavendish, who sat at the
bottom of the table, got up and gave " The Queen,"
whereupon we all stood up and drank her health. She,
of course, remained sitting, but, almost to my surprise,
blushed and looked quite shy as she returned the Duke's
obeisance. After a short interval he proposed H.R.H.
Prince Albert, and instantly, before any of us, up jumped
the Queen, which delighted me. At the second course
four enormous castles fully three feet high were placed
on the table. I suppose they were made of sugar, as
they were beautifully white, and they had loopholes and
battlements to admiration. On the two nearest the
Queen were a miniature Royal Standard of sugar, and
the others were surmounted by Union Jacks. I confess
that I did long to carry off one as a trophy. You see
that I give you all details, which I know you like. We
had not been very long in the drawing-room when
the illuminations began. I got into one of the library
windows with Lady Leveson and the Duke of Wellington,
as from thence we had the best view of the cascade, but
we migrated occasionally to the drawing-room to look at
the fountains opposite the east front. The whole scene
was like what one reads of in a fairy tale—the locale is
so perfect, because nowhere else in all England at all
events is there a cascade of that height close to the
house and surrounded by woods. It was illuminated

quite up to the top, and the appearance perpetually varied with the colour of the lights, sometimes white, then blue, and afterwards red, which was the prettiest of all, from the tints thrown on the trees. It was beautiful, though I think that I admired the fountains the most, as the effect of the sparkling water with the different lights reflected in it was quite indescribable. Nobody seemed to admire and enjoy it as much as the Duke of Wellington. He said it was the prettiest thing he had ever seen, and that he was sure he should never see anything at all like it again.

"For myself the evening concluded in an unexpected manner. Just before the party broke up the Queen came across from the further end of the drawing-room straight up to me. She inquired after my mother, and asked where she now was, &c., in the most gracious manner, although in so low a voice that it was difficult to catch her words quickly.

"The illuminations were not quite over as we drove back to Edensor, and the park being crowded with people, many even from Sheffield, made the whole thing very uncommon and amusing. On Sunday Mrs. Wilmot and I went quietly to church at Edensor, but Mr. Mundy accompanied Mr. W. to Chatsworth, where the service in the chapel was at twelve o'clock.

"We had great difficulty in getting post-horses on Monday, as the party broke up on that day, and we were obliged to start at eight o'clock in the morning; we just caught a glimpse of the Royal Train whirling over one of the railway bridges with the gilt crown on the state carriage.

"Your affectionate niece,
"HARRIOT G. MUNDY."

1845.

FROM THE HON. MRS. GEORGE DAWSON DAMER, OF CAME.

"*July*, 1845.

"When the King of Holland[9] was in England, a Review was ordered in Hyde Park for his amusement, and he was invited afterwards to a collation at Colonel G. Dawson Damer's, whose house in Tylney Street looked into the park, and to a luncheon at Lambeth Palace. He came later than he intended to the Damers, having by mistake been taken first to Mivart's Hotel, where he was staying. On arriving at Colonel Damer's, the King made his excuses to Mrs. Damer, stating that the Duke of Wellington, being deaf, had not understood him when he said he would go to Tylney Street. Upon which Mrs. Damer said, 'But could not your Majesty have sent word to the Duke by some one else your wishes, and told him that he had mistaken them?' 'O no,' answered the King, '*I* could not send such a message to the Duke, *I* was much too long under his command with the army to find it possible to go contrary to any order of his. Besides, I owe everything to him, my life, my comforts, my kingdom. I can never do otherwise than obey him.'

"Mrs. Damer, in talking to him, corrected herself in calling him King of the Netherlands. They were speaking of a Review not long before, in the same park, which was prepared for the King of Belgium. His reply was, 'King Leopold has deprived me of a Wife and of a

---

[9] Succeeded his father as William II., King of the Netherlands, 1843; died 1849. After the rupture of his engagement to the Princess Charlotte, he married, in 1816, Anna Paulovna, daughter of the Emperor Paul of Russia.

Kingdom, but I will never renounce the title of King of the Netherlands.'

" Of the Archbishop of Canterbury the King spoke in strong terms of affection. He was Regius Professor of Divinity when the Prince of Orange was at Oxford for his education ; the pleasure the King appeared to find in being again in England was very great."

The summer of 1845 was uncertain, and generally cold. The Queen's residence in the Isle of Wight made yachting, &c., more fashionable than ever.

The sailing of the Experimental Squadron of eight line-of-battle ships from Spithead was a beautiful sight which I witnessed.

The Queen in her little steam pleasure-boat, the *Fairy*, and a multitude of noblemen and gentlemen's yachts, making quite a large fleet of small beautifully shaped vessels, contrasted in a striking manner with the bulk of the line-of-battle ships.

The order given to sail by the Queen herself, the firing of guns, &c., when this order was given, &c., made the whole a very imposing sight. The day was fine, although rather too calm.

1846.

April 8th.—A droll circumstance illustrative of these odd times was told me this morning.

That there is growing up a considerable division amongst the lower Popish clergy in Ireland, who complain of their Bishops forbidding them to appeal to the Pope, excepting by petition through the hands of the Bishop.

These lower priests actually got up a petition nume-

rously signed, and had it presented in the House of
Commons to claim the assistance of that Body for the
obtaining leave to address the Pope themselves, when by
our laws the Government neither acknowledged their
Bishops as having any authority, and still less the Pope
having any jurisdiction in England.

THE END.

LONDON:
PRINTED BY GILBERT AND RIVINGTON, LIMITED,
ST. JOHN'S SQUARE.